19th Century
EUROPEAN
FURNITURE

A wonderful example of Venetian carving. This fairly useless but highly decorative walnut sideboard carved in a very free but eclectic Renaissance revival style is signed 'V. Besarel Venezia'. The almost naked figure who is trying bravely to support the weight of the upper part represents Hercules, wearing his lion's pelt and holding a large club. Typically there is a drunken scene of infant putti *with one leading a goat, another riding it while another tries to hold him on. The four outset winged chimera and sphinxes support stands for large porcelain bottles and would look highly decorative with the contrasting colours of the porcelain. An unusual and rare piece that is much underestimated by the northern European and Western market. At the moment this type of furniture normally goes back to Italy.*

1870s

19th Century
EUROPEAN
FURNITURE

Christopher Payne

Antique Collectors' Club

First Published 1981
© copyright 1981 Christopher Payne
World copyright reserved
First edition 1981
Second edition 1985
Reprinted 1989

ISBN 1 85149 001 9

Printed in England on Consort Royal Satin paper from the Donside Paper Company, Aberdeen
by the Antique Collectors' Club Ltd., Woodbridge, Suffolk, IP12 1DS

Antique Collectors' Club

The Antique Collectors' Club was formed in 1966 and now has a five figure membership spread throughout the world. It publishes the only independently run monthly antiques magazine, *Antique Collecting*, which caters for those collectors who are interested in widening their knowledge of antiques, both by greater awareness of quality and by discussion of the factors which influence the price that is likely to be asked. The Antique Collectors' Club pioneered the provision of information on prices for collectors and the magazine still leads in the provision of detailed articles on a variety of subjects.

It was in response to the enormous demand for information on 'what to pay' that the price guide series was introduced in 1968 with the first edition of *The Price Guide to Antique Furniture* (completely revised 1978 and 1989), a book which broke new ground by illustrating the more common types of antique furniture, the sort that collectors could buy in shops and at auctions rather than the rare museum pieces which had previously been used (and still to a large extent are used) to make up the limited amount of illustrations in books published by commercial publishers. Many other price guides have followed, all copiously illustrated, and greatly appreciated by collectors for the valuable information they contain, quite apart from prices. The Antique Collectors' Club also publishes other books on antiques (including horology and art), garden history and architecture, and a full book list is available.

Club membership, open to all collectors, costs little. Members receive free of charge *Antique Collecting*, the Club's magazine (published ten times a year), which contains well-illustrated articles dealing with the practical aspects of collecting not normally dealt with by magazines. Prices, features of value, investment potential, fakes and forgeries are all given prominence in the magazine.

Among other facilities available to members are private buying and selling facilities, the longest list of 'For Sales' of any antiques magazine, an annual ceramics conference and the opportunity to meet other collectors at their local antique collectors' clubs. There are over eighty in Britain and more than a dozen overseas. Members may also buy the Club's publications at special pre-publication prices.

As its motto implies, the Club is an organisation designed to help collectors get the most out of their hobby: it is informal and friendly and gives enormous enjoyment to all concerned.

For Collectors — By Collectors — About Collecting

The Antique Collectors' Club
5 Church Street, Woodbridge, Suffolk IP12 1DS, England

For my father
and to
Di, Belinda and Nicholas

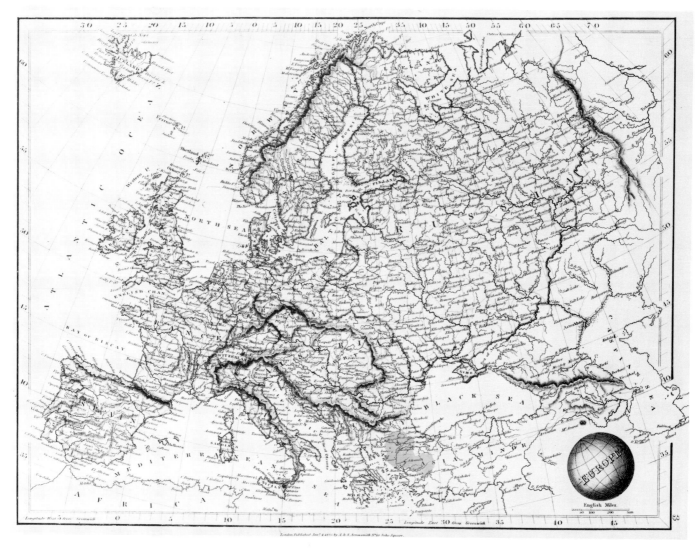

A map of Europe in 1825 published by A. & S. Arrowsmith of London. It shows Italy divided and the vast Austro-Hungarian Empire. Prussia stretches well along the Baltic coast into what is now Poland and Germany engulfs Czechoslovakia. Belgium at this time had not yet become a nation and is part of France and the Netherlands. Northern Germany extended into Schleswig Holstein.

Contents

Colour Plates

Acknowledgements

With thanks to Jonathan Bourne of Sotheby's, Clive Wainwright
of the Victoria and Albert Museum and Martyn Owen of the
Geological Museum for their guidance and suggestions.
Special thanks to the photographers and printers at Sotheby's, who
always undertook to help at short notice and produced usable prints
from the author's negatives.

Photographic Acknowledgements

Sotheby's Belgravia
Phillips & Phillips of Knowle
Bonhams
Christie's
David Barclay
Malletts
Mallett at Bourdon House Limited
James R. Lawson Pty Ltd., Sydney
Author's Collection
Harrods Ltd.
José Urbino
Antonio Galtier of Gal. Lé, Barcelona
Sotheby Parke Bernet & Co., London, Torquay, Chester,
    Monaco, New York, Los Angeles, Madrid, Florence
Musée National de Sèvres
Musée des Arts Décoratifs, Paris
Cliché Musée des Arts et Traditions Populaires, Paris

Preface to the second edition

The first edition of this book was published in 1981 under the title *The Price Guide to 19th Century European Furniture (excluding British)*.

It was hailed by critics as a substantial pioneering work on a subject that had not been tackled before. On the one hand this was not surprising as the amount of research needed was enormous. On the other hand the large amount of furniture on the market surely deserved more consideration than had hitherto been given to it by scholars.

Since the Antique Collectors' Club pioneered the concept of 'price guides' in the late 1960s, the words have increasingly become associated with publications of a less erudite form than those produced by the Club, and in which it is common for merely the bare bones of auction pictures, a few words of description and a price to be given.

So highly considered is the material in this book that the Club, in publishing a second edition, has decided it should stand in its own right as an excellent work of reference on a very difficult subject without mention of prices or values. However, for those who need such information price lists are published and revised annually in March.

Introduction

The style and form of furniture does not neatly follow man-made borders or boundaries imposed by transient governments and fluctuating politics. In the early years of the nineteenth century almost the whole of Europe struggled to get back on to a firm footing after the long ravages of firstly the French Revolution in 1789 and secondly the more wide-ranging consequences of the long Napoleonic Wars, whose effects were almost global, continuing from 1793 to 1815 with a brief two year interval of uncertain peace. The Industrial Revolution had been quickening its pace throughout the late eighteenth century and a huge industrial effort was needed to sustain such a long drawn-out conflict.

At the close of the Napoleonic Wars, Europe was able to settle down to a long period of unprecedented production, design and techniques. The old styles were initially forgotten. The elegant Directoire forms which ended the splendidly bold and ebullient years of the eighteenth century in France heralded a new, far more severe form at the turn of the century as the masculine, sometimes heavy, Empire style became commonplace throughout Europe. This style epitomised the rule of the first Napoleon, captured in the designs of Percier & Fontaine and the resplendent furniture of the Jacob Frères.

Modern taste at the beginning of the nineteenth century had shunned and turned away from Renaissance, baroque, rococo and pure neo-classical forms. As a direct reaction against the severity of Napoleonic rule and taste, the new Europe began to embed itself in a romantic revival and love of past history encouraged by writers such as Victor Hugo, Balzac and Sir Walter Scott. Designers were producing catalogues and drawings of revived Gothic and rococo forms even as early as the early teens of the English Regency period. This led to the muddled and eclectic forms of 'The Victorian Era'. The decade of the 1830s saw new prosperity and peace in a Europe which was now capable of large-scale manufacture and production of all household objects, including furniture.

The battered European aristocracy needed to replace their luxurious furniture of the previous century bought by special commission or directly from the *ébénistes* or from the discreet rooms of the *marchand-mercier*. Vast quantities of important and royal French furniture had been sold at public auctions, much of it forming today's important English collections such as the Jones Collection at the Victoria and Albert Museum, the Wallace Collection, Waddesdon and Strathfield Saye.

A new phenomenon, previously unknown, was emerging at first hesitantly but more and more boldly as economic life began to steady and grow on an unprecedented scale. The middle class had arrived. The explosion in population coupled with a new buying power created a huge demand for cheaper and more plentiful goods. These goods no longer needed to be individually made by experienced craftsmen but simply had to be produced in large enough quantities to satisfy a seemingly insatiable demand. The rapidly improving conditions for the average merchant and artisan meant that they could now afford machine-made, in some cases mass-produced, factory furniture. To a large extent the buyer was no longer willing or was no longer able to dictate to the supplier what his requirements were. No longer were Royal patrons dictating the transition and development of style. It was the astute businessman and manufacturer using widely printed furniture catalogues who were dictating the style and type of furniture available to the majority of the population. The shrewd producer would doubtless soon cease to market a style or object that was no longer in popular demand. The confines of patronage had become too narrow to satisfy the demands of an invigorated and comparatively wealthy populus. The donkey had very firmly grasped the carrot, which was proving juicier and even more insatiable than could have been imagined by the individual cabinet makers working at the beginning of the century.

The second half of the nineteenth century saw many new industrial and marketing techniques. Power was available to even the smallest workshop, firstly steam power and then, on an even wider scale, electric power by the late 1880s. No longer did the wealthy patron go to the merchant to commission a piece of furniture and to dictate his wishes to the supplier. The supplier or manufacturer was to sell his product to an intermediary who would sell the product at the most advantageous price, in the best possible market and to a new far wider clientele. The age of the showroom had arrived. A vast range of furniture was now put on display for all to see and there would be a choice of not only materials and price, but of style, available. These showrooms began to mushroom all over Europe. Many were simply selling furniture purchased from various makers from various towns. Others were showrooms financed and set up by the large manufacturing companies to sell their own goods exclusively. Certainly a large number of the bolder French makers set up premises in several major cities on the Continent, trading on the certain superiority and chic of Paris-made furniture and the advanced state of her industry compared with others by the middle of the century.

The new clientele had not the education or background to direct fashion and a proliferation of designs flowered catering for all tastes and flights of fancy, which enabled the producer simply to amalgamate the many styles of previous centuries into comfortable and more convenient forms of furniture. The spindly back legs of a late seventeenth century chair would be shortened to make the chair more robust. The highly decorative but rather formal and uncomfortable upholstery of previous eras was rounded off, inevitably incorporating a plasticity exaggerating the most profuse rococo elements of design. If a chair was to be sat *upon* in the eighteenth century, by the middle of the nineteenth century one was able to sit *in* the chair — modern taste was determined to have comfort together with what was considered to be style and fashion.

The upholsterer became by the 1840s almost as important as the *ébéniste* and a new sense of comfort was introduced. Even the greatest cabinet makers in France and England, for example Fourdinois or Wright and Mansfield, had by the late 1870s begun to call themselves Cabinet Makers and Upholsterers in the International Exhibition catalogues. The outside world had literally become cushioned by upholstery, tassels and fringes which hid the unsightly legs of not only the furniture, but also chimney pieces, a vogue highlighted by the mass of materials needed for the bustle on a lady's dress.

The culmination of this emergence of uncoordinated traditional designs was in the first of the International Exhibitions, the Great Exhibition at Crystal Palace in 1851. The revival of Louis styles proliferated in Europe as well as in England, who developed her own special brand of "Jacobethan" furniture, which covered the wide span of Gothic, Tudor, Jacobean and Stuart forms, normally including all the styles in one single piece of furniture. The Italian Renaissance re-flowered, occasionally in a new style, but more often than not in a pseudo traditional manner. France looked back to the turned balustrades and elegant columns of François Premier and Henri Deux.

Italy and France had dominated the Renaissance period of furniture making. The sixteenth and seventeenth centuries once again saw Italy as the dominant force, closely followed by France and the Low Countries towards the end of the century. During the early eighteenth century France quickly established herself as the leader of fashion and the most influential country, but by the middle of the century patronage in the vastly wealthy English industrial areas and attendant country houses had ascertained England as the most important influence on the rest of Europe.

By the late eighteenth and early nineteenth century England had achieved an unrivalled supremacy of fashion, style and cabinet making. France had begun to play a less important role, essentially following her eighteenth century traditions, basking in the reflected glories of Versailles. The later flowering industrial capabilities of America allowed her to become a major producer of furniture on a large scale, highlighted at the International Exhibition at Philadelphia in 1876. The remaining European countries, their political and designing influence long dissipated and Empires lost, played only a secondary role. Towards the end of the nineteenth century Germany and Scandinavia began to establish themselves as the major influences, laying down the principles and ground rules of modern design.

Architects, as in previous centuries, have always played a major role in furniture design and a continuity of feeling for houses and the furniture within them. It was the progressive architect designers in England during the middle years of the nineteenth century who were the reformers actively able to influence design, albeit to a limited extent. William Morris and his circle, William Burges and E.W. Godwin, and later Arthur Heygate Mackmurdo, Walter Crane and Charles Rennie Mackintosh with Richard Riemerschmid in Germany attempted to reconcile mass production to design and their individually made, singular designs began to have a wide and far-ranging influence on the rest of Europe which laid down the foundations of the Modern Movement. Samuel Bing, the German dealer whose shop in Paris had given the art nouveau movement its name, wrote in 1898 "When English creations began to appear, a cry of delight sounded throughout Europe".

Paradoxically enough it was two of these English reformers, Lewis F. Day and Walter Crane, who so viciously attacked the art nouveau furniture given to the Victoria and Albert Museum and now at Bethnal Green, after the Exposition Universelle of 1900.

Art nouveau designs were to run with the new modernist and functionalist furniture designs of Germany. At the same time, as the new century dawned, most European countries were still supplying well-tried neo-Renaissance, Gothic and Louis revival furniture in vast quantities to a market that demanded comfort combined with low prices and a certain durability mixed with a nostalgia for the past. Usually the past of the particular country concerned when it was at the height of its furniture making powers, be that the sixteenth century, the eighteenth or even the nineteenth. Contemporary furniture was born out of an amalgam that fused together the past, the present and the future.

* * *

The definitive book on nineteenth century furniture made on the continent of Europe, even if narrowed down to the last seventy years of the century, is the work of a lifetime. The chapters in this book cannot hope to give all the answers, but simply attempt to summarise in a logical format the vast creative output of both men and machines during this period.

Subsequent editions will contain additional facts, makers and corresponding photographs as the information becomes available and it is hoped that anyone who can add to the points mentioned in this edition or contribute information regarding uncharted territories will be forthcoming with their discoveries and conclusions.

Definition of Styles

It is quite possible for any potential student of the nineteenth century to commence his or her study without a detailed knowledge of developments in previous centuries. However, as a large proportion of nineteenth century art forms are borrowed from a bygone era it is important to have some recognition of the styles and artistic persuasions that prevailed throughout the years. Styles which were developed in one or other major country slowly filtered through to the more remote capitals, the provincial towns and rural areas. The very fact that the dissemination of new ideas and fashions took so long, especially compared to the speed of modern communications, means that there are no hard and fast rules as to when or where a style became *passé*. There are no dates to guide us, some rural pieces maintaining a particular style of decoration or form for many years after they had ceased to be fashionable in Rome or Paris. Consequently, until the early nineteenth century it is possible to find rather quaint, seemingly eclectic items of furniture which, at first glance, appear to be anticipating the eclectic and muddled styles of the industrialised second half of the nineteenth century. Upon investigation it is proved that these pieces are simply hanging on to an older, perhaps outdated fashion, more aptly named 'survival' rather than revival.

Given a complete understanding of styles it is possible to label most with a reign date of the particular monarch who was on the throne whilst the style was fashionable, or who possibly encouraged the fashion in his court and Royal palaces. Unfortunately, not even the death of the monarch necessarily meant the immediate demise of a particular style he preferred, although in France during the eighteenth century it is almost possible to date the start and termination of a style by the reign of a king. This is quite simply because the French kings led and dictated fashion throughout Europe for over a hundred years. Consequently, to call a piece 'Louis this' or 'Louis that' can on occasions be correct and can also indicate the style associated with that particular monarch, be it Renaissance or rococo.

It is only with this knowledge that the eclecticism of the second half of the nineteenth century can be identified as 'renoco', 'classical baroque', Jacobethan' or whatever other combination the designer's fancy has turned to.

A chart, following the styles from the early Middle Ages to 1900, and based on the French monarchies, is given overleaf, and is intended as a general guide to the influences on furniture in the continent of Europe.

* * *

Much of nineteenth century furniture design was a pastiche of the fashions and styles of past centuries. Designs were adapted to suit the needs and fads of the middle-class industrial era during the second half of the nineteenth century which had a love of improving well established and well tried principles of form and decoration. Therefore, in many cases furniture from this period has a distinctive style of its own and is easily labelled 'nineteenth century'. However, there were many exact and finely executed copies of earlier furniture made at this time. *Certain illustrations on the following pages have been marked with an asterisk* to denote that, in the author's opinion, they could be mistaken for original examples of their period from the evidence of the photograph shown or that they are exact copies.*

* * *

Style Chart

List of European styles from the early middle ages to 1900. France had the steadiest of monarchies during this period, the individual monarchs consistently exerting their influence on fashion more than those of other European countries. The style dates are approximate.

Style	French Monarch	Peculiarities
Medieval 1050-1300		Simple forms with polychrome decoration, 'romanesque' arches
Gothic 1200-1500		Lancet arches, crocketed finials, elaborate pierced carving
Renaissance 1500-1600	François I (1483-1547) Henri II (1547-1589) Henri III (1589-1610)	Fine and delicate intarsia, lightness, scrolling foliage, columns
Mannerism 1550-1650	Louis XIII (1610-1643)	Slight heaviness starting, profuse carving of figures and beasts
Baroque 1650-1720	Louis XIV (1643-1715) (Effectively reigned from 1661)	Massive architectural forms, full relief carving of figures and swags of flowers
Régence 1710-1730	Philippe d'Orléans as Regent (1715-1724)	Slight lightening of form with massive mounts, the cabriole leg appears
Rococo 1725-1750	Louis XV (1715-1774)	'c' scrolls, very light fanciful carving of foliage, no straight lines
Transitional 1750-1770	Louis XV/XVI	Reaction against excesses of rococo, restraint, mixture of Louis XV features and anticipation of Louis XVI
Neo-classical 1770-1790	Louis XVI (1774-1789)	Tapering legs and classical motifs, revival of Louis XIV side cabinet
Directoire 1790-1800	The Directorate (1789-1799)	Elegant simplicity, Etruscan decoration, evidence of English influence
Consulate 1800-1805	The Consulate (1799-1804)	Rectangular and architectural forms, plain woods with fine *guilloché* mounts
Empire 1800-1820	Napoleon (1804-1815)	Heavy architectural forms, often plain with massive ormolu mounts, masculinity
Restoration 1815-1850	Louis XVIII (1815-1824) Charles X (1824-1830)	*Bois clairs,* mass production, seeds of eclecticism, Gothic and rococo revivals
Second Empire 1840-1870	Louis-Philippe (1830-1848) Napoleon III (1852-1871)	Muddled eclectic designs, Renaissance and Louis revivals, exhibition era
Art Nouveau 1885-1910		Reaction to mass production and eclectic design, naturalistic and stylised plant forms
Modernism 1895-present day		Return to simple pure rectangular forms, fine veneers alongside a return to the 1820-1840 Biedermeier period

A very grand and imposing kingwood and purple heart bonheur du jour *in the finest Louis XVI revival style of the nineteenth century. The vase alone would be a highly prized collector's piece. The plaque on the frieze drawer is an unusual shape and beautifully painted. The plaques on the sides and frieze are all unusual and are rarely, if ever, seen on furniture. An amusing feature is the pierced urn stand on the platform stretcher. The quality of the mounts, porcelain, veneering and carcass are extremely fine. It is a pity that the complicated Ionic capitals and the fluted legs are a little heavy.*

c.1870

These three photographs show first of all France as it really was, secondly France as it was for royalty and thirdly, France as the nineteenth century imagined it to have been in the eighteenth century.

An engraving of an interior from the Nice and Savoy area which would at this time have been one of the states of Italy under the stern eye of the Austrian Empire. It shows the general living room of a house in the small village of Mont Bride in the vallée de Sixte. The style is totally that of the eighteenth century, showing how traditional styles continued to be used with comparatively little added furniture in the first twenty to forty years of the nineteenth century. The three beds set in the wall are very interesting, as is the enormous provincial long-case clock.

The Cabinet de Travail of Queen Marie-Amélie at the Tuileries, gouache by Jean-Charles Develly. The room is stuffed with furniture, including a late Empire settee and a pair of Empire arm chairs and foot-stools. On the left there are two Louis XVI centre tables and a Charles X chest-of-drawers. The bureau plat that the Queen is sitting at is also a Louis XVI original. The small guéridon on the right hand side of the photograph is in the new Gothic taste. Next to it is an upholstered méridienne. Apart from these three pieces there is very little new furniture. Dated 1841.

A wonderful romantic version of France in the high fashionable style of the second quarter of the eighteenth century, from a painting by J. Rivier. The room is full of asymmetrical rococo mirrors and wall panels. The billiard table is an inventive Italianate version of the Louis XV style that could only have been dreamt up during the nineteenth century. The stool that the onlooker on the right is sitting on could never have existed in the eighteenth century.

FRANCE

''The king is dead — Long live the king''. The ritual phrase that echoes the continued traditions of furniture making which rose to undisputed heights in the eighteenth century. The sun has never set on the Sun King — the reflection of his glorious patronage of the arts is still present in today's furniture making. The nineteenth century revived every style possible but without a doubt it was the Louis XIV, XV and XVI styles that predominated, remaining popular today whilst most other revival styles are lost to the increasing momentum of the Modernist movement.

The traditions of French cabinet making, learnt in the seventeenth century and brought to fruition in the eighteenth century, were continued through the long war-troubled years after the Revolution. France had for a long time accepted its monarchs as the precursors of fashion. The court and its many satellites down to the minor nobility, exiled in the provinces through being out of favour or through lack of enough income to sustain the rich life demanded at court, dictated taste and the contemporary styles were almost forced on a willing merchant class by the dealers.

Although at war with most of Europe, the enormous wealth of private patronage was just enough to sustain the furniture industry through British naval blockades and political uncertainty. The advent of Bonaparte led to enough stability to rekindle an industry which had been forced into hibernation during the revolutionary years. The cabinet makers who had supplied rich and extravagant furniture to the nobility were, if not targets of the revolutionaries as working men, forced to stop their work and their guilds were ordered to close down in 1791. Huge amounts of Royal and important furniture had been sold privately and by public auction, much of it to the English nobility, an extraordinary idea to contemplate today, considering the politics of the time and the war with England. The establishment of the Empire realised a need to re-furbish the looted Royal palaces under the excellent auspices of the Garde-Meuble Impérial and enormous sums were spent to achieve this.

At first mahogany mounted with breathtaking *bronze doré* was used almost exclusively, but as the century entered its 'teens the effectiveness of the naval blockade became more apparent and furniture makers were forced to look for alternative supplies of timber in the indigenous woods of Northern Europe. These were the *bois clairs,* sycamore, maple, ash, elm and *bois de citron.*

The influence of the Empire had been paramount throughout occupied Europe and beyond and furniture had taken on a severe, almost austere, outline. The sovereigns Louis XVIII and Charles X and also, to a limited extent, Louis-Philippe, had not attempted radically to change the styles of their immediate predecessors. The reduction in Royal patronage, although still apparent, coincided with a new elite, a new middle class whose wealth was fostered by the industrial and subsequent economic revolution. Far more people were able to buy furniture of a more sophisticated type, but their demands were for a far less ornate style of more practical items than previously supplied by cabinet makers under the banner of the highly specialised guilds. The new clientele's tastes were not as developed as the tastes of Royal patronage, and consequently the standards of design and manufacture were not as exacting. The Paris cabinet makers were in the perfect position to accommodate these new requirements and were able to form new small businesses and workshops combining all the necessary skilled craftsmen under one room for the first time, a practice not possible under the guild system.

Nineteenth century France inherited political uncertainty as well as the art of fine furniture making from the previous century. In July 1830, the incompetent Charles X abdicated under mounting pressure from the people of Paris who were making threatening noises against his politicians. The previously exiled Louis-Philippe, Duc d'Orleans, was proclaimed king and there were almost two decades of peace and prosperity.

However, by 1848 there was another revolution stirring in Paris and in turn Louis-Philippe was forced to abdicate and flee to England. The consequent political instability, mainly caused by a penal form of taxation, produced a brief Civil War in Paris. At this time many French cabinet makers and designers left for the stability of England and applied their trades in London. This merging of French and English design and furniture making techniques marked the beginning of the International Style.

The political unrest had established a need for a new type of rule in France and the machine to elect a President was set up. One of the candidates was Louis-Napoleon who, due to his rank and famous name, was surprisingly accepted greedily by the electorate and elected President Bonaparte by a landslide in 1848. French Royalist traditions soon rose above politics and in 1852 the President was proclaimed Emperor and the Second Empire began under Napoleon III. His marriage to Eugénie de Montijo in January 1853 set a seal of approval on the monarchy and fashion again began to be dictated by the monarch, as it had been in the eighteenth century. The Empress Eugénie had a love of anything to do with Marie-Antoinette and she set about re-decorating her rooms in the Louis XVI style marking the first step towards the Louis XVI revival that was to continue throughout the century until the present day.

The Franco-Prussian War in 1870 marked the fall from power of Napoleon III and the end of the Second Empire. France had been quickly and easily defeated and Paris itself threatened. The subsequent economic upset had a marked effect on the Paris furniture industry and it was to be several years before trade was on to an even keel. By this time Germany had established herself as a major furniture manufacturing power and the lead of France was lost, although her designers were still active, especially in the host of revival styles.

Napoleon III had not been a man of great taste or artistic ability but he did have a wide and genuine interest in the new and expanding commerce of France and of the possibilities of industry and machine power. Eugénie was a lover of showy goods and *meubles de luxe,* glitter was the Royal order of the day rather than style. This glitter was amplified by the cluttering of rooms with all types of furniture. Rooms were filled with *crapauds* and other comfortable chairs and everywhere there were small tables for different uses.

French furniture was by far the most expensive in Europe. It was well made and usually well designed and had a certain chic which made it more sought after than furniture in the French style manufactured elsewhere. For a good label purchasers have always been willing to pay more for their goods and the social cachet in owning 'a genuine French desk in the Louis XV style, made in Paris' went a long way to supporting French firms for the most part of the nineteenth century, even though they had become largely uncompetitive with England and Germany by the 1880s. Although the Paris furniture making industry was large, it consisted of numerous small firms in and around the Faubourg Saint-Antoine, many of which had been there for several generations, in small and overcrowded workshops that were hardly adaptable to the installation of modern machinery. Of course there were many exceptions to this rule, one of which was the firm of Krieger, with its retail outlets all over Europe. Line engravings of their workshops in the 1880s are to be seen opposite and overleaf.

Etablissements Krieger-Damon and Cie in 1884 had no less than six different addresses for their workshops, including upholstery, veneering, modelling, metalwork, tapestry weavers and designers. This was one of the larger firms whose range of products covered a wide sphere from the ordinary *meubles courant* to the very best *meubles de luxe.* Another large firm, the Maison L. Simon, had retail premises covering four houses in the rue de Rivoli and no less than seven in the rue François-Miron.

The furniture industry employed many workmen in Paris and by the 1880s there were 17,000 recorded. This compares to the 10,000 recorded in the first decade of the century. There were approximately 2,000 engaged in the making of the superior *meubles de luxe* and 14,500 employed in the manufacture of the less expensive and poorer quality *meubles courant.* This leaves a figure of 500 workers who were engaged in the fascinating world of the *trôleurs.* These were the men who made their furniture in small back-street workshops, even at home. Their products were not always made to the normal high standards expected of the French furniture industry. They did not have their own retail outlets so they plied the streets of the Faubourg Saint-Antoine with their wares on hand trollies, selling to whoever they could at whatever price they could obtain. These workmen quite often made their furniture in organised workshops, to varying standards but sold the pieces themselves to the highest bidder. They paid for their own materials and the use of the workshop and were at the mercy of the rich dealers as they lived from day to day, from hand to mouth, often being forced to sell their wares at cost in order to survive.

The *ébénistes* of *meubles de luxe* were in a privileged

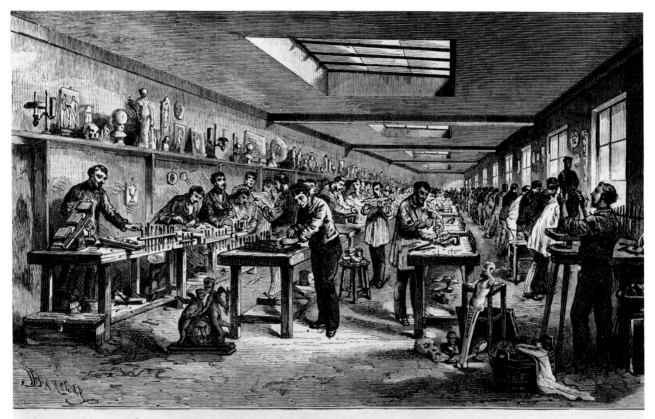

ÉTABLISSEMENTS KRIEGER-DAMON ET Cⁱᵉ (Un atelier de sculpture et de modelage).

A line engraving of one of the large workshops of Krieger-Damon & Cie. Two companion photographs are reproduced overleaf. The engraving was commissioned c.1884 and is an impressive picture of a large establishment's working conditions, conditions which would have been described in glowing terms by the employer. The relatively large areas of glass in the roof and windows allow a generous amount of light into the long gallery. There appears to be no provision for any form of lighting. It would be very difficult to work in any of the three shops illustrated after dusk. There were two grades of sculpteurs in Paris, the wood carver and the modeler. The wood carver was the most highly paid of all the general workers, earning 90 centimes to one franc 25 centimes per hour. The modeler, who prepared the clay models for the bronze mounts, can be seen standing on the left hand side of the engraving, putting the finishing touches to a figure.

position amongst the Paris workmen, making a varied selection of fine quality furniture, often for Royal patrons. They worked in the small workshops behind the large shops under the direct supervision of the main furniture retailers who did not have their own workshops.

The 14,500 ordinary cabinet makers were by far the greatest number and worked directly for the large shops or manufacturers, at home or in garrets. In many cases, the same man would spend the most part of his career making the same pieces of furniture day in and day out. This itself is an indication as to how long styles remained popular in the last thirty or forty years of the nineteenth century. These workmen or *spécialistes* more often than not worked in appalling conditions, in tiny rooms with poor ventilation. To increase their productivity and consequently their wages, they were often forced to make use of able-bodied

members of their family to do the laborious, time consuming non-skilled jobs, such as sanding and polishing. Notwithstanding these dire conditions, the Paris workman was well paid, especially when compared with his Continental counterpart. The highest paid were the wood carvers at 90 centimes to 1 franc 25 centimes per hour. The tapestry workers were next with 80 centimes to 1 franc 25 centimes. The cabinet maker averaged between 80 centimes and 1 franc 10 centimes per hour for the *ébénistes de luxe* and only 40 to 80 centimes per hour for the ordinary cabinet makers — pay that underlines their plight. The carpenter or *menuisier* earned between 70 centimes and 1 franc per hour, putting him almost on the same scale as the cabinet maker. The carpenter of the *meubles massif* was paid between 80 centimes and 1 franc 15 centimes. The chair makers, a separate section of the furniture industry, were paid between 70 centimes and 1 franc per hour for

ÉTABLISSEMENTS KRIEGER-DAMON ET Cie (Un atelier de mécaniciens).

A line engraving of one of the many large workshops of the firm of Krieger-Damon & Cie. It shows row upon row of ébénistes who were the skilled workers of the Paris furniture trade considered to be the true technicians, working with the skills of past decades. The cabinet maker was one of the highest paid workers at the time of this engraving in approximately 1884, earning 80 centimes up to one franc 10 centimes per hour. That was the going rate for the de luxe cabinet maker, the ordinary furniture makers, employing by far the most work-men, paid only 45 to 80 centimes per hour. Although Krieger employed many people it is difficult to accept the artist's impression of the row upon row of men so gainfully employed. There must be a certain amount of artistic licence — doubtless to please the patron!

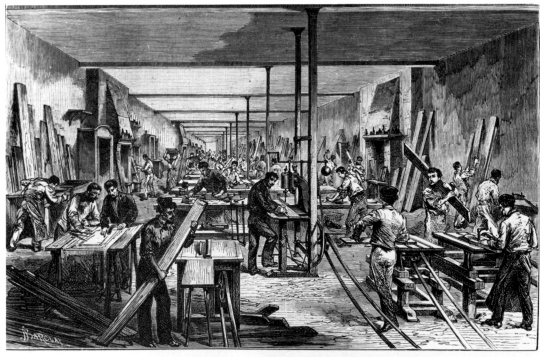

ÉTABLISSEMENTS KRIEGER-DAMON ET Cie (Un atelier d'ébénisterie).

A line engraving from the firm of Krieger-Damon & Cie showing one of the companion workshops to the cabinet shop. Both workshops with their rows of employees are considerably aided by the use of machines. There is a complicated arrangement of overhead pulley wheels, driving lathes and drills. How dangerous all these unprotected wheels must have been. There appear to be no guards or safety devices and all the men are wearing everyday clothes. A modern day factory inspector, or shop steward, would have a heart attack! The mécanicien was an integral part of the larger furniture manufacturer's establishment.

the *meubles de luxe* and a mere 45 to 65 centimes for ordinary work. This scale of wages is difficult to compare with those of today and the comparison is hardly relevant. Suffice to say that the skilled wood-worker or cabinet maker in today's age of the machine is valued far more highly than he was in the dawning era of machinery. An interesting comparison is one with craftsmen of similar skills during the same period in the 1880s in other countries. The going rates were approximately two thirds of the Paris wages in Germany and Belgium, with the unfortunate Italian craftsmen earning even less than their northern fellows.

However, the highest paid wood-carver or tapestry weaver earning 1 franc 25 centimes per hour was only able to earn, let us say for a modest, for the times, sixty hour week, 75 francs. The head cabinet maker to the Crown workshops was earning almost 400 francs per week at the same time, on a fixed monthly salary.

Paris was able to support approximately 1,200 different main employers and retailing outlets, who in turn employed the services of the 17,000 workers in the Paris furniture industry. Approximately fifty of these were the vendors of the *meubles de luxe,* many of whom appear in the retailers and makers list (q.v.), the rest being the ordinary shops throughout the whole of Paris but mainly in and around the Faubourg Saint-Antoine.

Nevertheless, the French craftsmen were not satisfied with their lot and in 1882 there was an unprecedented strike in the Paris furnture industry. Although the strike was comparatively short-lived, it allowed a vast amount of foreign goods to flow on to the French market. The newly established industries of the Second Reich in Germany were to take full advantage of this lull in French industry but the Belgians and the Italians also took the opportunity to exploit a greedy and weakened market. Foreign salesmen descended on the retailers with sophisticated catalogues of engravings and photographs and quickly took over a major slice of the market. This was not difficult as the lower wages of the other countries and the streamlined manu-facturing efficiency, especially of Germany, meant that the imported goods were far cheaper than those made in Paris. Furniture that was to all intents as well made as French furniture was imported at three-fifths of the price of local furniture. The French industry had been resting on its laurels for far too long. Competition from now on was to be international and furniture made in an international style.

Certainly the French had the monopoly of the small beautifully made *meubles de luxe* but this was a small part of a huge market. The average man in the street wanted an average piece of furniture at an average price and was not interested in the finer points of execution that a French craftsman might indulge in compared to a foreign craftsman. The general economic depression at this time, combined with continuing political instability, caused many furniture workers to leave Paris for other countries, further weakening France's position.

A need for change, fostered by the establishment of a new social order after the Napoleonic Wars, was echoed in the proliferation of romantic literature and a new desire for the historical background of the past. Designers' heads (although some would have it, their hearts only) were turned back towards the splendours of Versailles and even earlier to the for-gotten treasures of the Renaissance and towering spires of gothicism.

The published formal Empire designs of Percier and Fontaine were watered down by La Mésangère and the empire style doggedly continued until the very late 1830s. Without the massive bronze mounts of the true empire, this masculine style fought a losing battle with eclecticism and the potential plainness of pieces in the Charles era was relieved with inlaid Gothic arches or rococo foliage in woods such as lime and sycamore. Plain bourgeois taste had triumphed for a while but the vogue for dark woods and plain, beautifully figured red mahogany veneers, using simple empire forms, was never to be repeated. Mahogany was to be used less frequently, rosewood taking its place. Walnut, in plentiful native supply, was therefore a cheap and highly decorative wood for less important articles.

The harbours of Le Havre had become the ship-ping centre for a great deal of the woods imported from abroad, the more exotic woods from the West Indies and the Americas. As a large and geo-graphically important port, Le Havre served not only the Paris furniture trade but also much of the trade of the rest of Europe.

The need for large amounts of cheap serviceable furniture was becoming insatiable. The Paris population figures in 1830 were well under one million — by 1840 the figure had increased by over ten per cent. The industrial age of steam driven saws and veneer knives was fully equipped to deal with this unprecedented demand for furniture. Every household wanted and was able to buy more pieces than might be strictly necessary and by the middle of the century the move to overfurnishing, coupled with a desire for everything to be upholstered, including heavy curtaining, was well under way.

The emphasis was on comfort. Le Bouteiller describes France and England as "*...les deux royaumes bien aimés de la grâce, du luxe et du* comfort". The *Exposition Journal de l'Industrie et des Arts Utiles* of 1839 was translated into German, English, Russian and Italian.

The elegance of the beautifully figured rich mahogany veneers of the Charles X and Louis-Philippe period was an elegance intended for the new bourgeois market. The popular *fauteuil à gondole* developed an elegant swan's head terminal to the arms, a feature repeated on beds and the new conception of the wardrobe — *l'armoire à glace* — simply the logical step, in hindsight, of joining together a *psyché* or small toilet mirror, and a cupboard.

These plain but elegant pieces lent themselves to the new Gothic style. This influence, somewhat inexplicably known as *le style troubadour,* can be broadly divided into two factions in French furniture. The first is the elegant style of finely inlaid articles of a basically conventional type with tall lancet arches in a true *ogivaux* manner, the inlay being only thin strips of a *bois clair* and the edges of the piece inset with similar stringing. This pretty Gothic style popular under Charles X fell prey to the full ravages of the romantic revivalists and Victor Hugo. By 1840 Gothic had become much heavier, incorporating medieval and Louis XIII motifs without the lightness of form of the previous style or its English counterpart continued from the Regency Gothic to the designs of Pugin.

Furniture was now not solely a product for the home market but influences came from abroad too. The first, apart from a brief revival of Egyptian interest under Louis-Philippe, was Anglomania. The political strife in Paris in 1848 caused many artisans to leave France for England. The London makers welcomed a highly skilled workforce ready to interpret the highly fashionable French designers' work into fine pieces of furniture, often almost indistinguishable from French pieces.

Influences from France to England and *vice versa* were to remain interchangeable during the exhibition years of the third quarter of the century.

The end of the Empire influence and the Gothic coincided with the July monarchy of 1848. However, as early as 1840 the eclectic seeds of the Second Empire had been taking hold and the style to be known as Napoleon III was born.

The 1840s was the decade that set the seal of approval on the era of the revival. The innovative nineteenth century mind was ready and able to copy the styles of the past but always sought to improve upon them. A Henri II theme would quickly be adapted to suit the shape and needs of contemporary life. A Louis XIII chair would be reduced slightly in size and proportions. Renaissance details would find their way on to a transitional *bureau à cylindre* with a Louis XIV base. This unconscious need to amalgamate styles and motifs on forms of yet another era was totally accepted and approved of by the new clientele. It suited their needs of comfort and their romantic outlook on the past history and glory of France. Thus eclecticism was born and remained *à la mode* until the 1890s.

The intervening years were years of wealth and ambition based firmly on the traditions of art created for France by the great monarchs of the past. Design had to rest on its laurels whilst new revivals vied for recognition in a vague but discernible vestige of order. The great architectural restorer Viollet-le-Duc brought about a love of Medievalism echoed by Victor Hugo as well as the novels of Sir Walter Scott. This style never became the passion in France that it had been in England under the eye of William Burges. France was content, once again, to rest on her architectural laurels and simply restore the great Norman and Medieval churches of the north, which had so inspired Burges, who in turn influenced a few German cabinet makers for a short time.

This contentment was not so with the revival of interest of the Renaissance and Henri II's reign. Louis-Philippe had set his seal of approval on this style at the Exposition des Produits de l'Industrie in 1839, when he purchased a Renaissance cabinet from the Grohé Brothers. However, the designer Aimé Chenavard had expounded the return to Renaissance in *Nouveau Recueil d'ornements* published in 1835.

The Renaissance remained popular until the end of the 1880s in France. Alongside was the more positive French style of Louis XIII. Turning and balusters were all the rage, mingled with a Flemish heaviness and gadrooning.

The most complete example of 'Renaissance' furnishing in Paris must surely be the work of Maugin, the architect who designed the furniture for the Hôtel de la Païva on the Champs Elysées.

The Renaissance revival was to become the dominating style throughout most of industrial Europe. By the 1880s every shop included Renaissance style furniture in its stock and every catalogue was lavishly illustrated with these ornate and often heavy pieces.

'Renaissance' furniture, whether stylistically from the François Premier period, or the later mannerist styles of Henri II and Louis XIII was essentially furniture for the dining room, using walnut or other light woods.

Every room began to have its own peculiar style of revival furniture. Certain of the older styles, in their refined nineteenth century forms, were deemed suitable for the dining room, others for the boudoir. The drawing room or *salon* was always a complete mixture or muddle of the three Louis styles although by the end of the century most salons were to be furnished in a more complete Louis revival style, with a large suite of seat furniture directly copied from the eighteenth century and usually in the Louis XVI manner. The dining room lent itself perfectly to the Renaissance, with the *meubles massif* in oak and walnut with their roughed-out machine carving finished off by hand by the *sculpteurs*. The designs of game and sporting scenes by Liénard were perfect for the dining room of the second half of the nineteenth century, there was none of the morbid horror of trophies of dead game that would put the modern diner off his or her meal.

Bedrooms were furnished in a light and airy fashion with a great deal of attention paid to the mass of upholstery and a feeling of snug comfort, luxury and security. The lighter turnings of the Renaissance were ideal for beds. Conversely, the severe and plainer early Renaissance designs, as opposed to the later designs mixed with baroque for the dining room, were ideal for mens' clubs, studies and smoking rooms. These pieces of ebony veneer or *bois noirci* were decorated only with the contrast of the gilt mounts. The large *bureau plat* in either Louis XV or Louis XVI style, sometimes with a *cartonnier*, was suitable for a study.

The publication of *Cousine Bette* in 1848 refers to the Louis XV style and heralds the re-birth of the rococo. In French *rococo* simply means old fashioned or antiquated. The use of the word *rocaille* in France to describe the early Louis XV period is far more accurate, referring to the rockwork carving so popular on the carved frieze of a console table or the apron of a mirror. The eighteenth century designs of Meissonnier and Nicolas Pineau were revived with abandon. The Rococo Revival, surprisingly a much later one than the German *Zweites Rokoko* or the renewed interest shown by England's Prince of Wales at the Brighton Pavilion at the very beginning of the century, is almost certainly the most popular style today. Readily identifiable with all that is French and fashionable, Louis XV forms are always the most sought-after in shops and auction houses. Italian and Spanish artisans, living in secluded villages, are still today supplying the large city retailers with chairs in the rococo manner, directly copying the French style, rather than incorporating

their own local peculiarities as they would have done in the nineteenth century. This popularity was apparent during the Second Empire and, of a single style, Louis XV is by far the most commonly available and most asked for. The image of comfort combined with elegance and a casual 'prettiness' that fits so well with today's modern living was as vivid under the early years of the Second Empire as it is today. The wealthy *bourgeois* family popularised the style that was made and distributed throughout the whole of France. The rococo was the style for the *salon*. The comfortable chairs would be ideal for the relaxed but still formal daytime entertaining and the room would be liberally dotted with small tables or *guéridons*, with perhaps a *bureau en pente*, traditionally called a *bureau en dos d'âne*, at the side of the room.

The romantic writings of Balzac were not only confined to references to the rococo. The Pompadour Style had enjoyed a limited popularity under Louis-Philippe, a popularity brought to its zenith by the Empress Eugénie. The Empress delighted in all things connected with Marie-Antoinette and in the true traditional manner of French monarchy she fostered the revival of the Louis XVI style.

Victor Quetin, in *Le Magasin de Meubles, Journal d'ameublement* described the Napoleon III period as the ''Louis XV revival''. This was in 1865-67 and although his drawings show comparatively little Louis XVI furniture, the style must have been well on its way to eclipsing the rococo revival. The range of Louis XVI furniture was complete. From *guéridons* in the style of Weisweiler to *commodes à l'anglais* inspired by the same maker and from *bureaux plats* after Martin Carlin to the rarely seen dining table. The drawing room was either furnished in Louis XV or XVI taste, depending entirely upon the whim of the householder. Numerous pieces of porcelain mounted furniture, imitating Sèvres, were produced. The application of these panels, inevitably painted with a Watteauesque girl on a swing or a couple in a garden setting after Boucher, held by attenuated rococo mounts, watered down the severity of form of the Louis XVI period.

The Empress Eugénie's bedroom at Saint-Cloud shows a pair of lacquer *commodes a l'anglais* and a *guéridon* similar to that supplied by F. Dammanock to Queen Marie-Antoinette. The whole mood of her room is Louis XVI but with the comfort and plushness of upholstery that dominated the middle period of nineteenth century France.

The *bas d'armoire* and *meuble d'appui* that had their origins in the early eighteenth century but were popularised in the Louis XVI period became some of the most consistently popular items of furniture of the Louis XVI revival. They were also perfect targets for porcelain panels.

As Louis XVI furniture became more severe in the eighteenth century, so did its imitations towards the end of the Second Empire and the end of the nineteenth century. The simplicity of Jean-Henri Riesener's later work of the late 1780s is reflected in the popularity of the *bureau à cylindre* in the late nineteenth century. This severity suited the tastes for a gentleman's study.

Boulle furniture, discussed in detail on pages 31 and 32, was popular in the Napoleonic period and it is difficult to establish the timing of its prolific revival until it appears *en masse* during the Second Empire. However the revival of interest of the Louis XIV period, Boulle's royal patron, can be traced back to the reign of Louis XVIII. It was not until just before the Second Empire that the revival of Louis XIV became established.

Any confusion that may have occurred in the mind of the early nineteenth century furniture collector as to the date of the popular boulle *meuble d'appui* or *meuble d'entre deux* which were revived from the early eighteenth century by makers such as Etienne Levasseur in the 1770s, would have been heightened by the revival of the Louis XIV boulle style in the 1840s.

Apart from the myriad of boulle furniture, traditionally mis-spelt 'Buhl' in England during the nineteenth century, the Louis XIV revival was not as popular as the styles of the two subsequent Louis. Chairs were commonly made in Louis XIV style as well as side cabinets and low vitrines or *meubles d'appui*. In line with most of the earlier styles, the Louis XIV period was popular for the dining room. The large comfortable armchairs of the period were suitable for long meals and had a formality and dignity suitable for formal entertaining.

The Orient had been a mystical influence on the traders of the late seventeenth century and its romance was not lost on nineteenth century France. Alongside the Anglomania of the Louis-Philippe period Great Britain influenced France, bringing about a love of everything from the Far East. A direct influence was the imitation of *papier mâché* from the English factories. France paradoxically did not use *papier mâché* but favoured stained woods which were certainly more durable. These *bois noirci* pieces were commonly made of the readily available pear wood, stained, rather than the high gloss of lacquer, black. The decoration, in the Chinese manner imitating *lac burgauté,* consisted of mother-of-pearl inlay and a polychromatic decoration of

flowers. Small pieces in *façon de laque* were decorated with chinoiseries in gilt on a black lacquer ground, often highlighted with polychrome figures, unlike the Chinese export pieces popular at the same time and filling the same functions. A pair of small tripod tables or *guéridons* were supplied in 1839 to the Grand Trianon — a year after a pair of boulle tripod tables. These small tip-top tables, after an English mid-eighteenth century form, were commonly used as fire screens and consequently not many have survived today as their delicate construction was not suitable to withstand too much heat.

The Orient also brought about a revival of 'bamboo' furniture in the late 1830s. Popularised in England by the Prince of Wales when redecorating the Brighton Pavilion at the beginning of the century, large amounts of simulated bamboo furniture were made. Commonly 'bamboo' furniture in France was made of turned pine (*bois de pin*), although better quality pieces would be turned from beechwood. Tahan is known to have made small simulated bamboo pieces cast in bronze. At the end of the century rattan and wicker furniture enjoyed a tremendous vogue in a new era of aestheticism given impetus by the progressive English designers. Also at this time light framed 'bamboo' furniture, as well as rattan and wicker, was being exported to Europe from America and the exact origin of many pieces is in doubt.

The love of pastiche, to all intents and purposes in an almost chronological order, continued until the last decade of the century. After Louis XVI, predictably enough, came a revival of interest in the very Empire style that romanticism had fought against in the 'twenties and 'thirties. As the Second Empire waned the later Louis XVI revivals had become less eclectic and were truer in spirit to the original eighteenth century designs. The Empire style was copied perhaps more faithfully than earlier revivals, nurtured by the interest in Biedermeier that was beginning to revive in Austria and Germany and in the Regency period in England. Like the more severe later Louis XVI revival furniture, the Empire was confined mainly to impressive desks for the office or study, although eventually it became the ideal style for the formality of the dining room, remaining popular until well into the twentieth century and, like many other revivals is reproduced today but none with the true spirit of quality of the Napoleonic Era.

The revivals mentioned in France in the preceding paragraphs have been in some form of chronological order in their development in the nineteenth century. Unfortunately however, although a faint pattern of a chronological revival can be traced from the second quarter of the nineteenth century from Louis XIII to the Empire of the 1880s, the revivals cannot be so easily defined. Certainly their popularity can be traced chronologically, but their inspiration and their actual inception cannot.

A Louis XVI piece may pre-date a Louis XIV piece in the hectic revivalism of the early years of Louis-Philippe's reign. Baroque before Renaissance, medieval pre-dated by the love of all that is Gothic.

The *Expositions* in Paris of the 1880s were still the seed beds of eclecticism. The fashionable salon by this decade would be full of various styles of furniture and the tendency amongst the richer *bourgeoisie* to furnish rooms in a particular stylistic theme was diminishing. The various revivals would be proudly exhibited together. The craftsmanship, whether man-made or machine-made, was unquestionable. Certainly, the cabinet work of the nineteenth century maker was far superior to that of most eighteenth century pieces, with perhaps the exception of the royal commissions for Marie-Antoinette during the 1780s. Until the end of the century the interior and carcass work was definitely at its peak, with considerable attention to finish by the better Paris makers.

To the modern eye, machine-made furniture appears less attractive than the earlier hand-made examples but to the nineteenth century eye there was an undoubted feeling of pride in the achievement of production. After all man had made the machines to make the furniture and thus was able to make more of it to satisfy the immensely expanding market.

Towards the end of the Second Empire interior carcass work had reached the high standards of English equivalents and dovetails, whether hand-sawn or machine-made, were comparable, and indeed in many cases indistinguishable from, English work. This is the same for most of the north European countries, especially as machinery became standardised.

A mind that was able to operate with almost total independence from other furniture designers, due to generous patronage, was that of Rupert Carabin. He had designed stands at the 1889 Paris Exhibition and that year was commissioned to design and make a bookcase with no conditions as to the form, simply *'ce que vous aurez en tête'*. The result was a bizarre cabinet of walnut and wrought iron carved in full relief with naked female figures, applied with swaying bulrushes. Carabin's sources are those of sixteenth century baroque, enlarging naked female caryatid figures to extraordinary proportions, which

are either free-standing or their hair or feet 'growing' into the cabinet work. As a sculptor and furniture designer, Carabin completely eclipses the elegant sculptural table c.1865 made by Jules-Aimé Dalon for Madame de Païva's house, mentioned earlier.

Carabin's rare pieces of furniture (approximately only twenty were made) show an unprecedented freedom of design and execution but are of a style hardly acceptable to the commercial manufacturers of the day who were still deeply embedded in historicism.

Paris was by no means the only French furniture-producing city or town. Louis Majorelle had a large provincial business supplying furniture of all the revival styles and not simply in the new *art nouveau* style. There were large centres at Tours, Lyon and Toulouse with many small workshops throughout France producing quantities of furniture in the Paris styles.

Furniture in the regional areas of France continued to be made in a traditional manner, using well-tried techniques and in many cases simply continuing to reproduce the old regional styles of each individual area while new furniture could be purchased from the many furniture shops growing up in the larger towns, who bought their furniture from the main suppliers. In the area surrounding Nice, for example, locally made furniture continued to be made in a local Italianate style, although after France acquired the province along with the Savoy from Austria in 1860, Nice and many other regions began to look towards Paris for inspiration rather than their own essentially local styles.

The seeds sown by Viollet-le-Duc and Ruprich-Robert during the 1860s took a long time to germinate and it was not until the late 1880s that their work and the principles of design behind the Union Centrale des Beaux Arts began to take a definite form.

The rumblings felt throughout northern Europe (Morris and his circle in England, Van de Velde in Belgium and again later in Germany and the Munich designers) were no less apparent in France.

Flore Ornementale, published in 1866 by Robert, epitomised the naturalism that was to grow from baroque and rococo foliage. A cabinet in the Louis XV manner designed by Robert in 1852, on cabriole legs profusely inlaid with flowers, hardly anticipates the elegance of the high art nouveau period at the end of the century. The stylised plant forms of Viollet-le-Duc as illustrated in his *Entretiens sur l'architecture* of 1872, are the first true signs of what was to develop in France during the next thirty years. Gustave Eiffel, whose giant tower erected in 1889 is considered to be one of the earliest architectural indications of the new style, cannot really be considered a true originator of French art nouveau. His tower is a self conscious tribute to the revolution afforded by industry and new techniques and only the apparent effortlessness of the tower when seen from afar — possible with the use of steel — gives any indication of what was to come.

The Orientalism that had been repeatedly popular since the early years of the nineteenth century had become more clearly defined by the 1860s as a Japanese style. The light colours of Japanese design, combined with their extraordinary use of space and asymmetry, had attracted Samuel Bing, the Hamburg dealer who imported Japanese traditional ware to Paris. His Paris shop soon became a centre for all types of material, be it furniture, paintings, glass or ceramics, and he unwittingly named the new style that was developing from a mixture of Japanese forms and earlier naturalism when he named his shop 'L'Art Nouveau'. French Symbolist painters such as Gustave Moreau and Odilon Redon had already preached their ethereal wispy Symbolism, inspired by Blake and Burne-Jones in England, which indicates early French sources of the later art nouveau period.

There was no sudden change from the eclecticism of the industrial world to the naturalism of *l'art nouveau*. The naturalistic motifs, copied faithfully from nature, were slowly to become more and more stylised until the very plant forms themselves began to define the shape for the furniture, rather than merely decorating it. The rare furniture designs of Eugène Grasset in the late 'seventies and the early 'eighties were early signs of this stylisation, albeit mixed with the medievalism of the 'fifties. The sinuous furniture of Louis Majorelle and Alexandre Charpentier consists of broadly moulded and twisting supports holding wide lily leaves. This style of furniture had broken completely away from the earliest English influences of William Morris and the Arts and Crafts Movement, which advocated construction as a part of the overall design. The French plant forms appear to have literally 'grown'

into pieces of furniture. Their form was sculptural, many items were originally conceived in plaster mock-ups allowing total fluidity. Gallé was the past master of floral inlay but the foliate *bronze doré* mounts of Majorelle are impeccable, setting off each piece of furniture with a soft delicious gilding comparable to the best that the eighteenth century could provide. Although far removed from Empire forms, Majorelle's metalwork reflects the quality and contrast of Empire mounts against dark, rich mahogany.

The work of Hector Guimard, an architect designer and that of Eugène Vallin and Eugène Galliard, anticipates the Modernist movement of the early years of the twentieth century which eclipsed the art nouveau style as it reached its zenith at the Paris Exposition Universelle in 1900.

The furniture of Emile Gallé, founder of the Nancy School, had been profoundly influenced by Japanese artifacts. However his earlier furniture, some of which is in the Musée de l'Ecole de Nancy, is surprisingly eclectic. It is strange to see his stylised marquetry, of the finest quality, set into conventional eighteenth century forms, with obvious rococo and even Louis XIII shapes and motifs. It was the later work of Le Corbusier and Charlotte Perriand that laid the foundations in France of the modernist and functionalist principles that had been seized upon by the German and Dutch designers after the shattering effects of the First World War.

It is difficult to reconcile the fact that alongside the fresh new spirit of art nouveau and modernism most firms continued simply to manufacture and produce item after item of revival furniture, more often than not purely as a reproduction piece.

Occasionally the better makers, for example Linke and Zwiener, would introduce an extra spark of rococo roundness and ebullience into the shape of their more enlightened commissions, possibly inspired by the new freedoms in design but still totally 'Louis' in taste. The furniture of the people of France at the dawn of the twentieth century was still essentially eclectic, relying heavily and almost totally on the era inspired by the Sun King. ''The king is dead — Long live the king.''

Boulle Furniture

André-Charles Boulle (1642-1732) has become a household name for the furniture collector. All marquetry pieces, inlaid on to a tortoiseshell ground, are now termed 'boulle', regardless of whether or not the design is attributable to him, and regardless of the date of manufacture of the piece, or even country of origin.

Boulle furniture has remained the singularly most popular type of French furniture since its inception. It has been made continually since the reign of Louis XIV, only waning in popularity during the Napoleonic Era. These traditions were fostered by a direct link from Boulle himself from the 1690s to the 1840s. Boulle's son Charles-Joseph continued the workshops after his father's death in 1732 into the second half of the eighteenth century. These work-shops were responsible for the training of Etienne Levasseur who made and repaired boulle furniture during Louis XVI's reign. In turn Levasseur's son, Pierre-Etienne, carried on boulle techniques until the mid-nineteenth century. Lemarchand supplied a pair of *guéridons* to the Grand Trianon in 1838 and by this time most of the larger Paris firms were supplying boulle furniture.

Consequently a large amount of boulle furniture is seen on the market and despite the difficulty in repairing the inlaid surfaces, with their tendency to lift and peel away, boulle is always saleable.

During the second quarter of the nineteenth century machines had been invented to cut the tortoiseshell and metalwork mechanically. This enabled the smaller manufacturer to purchase ready-made sections of marquetry and veneer it on to a carcass of his own manufacture.

It is the technique itself which has become synonymous with the name of Boulle, although it was not his invention. Boulle himself simply developed the practice of inlay to an incredibly high standard of both design and execution. In his work-shops at the Louvre he made numerous monumental and magnificent cabinets and other pieces for the Sun King, Louis XIV. His work was readily com-missioned by the nobility and wealthy merchants, who appreciated the quality and intricacy of the marquetry, which was made in large quantities, mostly supervised, if not personally executed, by Boulle himself. He soon rose to become one of the most respected cabinet makers of all time.

The technique of inlaying tortoiseshell and pewter into a solid ground was of Italian origin, developing in the sixteenth century, the marquetry normally being inset into a solid palisander ground. The dawn of the seventeenth century saw the technique being more commonly used in France, as well as Holland and some parts of Germany.

The influence of the *Manufacture Royale des Meubles de la Couronne,* under the control of Charles Le Brun in the third quarter of the seventeenth century, is evident in the important designs of Jean Berain, a contemporary of Boulle who was responsible for the design of much of the latter's work, both in terms of form and decorative inlay.

Pewter, brass, silver, palisander, mother-of-pearl, ivory and tortoiseshell were all used in various types of boulle furniture. Various colours of tortoiseshell were used, including the practice of staining clear shell to the required colour or the far more subtle approach of inserting coloured paper under clear shell to obtain brilliant hues of green or any other desired colour. This practice was far more common in the period c.1700 than in the mass-produced industrial examples of the nineteenth century. It is most important to examine later pieces most care-fully. A practice has developed of very carefully simulating, by means of painting or even printing 'tortoiseshell' and covering it with a dull clear varnish or lacquer. Many provincial pieces were painted to simulate tortoiseshell in the early eighteenth century. This was done where the maker or his client could not afford the real thing, or the materials were simply not available. In later years it appears to have much more of an intention to deceive and can be very difficult to detect. Modern 'tortoiseshell' is quite often made of resin, usually in a far too bright Post Office red.

A red hot needle is a useful implement to decide whether or not a suspicious piece of boulle is real tortoiseshell or a more modern resin substitute. Tortoiseshell, when burnt, will crackle slightly and will not melt, giving off a proteinaceous odour like that of burning hair. Resin will melt like plastic, giving off a dense putrid black smoke.

Today a great deal of 'Boulle' furniture is being made in Spain, to quite high standards copying the styles of nineteenth century makers. Although it is not normally difficult to identify these pieces as modern, it is important that they are identified and that the would-be collector or dealer is aware of the lower prices realised for modern boulle. Doubtless modern prices will maintain a second-hand value as the popularity of boulle continues to increase, but as they become more used these pieces will become more and more difficult to tell from older items. It is evident in the saleroom that some bidders are not aware of these modern items, or they have a clientele that is indifferent to the age of a piece, provided it is in good condition.

Occasionally boulle furniture is seen in a 'matched pair' of cabinets or marriage coffers. The decoration or inlay on one piece will be a mirror image of the other. This technique is known as *premier* and *contra partie*. When a *marqueteur* is cutting out the design in, let us say, brass, of a small figure from a large sheet of material, he must cut an outline of that figure in the corresponding piece of tortoiseshell, subsequently laying the brass figure into the shell. Quite logically he is left with a large sheet of brass with a cut-out silhouette of the figure and a small image of that figure left over from the sheet of tortoiseshell. These two remaining pieces are then simply married up together, giving an opposing picture of the first assembled figure, with the figure in shell on the second piece and in brass in the first. The desirability of these 'pairs', made with the obvious advantages of reduced effort, saving time and waste, is high. Two identical commodes may realise twice the price of one, adding twenty to thirty per cent for the attraction of a pair, whilst a pair of commodes in *premier* and *contra partie* would cost at the very least fifty per cent more.

French Cabinet Makers, Designers and Retailers

At the beginning of the nineteenth century more than ten thousand workers and craftsmen were employed in the furniture industry and it is only practical to record but a handful here.

The names listed below act as a convenient guide not only to makers, but to the retailers and designers whose work is more commonly seen in salerooms, antique shops and private collections, or who exhibited in the major exhibitions of the period from 1830-1900.

I would like to acknowledge *Les Ebénistes Parisiens, 1795-1870* by Denise Ledoux-Lebard, De Noeble 1965, which considerably helped my research in compiling this list.

ACHARD. 119 rue du Faubourg Saint-Honore c.1860, no.75 from 1869. Carved oak pieces.

ALBRECHT, Albert (1786-1860). Succeeded J.M.A. Albrecht, born in Hamburg. In 1866 formed Company Leger, Albert Albrecht & Cie, exhibiting at the 1867 Paris Exhibition.

ALESSANDRI FILS. Exhibited at the Paris 1867 Exhibition.

ANDRE, Paris. Exhibited iron fireplaces and chimney pieces at the Great Exhibition, Crystal Palace 1851.

BALNY, Jeune. Took over from P.M. Balny in 1832, Balny Aîné from 1839. Gothic, Renaissance and rococo revival pieces. Exhibited Crystal Palace 1851, New York 1853 and Paris 1855. Published *Le Meuble* in 1853.

BARBALAT et Cie. Exhibited cast-iron furniture in 1855.

BARBEDIENNE, Ferdinand (1810-1892). Highly important and prolific bronze founder of furniture mounts and, more commonly, bronze sculpture including figures and animals. Produced catalogues of bronze reproductions of Greek and Roman classical sculpture and experimented with *champlevé* and *cloisonné* enamels during the third quarter of the century. Exhibited several pieces of furniture at the 1855 Paris Exhibition including an ormolu mounted oak dressing table and and ormolu mounted ebony veneered bookcase. Both pieces were executed in his favoured Renaissance revival style for furniture. However, furniture by Barbedienne is extremely rare and although mounts may have been supplied by his foundry for furniture makers, no *furniture* mounts have been seen by the author signed by this firm. Signature varied from hand written capitals to stamp in capitals, usually 'F. Barbedienne, Fondeur' or 'BARBEDIENNE PARIS'.

BARON. Association des Menuisiers en Fauteuils. 3 rue de Charonne. Exhibited 1867 Paris.

BAUDRY, François (1791-1859). Large scale manufacturer who exhibited at numerous exhibitions 1827-1855. 'Ebéniste du Roi, des Princes et des Princesses'. An inventive maker who later abandoned manufacture of luxury items for cheaper functional pieces.

BEAU FILS. Bordeaux maker exhibiting Renaissance furniture in 1855.

BECKER & OTTO. 79 boulevard du Temple from 1860. Exhibited imaginative furniture of a fantasy nature in Paris Exhibitions of 1855 and 1859, also in London in 1862.

BECKER, Jean (fl.1837-1855). A Royal furniture maker on a monthly retainer.

BECQUEREL (fl. during the 1850s).

BEFORT, Fils Aîné, also Befort Jeune, sons of J.P. Befort (fl.1836-1866). Boulle pieces. Also porcelain mounted pieces like their father in the manner of J.H. Riesner.

BELLANGE family. An important family of cabinet makers to a very high standard, comprising P.A. Bellangé, his son Antoine-Louis and his slightly younger brother L.F. Bellangé.

BELLANGE, Pierre-Antoine (1758-1827). Became 'ébéniste breveté du Garde — meuble de la Couronne'during the reign of Charles X. Prominent commissions include work for the Tuileries, the Garde-meuble and furniture for the Oval Room at The White House. Stamp 'P. Bellangé'.

BELLANGE, Louis-François (1759-1827). A pair of secretaires are now at Windsor Castle. Stamps — 'L. Bellangé' and 'Bellangé Faub. St. Martin No.41 Paris'.

BELLANGE, Alexandre-Louis (1799-1863). Worked with and succeeded his father and his uncle. Ceased working in 1855. Cabinet maker to the King in 1842. He kept his father's workshops open producing plainer pieces whilst in the rue des Marais he produced eclectic furniture in various revival styles, including boulle work. A pair of Louis XIV style consoles are at Buckingham Palace, other pieces in the Wallace Collection, Windsor Castle and Versailles Museum. Had many royal commissions for the Tuileries, Versailles, the Grand Trianon, Saint-Cloud, Fontainebleau and Compiègne. Stamps 'Bellangé Ebéniste du Roi', 'Bellangé No.33 Rue des Marais Fb St Martin A Paris', 'Bellangé rue des Marais 33 Paris' and 'Bellangé Ebéniste rue des Marais No.33 Faubourg St Martin A Paris'.

BELLERY-DESFONTAINES. Late nineteenth century designer in Paris in art nouveau manner of curvelinear moulded forms.

BENARD, Joseph-Marie. Exhibited neo-Greek, Egyptian and Empire styles in the Universal Exhibition of 1900. Also five pieces at the Musée des Arts Decoratifs 'Chefs d'œuvre des grands ébénistes', 1951.

BERTAUD (fl.1828-1872 onwards). Later Bertaud Frères. Chair makers and cabinet makers. Official commissions from Compiègne and the Palais-Royal. Exhibited in Paris 1855 as Caton et Bertaud and at the 1867 Exhibition as Bertaud Frères, Stamps — 'Bertaud rue Meslay No.57', 'Bertaud et Colonia' (1828-1834).

BEURDELEY Family. Important furniture makers to an exceptional standard and wide virtuosity, especially during the latter half of the nineteenth century. Three generations starting with Jean, his son Louis-Auguste-Alfred, succeeded in turn by his son Alfred-Emmanuel-Louis. Their cabinet making tradition lasted for ninety-one years.

BEURDELEY, Jean (1772-1853). Established in Paris by 1804. He slowly built up a modest business and reputation, the fruits of which were reaped by his son and grandson. No known or recorded examples of his furniture to hand.

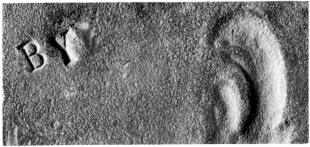

BEURDELEY, Louis-Auguste-Alfred (1808-1882). Married an American girl born in New Orleans. Commenced business at 32 rue Louis-le-Grand where he greatly built up his father's practice. He specialised in exact copies of period French furniture almost exclusively in a classical style from the Transitional and Louis XVI periods. However, a copy of a Louis XV bureau was sold at auction in 1895 and a painted card table in the same style is reproduced in *Les Ebénistes Parisiens*, Plate XVI. He became a principle cabinet maker under the Second Empire for the Garde-meuble.

Also three *jardinières* in Louis XV style were commissioned for the Tuileries. As well as commissions for the Tuileries he made furniture for Napoleon III to celebrate his wedding to Eugénie de Montijo. Exhibited furniture and works of art at the Paris 1867 Exhibition.

BEURDELEY, Alfred-Emmanuel-Louis (1847-1919). Worked at first with his father and eventually succeeded him. He kept the shop at rue Louis-le-Grand (The Hannover Pavillon) and had workshops at Nos.20 and 24 rue Dautancourt. The business continued in its traditional style with very few variations, until it was liquidated in 1895 and the remaining contents of the

premises and the principle part of his private collection was sold at the Galerie Georges Petit.

Alfred Beurdeley exhibited at the 1878 Exhibition, one major piece being an exception to the family rule in Renaissance manner. The stamps of both Louis-Auguste-Alfred Beurdeley and his son Alfred-Emmanuel-Louis appear to be the same and it is therefore not often possible to distinguish between the work of father and son. The normal mark is that of a *marque au fer,* or brand 'A Beurdeley A Paris'. Some pieces are simply stamped in the eighteenth century style, without being burnt in.

The ormolu mounts on Beurdeley furniture and the numerous smaller artefacts, often marble pieces, are almost invariably of an exceptionally high quality. The mercurial gilding and hand chasing are of a standard that makes them difficult to distinguish from late eighteenth century work. Occasionally, on the back of such mounts and more especially on the back of gilt-bronze items such as wall lights or barometer casings, a handwritten or incised mark 'BY' is found.

A highly important *succession* auction 'Collections Beurdeley' took place at the Hotel Druot in May 1979.

BIGOT, Clément-Louis (fl.1820-1855 onwards). Became C. Bigot et Cie. in 1855 and exhibited at The Universal Exhibition of the same year. Also exhibited at the 1827 Industrial Products Exhibition. Some Gothic, also boulle pieces.

BING, Samuel A. (fl.c.1895). Hamburg dealer whose Paris shop in rue de Provence became the centre for modern art. He traded under the name 'L'Art Nouveau' and from this trade name came the name which was applied to the new form of art fostered in the earlier teachings of Viollet-le-Duc.

BOUDOIR, exposé au Pavillon de l''Art Nouveau'. Bing en 1900.

A room at the Paris Exhibition of 1900 exhibited by the owner of the shop 'L'Art Nouveau', the Hamburg and Paris dealer Samuel Bing. The furniture is designed by Georges de Feure in a somewhat restrained manner based on traditional designs.

BLANCHET, Paul (fl.1844-1863). Primarily a shopfitter but exhibited a fine carved oak and marble bookcase at the 1855 Exhibition.

BOIN. Took over from the well-known shop of Mme. Veuve Desamaud-Charpentier in Paris, 1830.

BON MARCHE. A fashionable Paris shop c.1900.

BORGENAUD, Georges (fl.c.1900). Produced catalogues of mainly office furniture.

BOUILHET, H. Made castings with Christofle (q.v.).

BOUQUET, J.J. 6 rue Pavée. Exhibited at 1855 Exhibition several small pieces of furniture.

BROSSIER, Emile. A carved Louis XVI style cabinet from 8 rue Hélène, Paris 17e. c.1880?

BRULAND, Antoine (fl.1855-1867). Exhibited at 1855 Exhibition a Henri III style bookcase purchased by Napoleon III. Also exhibited in 1867.

CARABIN, Rupert (1862-1932). A sculptor from the Alsace whose extraordinary furniture was an independent, but early indication of art nouveau. fl. 1880s-1920. Incised signature with date.

CARRIER-BELLEUSE (1824-1887). An important Paris sculptor. Not known as a furniture maker but sculpted figures for a desk in the 1867 Exhibition.

CATEACCI (1816-1894). Maker of fantasy rococo furniture for the Crown.

CAVORET, Joseph (fl.1861-1867). Turning and cabinet maker. Exhibited at Industrial Arts Exhibition and 1867 Exhibition, furniture in imitation bamboo.

CHAIX Frères (fl.1844-1868). Two brothers Pierre-Ambroise and A. Chaix. Called Chaix Jeune from 1853 and from 1856 A. Chaix. The two brothers worked together but exhibited separately, becoming important makers during the Second Empire. The elder brother exhibited at the 1855 Exhibition, one piece being purchased by Napoleon III. Pierre-Ambroise also exhibited, gaining a silver medal in 1867. His younger brother sent furniture to the 1861 Industrial Arts Exhibition.

An oval collectors cabinet was exhibited in London at the 1862 Exhibition. The silver medal piece at the 1867 Paris Exhibition was a Louis XIII Renaissance revival *armoire* with panels after Jean Goujon. Several Renaissance style pieces are recorded by the brothers including a bookcase in the manner of Hans Vredeman de Vries, whose late sixteenth century publication of designers in *Differents Pourtraicts de Menuiserie* had influenced not only his contemporaries but must have been available to nineteenth century copyists. The Chaix Brothers also made articles in Louis XV and XVI style.

CHARMOIS, Christophe. Worked with his brother. Exhibited at the Industrial Products Exhibition in 1844, also at the Universal Exhibition in 1867. His partnership with the Poteau brothers continued into the beginning of this century.

CHARMOIS, Pierre. Exhibited bedroom furniture and boulle at the 1855 Exhibition.

CHARON Frères. These two brothers worked together from 1855-1860, then continued separately. Exhibited 1855. Their jewel box made for the Empress Eugénie was exhibited at the 'Chefs-d'oeuvre des grands ébénistes' and sold in the Farnborough Hill sale in 1927. Stamp in stencil form: 'Charon Frères FeursBtes de S.M.L'Empereur Rue de Braque No9 A Paris'.

CHARON, Aîné, Maxime. Continued until 1863 after ceasing to work with his brother. Supplied furniture to the Tuileries and Fontainebleau.

CHARON, Jeune. Continued trading until c.1866 and patented a sculpture in the round process.

CHARPENTIER, Alexandre. Primarily a sculptor and decorator. Made art nouveau furniture c.1900.

CHASTENET et Cie, Antoine (fl. 1849-1858). Exhibited 1841, 1851 in London and 1855 in Paris, selling a desk to the Empress Eugénie. Several pieces at Compiègne.

CHASTINET et Cie. Exhibited furniture from the 'Association of Working Cabinet Makers' at the Paris Exhibition, 1855.

CHERET, J. Known to have sculpted figures for a desk in the 1867 Exhibition.

CHEVALIER, A. (fl.1837-1853). Supplied seat furniture to the Tuileries.

CHEVENARD, Aîné (born 1798). Published the influential *L'Album de l'Ornemaniste* in 1835. Became inspector of the Beaux-Arts of the Maison du Roi in 1828. Made hundreds of designs for the Sèvres factory. A meticulous designer of furniture in the Renaissance, Gothic and Oriental tastes, also in the Louis XIV style.

CHRISTOFLE, P. (fl. third quarter nineteenth century). An important silversmith established in Paris. He often contributed fine silver and enamelwork to furniture (see dust jacket). Made castings for lady's writing desk for 1867 Exhibition and for a cradle purchased by Napoleon III.

CLERGET (fl.c.1845). Published an important and influential book of neo-Renaissance designs.

CORNU, Jeune. Younger brother of another cabinet maker, Louis. Exhibited at Bescançon in 1860 and Nantes in 1861. Boulle and other types.

CORROY, Fils (fl.1829-c.1860). Supplied furniture to the royal warehouse in Louis XV style and boulle.

COSSE (fl.1846-c.1860). Exhibited 1855. Son-in-law to Antoine Krieger (q.v.).

CREMER, Joseph (fl.1839-1878). Born in Luxembourg. Furniture supplied to Louis Philippe and the King of Holland. Specialised in marquetry. Exhibited 1839, 1844, 1849, winning a medal in each case. In 1855 he exhibited a suite as well as boulle furniture, also a table he inlaid for Tahan (q.v.). Stamp: A *marque au fer* 'Cremer Marqueteur', within a chamfered rectangle, also 'J. Cremer' incised in marquetry panels.

CRUCHET, Michel-Victor. Important sculptor and *papier mâché* maker. Supplied decoration for Empress Eugénie at Saint-Cloud, also work for the Tuileries and Fontainebleau. Exhibited 1849, 1851 and 1855. Succeeded by his son Albert until the late nineteenth century.

CRUYEN (fl. mid-1912?). 16 rue de Charonne, Paris. Henri II style chair with paper table.

DALOU, Jules-Aîmé (1838-1902). Important sculptor. Made a marble and precious stone table supported on the shoulders of two powerful male figures, now in the Musée des Arts Decoratifs, cast bronze plaques for certain pieces of furniture. Not known as a furniture maker.

DAMON & COLIN. Paris furniture makers who exhibited furniture in the chinoiserie style at the Paris Exhibition of 1900.

DASSON, Henry (1825-1896). 106 rue Vieille-du-Temple. Important furniture maker using the very finest ormolu mounts with high quality mercurial gilding. Specialised in copies of eighteenth century models, mainly in the Louis XVI vein. Exhibited Louis XV, XVI and pieces of his own modified eighteenth century design at the 1878 Paris Exhibition. Numerous *objets d'art*, including wall lights and candlesticks found. His work is now very popular in Great Britain but has never been held in such high esteem by French collectors and dealers. Dasson closed down his business in 1894, after which there was a large auction. Stamps: on carcass work, a simple *marque au fer* 'Henry Dasson'. On mounts, a script signature. In all recorded cases the Christian name is spelt with a 'y' at the end. The metalwork almost invariably incorporates a date after the signature, although this is not so common on the carcass. Sometimes the *marque au fer* is followed by 'A Paris'.

DEXHEIMER, The brothers Jean-Adam and Philippe. Worked together from 1856-1863 setting up a premises at 58 Upper Charlotte St. in London in 1862, soon moving to 27 Connaught Terrace on the Edgware Road. Exhibited Paris, 1849 and London, 1852.

DIEHL, Charles-Guillaume (fl.1855-1880). Maker of a varied range of furniture but small pieces and work tables most commonly seen. Exhibited Paris 1855, Industrial Arts in 1861 and the 1867 Paris Exhibition. Also made boulle and *pietre dure* furniture. Signature usually found on the lockplate in an almost Gothic script 'Diehl A Michel-le-Compt 19 Paris'. He had a unique exotic style of a Romano-Gallic nature, incorporating lavish, full relief mounts on to rectangular items of furniture, profusely inlaid.

DROMARD, L. 18 rue St. Lazare, Paris. Used an oval *marque au pochoir* and/or a *marque au fer* 'L. Dromard Paris'.

DUPONT. Paris makers of cast-iron furniture. Exhibited at Crystal Palace in 1851 and at the Paris 1855 Exhibition. Possibly Dupont et Cie, later E. Dupont of the rue Meslay?

DURAND, E.P. Exhibited a highly carved sideboard in baroque taste, hung with carved game and applied with portrait medallions, at the Paris Exhibition, 1851.

DURAND Fils, Posper-Guillaume. The son of an important early nineteenth century maker, Louis. He flourished from 1834 to c.1860. In the 1830s he supplied, with his father, numerous pieces for the Trianon, Saint-Cloud and other palaces. Made *Ebéniste du Roi* in 1839, he continued to supply the royal palaces. Exhibited at Industrial Products Exhibitions, 1834, 1839 and 1844, also the Paris Exhibition of 1855. Stamp: a *marque au fer* 'Durand', commonly followed by 'A Paris'. Most pieces seen are of plain mahogany veneers with ormolu mounts and plaques in a watered-down Louis XVI/Directoire manner typical of the fine quality furniture of the Louis-Philippe period.

DUVAL. A Paris upholsterer and chair maker, at the Beauvais National Manufactory. Possible address 6 rue Lenoir-Saint-Antoine from 1836. Exhibited at the Paris Exhibition, 1851.

ESCALIER DE CRISTAL. A shop started by Mme. Desaraud c.1847, continuing under various names until 1923. Furniture and objects copied from the eighteenth century. Stamp: 'Escalier de Cristal Paris'.

FAURE, Jean-Marie (fl.1844-1863). Chairmaker, exhibiting in London in 1852.

FISCHER, Fils Aîné. Worked with his father, Jean-Christophe from 1839-1848 and continued until 1863. During his father's lifetime all types of furniture were made, the son continuing to specialise in chairs and furniture mounts.

FLORANGE, The brothers Gaspard and Jean. Both flourishing from about 1836 to 1855, exhibiting in Paris in 1855, London 1852 and other minor exhibitions. Various types of furniture, especially beds.

FOSSEY, Jules (fl.1844-1861). Followed by his son also called Jules. Exhibited with Fourdinois in 1844, again in 1849 and by himself in 1855. The father made furniture in Renaissance and Louis XVI manner for Compiègne, the son supplied pieces for Saint-Cloud.

FOURDINOIS, Alexandre-Georges (1799-1871). A highly important maker under the Second Empire, guaranteed to make the eyes of the *cognoscenti* water. Exhibited with Fossey in Paris. His business at 38 rue Amelot was founded with Jules Fossey in 1835, moving to number 46 in 1853. His son Henri joined the business from 1860-1867. Important commissions for the Garde-meuble, Compiègne, the Palais-Royal, Saint-Cloud and Fontainebleau. Furniture executed mainly in Renaissance, Louis XIV and Louis XVI styles. Furniture by this maker, or his son, is rarely seen on the open market. Stamp usually the surname, with a *marque au fer*.

FOURDINOIS, Henri-Auguste, son of the above. Born in 1830, working until 1887. Worked in London for two years with Oliver Morel. Exhibited 1862, 1867 and 1878. Worked very much in the style of his father, favouring the Renaissance, with occasional forays into Greek revival. A cabinet with silver mounts sold at the Hôtel Druot in 1887 was signed on the silverwork 'H. Fourdinois', with ivory figures by Carrier-Belleuse. Also produced more ordinary Louis XV and XVI *fauteuils* for 1867 Paris Exhibition. Produced numerous catalogues. A magnificent Renaissance revival cabinet was purchased at the Paris 1867 Exhibition for £2,750 and is now at the Bethnal Green Museum.

FOURNIER, A.M.E. (fl.1860-1867). Exhibited seat furniture in 1867 Exhibition. Designs of an elaborate 'ropework' stool, one at Compiègne, are thought to be by this particular Fournier.

FROMENT-MEURICE. Paris maker of the incredible dressing table, made in silver for the Duchess of Parma and exhibited at Crystal Palace.

GAILLARD, Eugène. Helped Bing (q.v.) to collect items for his shop 'Art Nouveau'.

CHAMBRE A COUCHER exposée au Pavillon de l''Art Nouveau'. Bing en 1900.

A bedroom suite, designed by Eugène Gaillard, showing a striking use of contrasting woods. From a room exhibited at the Paris Exhibition of 1900 by Samuel Bing, owner of the shop 'L'Art Nouveau'.

GALLE, Emile (1846-1904). Highly important art nouveau designer and maker. Few furniture designs but a major influence on the interpretation of plant forms into art. Founded Nancy School. Designed furniture in Modernist style of later art nouveau.

GANDILLOT. Iron furniture mid-nineteenth century.

GARRAULT, Fils (fl.1827-1863). Carver and cabinet maker. Exhibiting carved furniture as early as 1827.

GERSON & WEBER. Small and fanciful articles and carving, exhibiting in 1861.

GIROUX, Alphonse, Et Cie. Business included his son, François-Simon-Alphonse and grandson Alphonse-Gustave. François was the principle businessman of the three, supervising the manufacture of small items of furniture and producing designs from approximately 1834 to his death in 1848. Alphonse-Gustave worked from 1838, exhibiting the next year, continuing until 1867 when the business was taken over by Duvinage and Harinkouke. Stamp: Normally a script signature engraved on the lockplate 'A Paris chez Alph.Giroux et Cie' or 'Alph.GIROUX et Cie., Paris'. Empire and chinoiserie pieces, small *nécessaires* and jewel boxes commonly seen.

GRADE, Louis (fl.1850s and 1860s). Made many pieces in boulle. Exhibited in 1855 and 1867.

GRASSET, Eugène. Teacher in the Modern Style, designed some furniture c.1880 in an early art nouveau vein.

GROHE, Guillaume and Jean-Michel. Working 1829-1861, the younger brother, Guillaume continuing until 1884. In 1847 became Grohé Frères with Guillaume the principle partner. Supplied many royal houses, including Queen Victoria, from 1862 onwards. Favoured Louis XVI style but made pieces in many different styles, exhibiting almost continually from 1834 to 1878. Stamp: 'GROHE' or 'GROHE A PARIS'.

GROS, Jean-Louis-Benjamin (fl.1850s). His son continued throughout the next decade. Exhibited 1849 and 1855. Boulle and Louis XVI pieces, marquetry. Stamp: 'GROS PARIS'.

GUERET, Denis-Desire and Onesime. Working from 1853 as Guérèt Frères and from 1867 Guérèt Jeune et Cie, continuing on to at least the 1880s. Exhibited 1855, 1867 and 1878 all types of furniture in traditional 'Louis' styles including rustic furniture in pearwood.

GUIMARD, Hector (1867-1942). Important architect/ decorator and occasional designer of furniture in the 'Modern Style' in a formalised art nouveau manner c.1900.

HERTEINSTEIN (fl.1836-1870). Exhibited in 1867 under name of Hertenstein Père et Fils.

HOEFER, (fl.1839-1855). Inventive up-to-date supplier, selling furniture to Louis-Philippe and the Empress Eugénie at the 1844 and 1855 Exhibitions.

HOPILLIART ET LEROY (fl.c.1900). A Louis XV style *table à ouvrage* with a *marque au pochoir* 'Meubles et Bronzes Anciens 12 rue des Sts. Pères, Paris'. Also paper trade label.

HUNSINGER, Charles (fl.1859-1878, d.1893). Renaissance style furniture. A piece at Vienna. Stamp: 'Hunsinger et Wagner' (Approximately from the late 1870s onwards). Also a label 'meubles de chez M. Hunsinger, 13 rue Sedaine' (from 1874 until presumably 1878).

IGNACE & PLEYEL et Cie. Piano makers c.1860. Later became simply Pleyel et Cie. who continued into the twentieth century.

JACOB Family. It is impossible to adequately summarise the work of this important and influential family of cabinet makers who led fashion and standards from 1765 to 1847. Ledoux-Lebard describes their work in fifty pages of *Les Ebénistes Parisiens (1795-1870)*. Georges-Alphonse Jacob Desmalter comes within the scope of this price guide, flourishing from 1830 to 1847. He exhibited at all the more important exhibitions, selling furniture to the royal family and receiving many royal commissions. His style was an up-to-date version of the Empire style typified under the Charles X and Louis-Philippe period, using indigenous woods and *bois clairs*. Stamp: 'A. Jacob', *marque au fer* 'A.Jacob Fs. & Cie. B. de Bondy 30' 'A-Jacob Desmalter A Paris' and from 1830-1847 'Jacob'. Lockplates were often signed 'A. Jacob-Desmalter' or, more simply 'A.Jacob'.

JEANSELME Family. Important makers who bought the thriving business of the Maison Jacob in 1847. The two brothers, Joseph-Pierre-François and Jean-Arnoux, worked together from c.1828 as Jeanselme Frères until 1848. J.P.F. Jeanselme continued the business and was

later joined by his son Charles-Joseph-Marie. From 1861 until 1871 the enterprise traded under the name Jeanselme Fils et Godin et Cie. There were many royal orders for the family, who exhibited widely. Their combined work was almost exclusively seat furniture and they described themselves as upholsterers. Much of their work was taken from the designs of Pasquier in *Cahier de Dessins d'ameublement*, published c.1840. Stamps: 1824-1840 'Jeanselme Frères' (*marque au fer*); 1840-1856 'Jeanselme' (stencil); 1856-1861 'Jeanselme Père et Fils' (stencil); 1861-1871 'Jeanselme Fils et Godin et Cie'. (stencil).

JEANSELME Jeune, Pierre-Antoine (fl.1848-1863). A carver and chair maker of no evident relation to the above. Louis XV reproduction and boulle furniture for the Tuileries and the 1855 exhibition.

JOLLY-LECLERC, Jean-Pierre (fl.1831-1853). A wide variation of styles including early examples of neo-Renaissance. Exhibited in London 1852. Also a rosewood cabinet in mannerist style in Paris in 1867.

KLAGMAN, Jules. Designer during the middle of the century. A pupil of Jean Fuchere, both contributed sound, inventive designs to the furniture industry.

KNECHT, Emile-Frederic. A Paris wood carver exhibiting at the 1851 Paris Exhibition, also in 1867.

KREISSER, E. Made a fine silver and gilt table exhibited in 1855. Given as a Christmas present by Queen Victoria to Prince Albert.

KRIEGER, Antoine. A major manufacturer during the second half of the nineteenth century. The company had changed its name several times by 1880, latterly becoming Damon et Cie. Exhibited various types of furniture in 1852 and 1855, making copies of eighteenth century

furniture, also modern interpretations of earlier styles. Later pieces appear to be comparatively poorly made, including the use of plywoods, with stained woods and mass-produced mounts. Some pieces with paper label, others signed with surname on metalwork.

LACROIX. Nice cabinet maker. Small pieces inset with average quality marquetry c.1860.

LALANDE, Maison (fl. early twentieth century). Louis XVI style.

LA MESANGERE, Pierre de. Published a highly influential book of designs in the *Journal des Dames et Modes* called *Collection de Meubles et Objects de Goût*, during the years 1802-1835. His clear, simple designs contrasted with the magnificence of the designs of the great Napoleonic designers Percier and Fontaine, suggesting the first indications of a romantic revival.

LAURENT ET LERUTH. Exhibiting in 1849 and in London 1851, small exquisitely made items.

LEFUEL. The architect responsible for re-creating the Louis XVI style. He designed the Marie-Antoinette rooms at the Tuileries for the Empress Eugénie in 1865.

LE MAGASIN DE MEUBLES (fl. late nineteenth century). A large house furnisher producing complete furniture catalogues.

LE MARCHAND, Louis-Edouard (fl.1815-1852). Son of an important maker Charles-Joseph. The business was continued by André and Henri Lemoyne until 1893. Le Marchand continued the traditions of his father and also copied several pieces from the fashionable plates of La Mesangère (q.v.), favouring the *bois clairs*. He also made

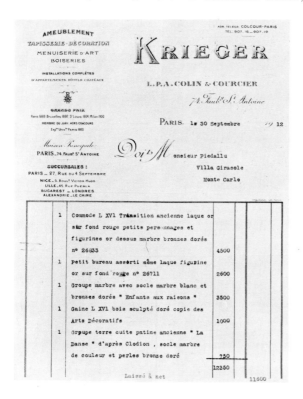

pieces in boulle, notably a pair of tripod tables for the Grand Trianon. His many Royal commissions included Louis XV style furniture and chinoiserie pieces. His arguably finest work was a magnificent ebony and oak lined tomb for the Emperor Napoleon in 1840. Few items by this maker were exhibited in major exhibitions and his work is rarely seen on today's market.

LEMOINE or LEMOYNE, André. Worked with Le Marchand from 1846, taking over his business in 1853. André Lemoyne's son Henri continued the firm until 1893. Many pieces were supplied to Napoleon III but not apparently after the 1850s. Several articles of furniture were exhibited in 1855.

LEPRINCE, Ringuet. Possibly of 6 rue Lenoir-Saint-Antoine c.1836. Exhibited a carved wood cabinet, in baroque taste, in Paris in 1851.

LES GALERIES DU LOUVRE (fl. late nineteenth century). A Paris draper, Chauchard, started an upholstery shop selling new and old materials. He also purchased sets of chairs with eighteenth century Beauvais and Aubusson tapestry seat covers, patronising fashionable Parisien cabinet makers.

LESAGE, Antoine-Nicholas (fl.1812-1841). Made several pieces for Louis-Philippe and the King of the Belgians. He was primarily a retailer, applying other smaller merchants' furniture with his label.

LEXCELLENT, E. (fl.1860-1923). Exhibited in 1867. He was a maker and retailer of good quality expensive pieces in all styles. Stamps: 'Lexcellent Paris' in stencil. Also 'Lexcellent, rue Breguet à Paris' (from 1867 on). See illustration from Paris 1900 Exhibition catalogue.

LEYS, Pierre-Jean (fl.1833-1861). Upholsterer and cabinet maker. Several royal commissions. From 1861 known as Leys and Violet.

LIENARD, Michel-Joseph-Napoleon (1810-1870). A designer in a florid Renaissance style. Published *Le Portefeuille, motif Décoratif inédit applicable aux Arts Industriels et Somptuaires*. Also *Spécimens de la Décoration et de l'Ornementation au XIXe siècle*, 1872.

LINKE, François (fl.1882-1935). 170 Faubourg Saint Antoine and by 1905, 26 Place Vendôme. Of Czechoslovakian birth, Linke is possibly the most sought

after cabinet maker of the late nineteenth and early twentieth century. Made a wide range of furniture mainly in the Louis XV and XVI styles, many copied directly from eighteenth century examples. However, some very fine pieces made in a more individual style, notably a magnificent, monumental display cabinet for the 1900 Exposition. His work is popular today in most countries, especially in France and the United States. Unfortunately there have been an increasing number of articles on the market during recent years, bearing Linke's signature, the quality of which leaves their origin in some doubt. More aware auctioneers have catalogued several pieces as 'bearing the signature Linke'. However there is no doubt that his work was made well into this century, after the First World War, when the quality of materials and standards of workmanship had generally fallen and it is certain that the too cautious are presuming these later pieces to be fakes, expecting the later, more commercially made examples to be of the exceptional quality of his early work, before he was able in any way to trade on his name. All his work has the finest, most lavish mounts, very often applied to comparatively simple carcasses of quarter veneered kingwood or tulipwood, without the embellishment of too much marquetry.

Stamp: A stencilled 'F. Linke Paris'. Engraved script signature on one piece of the ormolu, 'F. Linke', normally on the upper right hand side.

Exhibited at the Deuxième Salon des Industries du Mobilier, Grand Palais, 1905. After Linke's death c.1935, furniture bearing the Linke signature was still made for a time by his workshops.

The most notable feature of Linke's work, perhaps even more of a guarantee than a signature, is his continued use of a concave scallop-shell or *coquille*. The shell is held by delicate tendrils of acanthus, implying the shape of a crab with outstretched claws. A small *bureau plat* made considerably more than its estimate at auction in New York bearing this motif, although it was unsigned.

MAJORELLE, Louis. The Majorelle workshops were at 6 rue du Vieil-Aître in Nancy. At the beginning of the twentieth century there were also four showrooms in Nancy at 20 rue Saint-Georges, in Paris, at 22 rue de Provence, in Lyon, at 28 rue de la République and in Lille at 55 rue Esquermoise. Major exponent of art nouveau. A friend of Emile Gallé (q.v.). Worked at the Nancy school in various media, his furniture taking on stylised plant forms with fine bronze mounts.

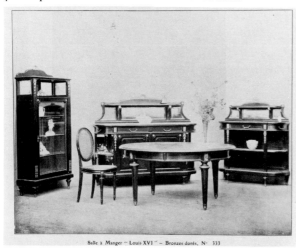

An interesting insight into a catalogue of Louis Majorelle produced in about 1905. This famous maker of art nouveau furniture also made a considerable amount of Louis revival furniture including meubles massif *as in this photograph and more elegant* meubles de luxe.

MATIFAT. Exhibited an ivory casket at the Crystal Palace Exhibition 1851. Paris maker.

MAUGIN. Designed furniture for Madame de Païva's house on the Champs Elysées, in the Renaissance style, with abundant use of ebony. An architect, he flourished c.1865.

MAZAROZER, Jean-Paul (fl.1850-1890). A wood carver who published a book of designs in Renaissance style. He exhibited machine carved furniture in 1855 and 1867.

MELLIER et Cie.: See Monbro (q.v.).

MERCIER, Claude (fl.1830-1870?). Exhibited widely in various styles and supplied furniture to the Spanish Court. Later examples have a small metal plate, inscribed 'Mercier', inside the carcass.

MILLET (fl.1853-1918). Copied Louis XV and XVI furniture. Amongst others a lacquer writing table made for Marie-Antoinette by Adam Weisweiller.

MILLOT, Théodore. Supplied furniture in the Louis XIV style for Compiègne.

MONBRO Aîné, Georges (fl.1832-1853). A maker and repairer of furniture, mainly to give a complete service to his various antique shops. Several Royal pieces. Maker of boulle furniture.

MONBRO, Fils Aîné (fl.1850-1868). Continued his father's shops and started a business in London in 1863 at 2 Frith Street near Soho Square. Executed fine pieces of furniture in most styles but items of boulle most commonly seen. Exhibited in 1855. A large collection of his boulle work can be seen at the Bowes Museum, Barnard Castle, Co. Durham. Stamp: *Marque au fer* 'Monbro Aîné'. Business taken over by Mellier et Cie.

MULLER, R. (fl.1850-1870). Porcelain mounted and boulle pieces in blond tortoiseshell. He also repaired antique furniture.

MUNIER, Charles (fl.1828-1863). Made furniture and supplied mirrors but was primarily an upholsterer and tapestry maker. Re-covered many chairs at Versailles. Stamp: 'CH.Munier'.

OSMONT (fl.1838-1860). Latterly as Mme. Vve. A.V. Osmont. Specialist maker of lacquer and patented a marble carving technique. Exhibited from 1839 to 1855. Established a branch of the business at 50 Frith Street in London.

PAPE. A maker with addresses in Paris, Brussels and London. Exhibited a metamorphic piano which closes to form a table at the 1851 exhibition.

PASQUIER. A designer, published a comprehensive book of chair designs c.1840 called *Cahier de Dessins d'ameublement* which was a major influence on the manufacture of chairs for everyday use.

PENON, Henri (fl.c.1880). A prolific designer and publisher of furniture designs.

PERCIER & FONTAINE. Architects to the Emperor Napoleon. Their publication of *Recueil de Décorations Intérieures*, first produced in 1802 and again in 1812, had a major and far ranging impact on European furniture and their traditional, heavy Empire style influenced design well into the 1840s.

PERET, R. Made small practical pieces of fine quality from rue Montmorency, St. Martin, 19 Paris between 1856 and 1864. Engraved signature on the lockplate.

PEROL Frères. Furniture makers in a watered-down commercial art nouveau style. Exhibited Paris 1900.

PETIPONT-FREQUANT, Charles. A firm started c.1800 which continued throughout the nineteenth century as Louis Soubrier et Cie. Designed all types of furniture.

PICARD (fl. third quarter nineteenth century?). A gilt-bronze *guéridon* in Louis XVI style seen incorporating an Imari style plate manufactured by Copeland's.

PIHET Frères. Makers of iron furniture in the mid-nineteenth century.

PUTEAU, L.F. (1780-1864). Furniture in the Louis-Philippe and French Biedermeier style.

QUETIN, Victor. 55 rue du Faubourg Saint-Antoine.

QUIGNON, Napoleon (fl.1850-1870s). Maker of chairs and beds. Exhibited in Paris and London. His son joined him in 1872.

REIBER, Emile. A furniture maker to Napoleon III.

REQUIER (fl.1806-1863). Makers and re-upholsterers of seat furniture. Their stamp with reversed 'P' in place of the 'Q' is found on earlier chairs made by other firms and re-upholstered by Requier.

RIBAILLER Aîné et Cie., Mazarol (fl.1844-1860s). An antique dealer who made furniture and large sculptural pieces in Renaissance and Louis styles, exhibiting at major events.

RIBAILLER, Jeune (fl.1843-1860s). Produced similar work to the above. Supplier to the Empress Eugénie.

RIBAILLER, Pierre (fl.1846-1870). Similar sculptural furniture to the previous two makers.

RIBAL, Frederic (fl.1848-1860s). One of the few makers of dining tables recorded. That elusive but useful item of furniture rarely appears on the market in a nineteenth century form. Exhibited internationally.

RINGUET-LEPRINCE, Auguste-Emile (fl.1831-1850s). A cabinet maker and upholsterer to the king. Made various types of contemporary furniture, including boulle, exhibiting in London.

RIVART, J.N. & ANRIEUX (fl.1850-1890). Specialised in porcelain mounted furniture, used trade labels.

ROLL, Joseph (fl.1844-1870). Made all types of furniture, exhibiting at major Paris exhibitions.

ROLLER & BLANCHET Fils (fl. mid-nineteenth century). Fine marquetry work. See a piano at Chantilly.

ROUDILLON, Etienne-Simon-Eugène (fl.1853-1890). Took over the business of Ringuet-Leprince (q.v.) c.1853.

ROUX, Frédéric (fl. under the Second Empire). Supplied fine boulle pieces to the Tuileries.

ROYER, Marie-Aubin (fl.1811-1840s). Fine quality maker in the Empire style who supplied various types of furniture to the crown. Stamp: 'Royer, *Sculpteur A Paris*'.

ROYER, Maison. Stencil recorded on the back of a cabinet by Beurdeley 'Maison Royer 14 Rue du Cherche Midi 6e'.

RUPRICH-ROBERT. Published *Flore Ornementale* in 1866, which underlined the work of Viollet-le-Duc (q.v.) in promoting the use of plant forms in design. Designed furniture in a florid Louis XV style and a severe Louis XIV style. Also a Dresden porcelain mounted cabinet in Louis XV style intended as a present from the King of Prussia to Napoleon III.

SANTI, M. Published *Modèles de meubles et de décorations interieures pour l'ameublement* in 1828. Influenced by La Mésangère (q.v.). Santi's designs were the epitomy of the period of heavily draped furniture.

SAUVREZY, Auguste-Hippolyte (fl.1840-1884). Sculptural furniture and pieces of Renaissance and Louis styles. Exhibited in Paris.

SCHNEGG. A Paris maker and repairer from 8 rue Craversière. Pencil signature seen dated 1892.

SIMON, L. (fl. late nineteenth century). Complete house furnishers at 1, 3, 7 and 9 rue de Rivoli and 39, 41, 43, 45, 72, 74 and 76 rue François-Miren.

SORMANI, Paul (fl.1847-1934). Owing to the long establishment of the Sormani firm which continued for eighty-seven years many items of furniture are seen on the market bearing their signature. Consequently, many pieces are presumed to be mid-nineteenth century as the firm continued to make furniture in a traditional style, it not being commonly appreciated that some pieces are in fact twentieth century and the more commendable for being so. From 1847 to 1854 the address was 7 cimetière Saint-Nicholas. From 1854 to 1867, 114 rue du Temple. In 1867 the firm moved to 10 rue Charlot where it stayed, continued by Sormani's wife and subsequently his son until 1934. Most signed items inevitably are from the latter address, which is included in the signature. Sormani exhibited in 1849, 1855, 1862, 1867 and 1878. A large amount of the firm's production was in copying Louis XV and XVI furniture but there are also numerous pieces in a modified Louis style. Boulle pieces are also found. The quality of the earlier pieces is very high, almost to the standard of Dasson's work (q.v.). Numerous pieces of good quality are seen today which, although very acceptable are not of this firm's first quality. It can only be presumed that these are later examples of their work, continuing nineteenth century traditional styles into this century without quite the same standards of finish. The wage bill of such an enterprise must have been far less *per capita* during the 1848

revolution than in the years following the Great War! Stamp: Usually an engraved signature on the lockplate, incorporating the address.

TAHAN, Alphonse (fl.1830-1880). A major maker of small items of furniture and cabinet maker to Napoleon III. He made a wide variety of items, using most techniques in common usage, including pieces cast in bronze to simulate bamboo. A great number of small ebonised pieces were produced inset with small Sèvres plaques. Stamp: Usually 'Tahan Ft.', 'Tahan A Paris' or, more rarely, 'Tahan, Fournisseur de l'Empereur'. Additional writing to the name is normally quite florid, the name itself with the strokes of each capital letter appearing to grow a circumflex. The business was continued by his son, Jean-Pierre. Exhibited work in an ornate naturalist style in Paris, 1855.

THERET, J. (fl.1840s-1850s). Specialist in mosaic, exhibiting in London in 1852.
THONET FRERES. The Paris showrooms of the Austrian brothers' firm was at 15 blvd. Poissonnière.
THUILLER. Continued the design work of Lemarchand (q.v.), the *Cabinet de dessins de fauteuils*.
TURINETTI, M.A. Signed with a *marque au fer*.

UNION CENTRALE DES BEAUX-ARTS *appliqués à l'industrie*. Started in Paris in 1865, became the Union Centrale des Arts Décoratifs in 1877. Formed to spread the word of art and design, bringing it into line with modern techniques of manufacturing.

VACHER FILS, Georges (fl.1830-1840s). Son of a royal cabinet maker. Supplied plain pieces of contemporary style to the Royal households.
VAN BALTHOVEN, Pierre (fl.1840s-1860s). Exhibited ebony and palissander furniture.
VERDELLET, Jules, (fl.1870s). A designer of upholstery who produced several influential publications.
VERVELLE, A. Aîné (fl.1804-1856). Made a wide variety of small pieces in differing styles. Published the *Bulletin du magasin des nouveautés* in 1830. Boulle and thuya furniture, also Renaissance style pieces.
VIARDOT, C. A maker of a distinctive type of chinoiserie furniture in a personal style but also made traditional reproduction pieces. Much of his work is found in the United States of America and he may well have had a shop there. Exhibited between 1851 and 1900. Stamp: 'C. Viardot'.
VIOLLET-LE-DUC (1814-1879). An architect who specialised in the restoration of early buildings. Also designed furniture for the Emperor's railway carriage. A leading teacher and exponent of plant forms incorporated into modern design, he sought to rationalise the use of machinery and its artistic vulgarities and to bring the craftsman back into favour.

WASSMUS FRERES, Jean-Henri-Chrétien and Jean-Henri-Christophe (fl. during the third quarter of the nineteenth century). Born in the Hanover area, the two brothers started business together in Paris in 1810. However, the driving force of the firm was from Henri-Léonard, the son of the elder brother. From 1853 the business traded from 146 rue du Faubourg-Saint-Denis, supplying furniture to the crown. He exhibited in 1855 and 1867 making furniture in all styles including boulle, Renaissance and Louis revival.
WIENER, Felix et Cie (fl. early twentieth century). Makers of Shannon Office Furniture at 3, 5 and 5 bis rue des Goncourt XIe.
WINCKLESEN, Charles (fl.1854-1870). Maker of fine quality furniture in eighteenth century style. At his death in 1870 the business was bought by Henri Dasson (q.v.).

ZWIENER. Of German extraction, he produced the very finest furniture copied from public collections in France. Between 1880 and 1895 he was at 12 rue de la Roquette. His work appears mainly to be in the Louis XV rococo manner, inset with fine marquetry, Vernis Martin panels and encrusted with gilt-bronze mounts, all to the highest standard. There is some uncertainty between the recorded stamp 'E. Zwiener' illustrated and the work of Julius Zwiener, a Berlin cabinet maker who made furniture in a very similar style, exhibiting in Paris in 1900 and making furniture for Wilhelm II. The connection is not evident to date but the similarity in style suggests that the two were brothers or at least of the same family.

Terms

Armoire. Wardrobe/cupboard.
Armoire à Glace. Mirrored wardrobe.

Baguette. Bead or astragal.
Barbière. Gentleman's mirrored shaving stand.
Barège Pompadour. Watered silk and woollen cloths popular in the mid-1830s for draping furniture.
Bas d'armoire. Low wardrobe.
Bergère à Transformation. Armchair with filled-in sides, opening to form a day bed.
Bibliotheque. Side cabinet glazed for books.
Billet Doux. Small screen with writing flap.
Bois Foncé. Dark stained wood.
Bois Noirci. Stained pear wood (c.f. with *papier mâché*).
Bonheur du Jour. A lady's small writing desk with drawers above a writing surface in the form of a flap.
Borne. A circular settee with an appliqué on the centre.
Boudeuse. Upholstered chair with two addorsed seats (see: *dos à dos*).
Bronze Doré. Gilt bronze fused by process of firing mercury. Mercurial gilding. Ormolu.
Buffet. Glazed or panelled *meuble d'appui* with shelves above.
Bureau. Flat top desk, often with trestle supports.
Bureau à Cylindre. Cylinder desk.
Bureau à Gradin. Flat desk with drawers above the pull-out writing surface (*bonheur du jour*) (q.v.).
Bureau à la Bourgogne. See: *bureau de dame.*
Bureau à la Capucin. See: *bureau de dame.*
Bureau de Dame. Writing desk with superstructure of drawers and pull-out writing surface.
Bureau en Dos D'Ane. Derived from a *table à écrire à gradin* (q.v.).
Bureau en Pente. Originally called a *bureau de dame* (q.v.).
Bureau en Pupitre. Tall writing desk to be used standing.
Bureau Mazarin. Writing desk designed mid-seventeenth century with two sets of four legs, each set joined by an X stretcher.
Bureau Plat. Flat top writing desk on four legs with three frieze drawers.

Canapé Médaillon. Louis XV style settee with oval central section.
Cannelures. Fluting, usually low, wide.
Chaise à Porteur. Sedan chair.
Chaise à Roulettes. Armchair with medallion back.
Chaise en Cabriolet. Cabriole chair.
Chaise Fumeuse. Smoking chair with yoke shaped padded toprail. Sit on in reversed position.
Chaise Gondole. Inverted U back leading to the arms, usually with sabre legs.
Chaise Lambrequin. Upholstered low chair with lambrequin frieze.
Chauffeuses. Low chairs or stools.
Chauffeuse Grecque. Button upholstered chair.

Chiffonnier. Six drawer chest.
Chûtes. Bronze mounts at top of leg.
Coiffeuse. Dressing table.
Coin de Feu. Small fireside chair.
Commode. A chest of drawers.
Commode à Deux Vantaux. Chest with two cupboard doors often below one long drawer.
Commode Secretaire. Desk with an angled flap above two long drawers.
Confidente. Settee with two long seats back to back and a seat at either end.
Console. Side table.
Console Desserte. Ditto with marble top for food.
Console Jardinière. Self supporting side table zinc lined for flowers.
Corbeille à Ouvrage. Work table.
Crapaud. Small button upholstered tub armchair with fringes hiding the legs and woodwork.

Dos à Dos. Upholstered small double seat, literally for sitting back-to-back.
Duchesse. A comfortable day bed.
Duchesse Brisé. As above but splitting into three parts to form a *bergère,* a stool and a small armchair. Occasionally found in two parts, forming two armchairs.
Duchesse en Trois. As above.

Ecran. Screen.
Escritoire. Davenport.

Fauteuil. Open sided armchair.
Fauteuil à Rampe. A generous 'U' shaped chair with a button-upholstered top-rail. Also *chaise à rampe.*
Fauteuil Anglais. An upholstered easy armchair, with only the moulded arm supports showing the woodwork.
Fauteuil de Bureau. A desk chair with one of the legs at the centre front.
Fauteuil de Cercle. Button upholstered easy chair.
Fauteuil de Repos. Easy chair (wood framed).
Fauteuil Voltaire. Button upholstered armchair with swan neck handles and tall back.

Guéridon. A small occasional table.
Guéridon à Abattant. Circular tip top tripod table.

Indiscret. Three seater settee.

Jardinière. Stand with zinc lined container for flowers.

Lit à Enroulement. Bed with overscrolled ends and cylindrical cushions.
Lit à la Polonaise. Arched and canopied bed.
Lit de Parade. Formal 'state' bed.
Lit Bateau. A bed with two ends of equal height, each end overscrolled.

Meridiènne. Chaise longue with a back support at one end only and half-back or day bed.
Meuble d'Appui. Side cabinet (often blind fronted). Taller version called *Meuble d'hauteur d'appui.*

Moiré Pompadour. Watered silk and woollen cloths popular in the mid-1830s for draping furniture. *Barège Pompadour* (q.v.).

Ottomane Corbeille. Oval button upholstered small *canapé* with no woodwork showing.

Panier à Ouvrage. Work basket.

Petit Milieu de Salon. Button upholstered centre seat for four.

Piquet. Folding *table à jeu* (q.v.) with interior wells for counters.

Pliante. Folding chair or stool.

Portière. Curtained and pelmeted doorway.

Pouffe. Small button upholstered box stool.

Psyche. Cheval mirror early nineteenth century.

Raffraichissoir. A small table including brass or zinc wells for cooling bottles.

Secrétaire à Abattant. Flat fronted desk with fall front writing surface.

Secrétaire à Abattant à Doucine. Fall front writing surface above two cupboards.

Secrétaire à Culbute. A *secrétaire en pente* whose whole interior folds down to make a small flat top writing desk.

Secrétaire à Dessus Brise. Angled fall front desk above cupboards.

Secrétaire en Armoire. Old name for *secrétaire à abattant*, normally intended to go against a wall.

Secrétaire en Encoignure. Corner desk.

Secrétaire Scriban. Angled fall front desk on two long drawers with cupboards above.

Secrétaire Violonne. *Secrétaire à abattant* waisted to form rough outline of a violin. For example see a lacquer *secrétaire* by J.F. Leleu.

Table à Ecrire. Flat top desk with pull-out writing (brushing) slide.

Table à Gibier. Long, low hunting table.

Table à Jeu. Usually large circular drum table.

Table à la Tronchin. Reading table on trestle supports with an adjustable centre flap.

Table Ambulante. Small light movable occasional table.

Table à Ouvrage. Work table.

Table à Volets. Sofa table.

Table d'Aquarelliste. Small occasional table for the amateur painter.

Table de Canapé. Rectangular table with small 'D' flap at either end.

Table de Chevet. Bedside table.

Table de Salon. Centre table.

Table Pliante. Small mobile table with two flaps at one side only.

Tables Gigognes. Nest of tables.

Tabouret. Stool.

Tabouret en X. X frame stool.

Travailleuse. Work table.

Vénitienne. Button upholstered double ended *chaise longue*.

Vieux Bois. A much favoured term for Flemish 'Jacobethan' furniture.

Vis à Vis. See *confidente* (q.v.).

Voyeuse. Low chair with padded back rail for leaning on.

BEDROOM FURNITURE

In the eighteenth century beds were almost always exclusively designed to be placed alongside the wall and they conformed with the decoration of the room, merging into a complete and uniform room design. Upholstery had taken over but by the turn of the century wooden framed and veneered beds and in some cases metal beds became popular. The lit bateau *began to take over from the exotic* lit à la polonaise, lit à la française *or the late seventeenth century styles of the* lit à l'ange *or* à la duchesse. La Mesangère *even designed a fanciful* lit en corbeille, *an all enveloping basket-shaped bed. Upholstery was still allowed to play a part, especially for the canopy, but beds became smaller and more movable not being dependant on the design of the room.*

1 An exceptional bed in cast-iron for the Great Exhibition of 1851 by Dupont of Paris. This is a most unlikely material for such a large object as it fractures easily and is very difficult to repair. (The fan shaped ends and canopy support are steel.) The decoration is cast with scenes of the chase and, typically of mid-nineteenth century morbid taste, there are cast panels of dead fish and game. These subjects are often found on the huge carved sideboards of the time and are bad enough in the dining room for modern day squeamish tastes — but in the bedroom! A very rare example of the wish to mass-produce furniture in modern materials. Doubtless only very few survive and in the end, probably few were made.

c.1850

2 A majestic tulipwood and king-wood double bed stamped 'Zwiener, Jansen'. The quality and finish of the woodwork and the mounts are first class but the overall design is not quite as gutsy as the pure Zwiener who always used the large cartouche in his designs, repeated here on the head and footboard but normally with more zest, like the early work of Linke (q.v.).

c.1895

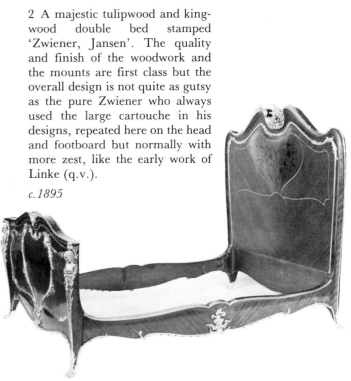

3 Another magnificent bed in a fussy, late Empire style. The dominant eagle on the headboard is a masterpiece of metalwork. The plum pudding mahogany *(acajou moucheté)* is a highly decorative feature. The bed is stamped 'Royer, Sculpteur A Paris'. His work is rarely seen and is of first class quality.

1820-1840

4 A large *armoire,* a companion piece to the bed on the previous page and also by Royer. The two pieces are not exactly the same but there are many similar details in the mounts. The plum pudding effect on the mahogany is not as marked as on the bed. Once again there is a large winged cresting, it would be interesting to see if this feature appeared on any other Royer pieces should they be found.

1820-1840

5 A charming mahogany cradle in a late Empire style. Perhaps not something that the modern mother would want to place her baby in nowadays — they usually end up filled with plants! The boat shape of the crade is very well designed but is let down by the very ordinary supports. The cradle is pure Empire of the early nineteenth century and the supports uninventive early 'Victorian'.

c.1840

6 A boulle bed — there is another one illustrated on page 55 in the boulle section. The half canopy is the owner's invention and not the designer's. Unlike the *lit bateau* this bed can be placed in the centre of a room, alongside the wall as with modern beds. The boulle work is not very good quality but a rare piece all the same.

c.1870

7 The headboard only is illustrated of a very well carved and gilt wood double bed with double caned panels. Double caning is always more popular than single caning, be it in beds or the popular 1920s drawing room suites. When fully restored with a new mattress and upholstery this bed will have a very light and charming effect on a bedroom.

c.1900

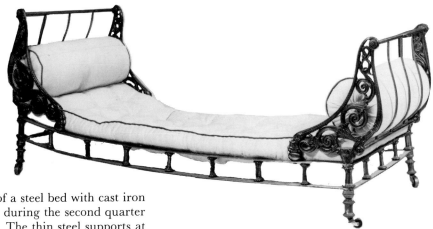

8 Another rare example of a steel bed with cast iron ends that became popular during the second quarter of the nineteenth century. The thin steel supports at the sides have been incorrectly designed and run on a flat horizontal plane which has caused the bend in the middle. A late nineteenth century bed would have angled steel or cast iron supports so that they could not bend. The generous scrolled ends imitate the *lit bateau*.

1850s

9 This is strictly speaking a small window seat probably intended for use in a bedroom with a matching bed. It is made of polished steel and brass. Once again there is an effect of the *lit bateau*. The swan became a very popular decorative motif during the second quarter of the nineteenth century.

1830s

10 A hideous walnut headboard. Could it almost be American? Certainly the style is a familiar American one but the addition of the winged cherub and the carved swags of flowers in such fine detail is not a particularly common American feature. The leaf finials at either side appear to have been arbitrarily truncated. The porcelain roundle is painted with a green-like 'heavenly' scene.

Mid-1870s

12 A typically French large and capacious *armoire* profusely inlaid but with mechanical flowers. The mounts are not very good quality although the asymmetrical acanthus cresting has an individual and almost over exuberant style not in keeping with the rest of the wardrobe.

Early twentieth century

11 A similar style of bedroom furniture, also made in walnut, with very American overtones in a neo-classical revival style with a little baroque thrown in for good measure. The top has a marble inset slab for use as a wash stand. There is a very definite feeling in both these two pieces of the 'Grand Rapids' bedrooms that were produced in quantity in Michigan.

Mid-1870s

13 The use of the vast new supplies of Dutch East Indies satinwood helps to date this piece towards the end of the nineteenth century but the style of the decoration and the columns with their extraordinary over-exaggerated entasis brings the design firmly into the early years of the twentieth century. Even though the design has a modern feel about it, the vases of flowers inlaid on the side doors and all the gilt bronze mounts have a traditional upbringing.

c.1910

14 A marquetry *poudreuse* in the Louis XV style. These toilet tables are extremely useful and capacious but have the distinct disadvantage that nothing can be placed on the top as not only does the centre section lift out to reveal a mirror but the two remaining side panels of the top hinge outwards to reveal wells. An irritating traditional factor is that on most of these tables the sides have to be lifted out before the centre panel can be lifted as it is held by small retaining pins.

1880s *

15 Another *poudreuse* of very poor quality, indeed with just a hint of marquetry on the top panels and the very thinnest and plainest of veneers on the sides. The mounts, for once, are too restrained, and of appalling quality.

1880s *

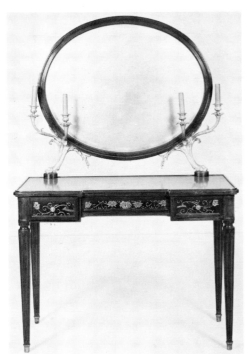

16 A very bold dressing table. One of the poor *bronze doré* mounts holding the candelabra was signed 'Linke'. Quite clearly, even from the evidence of a photograph, the quality of the base is far too poor to have anything to do with the fine workshops of Linke, even towards the end of his career in the 1930s. The two candelabra and their supports are of fine quality and were probably removed from another Linke piece and added to this inferior base with its unusual panels of coromandel lacquer on the drawers.

1920s

17 An unadventurous *armoire* of almost exactly the same form as the boulle *armoire à glace* no.28. The marquetry, instead of cut brass and tortoiseshell, is of various woods with kingwood and tulipwood veneers.

1850s

18 A mahogany *psyché* or cheval glass in a familiar English style. The trestle supports each have a small single candle arm. Although the supports must be solid to hold the weight of the mirror, the trestle is too massive to be harmonious and does not complement the strong architectural shape of the pediment.

1830s

19 A handsome toilet mirror in well figured mahogany that is only one stage removed from the Empire style. The lines, however, have become softer and far less severe and the woodwork has been left plain and not adorned with metalwork as a reaction against the overdecorated Empire period.

1830s

20 A very elegant *bronze doré* toilet glass with a very strong asymmetrical acanthus framework signed by Paul Sormani. If the better Paris makers could have produced more furniture and objects of this quality, nineteenth century furniture would never have developed the reputation for poor quality and design that it has been labelled with.

1860s

21 A carved walnut French provincial toilet mirror that no Paris maker would be proud of. It is interesting to see that the maker has used acorn finials on the walnut carcass. The flower head trellis is very French and the whole piece looks back to traditional French mid-eighteenth century features.

1860s

BEDROOM FURNITURE — A Linke Bedroom Suite

22, 23, 24 This page illustrates three pieces that form a part of a bedroom suite by Francois Linke of the Faubourg Saint-Antoine. The quality is very fine, the marquetry, veneers, mounts and carcass are all superbly made, the type of furniture that was made to last a lifetime but will last for ever. The overall feeling is, however, a little disappointing for Linke. It does not have the same superb quality that instantly lifts the furniture from his workshops to a special class of *meubles de luxe* that made the Linke name one of the most famous in turn-of-the-century French cabinet making. By most Paris makers' standards this suite would be considered as being in the *de luxe* category but for Linke it lacks the 'gutsy' swagger of his best exhibition work of the first few years of the century. There is little doubt that all the pieces are by Linke — all the bronzes are signed and each piece of the construction, taken individually, is of fine quality. The suite is a typical example of the type of good furniture that all the Paris firms were making as 'bread and butter' items that satisfied the huge demand for well made pieces in the old, well tried traditional shapes, in this case in the Louis XV style. The suite, which most likely was made with a dressing table could have been made at any time in the first thirty years of the twentieth century.

Early twentieth century

25 A very fine copy of a Louis XVI cabinet, with a *bronze doré* figure of the Sun King himself in the guise of Mars. The marquetry is of brass and pewter. A sumptuous piece and one of the finest nineteenth century boulle cabinets to come on the market in recent years. The mounts are signed 'F. Linke' and although this is an unusual piece for him to have made, his workshops are certainly capable of producing this and better quality. A copy of a cabinet inspired by a design by Boulle himself in the Musée du Louvre.

Late nineteenth century ✳

26 (left) A very unusual boulle dressing table, the base being a standard contemporary card table, although there was no indication that this piece had been made up. An uncomfortable mixture, but very useful and popular.

c.1860

27 (right) A cheval mirror or *psyche*. Another rare piece in boulle with very good quality inlay. Standing about five feet high it enables the narcissist to admire him, or herself from head to toe.

1850s

28 A small *armoire à glace* of the early Napoleon III period. Very little boulle of a very mechanical type.

1850s

29 These larger *armoires* are not seen very often and today, with the high cost of fitted wardrobes, they are surprisingly popular for their size. Again, very mechanical inlay and poor quality mounts.

1850s

A fine Augsburg table méchanique. The desk is illustrated in detail on page 363. The execution of the marquetry is exceptional, combining the best qualities of the French Louis XV style with the best German veneering and marquetry work. A fact that few people in Paris like to accept is that most of the best Paris made furniture in the eighteenth and nineteenth centuries was made so competently by the skills of the immigrant German craftsmen who imported marquetry from Augsburg, Ulm and other German centres.

1830-1850

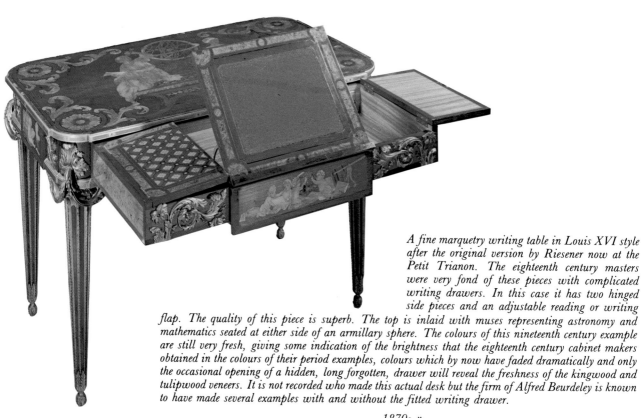

A fine marquetry writing table in Louis XVI style after the original version by Riesener now at the Petit Trianon. The eighteenth century masters were very fond of these pieces with complicated writing drawers. In this case it has two hinged side pieces and an adjustable reading or writing flap. The quality of this piece is superb. The top is inlaid with muses representing astronomy and mathematics seated at either side of an armillary sphere. The colours of this nineteenth century example are still very fresh, giving some indication of the brightness that the eighteenth century cabinet makers obtained in the colours of their period examples, colours which by now have faded dramatically and only the occasional opening of a hidden, long forgotten, drawer will reveal the freshness of the kingwood and tulipwood veneers. It is not recorded who made this actual desk but the firm of Alfred Beurdeley is known to have made several examples with and without the fitted writing drawer.

1870s *

30 A rare boulle *lit bateau* with quite well detailed marquetry, but of only average quality. Note that it is intended to be placed sideways against the wall, with no decoration or mounts on the far side. This limits its use for modern living.

c.1860

31 The squat form of the settee suggests an almost German origin, but the 'screw' feet are typical of the original Boulle period c.1700. Boulle seat furniture is rare.

All c.1850

32 Note that the maker has economised and has not inlaid the sides of this upright piano. The case is quite cheaply made with poor quality mounts. Signed 'Ziegler, 37 rue de la Chaussee d'Autin, Paris', manufactured for Abel and Sons, Music Sellers, Parade, Northampton. A poor quality export.

c.1850

33 A far superior version with inlaid sides and a serpentine fronted keyboard, held by child terms. Over decorated perhaps, but good quality and rare.

c.1855

34 Commonly called credenzas. This is an average quality example commonly seen but with the advantages of serpentine side panels. Good marquetry with quite good but rather mean bronze mounts.

1850s

35 Always less desirable with a straight front and convex glass sides. The boulle is of inferior quality with an extraordinary dance in the centre panel from the *commedia dell' arte*. The plinth, as is common, is of very poor quality indeed.

c.1860

36 Very similar quality to 34 but with an unusual copper-electrotype panel of a young couple in a garden setting.

1850s

37 Slightly smaller than the other examples and therefore much more convenient for modern living space. Very pretty twist turned outset columns interwoven with gilt bronze beading.

c.1860

38 Flat fronted and rather staid with an unusual mirrored superstructure which probably won't stay on for very long. Note the extremely weak mounts on the apron. The boulle inlay is simply long strips of purely mechanical marquetry. However, a useful cabinet.

1860s

39 Very unusual, with the earlier feature of bold acanthus mounts on the frieze which has three drawers below a marble top. The marquetry is highly coloured although the mounts on the doors and apron are rather weak. Useful, as drinks can be kept in the centre cupboard and the collector's glass or porcelain collection can be kept at either side.

c.1850

40 Another breakfront which compares almost exactly with 38.

1860s

41 Again flat fronted but with a much more interesting *contra partie* central door with a bird flying two feet off the ground and cherubs suspended from the heavens.

c.1860

42 A fine example of *contra partie* marquetry, the ground being purely cut brass. Again the earlier feature of a marble top above acanthus mounts on the frieze. The *bronze doré* mounts are of exceptional quality with the unusual 'C' scroll mounts at the spandrels. Under the lambrequin, the draped canopy, an allegorical group representing Wisdom and Religion is suspended in mid-air. The trophies of a palette and brushes, hunting horns and arrows are commonly seen on boulle pieces of the mid-nineteenth century. Unfortunately, yet again, the apron lets the whole piece down.

c.1850

43 A poor example with an ebonised top and very ordinary strips of 'token' boulle round the doors.

1850s

44 and 45 These two are very similar cabinets of the smaller type with only two doors. 44 has had the oval panels removed to make it into a slightly more expensive display cabinet, however the whole result is unsatisfactory. 45 is of very ordinary quality.

Both c.1860

47 A far more satis-
factory, earlier example
with good quality
mounts. However, one
is left with the feeling
that this cabinet is a
third of one of the larger
three-door cabinets such
as no.39.

c.1850

46 Very poor quality with no attempt whatso-
ever to decorate the sides. Purely applied with
mechanical strips of boulle.

1860s

49 An original decoration of a vase of flowers gives an air
of superiority to the inlay on the oval panel but the rest of
the piece is of the normal very ordinary quality produced
in large quantities. An interesting feature is the fact that
both the escutcheons are identical and no attempt has
been made to fill in the keyhole on the righthand side.
The apron and feet are the worst of their kind.

1850s

48 The serpentine shape is an added bonus but the
decoration and mounts are of very ordinary mass
produced quality. Not a very satisfactory shape, would
look far better as one of the larger examples.

c.1860

50 Refreshingly different, this cabinet is simply inlaid with brass on an ebonised ground. The decoration on the door panels is simple and effective and the mounts at least appear to fit, unlike some of the previous examples. The severity is relieved by an original white marble top of slightly serpentine outline.

c.1870

51 A similar theme where the decoration has been designed to enhance rather than smother the cabinet. However, the quality of this example is only average, which appears to be typical of French mid-nineteenth century pieces — this was stamped 'Maples' and therefore was an import probably made as late as the 1880s.

52 Another example of 'mechanical furniture'. Again this cabinet would be better if it were one of the larger examples.

1860s

53 The serpentine outline adds points to this two door cabinet inlaid in *contra partie* and is far more acceptable than the previous illustration.

1860s

54 (left) Here is an example of early eighteenth century *contra partie* work taken, probably, from the drawers of a *bureau mazarin*. The carcass is of exceedingly poor quality and the only advantage is that the overall effect is one of glitter. Made up mid-nineteenth century and could be used to remake an original boulle piece.

55 This is a mid-nineteenth century attempt to produce the same result as the previous example and is consequently far more satisfactory in execution. However, some of the inlay must have been salvaged from an earlier piece — the decoration on the pilasters changes direction half way down.

Mid-nineteenth century

56 A most superior serpentine cabinet but only brass inlaid into an ebonised ground. However, the whole effect is highly decorative with the central oval panel of naked *putti*. The sides are completely inlaid.

Mid-1850s

57 A serious attempt at recreating early eighteenth century boulle, some of the mounts (notably the hairy paw feet) compare directly to 25. The quality as a whole is very high, although the foliate decoration is rather stiff and inhibited.

c.1850 ✳

58 This *table à écrire* is inlaid with brass on an ebonised ground with no tortoiseshell in evidence. However, the inlay is restrained and could fit almost any other piece of furniture. These writing tables can be extremely difficult to use unless the legs are firmly set.

1870s

59 Neither a display cabinet or a writing table, this piece looks as though it will simply be a nuisance as the inlay starts lifting from the drawer. Not common, nor very useful.

1860s

61 (right) This cabinet on stand could also be from Southern Germany or Northern Italy. Inlaid with ivory on to an ebonised soft-wood ground, the effect is rather mechanical with little sign of quality. However, the boulle decoration is fairly consistent with the mass of French production.

c.1870

60 Inlaid with various decorative woods on to a walnut ground, this is an unusual example of wood boulle. The overall effect is quite pleasing but the shape is purely late seventeenth century. This cabinet could possibly be South German or North Italian.

c.1870

62 (left) A wobbly writing cabinet applied with indiscriminate mechanical boulle and capped by two rather silly vases. Quite a useful cabinet but one in which the decoration is usually found lying loose in one of the drawers.

1870s

63 (right) Much better quality, with an unusual angled flap. This hybrid desk is a mixture of Louis XV and XIV but the quality is good.

c.1860

64 and 65 Disappointing quality rather similar to 62, both examples of the type of boulle which rapidly sheds brass work.

Both c.1870

66 This is a fairly close copy of a Louis XIV boulle *bureau mazarin* in *contra partie*. The condition of this example leaves a lot to be desired.

c.1850

67 Although more obviously nineteenth century, the quality of this example is much higher, albeit with rather stiff mechanical brass foliage, on an ebonised ground.

1850s ✳

68 A rare example of boulle from the reign of Louis XVIII, this desk was bought by Baron Meyer de Rothschild in 1853 for £85. The provenance is reputedly from the Château de Neuilly and given to the Duc d'Orléans by Louis XVIII. The design is rather sophisticated with the unusual inclusion of twelve legs with the top itself resting on numerous *pieds de biche*. Almost a hangover from the late eighteenth century boulle revival but probably c.1820.

69 A very weak, poor quality *contra partie* example in appalling condition.

c.1860

70 A *bureau plat* looking directly back to designs of c.1710. Unfortunately the grotesque male masks at the knees are far too restrained and the legs have no sense of strength in their shape. The condition of this example is deteriorating rapidly.

1850s

71 A much smaller example more typically nineteenth century, with quite good quality inlay and bold naked *putti* at the knees. The top is also inlaid rendering it less satisfactory as a writing desk.

1850s

72 An even smaller desk intended for use as a writing desk with good quality *contra partie* inlay. The later castors give the legs a rather attenuated feel and the whole piece looks far too mobile.

1840s

73 A rather good quality example of Régence feeling with grimacing satyr masks. The frieze is inlaid with scenes from the *commedia dell' arte.*

1850s

74 A small writing slope which opens up to reveal pen trays. A small decorative piece of very little use in today's world. Again the maker has economised and left the sides undecorated.

1870s

75 A very fine quality desk set retailed by Aspreys but made in France. Although purely inlaid with foliage, the decorative effect is pleasing.

1870s

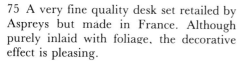

77 (right) A far superior piece in both outline and decoration. Although the legs are plain the brass stringing leading to the bronze *sabots* is a nice sign of quality. This piece was made by Paul Sormani and the signature on the lock is reproduced in the list of French cabinet makers on page 41.

1860s

76 A *bureau en pente* with token boulle inlay, the legs left undecorated for economy. A useful attractive piece but of very ordinary quality.

c.1870

78 Mechanical foliage is the only decoration to relieve the outline of this serpentine table which, without an inlaid frieze and legs, is one of the cheapest produced.

1860s

79 The paltry amount of brass inlay on this table is only slightly made up for by the quality of the acanthus mounts and the slightly smaller size of the table.

1860s

80 This is by far the most common type of boulle centre table and the condition must be checked very carefully. This example is in good condition and of quite high quality but note the way the brass decoration on the legs is simply cut off before the *sabots* and does not flow into them. This is the type of table which is being reproduced today in Spain, made of resin rather than tortoiseshell.

c.1870

81 The token amount of brass inlay on ebonised ground belittles the fine quality of this unusual centre table. The whole piece is made elegant by the cross stretcher and that extra little bit of scroll on the cabriole legs. The mounts are of good quality and the whole effect is much more pleasing and typical of the better Napoleon III furniture.

c.1860

82 Another centre table similar to 80 but of better quality in terms of inlay and the mounts.

Late 1860s

83 A smaller table in terrible condition that was not of a high quality in the first place.
1860s

84 Another direct comparison to 80 but in this instance with a gilt-tooled leather top intended for use as a writing table. Although these tables were made with leather tops, many of them have been converted as the brass inlay on the top had deteriorated and it proves cheaper to take all the decoration away and cover it up with a leather skiver. However, the condition of the remaining inlay on this example leaves a lot to be desired.

1860s

85 Another comparable table to 80 with the inlay on the top lifting. Slightly better quality.
1860s

86 Unfortunately this *table à volets* is in such poor condition that it is almost beyond repair and it would probably have to be used for 'spares'. Not only is the decoration lifting but the top is warped. The mounts are of very ordinary quality.

1850s

87 Small centre tables of this type are very sought after and are not very common. The inlay is in poor condition but of rather unusual quality, the foliage appears to tumble down the legs and is interwoven in an almost 3D effect.

1850s

88 A small serpentine *table ambulante*. The decorative effect of the top and the plain tortoiseshell apron is spoilt completely by the inlay on the platform stretcher. However, small and useful.

c.1870

89 Another *table à volets* with rather mechanical decoration and a vague attempt to emulate Louis XVI designs. Useful and fairly uncommon.

c.1870

90 The tops of nineteenth century card tables twist round and open up flat on the existing apron and therefore there is no complicated gate-leg or concertina action as on eighteenth century examples. It is important to make sure that all the apron is decorated, otherwise when the table is being used in the centre of the room the side that is normally against the wall will look very dull.

1860s

91 A fine quality top inlaid with figures and a horse drawn chariot that adds considerable value to this good quality card table in good condition.

1860s

92 The inlay of alternating brass and mother-of-pearl flower heads gives a very pleasing decorative effect to this table although the designer has been a little carried away by the accentuated shape of the front. The plain legs are in stark contrast to the top and sides.

1860s

93 Another standard card table, this time in less than perfect condition.

1860s

The colourful technique of inlaying or applying Florentine hardstones is most effective when contrasted against an ebony veneered or ebonised background. This, contrasted with fine quality beautifully chiselled bronze doré *mounts, gives a dramatic overall effect of colour. The cabinet was made in Paris and the door almost certainly imported from nearby Italy.*

1850s

95 A rather exaggerated shape with thrusting female caryatids in gilt bronze makes this an unusual example. Few card tables of this period have the luxury of a frieze drawer. The mounts generally are very bold and of good quality.

c.1850

94 Louis XV shapes are far more common and this card table, based on Régence lines is rather elegant and of good quality. Normally boulle this shape is a little earlier than Louis XV types, probably 1850s.

96 and 97 These are two photographs of the same card table which in overall shape and appearance is very similar to the centre table 81. This includes a frieze drawer and the cabriole legs have that elegant extra emphasis. Unfortunately the join of the brass work where the drawer works against the apron is of very poor quality and could quite possibly have been added at a later date. Also there are various mounts missing, the most important being the urn on the stretcher.

c.1860

99 A poor quality *table à ouvrage* with a lifting top and sliding work bag below. Indifferent workmanship and a singular lack of inspiration of design does not endear this piece to the heart of the average collector.

c.1870

98 A boulle *jardinière* will suffer greatly from water damage if careful attention is not paid when watering the flowers. This typical Louis XV shape has a removable lid and a zinc lined container.

c.1870

101 A pretty *guéridon* of good quality which would prove very useful in modern sized rooms. Is the leather top original or a replacement for deteriorated brass inlay? Unfortunately not very common.

c.1860

100 A large *guéridon* with a top lifted directly from the conventional centre tables on page 67. Its rather unsatisfactory placing on a generous baluster column and heavy legs makes it look particularly unstable. Average condition and quality.

1850s

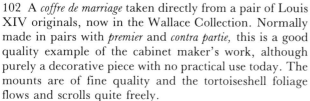

102 A *coffre de marriage* taken directly from a pair of Louis XIV originals, now in the Wallace Collection. Normally made in pairs with *premier* and *contra partie,* this is a good quality example of the cabinet maker's work, although purely a decorative piece with no practical use today. The mounts are of fine quality and the tortoiseshell foliage flows and scrolls quite freely.

c.1850 ＊

103 This tall attenuated shape was very popular during the reign of Louis XVIII. The *premier* and *contra partie* can quite clearly be seen on the overgenerously scrolled legs, *premier* on the left, *contra* on the right. Once again of fine quality and much earlier than most of the boulle that we commonly find on the market .

1830s

104, 105 and 106 A fine brass inlaid *gaine* or tall stand on the left, with good quality mounts that are not afraid to assert themselves. The central stand, by comparison to the other two, is a most miserable affair although well made. The stand on the right is one of a pair meant to be placed against the wall rather than in the centre of the room as with the others. Its proportions would be no less uncomfortable if stood upside down.

104 *1860s ＊*

105 *1870s ＊*

106 *1850s ＊*

104

105

106

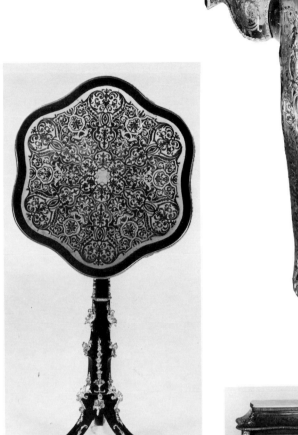

108 At first glance straight from the knacker's yard, this awkwardly shaped *console* appears to have been cut down from a centre table of the type in illustration 81. However, if so, it must have been done by the maker as the top is specially made, the decoration radiating from the middle back in conventional manner. Obviously needs to be screwed to the wall.

c.1860

109 Not as revolting as the English Edwardian 'revolving' bookcases but the quality of this circular *bibliothèque* lets it down somewhat. However, very rare and useful.

1840s

107 The numerous unidentified bits of bronze foliage applied to the rather elegantly chamfered column of this little *guéridon à abattant* rather spoil the effect of a comparatively early piece of boulle from the Louis-Philippe period. The column has a definite Gothic revival feel. The inlay on the top is somewhat repetitive, but a useful table, in good condition.

1840s

110 Not a chest of drawers but a *secrétaire à abattant,* the top three 'drawer' fronts are joined together to form a writing flap. Useful but very cheaply made, with only token mounts of appalling weakness.

1860s

111 and 112 Ready to leap like grasshoppers, these two *guéridons* are given the indulgence of a single page. Note the screw foot which compares to illustration 115. These odd little tables are copied from examples c.1700 to the last detail and there is a pair in the Jones Collection at the Victoria and Albert Museum. Placed in two corners of a room they are surprisingly useful. The dancing, in varying stages of undress in the right hand detail, is typical of that popular in the designs of Jean Berain. The long tendrils of foliage suggest a feeling of lightness not often seen in boulle designs of the nineteenth century. These are of exceptionally good quality and although in good condition were extremely difficult to date and were not immediately recognisable as nineteenth century.

1830s ∗

113 and 114 This console table with a detail of the top shown above, is another fine quality copy of a Louis XIV table. Note once again the popular screw foot and the decorative lambrequin on the centre drawer which was a very popular Louis XIV feature. The design is attributed to André-Charles Boulle from a template in the Boston Museum of Fine Art. In this copy the design is reversed.

1830s *

115 Another fine quality copy of an original table by André-Charles Boulle now in the Musée des Arts Décoratifs. Unfortunately the heavy marble top lets the design down and the stretchers are extremely weak. The urn on the centre of the stretchers looks decidedly out of place and is not nearly gutsy enough to be confused with the original design.

c.1840 *

CHINOISERIE

The vogue for l'orientalism began in the 1850s, having been popular in the eighteenth century and very early nineteenth century. However, by the middle of the century the vast European population became an ideal target for the huge 'production' capabilities of the Orient. Both China and Japan started to exploit the possibilities of the western world and exported a myriad of objects and domestic devices at cheap prices, which, like today, even with the distances involved, were still highly competitive on our industrialised markets. European manufacturers were quick to seize on the possibilities of the love of all things Oriental and designed charming items and decorative works of art, including furniture, in a watered down interpretation of the exotic arts of the relatively unknown Orient. The founder, Ferdinand Barbedienne, was a Parisian who experimented with imitation enamels and produced Chinese style bronze furniture during the late 1860s, an example of which can be found on page 148. Viardot was another maker who indulged himself in a very similar type of orientalism and his work is illustrated below.

117 (right) The base of this occasional table is exactly the same as the lower part of the *jardinière*. A very good way to economise, by making the various parts of his furniture of a standard form, attaching a different top to suit demand. Here the dragon is curling ferociously around the overscrolled end, the other end balanced by an asymmetric down-curved scroll.

116   Like the rest of the pieces illustrated, this is entirely made in the western world, no part being made or imported from China. The dragon is a typical trade mark of Viardot's work, always made in a fairly poor quality gilt-bronze. The charming naturalism of the casting is accentuated by the dragon wreathing in and out of the front of this *jardinière*. The heavily maned Burmese lions are another constant feature in his work.

c.1880

118 The materials used by Viardot are usually lightly stained beechwood or, in this case, pearwood, with dipped brass for the mounts — well cast but not the best material. There is often a little additional inlay, usually of an Oriental nature but here with a Spanish flavour of a guitar and fan. Economically the base is identical to the previous two even though the theme is Spanish! Little pieces of mother-of-pearl have been used to heighten the decoration.

1880s

Viardot exhibited at Crystal Palace in 1851 and at the Paris Exposition of 1900, alongside Linke and Majorelle. A fine and unusual cabinet in Oriental style was purchased by the Victoria and Albert Museum and is now in the Bethnal Green Museum. The quality is far higher than most Viardot pieces which are comparatively rare but normally not exceptionally well made.

119 Part of a large suite of red lacquer furniture in a full-bodied Chinese style. The black lacquer panels are in a very stylised western European style imitating Chinese lacquer but not successfully enough to be confused with the Oriental version. This suite bears an Italian retailer's label but to date there are no Italian firms making Chinese style furniture at this period on record. The furniture could conceivably have been made in the North of Italy, but is very well finished — too well for most Italian firms. It was most probably made in Paris as a later and more international version of chinoiserie to that of Viardot. Wherever it was made, it is very rare to be found in a suite of so many pieces.

1910-1930

COLUMNS

120 An elegant corinthian column, the yellow marble support stop-fluted.

c.1900

122 The redeeming feature of this rather unattractive column is the thirty-six cross sections of marble and alabaster. The overall effect is poor.

c.1900

121 A far dumpier alabaster column, but at least with a revolving top useful for displaying sculpture.

c.1900

123 No amount of gilt-brass and green onyx can make this spindly example attractive. The mounts are very weak and almost an afterthought.

c.1900

124 A highly decorative marble column with a revolving top, the base applied with a bronze relief.

c.1910

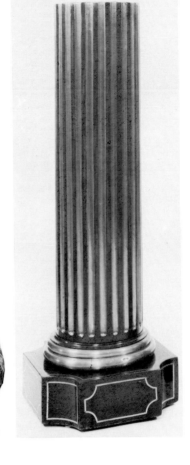

125 Cut short in its prime, this mahogany example with fluted brass fillets has pretensions to elegance but is let down by the rather heavy unthoughtful base.

1880s

126 Not the publisher rolling up his sleeves to correct the author's proofs, but an oak carving from northern France of a male terminal figure symbolising the arts. Probably part of a fireplace surround or a seventeenth century revival bed.

1850s

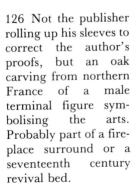

127 A ship's figurehead brought to rest on dry land and rather clumsily made into a *torchère*. Various traditional French features have been incorporated — the rather brazen caryatid above a musical trophy and a short fluted support on exaggerated *pieds de biche*.

128 This dumpy tulipwood and kingwood three drawer commode is more characteristic of the Régence period, giving it an almost Danish or Scandinavian flavour. The mounts are of extremely good quality and it is interesting to note that a bronze moulding is applied to the whole outline.

Third quarter nineteenth century

129 A conventional two drawer purpleheart commode. The proportions and small size are typical of nineteenth century re-creations which were made in this style from 1850 onwards. Signed by Schnegg on one of the drawers.

c.1890 *

130 A handsome parquetry commode in kingwood let down by the rather weak mounts which give it an undeniable nineteenth century air. Signed 'Pretot'.

1860s *

131 A well proportioned kingwood commode, the drawers slightly disguised by the *sans traverse* inlay of flowers. The mounts are of fine quality typical of the maker, Millet. Unfortunately the scagliola composite marble top spoils the whole effect and is possibly a replacement.

1860s

132 The striking decorative figuring of the kingwood is unusually marked on this commode with two bombé cupboard doors, each inlaid with a rather restrained cartouche of figures in garden settings in rather an unusual manner.

1880s

133 A Chinese lacquer commode decorated *sans traverse* similar to a commode made by Jean Demoulins for the Duc de Choiseul. The mounts once again are weak without the ebullience of Louis XV examples. This is the final evolvement of the Louis XV style commode.

c.1870 *

134 The drawers on this example are decorated in a very crude Chinese manner but at least the mounts are bolder and a part of the whole decoration rather than just an afterthought. Stamped: 'Jacob Maitre Ebeniste'. The maker at this period is unrecorded. Possibly some uninspired retailer thought that the guild stamp, abolished in 1797, *JME* stood for Jacob!

c.1900

135 The good contrasting light and dark bands of tulipwood and kingwood are of a better quality than the mounts which are only half successful. Note that in typical fashion of the mid-eighteenth century the scrolling acanthus mounts are also used as handles. The marquetry cartouche is rather indifferent.

1890s *

137 The more developed shape of the Louis XV period on this commode is slightly unsatisfactory and the whole piece appears to be bracing itself. The mounts are quite florid and the central panels inlaid with a contrasting kingwood trellis.

1850s

136 The three long serpentine drawers of this rather heavy piece are a reflection of its Régence origins from the 1730 period. Not very good quality with rather restrained mounts.

1850s ✳

138 The mahogany veneers of this example are so thin and of such poor quality that it suggests a much later date. The trailing acanthus mounts are a weak attempt at decoration.

c.1900

139 A fine kingwood veneered commode with the unusual arrangement of one wide cupboard door, taking up two thirds of the front, with a small door taking up the remainder. The gutsy mounts are signed 'F. Linke' and are strongly designed without being of the very best quality, but better than most. The Chinese panels of carved coromandel lacquer in various colours are not particularly well drawn and have a stiff feeling that was typical of later Chinese export ware.

1880-1900 ✳

140 The extraordinary elongated shape of this oak two door cupboard suggests a totally provincial origin and would be very useful for disguising a radiator. Note the typical provincial outset hinges with turned finials, usually made of brass. The doors are dowelled together in eighteenth century fashion.

c.1900

142 Another long oak cabinet with three rather strange drawers in the slightly serpentine centre. Typically provincial, this piece has been rather over-decorated on the centre drawers with unnecessary mounts.

Late nineteenth century

141 An eighteenth century invention, the *encoignure* usually has one or two doors. The swirling mounts disguise the join of the doors at the top. The marquetry is unusually good using contrasting grain and colours.

1870s

143 Another *encoignure* copying those of the slightly later almost Transitional period of the late 1750s. The whole effect of the marquetry vase of flowers is quite pleasing but the design lacks strength with the unusual inclusion of a wood top rather than marble. However, small and easy to place in a room.

1870s ∗

85

144 This fine quality Louis XV style commode is characteristic of the period 1750-1755 and similar to the work of Pierre Roussel. The quality and proportions are without fault — only the marble top could be slightly better quality.

1860s ∗   *£3,500 — £5,000*

145 This exuberant kingwood commode is surprisingly an exact copy of one by the master of the satisfactory combination of *bronze doré* on carcass work. Charles Cressent was *ébéniste* to the Regent Philippe d'Orléans. The original by Cressent was sold at the Hamilton Palace sale in 1882 and is now at Waddesdon Manor. Presumably the many copies were inspired by the 1882 sale.

1890-1900

146 This extremely fine quality commode is one of a pair by E. Zwiener. The flowing mounts are in harmony with the whole shape of the commode, framing and enhancing the delicate marquetry flowers.

1880s ∗   *£10,000 — £15,000 a pair*

147 A famous copy of an extraordinarily heavy Régence *cabinet à pans* in the Hôtel de la Monnaie, Paris. It is a faithful if rather stiff copy of the eighteenth century. This one was signed by Henri Dasson on the mounts but unfortunately no record was made of the date that usually accompanies his signature.

c. 1880

148 There is a lively elegance about this three drawer commode copied from the period of the mid-1750s. This is signed on the metal work by F. Linke and his familiar scallop shell can clearly be seen at the centre of the apron. Also the central cartouche effect given by the swirling bullrushes is typical of Linke's work and compares to similar features on the Dining Room illustration no.358. Note that an attempt has been made to disguise the drawers — a typical feature of the mid-eighteenth century.

c.1890

149 The shape of this ornate commode is almost Transitional in style but the legs have been made in far too heavy proportion and the mounts, although of good quality and detail, are very stiff. The inlay of naked *putti* studying architectural ruins makes a charming diversion from yet more flowers.

c.1890

150 It is surprising, with its fine quality mounts and marquetry, that this commode has not been signed by its nineteenth century maker. The heavy marble top is of a good purple and white colour with generous mouldings and a thickness almost impossible to obtain within the last thirty or forty years. It is interesting to note the unusual use of bullrushes although this in itself would not be enough to attribute it to the maker of 148.

c.1880 *

151 The decorative effect of the inlay disguises the fact that the maker has used very little bronze in his mounts and the normal cartouches are framed with parquetry acanthus. The bottom drawer opens out completely including the apron and in a manner popular c.1750. The light colours of the veneers, thinness of the top and rather mechanical inlay suggest a rather later date — probably c.1900 *

COMMODES — Louis XV Petites Commodes

The following three pages show twelve different small commodes, all of Louis XV style and inspiration, that were made in very large quantities in the latter part of the nineteenth century and are still being made at the present time. Their small size makes them far more convenient for modern living than their larger brothers on the previous pages. Unfortunately their quality is often indifferent with extremely thin veneers, machine cut marquetry and thin marble tops. Their reduction in size often leaves rather ungainly proportions.

152 (left) The marquetry on this is in a similar vein to that on the right. The drawers are rather ill fitting.

c.1900

153 (right) Better quality, but only just. The marble top has more colour but the mounts are extremely mean.

c.1900

154 (left) Once again the parquetry trellis is a welcome relief from the mass of summer flowers but the whole effect is of poor quality. Notice one of the *sabots* is missing, which is a habitual problem as they are very light and usually badly pinned on through the veneer to the softwood carcass.

c.1900 ∗

155 The marquetry again compares to illustration 152 and the effect is the same. The legs are rather too thin and pinched.

Early twentieth century

A very unusual kingwood bas d'armoire, *very much in the manner and style of Charles Cressent. The doors are quite delightful, applied with infant* putti *playing cymbals and pipes with dancing dogs and monkeys swinging from ropes. The female mask mounts at the sides are very similar to those on the* bureau plat *in the style of Cressent illustrated on page 104.*

1870s

One of a pair of very fine tortoiseshell side cabinets in Louis XIV style. The doors are inlaid with very bold pewter and brass strapwork and foliage. The bronze doré mounts are extremely well executed. It is very rare to find such a subdued pair of cabinets, and to find a pair of anything of this quality is becoming increasingly difficult. Many of the bigger makers in Paris made similar quality Boulle pieces, especially Sormani and later Linke.

1860s

157 The unusual proportions of this have the bottom drawer opening with the apron. The marquetry is unusual and attractive but still slightly formal in execution.

c.1900

156 Another example with slightly better marquetry at the sides.

c.1900

159 The sides of this are simply veneered with no marquetry and note there is a wood, rather than shaped marble, top.

Early twentieth century

158 A good example of machine made furniture.

c.1900

160 The plainness of this commode is a welcome relief but the mounts do not do it justice and the mahogany and tulipwood veneers are plainly of rather poor quality.

Early twentieth century

161 Veneered in rosewood and quite delicately inlaid with flowers but the overall result is not very successful. The drawers are ill fitting and the original purpose of design of the 1740s has now been completely lost.

Early twentieth century

162 By now a familiar shape with the tall attenuated legs and weak mounts with mechanical marquetry.

Early twentieth century

163 Another similar example.

Early twentieth century

164

165

166

164, 165 and 166 To all intents and purposes three identical commodes copied from one by Riesener (The illustration of 166 has been inadvertently reversed showing the ewer in a different light). There are three gradations of quality, 164 being perhaps the best, although the addition of swags of leaves and berries is not necessarily an improvement to the original. Also the maker of this one has deemed it necessary to change the decoration on the sides of the frieze drawers. Notice that both 164 and 165 have far superior *bronze doré* feet to those of 166 and the latter does not have quite the same exuberance in the marquetry. 165 is stamped 'Boudei', an unrecorded maker.

164 *c.1900* *
165 *c.1880* *
166 *c.1900* *

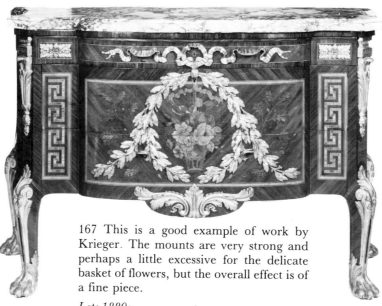

167 This is a good example of work by Krieger. The mounts are very strong and perhaps a little excessive for the delicate basket of flowers, but the overall effect is of a fine piece.

Late 1880s

168 A characteristic breakfront commode of the period between 1760 and 1770 was often reproduced in the latter part of the nineteenth century, but is not particularly popular today. This example makes a poor attempt at quasi-classical marquetry. As with some of the earlier Louis XV style commodes, the lower drawer on most of the transitional breakfront examples opens in conjunction with the apron. This one is kingwood with the unusual addition of ash legs.

c.1900 *

169 A very plain example, almost entirely neo-classical in its decoration, stamped with the *marque au fer* 'M.A. Turinetti', an unrecorded maker.

c.1890 *

170 The style is similar to that of J.F. Leleu of c.1770. Severely classical in decoration of good quality but a rather thin top.

c.1900 *

171 The cube parquetry is a highly decorative feature on this commode, but the whole effect is not one of a very strong design.

1880s *

172 The combination of good quality *bronze doré* Vitruvian scroll frieze mounts and a marble top that won't slide off make this small commode an unusual and decorative piece. For some reason the maker has decided not to have the bottom drawer opening with the apron. An extra bonus is that the metalwork on the knees continues to the *sabots*.

1880s

173 Unfortunately this has to be one of the worst examples illustrated. The warped top would be extremely expensive and difficult to straighten and there are several pieces of veneer missing from the crossbanding.

c.1890

174 and 175 These two *petites commodes* are almost usable as *guéridons*. 174 used the space at the sides of the drawers by incorporating cupboard doors. Both are rather plain, but the former is definitely of better quality.

Both 1890s

176 An unusual example with rococo mounts at the knees. A good medium size and the maker obviously intended it to have a wood, rather than a marble top. Quite pretty.

1880s

177 Another wooden top — a rare sight on eighteenth century originals. This is a wholeheartedly nineteenth century example in well figured kingwood. Probably a provincial piece.

1880s

178 A traditional eighteenth century design, although just slightly mean in decorative content.

1880s *

179 Although just conceivably an English copy, it is more likely that the stamp on the back of this commode, that of 'D. Carpenter, Nassau St., W.2612', is purely a retailer's stamp. The quality of the mahogany veneers is not very high, but the effect of the vase of flowers on the sycamore ground is good.

c.1900 *

180 A small commode with the unusual addition of three drawers cutting the hanging basket of flowers mercilessly into three.

c.1900

181 An attractive *demi-lune commode* using a similar Vitruvian scroll decoration to that in illustration 172. The simulated fluting is typical of the later Transitional period.

c.1890

182 Another *demi lune* but sadly underdecorated, strictly speaking a *meuble d'appui* the cupboard door of which would prove most awkward to use.

Early twentieth century

183 The *sabots* have been seen before on the 'Carpenter' commode no.179 and the urn of flowers, although of different colours, is otherwise identical.

c.1900 *

185 Resting its design on traditional English lines and arrangement of drawers, this 'chest of drawers' was made by G. Joffroy, numbered SD4 and the metalwork stamped 'De Launay'. Retaining traditional Transitional and rococo side mounts, the handles are decidedly 'modernist'. Good well-figured walnut veneers typical of the early twentieth century French makers' renewed interest in fine quality woods.

1900-1910

184 A kingwood *semanier,* one drawer for each day of the week, not a very inspired piece.

c.1900

186 Probably the same date as the previous example but very boring veneers.

Early 1900s

187 Purely a nineteenth century invention, this three drawer chest has a rather squat display cabinet above. The marquetry is once again rather mechanical, but quite a useful piece.

c.1870

COMMODES — Louis XVI style

The final development of the commode is clearly seen on this page. The fluted columns and toupie feet, together with the rectangular outlines, are common features of the period, also three of the examples have similar tasselled and draped swag mounts.

188 A massive commode approximately 220 cm wide. Modelled after an example by Stöckel.

1880s ✳

189 Another variation of the same theme, incorporating 'Wedgwood' or jasper panels on an adam green ground instead of the bronze panels after Clodion of the previous example. The wood is far lighter and not french polished as the other one appears to be. Both these examples have two frieze drawers above a seemingly useless fall front.

1880s ✳

190 The famous *ébéniste* Martin Carlin supplied the original example of this important commode to the daughters of Louis XV at Bellevue in 1785 and it is now in the Louvre. The Japanese black and *nashiji* gold lacquer panels have been faithfully copied from the original and the overall effect is fairly light. This huge commode is over 220 cm wide.

1850s ✳

191 The commode with a pair of bow fronted glazed side cabinets is called a *commode à l'anglais*. This is copied from an original by Guillaume Beneman for the Salon de Jeux at Compiègne. The quality is outstanding, although again a massive piece. The mahogany is of the plum pudding variety.

1860s ✳

192 A simple, plain three drawer commode quarter veneered in *bois de citron* and left uncompromisingly plain. Useful but late.

Early 1900s

193 The extremely dark mahogany is intentional to form a contrast with the good quality *bronze doré* foliate mounts.

c.1900

194 The Louis XVI origins of this example are disguised by the typically 'Edwardian' handles in an otherwise early Directoire form.

1890-1910

195 The general standard of workmanship on this small *demi-lune* commode is qualified by the stamp of Sormani. Note the decoration of the Vitruvian scroll found in bronze on example no.179.

1880-1900

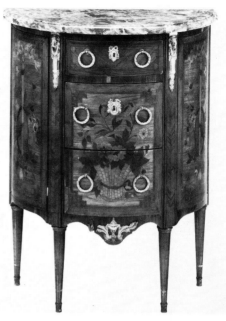

196 The fine quality of this mahogany three door commode — a common feature of the Louis XVI period — makes it difficult to tell from its eighteenth century original by Adam Weisweiler. Elegant, well made but large.

c.1870 *

197 Another small *demi-lune* commode with the advantage of side cupboards as well as drawers. This is copying a very early Louis XVI example but is of a workmanship lacking in quality all too common in commodes of minor makers during the last twenty years of the nineteenth century.

1880s

198 Several examples of this three drawer commode after an original by J.F. Leleu have been stamped by the Beurdeley family, although this one was not signed. The mounts are not of the quality one would expect from Beurdeley in this instance. The circular tapering legs on Louis XVI commodes of this type or later copies always look very unstable and out of proportion.

1870s *

199 A small breakfront commode with a hangover from the Transitional period. The fine quality marquetry consists of a holly and ebony trellis on a *bois de citron* ground. The frieze panel of frolicking *putti* is often incorporated into frieze drawers on *bureaux plats*. Although good quality, probably later than it looks.

c.1890

200 This dark *bois de rose* commode is a mixture of Louis XV and Transitional decoration and is typical of a type popular for bedroom suites at the beginning of the twentieth century. Not very elegant and rather massive but a useful storage unit.

Early twentieth century

201 A wonderful but honest example of late nineteenth century rococo when the love for asymmetry was at its height. A similar feel to the previous example but much more exotic and consequently far more popular.

Early twentieth century

203 An extremely fine amboyna veneered development of the Louis XVI commode with contrasting purple heart bandings. Again rather too big for modern houses but very elegant. The companion piece to a secretaire on page 137.

c.1880 ✱

202 Every available amount of space has been used in that even the apron is in fact a drawer. The mounts are simply dipped brass and would probably be better employed somewhere else. The mechanical aspect of the scrolling foliage, although quite free in its design, can be seen to be an exact repetition in all of the eight drawer panels. Quite striking.

1880s

204 A typical product of the machine made era using good quality walnut veneers and a token decoration from the Louis XVI era. *Semaniers* of this type were often part of a bedroom suite.

Early twentieth century

205 *En suite* with no.202 on the preceding page and the same comments apply.

1880s

206 A *semanier* in *bois noirci* of an international type locking in the same way as a Wellington chest. The beechwood inlay is of a very poor quality produced from 1880 onwards.

1880s

207 Quite possibly of German extraction, this small bedroom piece borrows the quadrant fluted columns from the Stöckel commode illustrated on page 98, nos.188 and 189. The inlay is ivory and is a better quality than the carcass. Not popular in black.

c.1870

DESKS
Régence and Louis XV bureaux plats

The bureau plat developed in the first few years of the eighteenth century and some of the earliest known designs are by André-Charles Boulle. This form of flat top desk, originally with a central frieze drawer and three drawers at either side, had itself evolved directly from the bureau Mazarin of the mid-seventeenth century. It was a natural progression for the design to lose the two spindly sets of legs joined by stretchers, see Boulle page 64 illustration no.66. The tops were invariably of rectangular form; the knees of the cabriole legs became more exaggerated during the Régence period and by the time of Charles Cressent they were applied with brazen espagnolettes or female busts. The quality varies enormously and these desks are still being made today, see page 311. The late Louis XIV and Régence bureau perhaps epitomises all the best qualities of French furniture of the eighteenth century and a well made boldly designed example will be highly sought after whatever its date.

208 This small writing desk is of an eclectic Louis XIII form inlaid with a mixture of renaissance and baroque ivory marquetry on an ebony veneered ground. The elegance of the legs is spoilt by the superstructure which was a favourite addition of the mid-nineteenth century 'to improve the earlier design'. Good quality but not very satisfactory as a desk.

1880s

209 This finely veneered kingwood writing desk incorporates the screw foot so popular in the late seventeenth century. The design has become a little muddled with cabriole and square tapering legs together with the normally later feature of a ram's head. Good quality but again not very practical as a desk.

1870s

210 This single drawer writing table follows the inspiration of the designs of the 1720s and is unusual for its small size. However, the mounts are not of very good quality and the *pieds de biche* are terribly flat footed.

c.1860

211 This parquetry veneered kingwood desk is an uncomfortable copy of the early eighteenth century *bureaux plats* and the *bombé* sides and drawers have become a little out of proportion. The *espagnolettes* have unfortunate grimacing features and show up the poor quality of the mounts.

c.1890

212 A very sophisticated Régence style *bureau plat* at the height of its development. The fine quality ebullient mounts are reminiscent of Charles Cressent. The whole design has an air of well being and elegant sophistication. Note the similarity in the frieze mounts to this and the next example.

Mid-nineteenth century ∗

213 Not quite the sophistication but considerable quality can be seen in the fine *bronze doré* mounts signed by F. Linke. Once again the *espagnolettes* are in the style of Cressent. Note that there is slightly more curve to the apron and on this example the top has a less practical parquetry veneer rather than a fine leather top.

1890s ∗

214 The frieze of this desk is attractively inlaid with a trellis filled with small flowers although the mounts are rather restrained.

1860s

215 The *espagnolettes* are surprisingly small and restrained when compared with the exuberant foliage applied to the frieze. The generally high quality of this piece is of a type that normally bears a signature and if an unscrupulous party was able to add a signature on the mounts or a *marque au fer* to the carcass the provenance would be difficult to dispute.

1880s ∗

216 A very handsome desk with fine male terms at each corner representing the four continents. The exaggerated inverted serpentine shape is typical of the earlier eighteenth century *bureau plat,* and the style has been faithfully copied. The mounts are very lush and unusual. *c.1870*

217 The flowing outline of this desk is marred by the weakness of the mounts and the benign faces of the female heads. The general lack of sophistication suggests a later date, probably c.1900. ∗

218, 219 & 220 The fine chiselling and realistic happy expression of the *espagnolettes* give a much more satisfactory feel to the design of this desk which is to all intents and purposes applied with the same details as the previous example which lacks totally the same sense of 'oomph'.

c.1870 ∗

The two best examples of nineteenth century reproductions of the *bureau plat* of the 1720s are illustrated in colour on page 108.

221 Another handsome and beautifully made desk by Krieger. The mounts are a delightful dusty gold *bronze doré* of the finest quality mercurial gilding which contrasts considerably with the dark tulipwood veneering. Krieger was capable of producing fine quality work, putting him amongst the leaders of Paris cabinet makers in the late nineteenth century but his workshops also produced many much poorer examples of craftsmanship and also sold dubious pieces of furniture in the eighteenth century, especially Louis XV, style that were very loosely described on their bills and can only be described as fakes.

1880s *

222 An exceptional *bureau plat* by François Linke mounted with his familiar powder blue jasper ware plaques. This desk compares exactly with the main part of the *bureau plat* by the same maker illustrated in colour on page 108. It is not known how many of these desks Linke made but this is the fourth seen by the author. In this example the top has not been inset with leather but has been exquisitely inlaid in a highly detailed marquetry. This desk, like its counterpart with the leather top, was signed on the metalwork and also stamped with a *marque au fer*. Guillaume Beneman copied this from the base of the bureau du Roi by Oeben and Riesener, now at Waddesdon, in 1786.

1890s *

The next two pages show lesser quality bureaux plats, *a feature which, generally speaking, seems to go hand in hand with desks of a smaller size. The nineteenth century cabinet maker, like his earlier counterpart, tended to make the larger desks as a form of* chef d'oeuvre.

223 Nicely quarter veneered in kingwood with a good bold and moulded brass banding to the top. This is a small and practical desk with slightly more restrained mounts than previous examples. The drawers are no longer outlined in *bronze doré* and *espagnolettes* have given way to full rococo foliage.

1860s ∗

224 A very similar desk of slightly weaker execution. *1860s* ∗

225 This *bureau plat et cartonnier* is of massive proportions. The addition of the *cartonnier* means the desk needs even more room to stand in without being cramped and many similar pieces have been separated from their bases. Two further examples of *cartonniers* are illustrated on page 268. This large desk has good quality mounts but the contrast of the kingwood veneers and ebony crossbanding is too marked. One always has the feeling of not knowing quite where to sit at these desks; if one sits at the side one can't open the leather lined *cartonnier* drawers and if one sits at the end one can see the clock but can't get to any of the drawers.

c.1890

226 An average quality small desk but the decoration of the drawers is very weak. Note that the boldly scrolling side drawers open with their apron which can be used as a hand-hold as in no.224.

1860s

A rather heavy but extremely well made bureau plat *by François Linke. It is similar in execution to the companion piece for the enormous* bureau du Roi *at Versailles and there is an almost identical example at Waddesdon Manor, catalogue no. 94. Linke made several versions. Another is illustrated on page 106. This was unusual in that the drawer was stamped 'F. Linke', contrary to his normal style of signing the* bronze doré *mounts.*

Left top: A very strongly modelled Régence style bureau plat *similar to a rosewood* bureau plat *at Clandon Park. The whole design is extremely gutsy with strong legs and heavily modelled* bronze doré *mounts, which in every way are made and designed for the desk and are not, as so often is the case, chosen from a box with assorted mounts and placed on in an* ad lib *fashion. The drawer has a hinged leather reading flap. As is often the case, even with these large French desks, only one side has drawers, the others being dummies.*

1850-1870

Left centre: Once again an almost identical shape, extremely well modelled with bold bronze doré *mounts. See how similar the mounts bordering the writing surface on the frieze and on the legs are to the desk above. This is exceptional, being veneered in ebony which gives an overall impression of a black colour but in fact ranges from black through to green and an almost mahogany red. The kingwood and tulipwood bandings bordering the leather top are a highly effective colour contrast.*

1850-1870

227 The attractive and unusual use of rosewood veneers on this desk is spoilt by the quite appalling quality mounts that have not been designed for the desk but purely attached in a 'meccano' fashion.

c.1890

228 How much nicer this desk looks with its gently serpentine frieze and heavy but honest nineteenth century egg and dart moulding. The restrained use of the mounts gives the desk an air of elegance although the gilt bronze beading attached to the sharp edge of the apron and legs is always susceptible to being pulled off by clothing and furniture removers.

c.1870

229 Unpretentiously nineteenth century, this small walnut desk has good bold rococo marquetry at each corner on the top, which is complemented by the mounts. There is no attempt here to emulate the Louis XV style but only to re-create it in a light and small practical piece of furniture of the 1860s.

230 This is a very poor quality example of another unashamedly nineteenth century desk. Notice how the drawers have become chipped where the diagonally placed veneer meets the drawer edge without the protection of bronze mouldings or the more normal crossbanding of an English drawer.

Late nineteenth century

The next six bureaux plats *make no pretensions of being eighteenth century examples in the fully developed Louis XV style of the 1750s. They all follow the general outline but the decoration is purely nineteenth century imagination.*

231 The execution of the marquetry on this desk is beyond reproach although the design is a little cramped. Annoying to use as a desk with the beautifully figured quarter veneered walnut top but a very decorative item and small enough to use in the home.

c.1860

232 The practical use of this desk is also limited and again the execution of the marquetry is unusual and to the very highest standards. The *marqueteur* has cleverly interlaced ribbons in and around the flowers giving a wonderful 3-D effect.

Late 1850s

233 The maker has sensibly included a token leather top so that this can be used more effectively as a desk. The inlay is restrained and not of the quality of the previous two examples but the use of sycamore on the drawers gives an added decorative effect.

1860s

234 Good quality marquetry decorates the drawers and wide top banding on this desk but the inlay is not of the highest quality. Once again the *marqueteur* has endeavoured to give the flowers a more striking and decorative effect by setting them into a contrasting ebony ground. Note that one of the *sabots* is missing which is an all too frequent problem, especially if they are of the type that is applied and pinned and doesn't have the added purchase of those in the next illustration. The legs of this example have become rather heavy.

1860s

235 A good quality desk probably made in large numbers by one of the smaller Paris workshops but again not of the superlative order of marquetry occasionally seen on nineteenth century furniture.

c.1870

236 The marquetry in the frieze is of good quality but doesn't quite reach the 3-D effect of no.232. The walnut carcass has been stained to give a contrast to the flowers.

1850s

237 It would be difficult to use this small marquetry table as a desk and equally a pity to cover the top up. The marquetry is attractive and inventive and once again unashamedly nineteenth century.

1860s

238 This is an example of a later nineteenth century version with the asymmetrical cartouche on the top and the rather poor quality kingwood veneer.

1890s

DESKS — Louis XV bureaux en pente

Commonly called a 'bureau de dame' which has become an almost accepted misnomer for a bureau en pente, i.e. a desk with an angled writing flap raised on cabriole legs.

239 The extra swell of the *bombé* sides of this desk are an added decorative feature on what is otherwise a fairly ordinary quality desk. The bronze and porcelain mounts are not up to the standard of the veneers. English?

1880s

240 The well faded veneers and marquetry contribute to the fine looks of this desk whose decoration is discreet and not too overdone. As on eighteenth century furniture, patination plays an important part on the overall look of the piece.

1860s *

241 (left) Although the marquetry panels are quite inventive they have a stiffness normally found on machine cut inlay. The colours are almost too bright and fresh and the mounts have a stamped out, rather than individually cast, quality.

c.1890

242 (right) A most extra-ordinary shape but very good quality sliced kingwood and tulipwood veneers. The tall top looks ungainly but will allow a larger flap and writing surface. There is no sensible explanation for the gilt bronze banding underneath the flap which appears to have been put on upside down. This desk was retailed by James A. Butti, 7 Queen Street, Edinburgh.

1880s

243 The rather extraordinary indentation at the top of this desk is a rare feature of later desks. Not very good quality however.

c.1920

244 Almost identical to the desk below but better quality and in superb condition. The elaborate gilt-bronze around the gallery is the hallmark of the neo-classical revival that was popularised at the 1876 Philadelphia Exhibition.

Late 1870s

245 (above) The flat sides and front are those of a much cheaper bureau than the serpentine and *bombé* forms seen earlier. However, the marquetry is quite good with an attempt at 3-D.

1860s

246 (right) There is considerable movement to the shape of this desk which is veneered in warm red tones of burr chestnut but unfortunately this has been contrasted with the ebonised pearwood framework which gives a rather sombre effect.

Late 1870s

247

247, 248, 249 and 250 These four marquetry *bureaux en pente* are all of the same basic shape with very slightly shaped side aprons and reserves of flowers. Nos. 247, 248 and 250 are of almost identical quality with little variation in value or date. The only difference would be the condition.

All 1880s

248

249   250

251 This example corresponds very closely to those on the previous page.

1870s

252 This is an example of the very poorest grade with very little movement and the worst possible quality marquetry — its only advantage being that there is little of it.

c.1890

253 A quite good example with nice clean lines and boldly figured oyster cut kingwood veneers that have the same sophisticated look as no.240.

1860s

254 Machine made mahogany veneered furniture at its very worst. This desk has little to say for itself except that it is eminently practical. The veneers have an early twentieth century 'bedroom suite' quality that leaves a lot to be desired.

Early twentieth century

256 Neither the veneer nor the porcelain have the same effect and quality as the previous example. The writing compartment is in the frieze drawer and everything has to be moved from the projecting table top to open the cupboard doors, which makes it rather impractical.

1860s

255 A fine quality writing table with Sèvres apple green porcelain mounts. Notice the rather extraordinary way that the frieze drawer fits into either side of the apron with a suspended section of diagonal veneer.

1860s

257 This uncomfortable looking piece of furniture is an attempt to marry a hanging cabinet to a small writing desk carried out at some unknown time in the latter part of the nineteenth century. Both sections were executed as different pieces of furniture at approximately the same time.

1860s

258 The lavish brightly gilt mounts and red highly decorative kingwood veneers and blue porcelain mounts at first take the eye away from the extraordinary shape of this cabinet. It is not a photographic illusion — the front for some reason is narrower than the back. A very unusual piece of furniture and a better variation of illustration no.256.

c.1860

259 Great effect is made of contrasting tulipwood and kingwood veneers and this writing table is a fairly satisfactory development of the mid-nineteenth century along Louis XV principles.

1860s

260 This desk has nothing of the quality of the previous example and the proportions are rather awkward. The porcelain mounts are too small on the cupboard doors and too big on the drawers for comfort.

c.1870

261 This desk is typical of the type of furniture imported into England by the antique dealer and modern retailer Edward Holmes Baldock, whose *marque au fer* it bears. The proportions are good with good quality porcelain mounts making a useful and highly decorative desk. The only disadvantage is the three quarter brass gallery which all too often gets in the way of elbows and is unnecessarily applied by the makers, as in the previous illustration. The leather is extremely distressed on this example.

1850s

262 Another good quality small and attractive desk that can be fitted easily into a modern room plan.

1850s

263 An ugly and uncompromising desk in *bois noirci* with the very worst mass produced transfer printed mounts in Sèvres style.

1870s

264 Fairly sombre in decoration, this desk is veneered with amboyna on a mahogany ground. Note the repetition of the tasselled gilt metal swags on the gallery which must have been produced by the mile throughout the second half of the nineteenth century.

1890s

265 Not the same piece but almost certainly from the same workshops. The condition looks very slightly better than the previous example.

1890s

266 The shape of this desk is slightly unusual, the *demi-lune* writing surface not quite in harmony with the upper part. Quite good quality with well contrasted kingwood and tulipwood veneers on the frieze.

1860s

267 An unusual but rather elegant writing table in king-wood and tulipwood, the two reserves on the top lightly inlaid with flowers. The underside is stamped with the *marque au fer* of G. Durand and is possibly that of Posper-Guillaume Durand.

Late 1850s

268 Another kidney shaped writing table with the elongated trestle support popular during the third quarter of the eighteenth century. The absence of a pole stretcher gives the piece a certain elegance but renders it very unstable in use. The construction of this piece was such that it was extremely difficult to tell from an eighteenth century example and consequently may well have been a provincial hangover made in the second quarter of the nineteenth century. *

270 Another plain and elegant desk, the only decoration being the carefully selected segments of kingwood.

Mid-nineteenth century *

269 Similarly, this desk is of a type looking directly back to the 1760s and with the incorporation of eighteenth century book spines applied to the cupboard doors it may well have been made to deceive the unwary.

Mid-nineteenth century

These four writing desks are all well made and are of an extremely popular type based loosely on the principles of an English Carlton House desk with the drawers in the last two examples curving round to encompass the writer.

271 The tiny doors on either side of the clock lead into cavernous bulbous cupboards of the most unnecessary shape.

1860s

272 Once again there is rather an unnecessary and exaggerated shape to the superstructure but the whole feeling is lighter than the previous example. The love of rather eccentric Louis XV revival shapes tended to regain popularity in the latter years of the nineteenth century.

1880s

273 Less exuberant but a much smaller desk, which is an important feature. The leather has been well worn. The mounts are only a shadow of the real McCoy.

1890s

274 The practical application of the candle arms is doubtful — at the height that these are set little light would fall on the writer — only wax. Note that the maker has economised and only put a timepiece movement in the superstructure, unlike the two examples above. At least there would be no intermittent striking to disturb the concentration.

c.1880

275 and 276 An extremely fine example of a kingwood and marquetry *bureau rognon* and one of the masterpieces of François Linke. This ebullient style is typical of this maker's design. Linke was fond of highly detailed naturalistic marquetry and scrolling serpentine and *bombé* form. The naturalism certainly has an eye towards the art nouveau forms that were popular when this desk was made but the shape and essence are wholly traditional. The mounts are quite exceptional, almost in full relief in places. The decoration to the back is every bit as good and detailed as the front, with the unusual addition of two *putti* holding a trailing lambrequin. Very cleverly, Linke has

arranged a delicately scrolling border and crossbanding on the back and sides which almost imitate bronze. The central medallion of winged female sphinxes is exceptional, the female heads are very delicately chased and must be sensitive portraits taken from real life. Even to those who do not favour this ornate style of furniture which typifies the early twentieth century, the quality and finish must be appreciated. To those who admire this type of design this desk is a rare example of a practical piece of furniture that is almost a standard for French furniture in the traditional style as the new century approached.

1900-1910

277 A good quality *bureau rognon* with a heavy pull-out writing surface above the drawers. The leather faced drawers in the superstructure are imitating those of a *cartonnier* and the whole shape is similar to that of the next illustration. The lost candle arm will be expensive and difficult to replace.

1870s

278 Ugly in the extreme, the only writing surface being a pull-out slide in the frieze. These *cartonniers* were intended as filing cabinets and one on a stand such as this may even have been used alongside a *bureau plat.*

1880s

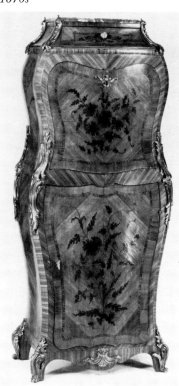

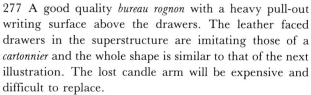

279 (left) A wonderfully exaggerated Louis XV shape with a light and effective decoration of marquetry and contrasting veneers. Cupboards are never particularly successful below a writing surface as there is no possiblity of opening them without the sitter moving away.

c.1870 ✳

280 (right) Again cupboards hamper the usefulness of this small lacquer secretaire decorated in the European fashion imitating Chinese lacquer. The condition has to be carefully watched in modern centrally heated rooms and although it is possible to repair, it can prove expensive.

c.1880 ✳

DESKS — Transitional secrétaires à abattant

The fall front secretaire became a highly popular item of furniture in France during the middle of the nineteenth century. It has never been particularly popular outside France because of the rather ineffective method of supporting the flap below the hinges against the fitted interior when the flap is down. This makes the writing surface unstable and the writer is inhibited about leaning too hard or piling books on the surface. Occasionally the first frieze drawer will pull out to support the flap which eventually leaves a mark on the decoration of the flap. The well tried English variation with lopers seems a much more satisfactory and sturdy mechanical arrangement.

282

281

281 and 282 The marquetry on both this and the following example is of a tired and mechanical quality. It is interesting to see the swell of the sides in the lower third of this cabinet repeated in the middle of the next one, indicating that although the mechanical reproduction of the marquetry is extremely similar at least the individual workshops still created their own designs.

Both 1890s

283 Here the swelling at the sides has reached the top, creating rather a severe and overburdened form. However, the quality of the individual flowers contrasted against the rosewood ground can clearly be seen and the scrolled acanthus mounts merely help to complete the overall outline rather than add to it.

1870s

284 The brutish quality of this tall stark breakfront form has not in this instance been relieved by marquetry flowers. The designer has decided that the contrasting woods are enough decoration. This normally good decision is perhaps wrong on such a severe piece.

1880s

285 The plum pudding effect on the quarter veneered flap draws one's attention to the otherwise barren surface like a scene from a science fiction film. This is the very type of poor quality wood and crossbanding used at the turn of the century. The unfortunate feature of the rather short cabriole legs so popular during the Transitional period gives the impression that the desk is about to hobble away.

c.1900

286 The musical trophy relieves the severity of the poor quality kingwood veneer, the only problem being that once the desk is being used and the flap is open, the decoration is lost.

1900s

287 and 288 These small marquetry writing desks were a speciality of Charles Topino c.1760 and were fondly reproduced in the middle of the nineteenth century. The marquetry in both cases will have been cut by hand, probably in a small dingy workshop, from where the cabinet maker could order any shape or size of pot, teacup or other domestic utensil. To all intents and purposes both pieces are decorated exactly the same but they have been applied slightly differently. In both cases the gilt bronze banding and galleries are identical, as are the mounts at the knees, although a different set of *sabots* has been used. The drawer handles and escutcheons are also different. Rather naïve and amusing. Probably made as fakes.

Mid-nineteenth century *

DESKS — Transitional secrétaires à cylindre

The invention of the cylinder bureau was a fortunate one for today's restorers, who spend a considerable amount of their time trying to unjam the cylinder which, in the better examples, works in conjunction with the pull-out writing slide. Changes of atmosphere, central heating and people who insist on opening the cylinder using only one handle, can easily damage the mechanism. Their main advantage is that a mass of untidy papers can be easily shut away, providing of course that the mechanism doesn't jam if the cylinder is closed too quickly. Several examples have a tambour action which consists of numerous slats of tongued and grooved wood held together by a backing of heavy canvas as in illustration 290. These are even more fallible and have to be kept in good working order.

289 (left) Almost the same metal gallery has been used as for the two small desks in illustrations 287 and 288. So much care has been taken to present us with a flower head trellis inlaid into a multitude of different veneers and cuts of wood that the application of the design to the desk as a whole has become rather unsatisfactory.

*c.1880 *

290 (right) This extremely handsome brute, after an eighteenth century model of c.1775 by Jean-Henri Riesener, is signed in several places by Henry Dasson and dated 1879. The quality of the mounts and the mahogany veneers is of an extraordinarily fine standard, the burnished mercury gilded mounts contrasting with the dark wood. The interior cabinet work is so fine that a rush of air can be felt and even heard as the drawers are closed. The overall size is difficult to imagine as it is nearly two metres wide and should the tambour jam, it would take four men to carry the piece to the restorer.

*1879 *

291

292

291 and 292 Another example of two *almost* identical desks, probably produced by the same workshops. No.291 is of inferior quality, the mounts are dull and were not gilt to the same standards. The main difference is that the inlay on the cylinder and drawers is on a cube parquetry ground on the latter example and a plain ground on the former.

1880s

293 A plain and severe desk with little movement on the rather restrained apron — a danger warning on the cylinder can just be discerned in that where the cylinder meets the frieze at each side there is less of a gap than at the centre, suggesting that the cylinder is warping slightly and may jam at any time.

1880s

294 A small and plain version but at least the width of 74cm measured at the widest point on the cabriole legs is considerably less than previous examples. Only the front has been decorated.

1880s

295 The curved moulding at the edge of the top of this *bureau plat* gives it an unnecessarily ugly appearance. How much better the edge would look with a simple gilt bronze banding or a rectangular finish. The mounts are however of very good quality but generally not a very successful design.

c.1900

296 The narrative on the flap of this secretaire is a familiar one, the young cavalier courting in a garden setting amidst classical ruins. The *marqueteur* was quite brave to attempt such a complicated story but the final execution is not particularly competent and the whole thing is let down by the extremely thin and weak foliate borders to the marquetry reserves which are inset into satinwood.

c.1900

DESKS — Louis XVI bureaux plats

The severe rectangular forms and straight tapering legs of the fully developed Louis XVI period are clearly shown on the following pages. The subtle plasticity in the Transitional shapes has now disappeared and the era of neo-classicism has now arrived. The emphasis under Louis XVI was one of contrast in materials and the very high standard of workmanship which is normally reflected in nineteenth century copies.

297 (above) and 298 (right) The similarity between this *bureau plat* and *bureau plat et cartonnier* is immediately apparent. Both are made and stamped by F. Durand et Fils who would have made several similar writing tables, adding the *cartonnier* if required. The plaque in the frieze is identical and is repeated on many desks of the period. A simple but very decorative feature is the flowering stem which issues from each corner and grows under the metal banding on the apron towards the centre of the table. All the leading edges have been covered with the finest *bronze doré*. These desks are an example of French mid-nineteenth century craftsmanship at its best.

Both late 1850s ∗

299 The elongated legs make this desk a little heavy but the quality of the mounts and of the porcelain on a deep blue ground are to a high standard. The leather is splitting along the planking of the carcass which is often all too common as the wood moves in changes of atmosphere.

1860s ∗

300 This very handsome desk is consciously trying to be an original Louis XVI piece from the 1780s. There is a completely false stamp of 'E. Levasseur, JME' on the underside and it is very important to look further than the stamp when dating such an item. There is nothing that one can tell from a photograph to help date an exact copy such as this. The drawers were badly made, the leading edges were not rounded off in the more normal eighteenth century manner and the porcelain plaques were of a type produced in the second quarter of the nineteenth century.

Probably c.1830 ∗

301 and 302 A majestic *bureau plat et cartonnier* in the Louis XVI style imitating with some grandeur the style popular in the 1780s. The *cartonnier* by itself is a useful side cabinet but unfortunately without cupboard doors or any drawers below the open pigeon holes, so that if placed against the wall with the desk in the middle of the room, it becomes a rather large decorative piece and not as capacious as it should be for its size. This is a well made desk and cabinet but the design is a little restrained and not perhaps as exciting as one might hope for. There is little sense of the adventure that some of the better makers employed at the end of the nineteenth century. The candelabra are too small and weak in comparison with the large clock. The studious looking naked *putti* surmounting the clock is flanked by a large figure of a cockerel stealing away with something under its wing — the bird appears to be about to take flight. An identical desk by Sormani was exhibited at the Paris 1900 Exhibition copied from a period desk in the Hamilton Palace sale, 1882.

1880s ✳

303 A rare example of the firm of Beurdeley's use of porcelain mounts in the early Louis XVI style but perhaps more consistent with the style of Bellangé c.1820. The cabinet work and mounts are of very good quality but not to the normal extremely high standards of Beurdeley. The painted porcelain panels are exquisitely decorated and help date the furniture. As this is one of the rather earlier pieces by Beurdeley made under the father's supervision, it probably explains the slight lack of quality compared with the work under the son's management, the son being the power behind the throne that made the Beurdeley name so famous.

1860s

304 A large mahogany *cartonnier et bureau plat* in the Empire style, with decorative features that are more in keeping with the very late eighteenth century rather than the full flight of the Empire under Napoleon. In this example the *cartonnier* has to stay with the desk. There is no question of separation.

1880-1900

305 The ribbon tied drapes heavy with summer flowers cling precariously to the frieze of this awful little writing desk. Although some of the mounts are of quite good quality the carcass is veneered with a very cheap and nasty mahogany. This small desk normally has one drawer opened by a spring operated button on the underside of the apron.

c.1900

306 The drapes are identical to the previous desk but are more in keeping with the size of the frieze. The decoration of trophies applied to each leg is generous and all four sides have applied mounts — not just each of the two outside edges. The drawer will open the same spring operated device as mentioned in the previous illustration.

1880s

307 The carcass underneath the leather top has settled creating an uneven writing surface. There is a lot of work in the crossbanding of the drawers and legs but the effect is one of a rather heavy uninspired desk.

1860s *

308 Again a spring operated drawer with a variation of frolicking *putti* to the frieze plaque on no.306 and 297 and 298. The top is inlaid with a marquetry trellis which has become very faded in patches and will have to be repolished.

c.1870 *

309 The dotted trellis work on the frieze and top of this desk became very popular in the late 1780s and was often used by the master craftsman Jean-Henri Riesener who would not have liked this desk with its heavy rather awkward legs. Once again the panelling under the leather has moved, giving the desk nothing but an 'antique' look. Compare with the English pieces on page 315.

1860s ✻

310 Another rather heavy desk with gilt fluted channels. The capitals of the legs have yet more of the gilt metal tassel and drape banding which is repeated time and time again. At either end there is a small ring handle for pulling out the brushing slide which gives more working space when required.

1860s ✻

311 This small exquisitely made writing table in mahogany with slight burrs was made by Grohé à Paris and is a good example of the high quality of workmanship that can be achieved in the best nineteenth century workshops. The legs, however, are very thin and this little *table à écrire* has little practical use.

1850s

312 The bronze mounts contrast sharply against the fashionable *bois noirci* ground. At some stage the brass fillets in the fluted legs have been repinned rather crudely and the legs themselves seem rather unsteady. Stamped on the underside 'Lefort Jeune', an unrecorded maker to date.

Late 1860s

313

315

314

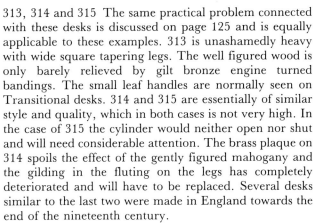

313, 314 and 315 The same practical problem connected with these desks is discussed on page 125 and is equally applicable to these examples. 313 is unashamedly heavy with wide square tapering legs. The well figured wood is only barely relieved by gilt bronze engine turned bandings. The small leaf handles are normally seen on Transitional desks. 314 and 315 are essentially of similar style and quality, which in both cases is not very high. In the case of 315 the cylinder would neither open nor shut and will need considerable attention. The brass plaque on 314 spoils the effect of the gently figured mahogany and the gilding in the fluting on the legs has completely deteriorated and will have to be replaced. Several desks similar to the last two were made in England towards the end of the nineteenth century.

313 *1870s* ∗
314 *c.1900* ∗
315 *c.1900* ∗

316 This is another example of the tambour cylinder in a similar style to that of 290. It is of good quality, finished to a high standard.

1880s ∗

317 This is a very popular desk, again after a model by Jean-Henri Riesener c.1780. The quality of metalwork and veneering is very high, although it is important to distinguish between a late nineteenth century example and a modern reproduction. It is almost impossible to reproduce metalwork on a commercial basis to compare with nineteenth century mercurial gilding and modern marquetry panelling is usually very half hearted with brash unacceptable colouring.

1880s *

318 Completely inlaid although the decoration on this small desk is rather crude, the skill being in applying the veneers so successfully.

c.1890

319 A terrible, dark mahogany desk inset with shaped milled bandings. The lower half of the cylinder opens outwards and downwards to form a writing surface; the upper half rolls into the carcass in the normal way. These small desks are often seen with Vernis Martin panels. An interesting feature is the fine multiple bands of stringing on the circular tapering legs which seems to be an unnecessary decoration on such a plain piece.

c.1900

320 Another variation of the previous desk decorated with Vernis Martin on the flap and simulated *verre eglomisé.* It is difficult to decide which is worse, the previous example of forbidding dark wood or the excessive decoration on this one.

c.1900

DESKS — Louis XVI tables à écrire

These tall tables à écrire *became popular in the nineteenth century under the Second Empire. Raised on tall thin legs, they are often very shaky and unsteady on their feet and the taller the superstructure the more out of proportion they become. They are quite frequently inlaid profusely with strapwork and flowers but their use is decorative rather than practical.*

321 (left) The finials on the superstructure are belching out copious flames and are totally out of place compared with the heaviness of design of this desk. The whole gallery is an unnecessary decorative feature. The quality of the mounts is very poor and there is too little contrast in the marquetry to clearly show the unusual and more adventurous design.

1880s

322 (right) Without the finials this piece looks slightly better. The marquetry is good and inventive, if a little over fussy. The hinged writing surface makes this desk a *bonheur-du-jour,* the disadvantage being that any object or ornament on the surface has to be removed before the desk can be used.

Late 1860s

323 (left) Another *bonheur-du-jour,* extremely difficult to use with the wide cupboard door which has a quite good quality marquetry musical trophy. For some reason the maker has seen fit not to continue the decoration below waist level and at the last moment has added an urn of minute proportions which would look better on the cresting rather than the cross stretchers.

1870s

324 (right) A much plainer writing table with unfortunately heavy legs once again. The mounts and drawers as well as the legs seem ill fitting. Not a particularly satisfactory or useful desk. In an attempt to continue the decoration the turning at the bottom of the legs, totally out of keeping with the channelling, appears to go on and on.

1870s

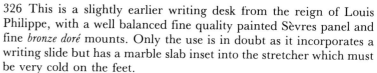

325 A kidney bureau finely made with kingwood veneers and over-elaborate swags of gilt-bronze roses.

c.1900

326 This is a slightly earlier writing desk from the reign of Louis Philippe, with a well balanced fine quality painted Sèvres panel and fine *bronze doré* mounts. Only the use is in doubt as it incorporates a writing slide but has a marble slab inset into the stretcher which must be very cold on the feet.

c.1840

327 If unable to write thank-you letters, the user of this desk could simply look at his own reflection in the central mirrored panel which is flanked by *verre eglomisé* panels. There is no reasonable explanation for the differing style of handles on the three frieze drawers.

1880s

328 An honest but very poor quality mahogany writing desk with yet more tassel and drape banding around the gallery. The arch in between the sets of drawers retains a Gothic element not normally present in neo-classical shapes.

c.1880

329 and 330 These two small writing tables are superb examples of workmanship under Napoleon III. They are based, with numerous variations, on a small table supplied to Marie Antoinette for the Château de Saint-Cloud in 1784. The design is by Adam Weisweiler and the *bronze doré* fittings are attributed to Pierre Gouthière. The example on the right is by Henri Dasson, signed and dated 1879. The one on the left, which should have a basket on the stretcher, is of approximately the same date, perhaps slightly earlier, i.e. the 1860s, and is stamped 'Millet à Paris'. The former example pays more attention to details of the original in that the lacquer panels are identical and the Syrian sphinxes on the frieze drawer are the same rather than Dasson's own creation of *putti* amongst foliage. *

331 This unusual little desk, again with the tassels and drapes on the gallery, has an adjustable fire screen to shade the face or the legs of the writer. If things become too unbearable the whole writing compartment unhooks and can be moved to another part of the room with the aid of the carrying handles. The mounts are of nice quality with *acajou moucheté* panels.

1880s *

332 A fine quality *bureau à gradin* stamped with a *marque au fer* 'F. Durand et Fils'. Both the woodwork and the metalwork are of the high standards expected of this maker.

Late 1850s *

333 (right) A good quality copy of a mahogany desk in the style of Adam Weisweiler, the original version would have been made in the late 1780s. The decoration is now much more severe, relying almost entirely on the mounts and veneers. The interlaced cross stretchers are typical of a kind habitually attributed to Weisweiler — compare the two small *tables à écrire,* on page 77 (114 and 115). The stretcher is a little too lumpy on this copy.

c.1880 ∗

334 (above right) Elegant severity again on this writing desk, the writing surface is in the form of a brushing slide below the drawer. The mounts by now are familiar and are identical to the two *tables à écrire* on the previous page. The beautifully chiselled caryatids are in the style of Pierre Gouthière. The cherubs, hovering in mid-air on the drawer, are similar to those on the Dasson desk.

c.1880

The comparative plainness that became the fashion in France before the Revolution, using to good decorative effect the mahogany veneers, is an indication of the influences that prevailed from England during the late 1780s. One hundred years later, when these copies were made, the French craftsmen were simply copying old French styles and were not displaying a love of all that was English.

335 A very plain and dull secretaire. If this is the result of English influence then there is nothing to be proud of. The severity is overwhelming and that, coupled with the poor quality workmanship, notably the metalwork, and the squashed toupie feet, render this type of furniture relatively undesirable at home and abroad. However they do make cheap desks.

1890s ∗

336 A fascinating study of overdecoration combined with fine quality mounts and porcelain panels applied to a parquetry trellis that almost looks like basket weave it is so realistic. The shape is typical of that of the Louis XVI period but the decoration is more reminiscent of the Louis XVIII popular revival that so loved porcelain panels of a more discreet nature than some of the excess of the 1770s.

c.1830

DESKS — Later secrétaires à abattant

337 (left) The Louis XVI style has by now suffered the vagaries and 'improvements' of the later nineteenth century designer. The only good point in this secretaire's favour is that it is smaller than the original versions and consequently more suitable for modern rooms. The thin white marble top, which seems to be sitting spuriously on a perfectly suitable wood top, is indicative of the thinner marbles used towards the end of the nineteenth century — they were much cheaper. The machine made decoration is only a token gesture to take the eye away from the mean mounts and poor quality ebonised carcass.

1880s

338 (right) A much better try, the decorative content being much more effective but still not of particularly good quality. Note that the mounts are identical on the canted corners to those on the pilasters of the previous piece.

c.1880

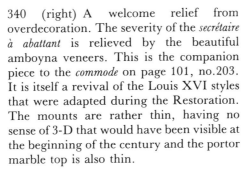

340 (right) A welcome relief from overdecoration. The severity of the *secrétaire à abattant* is relieved by the beautiful amboyna veneers. This is the companion piece to the *commode* on page 101, no.203. It is itself a revival of the Louis XVI styles that were adapted during the Restoration. The mounts are rather thin, having no sense of 3-D that would have been visible at the beginning of the century and the portor marble top is also thin.

c.1880 ∗

339 Little can be said on the plus side about this desk. Even the photographer has not managed to capture more than an image of this badly made half-hearted piece. The interior is veneered in burr-ash in an attempt to show willing. The only plus sign is that the manufacturer has condescended to make the desk of a serpentine outline, which costs more.

1880s

341 A revival of the late Directoire style of c.1800 that became popular at the end of the nineteenth century. Like the desk on the previous page, the mounts are thin and have simply been 'stuck on' rather lifelessly. This is an average quality desk.

c.1890

342 A combined *bonheur-du-jour* and *table à ouvrage* guaranteed to make any competent cabinet maker weep. This summarises all that is wrong with nineteenth century design and workmanship. The workshops must have had two pineapple finials left over from another piece of furniture, but nothing suitable for the centre of the stretcher. 'Bois nasty' at its worst.

1850s

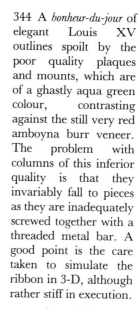

343 This *bureau à gradin* is plainly veneered in well figured walnut of the kind very popular in England in the middle of the nineteenth century. That is where the comparison must end. The maker must have been aware of the medieval interests of Viollet-le-Duc with the block feet. The pull-out writing slide is an essentially French feature. At least an honest practical desk.

1860-1880

344 A *bonheur-du-jour* of elegant Louis XV outlines spoilt by the poor quality plaques and mounts, which are of a ghastly aqua green colour, contrasting against the still very red amboyna burr veneer. The problem with columns of this inferior quality is that they invariably fall to pieces as they are inadequately screwed together with a threaded metal bar. A good point is the care taken to simulate the ribbon in 3-D, although rather stiff in execution.

Late 1860s

DESKS — Decorated desks from the later 1850s

All the desks on this page are finely inlaid with profuse amounts of foliage reminding us of heady summer days and the whole feeling is surprisingly light taken as a whole, considering that there is not very much space left that has not fallen to the knife of the marqueteur, *be he man or machine. This type of marquetry was the speciality of several houses, the most important being those of Giroux and Grohé. Most of this work was produced, seemingly, after the Paris Exhibition in 1855 for a period of about five to ten years before the Louis XVI revival took hold. The love for overdecoration can be directly compared to English papier mâché that also began to wane in popularity at the same time. One cannot help but appreciate the fine quality of the workmanship which complements the design of flowing outline.*

345 (left) Almost certainly by Giroux, this *secrétaire à abattant* disguised as a *semanier* is a highly decorative conveniently sized and useful item of furniture. However, the quality is not of the standard of the two writing tables illustrated below. The inlay is stiffer, and totally repetitive, indicating the unsympathetic use of machinery. *1850s*

346 (right) The addition of cherubs riding the wild sea horses must have been the crowning triumph when the work on this secretaire was finished. The shape and proportions of the top to the bottom are ridiculous — a monstrous piece applied with monsters. Despite the numerous goings-on, the quality of the marquetry is disappointing but the maker has cleverly created so many diversions that one dare not inspect the inlay too closely.

c.1860

347 and 348 These two desks are fine examples of craftsmanship. The one on the right is possibly the earliest, that on the left later, with its more restrained decoration. The later one bears the label of Giroux.

In both cases the galleries are identical but not the rest of the mounts. The earlier desk has the rather unnecessary addition — a contemporary one — of *putti*. The centre door panels of the right hand desk are exquisite but close inspection reveals that the remaining marquetry is not as good as it first indicates. On points the Giroux version must come out on top.

347 *c.1860*
348 *c.1855*

349 'La Forêt Lorraine'. A carved fruitwood desk with marquetry decoration, designed by Emile Gallé and exhibited by him at the Exposition Universelle, Paris, 1900. The Gallé workshops made a small number of these desks, all of identical structure but varying in the marquetry decoration. As is all too common with French art nouveau, the designers used and adapted traditional forms. This desk is simply a standard *bureau en pente,* albeit with delightful marquetry and rather contrived legs.

DIEPPE IVORY

350 Author and publisher have allowed themselves a major indulgence in including two identical chairs on one page. It simply proves that it was possible to make two particularly unpleasant and wholly impractical chairs when one would have been quite sufficient. Nevertheless, these Dieppe ivory chairs are extremely rare examples of regional craftsmanship from northern France. Each chair frame is 'veneered' in small carved 'leaves' of ivory, pinned on almost like a tiled roof. The crest on the toprail bears the same motto as countless mirrors made in the same material — 'Montoye St. Denis'.

c.1860

351 Another magnificent example of the ivory carver's art but with none of the beautiful and subtle elegance of the Dieppe ivory figures that were carved to imitate French nineteenth century romantic sculpture, in a method and medium of pure white ivory that competes successfully with contemporary bronze figures of the same subjects. The leaves are the same as the mirror and chairs on this page. The ferocious scaly fish heads joining the pole stretcher are highly individual. The apron bears the initials 'M.A.' which can only refer to a well documented patroness of furniture and the arts who lost her head some seventy years before this dressing table was conceived!

c.1860

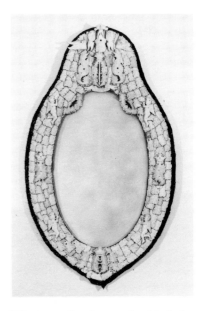

352 A small mirror of a kind that appears on the market, in similar form to the swing mirror on the previous dressing table, with some regularity. These mirrors must have been made in their hundreds for the wealthy visitor to Dieppe to take home as a sample of local craftsmanship. The crest appears yet again.

1860s

A similar technique to that of the colour illustration on page 244 has been used on this Louis XIII revival cabinet which has been lavishly applied with Viennese painted enamel mounts. The panels are painted and enamelled on copper and the execution is always impeccable. Once again, the carcass is disappointing, being very thinly ebony veneered on to a shaky pine carcass. This cabinet has a practical application with the angled writing flap and the interiors of the drawers are similarly applied with panels, as are the numerous interior drawers. This type of enamelling went on being made for some considerable time and is difficult to date particularly accurately.

1880-1910

THE DINING ROOM

Comparatively few dining tables of French origin come on the market in England. Subsequently they are normally rather expensive, as they are highly sought after today to go with decorative interiors in the French style.

353

354

355 This uncompromising Louis XV style dining table is made of carved oak with a quarter veneered oak top. It has none of the advantages of the English equivalent which at least in part can be folded away when not in use. This was stamped with a *marque au fer* 'J. Sarazin'.

c.1900

353 and 354 This uncompromisingly ugly sideboard is in the combined Directoire and Empire styles of c.1800 that became popular again from c.1880 onwards. Both the sideboard and dining table are of an average standard but surprisingly were retailed by Krieger Ameublements of Paris. This maker's earlier work is normally of a far superior standard and it is possible that he simply retailed these pieces.

c.1900

A set of eighteen dining chairs of the same suite are on page 193 illustration 547.

356 A very superior mahogany veneered dining table with six extra leaves. Unfortunately the centre pedestal is totally uncompromising and seems to be unnecessarily massive and completely out of keeping with the more slender legs that were popular c.1840, although this table must date from 1880 onwards which is an indication of how some motifs continued for many years, even in the rapidly changing nineteenth century.

1880s

All four illustrations on this page are by the same maker, F. Linke. 358, 359 and 360 are all from the same suite and are of the very finest quality that this maker's workshops could produce. The illustration 357 is an extraordinary example of his later work, probably as late as the 1930s when his workshops continued signing comparatively poor quality furniture with his name even for a short while after his death.

357 This sideboard with a heavy *brêche violette* marble top and a cartouche is well made by normal standards but not by the standards of Linke. Nevertheless it is a useful piece of typical French reproduction furniture.

Twentieth century

358 This *console desserte* is of a wonderfully exaggerated Louis XV style that must be admired for its boldness. The legs have to be strong to support the marble top and the mass of *bronze doré*. Signed on the mounts 'F. Linke'.

1900s

359 A dining table *en suite* with the previous illustration, again heavy but of very fine quality; also signed.

1900s

360 One chair from a very rare set of twelve kingwood veneered chairs showing quite clearly the central acanthus motif so regularly used by Linke on the centre of the apron. Very good quality although the rather boldly cast female mask on the top rail must be somewhat uncomfortable.

1900s

361 The plainness of the Louis Philippe period is almost a relief and there is almost an English feel about the well figured mahogany veneers. This small *console desserte* is useful and will fit most decorative schemes.

1840s

362 The decorative intent of the frieze and thin legs with bare breasted Assyrian sphinx capitals is completely let down by the base, as seems to be so common in a lot of furniture of the second half of the nineteenth century. This is a typical example of a revival of late eighteenth century decoration popular in the last twenty years of the nineteenth century. The mounts, although quite well cast, are simply 'plonked on'.

c.1890

363 The baroque revival, revived but not revitalised in this walnut and burr walnut sideboard of gigantic proportions, with applied machine carved decoration of fruit and flowers of a type popular for dining rooms of 1850 to 1880.

364 Either a commode or a sideboard with one huge drawer under a moulded serpentine *breccia* marble top. The mounts are of good quality and the overall effect is not dissimilar to the dining room suite by Linke on the preceding page.

c.1900

ETAGERES

The whatnot seems an odd word to apply to a table in the English language. It is uncertain how the term came into general use at some unspecified time in the nineteenth century. Possibly the nouveau riche factory owner could not cope with the seemingly apt word that the French had invented — the étagère. *The term is generally applied to small tables with two or more tiers for displaying objects or for serving food. Their uses are many, some even have the top tier as a removable tray.*

365 A fine example, the *bronze doré* mounts signed by F. Linke. The standard of workmanship is apparent in the photograph with the finely chosen kingwood veneers and uninhibited, bold purposeful mounts. The two handles are to enable the piece to be gently pulled around the room on the castors. The castors spoil the line of the legs and, although the *étagère* was obviously intended to have handles and therefore, presumably, castors, these have simply been screwed on without consideration. Linke's workshops would have more than likely made the handles but the size, form and shape of the castors appear to have been out of his control. The jasper plaque imitating Wedgwood is a fairly common Linke feature. This example has a brushing slide at either end for extra table space.

c.1910

366 A poor relation to 365 and 367 but nevertheless a useful and stylish article of furniture. The veneers are segmented, giving a radiating pattern of king-wood on each shelf.

1890s

367 Much cheaper veneers but very good quality mounts of a standard that is always thought to be that of Linke's work until it can be compared with the far superior real thing. Generally this example is far less lavish but better proportioned than 365.

c.1900

368 The mahogany veneers on this example are very thin with an uninteresting grain. The mounts are of dipped brass and are extraordinarily weak and un-inspired. The whole effect is merely an image of the other three.

Early twentieth century

369 Whoops! Someone was a little carried away with the almost articulated design of this hybrid table. The three tiers of joined 'S' scrolls that form each leg are each formed from one piece of wood for strength. The overall design is unusual with a trellis on each tier. The mounts appear to have been liberally scattered wherever the maker pleased.

1850s

372 Another mixture between a small occasional table and *étagère*. The mounts are quite good quality — better than the pearwood supports. The two tiers are inlaid with a mechanical parquetry trellis.

1860s

370 Cast-iron at its best. Like the previous *étagère*, this rococo extravaganza would have doubtless been called 'Louis XV' in the nineteenth century. The pattern is made up of standard naturalistic motifs. The weight of the iron makes for a sturdy but brittle table.

1850-1890

373 This weakly designed and finished piece was very crudely signed with a bogus signature of F. Linke. The engraving was carried out in a very shaky hand and was not convincing. Neither the woodwork nor the mounts are anything like good enough for Linke's workshops. The mounts on the frieze must have been all that were left in the workshop.

1880s

371 An uninviting table/*étagère* of indifferent quality. The mounts are poor quality brass and each tier is very thin and has warped without enough lateral support.

c.1860

374 A long hard look at the construction underneath the lower tier finally convinced the author that the legs were original to this *étagère* and not two trays with legs from another piece of furniture. The legs do look a little awkward but it is a well made piece with little coherence between the legs and the turned supports. Possibly English.

1850s

JARDINIERES

375 The legs of this tulipwood *jardinière* hardly look strong enough to cope with the exaggerated proportions of the upper part. The mimsy porcelain plaques are more typical of English pieces in the French style. However, the overall effect is one of good quality. The platform stretcher is prettily inlaid with flowers.

1850s

376 The designer has become even more muddled with the legs which seem to be extraordinarily complicated, although the basic idea is the same as the previous·example. The fine quality satyr mask is so out of proportion that it looks as though it will pull away the apron.

1850s

377 Slightly below average quality in simple Louis XV style, the maker has not even attempted to quarter veneer the frieze to save money but at least it is decorated all the way round. It is surprising that so many of these *jardinières* have retained their removable lids and one must only presume that they were never constantly in use.

1860s

379 This is a small kingwood table *jardinière* with corner mounts of Sèvres style porcelain. The central porcelain panel is of the same size as those used on 375 and 376. However, the quality is not high but a useful small piece that is comparatively hard to find, and the proportions are less uncomfortable when filled with flowers.

1860s

378 A very rare and stylish *jardinière* by Charles-Guillaume Diehl. A mixture of neo-classical motifs, the result is not particularly elegant but at least it is an attempt to design in a more original vein. Diehl's work is invariably of good quality in both the cabinet work and the metalwork.

c.1870

380 An incredible eclectic mixture of Italo-Chinese origins. The *pietre dure* Florentine mosaic, although of good quality, lets down the exotic *bronze doré* framework with jewelled elephants' heads leading to weak and not very ferocious dragons. The chinoiserie effect compares with the work of Viardot, whose work is illustrated on page 78. However, the metalwork is typical of the bronze foundry of Ferdinand Barbedienne (q.v.) in the late 1860s and the early 1870s.

381 Quite the worst designed piece of any country or period. Not only are the legs weak and the mounts token gestures, but the urn appears to have been added as an afterthought with the finial of an English Queen Anne toilet mirror added as a final triumph. The framework is of *bois noirci* inset with bands of thuyawood.

1870s

382 The only candidate for a design worse than the previous one is this *jardinière* which also appears in a Price Guide to *English* Furniture by a well-known publisher. The mounts are of the worst possible quality of horses' heads and the inlay of burr chestnut is poor, mechanical and uninspired. The whole rickety piece appears to be loosely held together by inadequate chains that are reminiscent of Roman originals.

1870s

383 Reflecting the severity of the late Directoire era of the eighteenth century, this copy has none of the quality of the earlier period. The stretcher is of a type favoured by Adam Weisweiler and Marie Antoinette who used it habitually on pieces such as dressing tables.

1880-1900 ∗

384 A weak interpretation of the Louis XVI style with a heavy domed top which is far heavier than the spindly legs. It is difficult to understand the need for the small cylindrical section immediately below the frieze and above the cubes that lead to the fluting. The mounts, wood and marquetry are cheaply done. This *jardinière* has the novel advantage of a lockable lid.

c.1870

386 Another similar cabinet but with even less decoration and with peeling veneer. The glasses and decanters are mass produced and moulded.

1860s

385 The worst results of factory production can be seen in this poor quality cabinet whose only real decorative feature is that the removable tray of decanters and glasses is almost complete. Thinly veneered in amboyna and ebony on to a soft wood poorly made carcass. This is the French equivalent of the tantalus but with the temptation securely locked away out of sight.

1860s

387 A tea caddy of a very assured and assertive bombé form, typical of the mid-nineteenth century in imitation of the 1720s. As with the previous illustration, the coloured marquetry is deteriorating rapidly and will be expensive to restore.

1850s

388 A rare example of a miniature boulle table of Régence form popularly revised in the middle of the nineteenth century. The lid lifts to store anything that the owner fancies. The decoration is of coloured ivory and bone on a brass and tortoiseshell ground and fully restored it would be a pretty although not very useful collector's piece.

1850s

LONGCASE CLOCKS

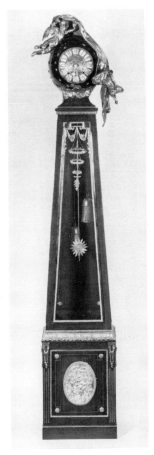

389 The exaggerated proportions of this king-wood and tulipwood quarter veneered clock suggest a German or Scandinavian origin although this is difficult to prove. By the mid-nine-teenth century most clocks in French style made in Europe would have a good chance of incorporating a French movement. The good quality mounts certainly have a lot of guts and the whole effect is only let down by the disappoint-ingly poor quality dial.

c.1880 *

390 The celestial frolick-ing of two cherubs almost disguises the function of this item of mahogany 'furniture'. The cresting is a perfect example of the Danish 'Klunkertid' or the age of tassels as described by Egon Friedell. The pendulum is almost pathetic in its size. Nevertheless a rare and sought after clock with Louis XVI pretensions.

c.1900 *

391 Take the stand from page 214 illustration 639, cut out a door, add *toupie* feet and a clock move-ment surrounded by clouds and cherubs and you have a very fine Louis XVI style *bronze doré* longcase clock by Paul Sormani — who would have made only the case and metalwork, inserting a standard French movement. Occasionally this model is seen with a matching barometer. They are copied from a clock in the Louvre attributed to Martin Carlin.

c.1865 *

392 A rather uncom-fortably constructed ordinary quality clock with no attempt to join the three main sections of the body in a satisfactory manner. Régence in inspiration, executed 1880s. *

395 The exuberance and carving of this boxwood barometer are typical of the high standards of workmanship but sometimes rather excessive design of the Beurdeley family. No feature has been left out from the Apollo mask in the heavens to caryatids holding a pair of billing doves. Tassels, too small to see on the page of a book, adorn the sides. This barometer was exhibited in the Paris Exposition Universelle 1878.

The size is misleading, it is 2.34m high.

393 A very similar shape to 391 the previous page. The exaggerated oyster kingwood veneers, however, give a far better decorative effect.

1860s ✶

394 Renaissance revival with a clock and an aneroid barometer in a carved walnut case of little merit. However, unusual which is always a bonus.

c.1900

396 A matching clock and barometer, each with a centigrade thermometer. The quality of the mounts is quite high but the overall design is slightly messy. Rare and very desirable.

1880s

152

397 This fine *meuble d'appui* is 'by' the widow of Paul Sormani and the lockplate is signed accordingly 'Vve. P. Sormani & Fils, 10 rue du Charlot, Paris'. The whole cabinet is veneered in ebony with very fine chiselled *bronze doré* mounts. The decoration is in a traditional Louis XIV style with a shape of cabinet taken from Louis XIV's reign but adapted to Louis XVI proportions. The single figure of Summer represented as harvest suggests that the cabinet was one of a pair, Spring probably being the companion piece — Autumn and Winter were often studiously avoided.

c.1880 ✷

Under the influence of Etienne Levasseur c.1770 there was a revival of interest in the work produced under the reign of Louis XIV. Levasseur himself was a pupil of one of André Charles Boulle's sons and many 'Boulle' cabinets were made during the third quarter of the eighteenth century. The shape and form of these cabinets were very similar to those of seventy years before and deciding the exact date of origin is not always easy. The cabinets were not only made in brass and tortoise-shell but in kingwood and with porcelain mounts as well.

399 This cabinet, stamped with a *marque au fer*, is by Pretot who worked in Paris between 1836 and 1853 before his firm was taken over by Frederick Roux. The date therefore must be before 1855 and from the shape is unlikely to be earlier than 1850. The carved ebony panel is late seventeenth century.

Early 1850s

398 This brass inlaid cabinet is a mixture of the styles of all the eighteenth century Louis. Many of the larger furniture makers in the second half of the nineteenth century made their own bronzes and the two plaques of Venus and Cupid and a female satyr and her infant are probably 'home made'. The inlaid brasswork is, of course, inspired by Boulle. All the applied foliate mounts are very weak and weedy and the apron is terrible.

1850s

400 This ungainly cabinet is very well made and inlaid with delicate brass tendrils. The fussy overall decoration belies the severity of the door panel. The shape and quality are similar to a cabinet by Diehl illustrated on page 177. Diehl, like many other older French firms signs on the lock, which in this case is missing — which in itself could be an indication that some unscrupulous vandal may have removed the signed lock and added it to a more saleable piece, thereby increasing the latter's value. The escutcheon is typical of Diehl, but is also seen on other makers' work.

c.1850

401 A kingwood and porcelain cabinet that has a very curious non-French feel about it, yet the porcelain plaques and the lock are French. The long 'C' scrolls are almost pressed brass and have a Dutch or certainly north European quality about them. This type of furniture was popular in Scandinavia as well as Russia but the shape does not have the eccentricity of similar Russian pieces.

1860ᶜ

402 A highly individual cabinet with three good lacquer panels held by gutsy mounts. The single door is surrounded by kingwood veneer with tulipwood cross-banding. Lacquer panels are comparatively rare and highly decorative.

1860s

403 The workmanship of this *meuble d'hauteur d'appui,* with the par-quetry veneers and restrained mounts, is similar to the later work of the Sormani firm. In fact, the lock is signed 'Millet à Paris' and is not the high grade of quality one would normally expect from this firm although a possible explanation is that it is much later, remembering that Millet continued until 1918.

1880-1910

404 A striking example of quarter veneering — the trade mark of French *ébénistes*. The irregular lozenge shape of the panels is an added decorative feature but so much more desirable than a mediocre outline of gilt-bronze mounts. A nice plain piece — ideal to hide a television and would fit in well with an eighteenth century decor.

1880-1900 ✳

405 (left) A well made two door cabinet, well proportioned although looks a little as though it has been holding its breath for a long time. The contrasting marquetry inlay of leaves is very delicate.

1890s

406 A decorative cabinet with very bright lacquer panels, in this instance imported from China.

1880s

407 (right) The work of the *marqueteur* is made far more difficult when he has to inlay the slats of a tambour cupboard. The strips are backed by canvas and, when opened, the upper doors slide unobtrusively away into the compartment. The lower doors are simple cupboard doors. This cabinet is provided with a brushing slide and this, combined with the tambour, suggests that the piece was made as a 'drinks' cabinet. The tambour, sliding away, means that opening the top cupboard does not interfere with bottles or glasses left on the brushing slide. The whole effect is delightful and typically French in style. A paper label on the back reads 'Ameublements de style, Meubles, Sièges, Tentures, Mercier Frères, 100 Faubourg Saint-Antoine 100, Paris' — a fine firm of makers who are still at the same address today.

1900-1930 ∗

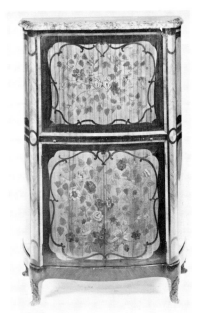

408

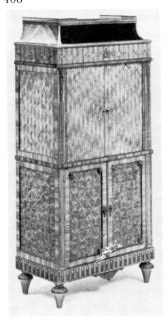

409

408 Another tulipwood cabinet with two upper tambour doors but no brushing slide. The 'feathered' banding of the upper section is unusual, the trellis is more typical. An attractive piece of furniture but not very well designed. The tambour has never been very popular in England and a cupboard of this type has to be of the very best quality to be valuable.

1920s

409 A nice quality D-shaped *meuble d'appui* on a poor stand, continuing the tradition established by Paul Sormani. This is signed by his widow from the Rue Charlot. She always signed the pieces made in her workshops after her husband's death with the prefix 'Veuve', or Widow, before her surname.

c.1900

410 All the mounts have a certain restraint and subtle quality on this *meuble d'hauteur d'appui* by F. Linke. If all mounts were of this quality on late nineteenth and early twentieth century furniture there would be far less room for criticism. The raised marquetry panel representing architecture and the sciences is good, without being of first class quality. Large, tall side cabinets of this type are not popular in England but complete the formal French dining room.

1900-1930

411 A poorly made cabinet with very indifferent mounts and marquetry. The veneers are very thin and poorly applied — they can be seen chipping away at the base of the apron. Note the thin Spanish brocatelle marble top which is at least a centimetre thinner than the previous example. However, a useful cabinet for modern living, be it for drinks or television.

1950s

412 A poor quality *bois noirci* cabinet on stand. The panels are quite attractively painted with courtiers and flowers but they cannot make up for the wobbly, badly designed cabinet which has little use in today's decorative schemes.

c.1870

413 Another ideal television cabinet, again with the tambour above a pair of cupboard doors. This one was fitted with a radio! The veneers on the side panels and cupboard doors are quite well figured but with very poor mahogany crossbandings. The Spanish brocatelle marble top is very thin with average quality mounts.

1920-1940

A page of eclectic cabinets in a mixed Louis XIV and Louis XVI style. These small meubles d'appui were made normally in pairs but have in most cases been split up.

414 The bronze plaque of frolicking *putti* and the pierced strapwork mounts on the canted corners are the only good quality features on this cabinet of ebonised pearwood. At least the maker has decorated the plinth which is so often neglected.

c.1850

415 A fine quality example bearing the *marque au fer* of 'Monbro Aîné'. The *contra partie* brasswork is of delicately trailing leaves. The mounts are very bold, especially the acanthus cast paws holding the central door which is applied with a fine sand case gilt bronze plaque of a Roman soldier escorting a young maiden away from her house. Once again the apron is neglected. The *verde antico* marble top is a twentieth century replacement, the original was probably a white or St. Anne marble.

c.1860

416 There is a lot of work on the parquetry trellis side panels and the door is finely inlaid with a complicated urn within a swagged reserve. It is important to look very closely at this type of marquetry as, especially towards the end of the nineteenth century, it is quite often etched very cleverly and not marquetry at all.

c.1870

417 A large quantity of these bronze plaques must have been made to apply to furniture. In the Beurdeley Succession sale in Paris in May 1979 there were several plaques of this type sold separately, bearing the Beurdeley mark. With the exception of the finer houses these plaques were often far better quality than the rest of the piece, as in this case. Note the white marble top as in the previous example which would have been originally on the Monbro piece above.

c.1870

418 A finely made kingwood and tulipwood side cabinet applied with beautifully painted Sèvres panels of flowers and birds, although the door with its trailing mounts holding on the porcelain plaques looks rather messy. The top, with its inlaid marble, is an Italian twentieth century replacement and is extremely thin, in keeping with modern marble slabs.

c.1850

419 The well figured *bois de rose* veneers lead the eye to the high decorative Sèvres plaques with *bleu du roi* and apple green borders. The whole piece is of very good quality. The pierced tendrils of small roses on the frieze are most unusual and are exceptionally free and naturalistic for the mid-nineteenth century.

c.1850

420 Another kingwood and tulipwood *meuble d'appui* with finely painted porcelain panels and a repeat of the unusual feather or herringbone banding seen earlier. The *espagnolettes* are individual and bedecked with a double string of 'pearls'. Their tapering columns are painted porcelain, as are the *patera* above the gilt bronze acanthus feet. An elegant and rare piece but unfortunately with a replaced, exceptionally thick, marble top.

c.1850

421 The porcelain and gilt-bronze mounts are much meaner than the previous examples but at least the kingwood veneer is very well figured and matched.

1860s

An exceptional ivory inlaid and ebony veneered writing cabinet by G.B. Gatti. It bears his signature, 'Gatti F. Fec. Roma', and is dated 1855. It was in this year that the cabinet was exhibited at the Paris Exposition Universelle where it was awarded the First Class medal in the class of Industrie concernant l'ameublement et la décoration. *This cabinet is unique, in that it has an accompanying letter in the maker's hand, 'Work executed by me, Gio. Batt. Gatti, for the Great exhibition in Paris 1855 upon commission for Mr. Wright Post'. The cabinet obviously at one stage had travelled across the Atlantic as it bears a pencil inscription on a drawer, 'Repaired by John A. Frank, New York City'. The cabinet caused quite a sensation at the exhibition and is one of the finest examples of Italian craftsmanship, far and above the quality of most Italian makers. Details of some of the marquetry can be seen on page 441.*

Dated 1855

422 A kingwood and tulipwood two door cabinet which would be much better without the porcelain plaques and their added fripperies which are far too mean. Even the gilt bronze male terms would be better removed. It is strange that the maker made no attempt to match the mounts on the apron, or at least the bottom of the pilasters.

c.1870

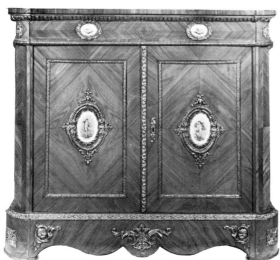

423 One of the worst possible examples of French furniture that has little popularity in today's market. The mounts and plaques are of the same appalling quality as the ebonised pearwood cabinet work. The top is wood and there was never any intention to fit a marble top. The apron appears to be much larger in proportion to the rest of the cabinet and unbalances the whole effect. The ridiculously small mask in gilt bronze applied to the sides is a very half-hearted token gesture.

1860s

424 A well made kingwood cabinet with rather poor and small porcelain mounts, although the gilt bronze leaf cast metalwork is of quite good quality. Unfortunately it was not possible to inspect this piece and it is quite likely that it will have a simple English lock with good quality English brass hinges. It is difficult to tell whether or not there was originally a marble top and if an English cabinet maker has made a wooden top veneered and crossbanded in kingwood. On balance, this cabinet should possibly be in an English category and the evidence for this — purely on the evidence of the photograph — is firstly the crossbanded kingwood edge for the top and the water-gilt egg and dart banding underhanging the edge, neither of which are French features. The plaques look as though they could possibly be Minton but it is difficult to tell from the photograph. Without doubt it will always be called French by collector and dealer alike, regardless of any alternative evidence.

1860s

425 A very messy ebonised cabinet that looks as though an apprentice has been given a plain cabinet and a box full of mounts and porcelain panels to apply as he thought fit and his supervisor forgot to inspect his work before the piece was let out onto an unsuspecting and undiscerning public.

1850s

426 Once again a fine bronze plaque in eighteenth century style. The terminal figures and *guilloché* are of good quality and superior to the rest of the piece. The black marble top with its soft moulded edge is unusual and almost certainly a replacement in the early twentieth century.

1850s

427 A good quality *meuble d'appui,* this time veneered in ebony rather than simply ebonised. The two female portrait heads would make most decorative busts by themselves and they, like the rest of the pierced and chiselled mounts, are of unusually good quality with mercurial gilding. This slightly larger cabinet at least has two side doors, a feature so often irritatingly forgotten on French cabinets. The late romanesque/Gothic pierced banding along the apron is very unusual, suggesting a hangover from an earlier decade.

1840s

428 A *meuble d'appui* with two corner *vitrines* that again looks as though it has been liberally applied with plaques and mounts from an assorted box of spares. The ebonising is in fact very thin ebony veneer. Quite possibly this cabinet is English but there were no locks to help prove this theory. The only real evidence is the gilt bronze banding holding the top, which is normally considered to be an English feature.

c.1870

429 A dramatically decorated side cabinet with an exceptionally large *bois durci* head. *Bois durci* panels were infrequently applied to French furniture to give the feeling of the ebony panels popular in the late seventeenth century. They were made by compressing ox blood and sawdust into a mould and are extremely hard and durable with no grain and a highly finished surface. The cabinet has the unusual *marque au fer* of 'Cremer marqueteur' but oddly there is no marquetry on this particular cabinet.

Late 1840s

430 There is a large amount of painstakingly applied marquetry on this large cabinet but the effect is purely one of three small side cabinets being stuck together. The flanking panels are not doors and are purely decorative. The only access to the sides is through the glazed end panels which have little use for display. It is unusual to see well figured burr walnut on French mid-nineteenth century furniture. This is a much more common English feature but in this case the maker, who was perfectly French, must have just been copying the English fashion or at least he made a token gesture towards it.

1860s

431 A very nice small and compact *meuble d'appui* bearing the *marque au fer* 'A. Beurdeley, Paris'. The lacquer panels are unusual for Beurdeley. The mounts are very well cast but not quite as well chiselled as one normally expects from the Beurdeley workshops. However, a tremendous change will take place if the mounts are carefully removed and professionally cleaned. Notice the good thick St. Anne marble top.

1860s ∗

432 A finely made side cabinet with good quality parquetry veneers and finely chiselled *bronze doré* mounts. The leaf clasped *flambeaux* on the narrow side doors are identical to those on the cabinet 427 on page 161.

1860s

433 The mounts and veneers are well executed on this cabinet but for once the whole effect is too restrained and somewhat inhibited. The tremendous contrast between the kingwood parquetry and exceptionally dark tulipwood framework is not in this case particularly attractive. The ribbon tied basket of flowers is amusing but out of proportion.

1900s

435 A parquetry *meuble d'hauteur d'appui*, the upper part very similar in form to the previous derivation of the *commode à l'anglais*. The lock in this instance was signed by Paul Sormani and the parquetry work is typical of his later furniture, which is always a little boring, although the mounts are always well proportioned and of good quality.

c.1880

434 A well made, rather plain, side cabinet inset with a Chinese coromandel lacquer panel and rather crudely carved, of a type exported in large quantities to Europe, mainly in screens, around the turn of the century. A good decorative effect has been made of the well figured mahogany panels and banding around the door but the mahogany used for the framework and legs is of an inferior quality. The shape of this cabinet is derived from the *commode à l'anglais* popular in the late 1770s.

c.1900

436 A good quality cabinet with fine foliate inlay in a restrained Louis XVI style form. The brass mouldings are not of the best quality and soon become dented and loose.

1870s

437 The contrast between the *acajou moucheté* and the finely chiselled *bronze doré* mounts is very effective in this cabinet on stand inspired by Adam Weisweiler, although the outset columns are taken from a large lacquer commode supplied by Martin Carlin in 1785. Even a sophisticated and well made piece such as this has got the inevitable tassel and drape banding which is of inferior quality compared to the rest of the mounts. It would be only too easy to imagine the base of this piece of furniture becoming wobbly and ten or more years ago, when the value and popularity of such a piece would have been very low, it would have been divided into a marble top console table and a separate low side cabinet by the simple addition of a plinth.

c.1880

438 A very fine purpleheart and amboyna cabinet by Henry Dasson. The central painted panel is a worthy item in itself. This cabinet is an exceptional example of Dasson's work in an individual and imaginative interpretation of the Louis XVI style. The incorporation of the painted panel may well have been at the whim of the patron who commissioned the cabinet. It is certainly an unusual idea and very successful. The free standing female figures are good examples of the combination of the work of the *bronzier* and *ébéniste,* the sculptor and the carpenter. The cabinet was made in the year of one of the most splendid *Expositions* and it would be intriguing to know if it was an exhibit.

Dated 1878

439 A burr-maple cabinet of the Louis-Philippe period. The interior is a strongbox to contain papers, jewels and the accoutrements of royalty. The style is essentially Biedermeier with little decoration, before the time that designers became tired of plain furniture and started to inlay the plain pieces so popular only a few years before. In this case the decoration is solely restricted to the natural grain of the wood. The small apron is a half patera or flowerhead that almost seems to anticipate the work of the early English Arts and Crafts designers such as Charles Bevan.

1840s

440 An eclectic mixture with Louis III legs and an overall Louis XVI form. The proportions are a little odd and there is a distinct feeling of a vacant space in the lower part. Such a cabinet has little use and is purely a decorative storage cupboard.

1860s

441 A finely made side cabinet by the firm of Krieger in an exotic Louis XVI style. The florid boulle and large sculptural female figures are strongly reminiscent of the Louis XIV period. A nice touch is the way the swirling patera in each corbel appear to grow into the boulle. An exotic piece, hardly likely to appeal to the average householder looking for a little extra storage space but a fine example of the cabinet maker's art and a late monument to the French furniture trade.

c.1900

On this and the following page are illustrated four magnificent side cabinets, big enough to dominate every room and certain eye catchers. All are beautifully made, the first two by Beurdeley and the last two by Linke.

442 Beurdeley here must have been dreaming of the large Louis XIV side cabinets that were so popular at the very beginning of the eighteenth century and which later became revived in the Louis XVI period. This is very much in the style of Charles Cressent in the early 1730s. The parquetry trellis is normally associated with slightly later furniture from the 1760s onwards. Once again the quality and the craftsmanship are superb. A very interesting feature is that all the bronze mounts on the central door are applied to crossbanded woodwork outlined with thin ebony stringing which gives an almost shaded effect — a very unusual feature and involving a lot of extra work.

1880s

443 Another *meuble d'appui* in an exotic Régence style with a rather eclectic figure of a lute player *à la Turque* but with chinoiserie influence. The quality is not quite so stunning as the previous cabinet. Neither the bronzes nor the veneers are quite as well finished. The outset and pierced legs at the side are an unusual feature.

1880s

444 Everything about this most exotic *meuble d'appui,* which presumably could also be used as an *armoire* in a bedroom, begins to shout the name of the maker — François Linke. The attention to detail is quite stunning and it is difficult to know whether to look at the incredible marquetry or the finish of the bronzes. The whole exotic style typifies the mind of one of the greatest French Revival designers of the late nineteenth and early twentieth century. The mind boggles at what Linke would have been able to achieve had he been working for the Court of Versailles over 150 years earlier. The combination of Royal patronage and Linke's imagination would have been fascinating. This cabinet has the familiar Linke feature of water being poured from the cresting through the waterfall and over the unhappy looking mask of Neptune into the sea below. The sea of course is inlaid with octopi and deep water fish. The two rather laconic sirens flanking Neptune appear to be sucking their thumbs. The waterfall landscape is a bronze study of Japanese lacquer panels, popularised by Marie Antoinette in the period c.1780 and is a work of art in itself.

c.1900

445 A fine *bibliotheque* by Linke in the same vein as the desks illustrated on pages 106 and 108. The lion masks, each with its own pelt, and the jasper panel are identical. The marquetry panels in the doors and the sides follow the very best marquetry styles of the third quarter of the eighteenth century.

1890s

446 A nineteenth century 'improvement' on the Louis XV style. The frieze is weak with the thin white marble top above the plain section of rosewood veneer. Otherwise it is a good little cabinet, with the extra bonus of a serpentine front that is wholly 'Victorian' in feeling, small and practical with an attractive decoration of flowers.

c.1860

447 A provincial D-shaped cabinet with a *breccia* marble top. It is uncertain where this type of furniture was made — it could have been made near the marble quarries in the South of France but also it has a lot of Flemish or Dutch influence, especially in the chequered banding and the simple tapering legs.

1870-1900

448 This exotically inlaid cabinet is a horticulturalist's dream. The profuse floral arrangements are delicately shaded and coloured with numerous stained woods, the door panels being an almost but not exact reverse of each other. The bold strapwork borders are very similar to English marquetry of the same period that imitated the French style. The English examples, however, rarely have foliate scrolls within the strapwork. The top is a wooden replacement for the original marble.

c.1850

449 (left) This style is loosely based on the Louis XVI classical style and where it lacks the bold lines of a serpentine form it makes up in the very good quality marquetry urn of flowers. This cabinet has been cleaned and fully restored giving an overall illusion of a better finish.

1860s

450 Floral marquetry from one extreme to the other. This art nouveau side cabinet of traditional shape has stylised panels and the details of the overall design are naturalistic in the highly stylised form that typified the early forms of art nouveau. Ash panels have been used as the ground for the long tendrils of grapes and other budding fruits, the highly figured ash heightens the feeling of lightness and naturalism.

c.1900

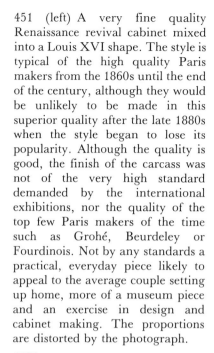

451 (left) A very fine quality Renaissance revival cabinet mixed into a Louis XVI shape. The style is typical of the high quality Paris makers from the 1860s until the end of the century, although they would be unlikely to be made in this superior quality after the late 1880s when the style began to lose its popularity. Although the quality is good, the finish of the carcass was not of the very high standard demanded by the international exhibitions, nor the quality of the top few Paris makers of the time such as Grohé, Beurdeley or Fourdinois. Not by any standards a practical, everyday piece likely to appeal to the average couple setting up home, more of a museum piece and an exercise in design and cabinet making. The proportions are distorted by the photograph.

1870s

452 Enamel, mother-of-pearl and brass make up the decoration on this ebony veneered cabinet in the style of the full flowering of the mid-nineteenth century 'Renaissance'. This fine quality piece was made by Courmont et Cie. The finish and overall decorative effect are superb, with a fine quality carcass but it is not a very useful piece. It is a pity that the makers have been forced to economise by cutting down on the marquetry and leaving the lower part inlaid only with stringing. Standing next to a piece the eye may miss the lack of detail to the base but from a viewpoint at the other end of a room or from a photograph it becomes more obvious.

Dated 1880

453 A fruitwood copy of a Breton cupboard of the late seventeenth century. French regional furniture is a study in itself, each area having distinct local peculiarities. There are hundreds of small turned balusters on this cupboard, which is ventilated by the gaps in the turning, for the storage of food. A charming rustic article of furniture but large for modern rooms.

c.1900 *

454 An extravaganza of baroque carving incorporated into a huge architectural form. This is the French answer to the designs of Protat and carving of Cooke of the English 'Warwick' school. The numerous hunting trophies of hounds, stags and game were ideal, to the mid-nineteenth century eye, for decorating the dining room. The thought of dead game in the dining room during a meal is far from popular today but it filled the romantic ideal of the wealthy businessman steeped in romantic literature and the world of hunting. This example could not resist the two beautifully carved female terminal figures flanking the lower doors taken from the late seventeenth century.

1850s

MEUBLES D'APPUI — Later Gothic meubles d'appui

The light elegant Gothic revival forms that were applied to furniture in the third quarter of the eighteenth century and the early years of the nineteenth century are highly popular today and are usually small and useful pieces. The troubadour *style, as the French Gothic became known, also developed many heavier forms which were intended to be exact copies of late fifteenth century examples, which became weaker and less commonly based on period examples towards the middle of the nineteenth century.*

455 An oak cabinet of huge proportions — almost three metres high. This cabinet has been attributed to Mazaroz-Ribailler & Cie. who specialised in Gothic and Renaissance style furniture from 1863. This finely made cabinet is clearly based on modern ideals of the nineteenth century reformers such as Viollet-le-duc in France and A.W.N. Pugin in England, whose influence and designs from the 1830s onwards were widespread throughout Europe. There is a large amount of medievalism present in this design (the roof, the castellation and the hinges) mixed with the Gothic arches and tracery.

Late 1860s

456 A far purer Gothic cabinet carved in walnut by Lerolle, Fabricants des meubles d'art, St. Rue des Sts. Pères, Paris. The clean shape is restrained and in a recognisable style from the late fifteenth century and is compatible with the attractive tracery. The cabinet is made entirely from walnut and has developed a fine dull yellow patination. A beautifully made piece without any pretence to disguise the fact that it is purely nineteenth century, a copy admiring the past and not a 'fake' piece.

1880s *

457 (left) A muddled eclectic Renaissance revival cabinet on stand with a carved centre panel of a 'sixteenth century' fireside scene. This type of conversation piece was so loved in the nineteenth century, in carving, paintings and on most suitable art forms. The characteristic heads are an amusing portrayal of personalities in the imaginary French court of three hundred years before. Once again carved from solid walnut and very well made.

1870s

458 (right) A rather dry and severe example of the Gothic revival, attempting to be an authentic piece, not in the way it has been constructed but in its style and overall appearance. The lock is quite convincing but the hinges are very new looking. The base looks like an afterthought, as do the heads hanging uncomfortably from the overhang.

1880s

MIRRORS

459 Strictly in the Louis XVI style, this mirror could be an exact copy of a period example. The sharply bevelled mirror plate is obviously a nineteenth century addition but of course this is no guarantee as to the exact date. The carving of the billing doves and flowers is rather too stiff and if the cresting was taken away, one would be left with simply a good picture frame.

Late 1870s ✳

460 Inspired by northern France of the late seventeenth century, this *repoussé* brass mirror was copied continuously throughout the second half of the nineteenth century. The quality varies enormously and certain mirrors of this type can be almost impossible to tell from original examples. Once again the cresting is simply attached and not an obvious part of the original concept.

Late nineteenth century ✳

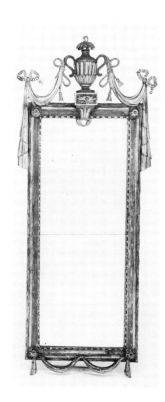

461 (left) A wood carver's nightmare and an impossible mirror to handle. When inspecting and valuing mirrors of this type they are always very firmly screwed to the wall and quite obviously re-gilt. This renders them impossible to date and even after the lengthy process of unscrewing them from the wall, pulling out plaster and rawlplugs, one can find to one's embarrassment that the question of date has not been answered. As a rule of thumb it is often quite useful to inspect how many birds wings or leaves on the outer extremity of the mirror have been broken and subsequently repaired.

1880-1900

462 (right) A provincial mirror in Louis XVI taste that is quite possibly an example of provincial survival rather than mass produced revival. The naïve application of the central urn and rather stiff drapery suggests the provincial air. Do not be deceived by the divided mirror plate which is by no means a guarantee of eighteenth century origin. Possibly first half of the nineteenth century. ✳

PIANOS

Certainly 'grand' on this page with two incredible examples combining the achievements of the Martin Brothers, Louis XIV, XV and XVI with the brushes of Berain and Watteau.

463 The whole surface of this piano is painted with a gold craquelure, decorated with every scene from the *commedia dell'arte*. The legs are 'jewelled' for good measure. Signed, inexplicably, 'Martin, B.', this piano was delivered to Lord Rosebery at Mentmore Towers in 1867.

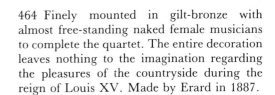

464 Finely mounted in gilt-bronze with almost free-standing naked female musicians to complete the quartet. The entire decoration leaves nothing to the imagination regarding the pleasures of the countryside during the reign of Louis XV. Made by Erard in 1887.

465 A slightly less grand piano signed on the mounts by F. Linke and made by Erard at the turn of the century. The quarter-veneered tulipwood is very plain in comparison with the previous examples.

c.1910

466 Queen Maria Pia of Portugal was given this painted amboyna piano as a wedding present in 1878. The quality is unsurpassed but the effect is spoilt by an attempt to cram every available space with paintings by Juan Antonio Gonzalez that would be easier to see on the wall.

467 An attempt to economise results in the decoration is parcel-gilt and not *bronze doré*, with a walnut frame. To lighten the visual load the carver has 'double-pierced' the massive legs.

1880s

468 English influence has restrained the decoration on this baby grand to a form of Angelica Kauffman revival on a Dutch East Indies satinwood ground. Made by Kaim in Germany 1890-1910.

469 A musical box, made in Switzerland, with a presumably French case of *bois noirci* and thuya veneers. Extra tunes are stored in the frieze drawer and the legs are built to take the weight.

1850-1860

470 Rossi Peppera and Sons of Lugano were responsible for the movement of this coin-operated piano organ. No one to date has come forward to claim responsibility for the faded maroon stained softwood case with such a sad face. The case looks almost Germanic in its proportions.

1890s

471 Erard were once again responsible for this rococo baby grand. The gilding is on wood and not metal.

c.1900

See also boulle pianos, illustrations 32 and 33.

472 A good quality parquetry kingwood grand piano with lavish *bronze doré* mounts but comparable in spirit to 465.

1890s

473 (right) A Pleyel piano, simply parcel gilt wood and Vernis Martin, as 467. The small boudoir grand size makes it useful and popular.

1880s

474 A good quality Pleyel piano of Louis XVI pretensions but the Vernis Martin decoration has deteriorated.

c.1900

475 Not a piano but an organ with transfer painted Sèvres plaques and the ubiquitous Vitruvian scroll. A very unusual example in poor condition that will be expensive to restore to full working order. This one had several fake eighteenth century *marques au fer*, including one purporting to be the signature of Jean-Henri Riesener.

1860s

PIETRE DURE

Pietre Dure, *strictly speaking, refers to the Florentine mosaic of hard and precious or semi-precious stones in a technique practised at the beginning of the seventeenth century. Large amounts of ready cut stones were exported from Italy during the nineteenth century and mounted with varying degrees of success on furniture, usually side cabinets. Most pieces commonly found are of French construction. However, detailed inspection of the locks and hinges may reveal some of English manufacture. The major disadvantage to modern taste is that all the cabinets were made of ebony veneers or* bois noirci *so that the black would contrast with the rich colours of the stones (see colour illustration on page 69) which, for the most part, are soapstones. The stone is either simply glued to the surface or in more sophisticated cases let into the veneer. Changes of atmosphere and central heating are the enemies of* pietre dure *and care must be taken not to pull the stones out when dusting. Quality varies enormously and condition is most important.*

476 (right) A marble top column with tired lions supporting the weight. Several leaves are missing and the gilding is dull.

1850s

478 (below) Another, smaller, *table à écrire* with rather weak vases of flowers; note the sides of the cabinet are not applied with *pietre dure*. This desk is English but has been included here to illustrate the similarity between French and English examples.

c.1870

477 An unusual *table à écrire* of Louis XVI inspiration. The *pietre dure* consists of rather squat vases of flowers but the four moths are a welcome addition.

c.1870

479 A good quality *meuble d'appui* with a bold, profuse vase of flowers and the added luxury of a bird, with useful glazed side cabinets divided by good quality oversize *bronze doré* columns on tiny legs. The plaque of *putti* learning the arts was more commonly applied to *bureaux plats* (see illustration no.306).

c.1860

480 and 481 At first glance almost identical, although 481 has a token gesture of boulle in the spandrels. However, the bird appears to be about to fall out of the tree. The quality of 480 is generally better, with a superior line.

both c.1860

480

481

482 A bold design but rather wispy *pietre dure* panels and spandrels. The jet black marble top is far too severe and probably a replacement. On many *meubles d'appui* of this type the brass apron stringing and veneer deteriorates rapidly. The mounts are very weak.

Late 1850s

The difference in technique of English and Florentine stone inlay is illustrated on page 496.

483 The maker was economising here on imported *pietre dure*. A cabinet with a mirrored top will sooner or later end up in two pieces. Note the similarity of brass stringing with 477 and 480.

1860s

484 The proportions are unusual and the mounts are of good quality with bold *pieds de biche*.

Late 1850s

485 (right) The inlay is true *pietre dure* of inlaid mosaics of semi-precious stones in the style of the early Florentine craftsmen. The mounts and general quality of the cabinet spoil the piece and the comparative scarcity of true *pietre dure*.

1850s

486 A well designed cabinet with unusual 'C' scroll mounts at each corner of the door. The acanthus frieze is normally found on the earlier nineteenth century boullé and *pietre dure* cabinets. The panel is damaged and will be expensive to repair.

c.1850

487 (right) A fine quality cabinet, the lock engraved 'Medaille à L'Exposition Universelle 1855 manufacteur des meubles, Diehl, rue Michel le Compte 19, Paris'. Unfortunately, whatever the *putti* were holding on the cresting is missing but nevertheless a good piece by a respected maker.

Late 1850s

488 and 489 Two photographs of panels of Florentine stonework, incorporated on an English side cabinet. The bird in the tree is a comparatively common design — often used on panels of applied hardstones. The camel is a reminder of the camels that were introduced into Italy during the Renaissance — the water buffalo looks terrified of it.

1850s

SCREENS

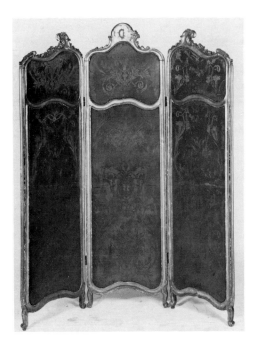

490 All the worst features of the nineteenth century rococo revival incorporated into one piece of furniture. The asymmetry of the crestings is far too heavy with little freedom of movement. The cherubs appear to be falling out of the sky with the weight of their stolen flowers and fruits.

1880s

491 Once again dull, rococo asymmetry on the giltwood frame, in this case in rather poor condition and the cost of satisfactory regilding would be very high. There is nothing worse than seeing these frames repainted with picture frame gilding. The expensive green silk damask is beginning to deteriorate.

c.1890

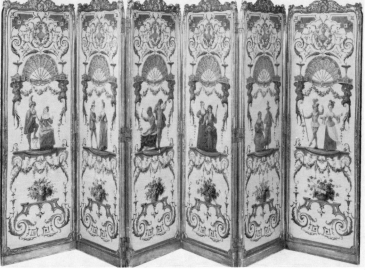

492 A good quality screen made entirely from wood with quarter veneered kingwood being used to heighten the decorative effect, although one feels the centre of each panel should have been inlaid.

c.1900

493 Painted screens of this size with interesting early eighteenth century pastimes depicted on each panel are extremely popular, although the overall decorative effect is a little too 'ritzy'for some tastes. The reverse of a screen of this quality will probably be fairly plain, lightly decorated with flowers and scrolls.

c.1880

494, 495, 496 All fire kerbs, *chenets* and fire irons are greatly sought after. The quality varies considerably from mercurial gilded *bronze doré* as in 495 to dipped brass in 494 and 496. As all the individual pieces are separately cast and screwed together, many pieces become detached and have gone missing over the years, especially in the case of 496.

494 *c.1900*
495 *1870s*
496 *c.1900*

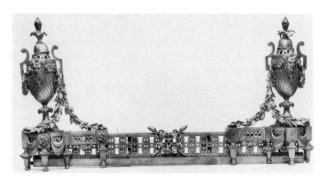

494

496

497 A carved and giltwood fire-screen, the weight being supported by grimacing lions raised on white ceramic casters for ease of movement. The centre would normally have a decorative needlework panel. An uncomfortable design but good quality.

Late 1840s

498 This screen, like the fire kerbs, is made of individually cast *bronze doré* pieces. In this case the oval bevel glazed centre panel is intentional so that the heat of the fire can be screened but the flames still be seen. Individual pieces of casting were all stamped with a B and a serial number which to date has not been explained.

c.1880

499 A fine example of the high standard of craftsmanship obtainable in the Atelier des Ciseleurs in the Beurdeley workshops. The finely chiselled mercurial gilt bronze frame is set on to a very deep dark blue *tôle peinte* ground. The mounts at the sides are in the style of Pierre Gouthière. This screen was offered for sale in the Beurdeley Succession auction in Paris in May 1979 and has subsequently been restored to its original exquisite condition.

1880s

SEAT FURNITURE — Louis XIII to Régence Armchairs

The chair, at the beginning of the seventeenth century, was a rare item of furniture, reserved for the very rich. Design soon blossomed, and by the middle of the century most houses could afford the small, low backed chair or armchair which often had twist turned arm supports, legs and stretchers. By the time Louis XIV was old enough to assume the throne chairs had assumed generous proportions with curved arms and flower carved turned stretchers. Chair backs became higher and the stretcher formed an 'X' rather than the earlier 'H' shape. The high chair back soon disappeared and by c.1700 had been lowered to the height of the 1660s but instead of a rectangular back a gentle arch had developed and the whole frame became more curvilinear. Slowly but surely the stretchers began to disappear altogether as the Régence period developed into its full rocaille *glory and more and more woodwork was exposed to the devices of the carver.*

500 A fine example of eclecticism. A walnut *fauteuil de bureau* in an early Louis XIV style. These desk chairs were always distinguished by their 'extra leg' at the front and appear in all the Louis styles. This is a rather handsome example in a very soft walnut. The decoration on the splat just peters out at the top appearing unfinished.

c.1850?

501 This is a giltwood copy of a Louis XIV chair c.1690. This amply comfortable type of chair was made in large quantities throughout the second half of the nineteenth century and can be very difficult to date between 1850 and 1920. The gilding on this one is in poor condition and appears to have been rather crudely repainted at some stage. Comfortable but very large for modern rooms. This one probably c.1900.

502 This chair reproduces one of the early Régence era. The carving has none of the depth or vigour of an eighteenth century original and the stretchers are very plain and heavy. The chair still retains the straight uprights holding the back to the seat that by the second quarter of the century had developed into a subtle 'S' scroll that typifies French chairs and sets them apart from England and most other countries. The Gobelins tapestry is in poor condition and contemporary with the chair.

c.1880 ✱

Nineteenth century copies of chairs from the Louis XIV to Louis XVI periods were often made in quite large sets comprising anything from seven to thirteen or seventeen pieces.

504 Stretchers have now disappeared and the early style of the Louis XV chair has now developed. Some period chairs — and a few copies — have wooden butterfly toggles at the back of the padded back which allow the upholstery to be completely taken out for ease of cleaning or repairing. The upholstery is of a type that some will love and others will be offended by.

1880-1900 *

503 Copied from a chair of the 1690s with weak and simple carving that compares to the previous example. The upholstery, however, is early eighteenth century Gobelins.

1880-1900 *

505 (left) Although the carving is not very deep it gives an exaggerated effect to the already scrolled and vigorous frame. Note that the back supports have become the shape of an inverted 'S' and the seat rather unusually is of the stuffed drop-in variety. The bold cartouches framing the sprays of roses make the chair very attractive and of course condition is all important. The chair and upholstery are third quarter of the nineteenth century. *

506 The elegant fluid line of this grey painted armchair is totally Louis XV. The upholstery in muted tones of red and verdure is good quality and nineteenth century, copying the style of a hundred years before. The frame c.1880. *

The condition of gilding is very important on all furniture but especially chairs, which are being constantly handled and moved around a room and the legs kicked by passers-by. Therefore condition of gilding is most important and whereas small chips can be filled in and re-gilt quite satisfactorily — almost by the amateur — once the gilding deteriorates to any substantial degree to bring it back to a satisfactory condition will prove to be very expensive. For a single chair, let alone a set, to be completely re-gilt to the standards of the mid-nineteenth century is extremely costly indeed, not only in terms of labour but also materials. Gold leaf is no longer a cheap commodity. Bad re-gilding can be heartbreaking and it is important to establish the quality that the restorer intends to apply. Picture frame gilding is cheap and is guaranteed to ruin the value of a chair.

508 Again good quality Régence carving but the gilding is rapidly deteriorating and will need immediate attention. A very generous chair but almost too wide for comfort.

c.1880 ✳

507 A good, solid and comfortable chair ebonised and parcel-gilt in mid-nineteenth century taste. The carving is very good and free with a delightfully unnecessary acanthus circlet on the top-rail which will surely get damaged quite regularly.

1850s ✳

510 A vigorously moulded chair with unusual extra shaping to the back. The carving is only average although the top-rail is quite spirited. A good practical chair which looks very comfortable.

1860-1880 ✳

509 (left) What a lump. The original flowing intentions have been completely lost and are let down by the very heavy mouldings and thick legs which have not been counterbalanced by the thin top-rail. The gilding looks quite horrible.

c.1900 ✳

In the second half of the nineteenth century the fashionable all had their drawing rooms furnished in 'the Louis taste', a fashion which continued until the Great War. Fine copies were made in large numbers with good quality upholstery imitating that of the eighteenth century. The scarcer the original sets became increased the demand for copies. Those who could afford to buy eighteenth century upholstery in good condition would have their nineteenth century suite upholstered in the earlier work — a fact that many upholsterers and restorers overlook today, wrongly advising clients that their suite is 'genuine' throughout.

511 Average quality carving on an oak frame. The gilding on this chair is thin but applied directly to the frame it will last for some time. The upholstery is machine woven and although picturesque has faded considerably. A cockerel and a wide eyed undernourished bird of paradise are perched on a well head on the back panel.

1880-1900 ✱

512 A very strongly designed chair. The carving is not very deep but there is plenty of decorative strapwork on the framework. The Beauvais tapestry is prettily worked with birds, squirrels and other animals in delicate colours that are not too faded.

c.1880 ✱

513 The Gobelins upholstery on this chair is from the middle of the eighteenth century. The chair frame has probably been made to accept the older upholstery, as the back cartouche held by toggles and the seat of the drop-in variety both come out easily. The frame is well moulded with not a straight line and the flowers — marguerites — are boldly carved.

1860s ✱

514 Look how weak the frame is compared with the previous illustration. Only on the top-rail does the carving stand proud of the moulded frame. On the legs and apron it is cut *into* the frame and is not very deep. The upholstery is contemporary with the chair. c.1900. ✱

The moulded frames of seat furniture are either gilt on to a gesso base, i.e., a carved frame gilt over plaster, or, towards the end of the nineteenth century and the beginning of the twentieth century, simply applied with gold leaf directly to to the frame. Earlier chairs and almost all gilt gesso chairs are made of beech and later chairs of oak, the grain of which very quickly shows through the thin gilding.

515 A dark foreboding ebonised beechwood frame that has none of the light of previous examples. It is a stiff interpretation of Louis XV rather than a direct copy. The carving on the top-rail is quite bold but very formal. Not an elegant chair. It would need expensive upholstery to bring it to life.

1850s

516 What a difference the parcel gilding makes to the whole flow of the moulding on this chair. Unfortunately it is in poor condition but the Aubusson seat covers are not too dull or worn. Compares with the quality of a Transitional chair illustrated on page 192.

1850s

517 The shape of this chair is Louis XV although the back is taken from a slightly later era. The walnut frame is of fine quality with well cast but discreet *bronze doré* mounts of ribbons and marguerites.

1870-1890

518 A very comfortable looking chair of beechwood stripped of its original gilding. The addition of a loose squab cushion filled with feathers makes the chair look particularly inviting and less formal than most, rendering it more suitable for the relaxed slouched attitude needed to watch hours of television. It is a pity that the leaf carving on the arm terminals is cut off abruptly by the supports and not continued.

c.1900

519 Régence in style but far too crudely carved to realistically be taken for that period. Very generous proportions and very comfortable.

c.1910

520 The legs are heavy enough to take all comers without undue concern. The ebonised beechwood has a token decoration of gilding throughout the frame in an attempt to relieve the severity.

c.1860

521 (left) This delightfully light armchair almost anticipates the transitional style. The decoration is still however that of the late rococo era. Unfortunately the frame is white painted, which limits its appeal but at least the carving has been parcel-gilt.

c.1900 *

522 A very dark walnut frame almost makes the eye turn away from this chair. The richness of the wood has not been captured on the photograph. The wood, combined with quite good quality discreet carving and an elegant frame sensing the transitional style, makes for a good and acceptable, comfortable chair.

1880s *

523 (left) The rather stiffened lines of this chair are an attempt to copy the transition from the gently flowing lines of Louis XV to the more formal neo-classical lines of Louis XVI. The oval of this *fauteuil à médaillon* and restrained cabriole legs are indications of the transition. The *bronze doré* is finely chiselled and of very good quality. The scallop shell with 'crabs' claws' of acanthus suggests the work of Linke and this chair could possibly be from his workshops, made towards the end of his career.

Probably 1920s

524 (right) Boldly carved but what an ugly chair. The belligerent rams' heads are far too large, the legs clumsy and unnecessarily hung with tassels. The profuse tumble of marguerites on the ribbon moulded top-rail and back supports are typically French. If it were not for these features the chair could easily be Danish or Swedish. It is a poorer relation to the chair below.

c.1900 ✳

525 Here the transition is complete with no traces of the *roçaille* left. The sturdy all-embracing arms look heavy on the decisively twisted legs. There is a lot of expensive carving on the frames and the intricacy of the flowerhead *guilloché* moulding on the seat-rail is competent. The Aubusson upholstery is becoming thin and will soon start to look shabby.

1880s ✳

526 There is not quite the heaviness of the almost identical chair illustrated as 524. The rams' heads appear smaller and far less stupid. The back supports, although thicker, are more florid and in keeping with the rest of the chair. The light bright gilding and decorative upholstery make for a more expensive chair. On this example the backs are upholstered in late nineteenth century Aubusson and the seats in remnants of eighteenth century material. This chair is part of a suite copied from a period one in the collection of Mme. d'Yvon and was sold in the Galerie Georges Petit in Paris in 1892. It is possible that the sale inspired these copies to be made.

Late 1890s ✳

SEAT FURNITURE — Louis XVI Armchairs

In the middle of the eighteenth century seat furniture was popularly painted a delicate off-white or grey, especially in provincial areas or for patrons who could not afford expensive gilding. This practice was revived throughout the second half of the nineteenth century but more especially in the last few years of the century. Late nineteenth century chairs painted in this manner are often delightfully coloured in pastel shades and the paintwork, if looked after, can last for a long time. The colours contrast well against the brightness of French tapestry woven upholstery, the two complementing each other.

527 (left) A very similar chair to the next example with not quite such a wide seat and a bow fronted rather than an outset apron. The back and seat upholstery probably belong together and are original to the chair.

c.1900

528 The medallion back is less formal than the later square back although both types were copied during the second half of the nineteenth century. This chair is of a type of which thousands were, and are still being, produced. The carving is quite good by modern standards but must have looked sub-standard compared with the available workmanship of the late nineteenth century. The seat cover would have been replaced and looks to be of an earlier material than the back.

1890s

529 (left) When the reader's eye settles down and is able to focus on the carving rather than the upholstery of this chair, the mechanical but quite deep ribband moulding can easily be seen. The outswept arms are quite generous but the whole frame lacks life and is clearly a pastiche.

1920s

530 (right) Another very similar frame but slightly heavier, which gives it a better sense of proportion. The attractive upholstery makes all the difference to the value.

Early twentieth century

531 A similar chair to those on the previous page with delightful upholstery, unfortunately wearing a little thin on the seat cover.

Early twentieth century ✳

532 The lightness of the ribband back is spoilt by the severity of the fluting on the arms and the heavy tapering legs. The gilding is in poor condition and will need attention if it is not to be hoovered up for the next few months while it slowly chips away with use.

c.1900 ✳

533 This very plain chair is made of darkened beechwood which presumably was not properly seasoned before use. Both the front legs are slightly unsure — the right one definitely bending outwards. On this chair it can clearly be seen that the front legs consist of the stop fluted tapering column *and* the capital carved wood *patera*. This is then morticed into the arm support and seat-rail. Plain and rather dull. At least it will not have to be re-gilt.

Early twentieth century ✳

534 A rather scruffy chair illustrating the square tapering back of the late Louis XVI period. The finials are decidedly tired and are out of proportion with the rather weakly carved ribband top-rail. The chair generally needs attention although the sagging upholstery is still in good condition. Note that the 'S' shaped back supports have disappeared.

1890s ✳

189

535 A square tapering back similar to the previous example and also with scruffy gilding. An elegant chair, however, with an upholstery that can be placed in most decorative themes.

c.1900 ∗

536 Carved walnut becomes dark quite quickly when constantly handled and this would be especially so with a chair frame which in this case has been stained slightly. The trophy of a crossed quiver of arrows and a *flambeau* tied with ribbons makes an attractive cresting. There is also considerably more work in making the outset fluted columns that support the back. The *chapeau gendarme* finials can just be discerned at the top of the columns.

c.1900

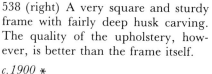

537 (left) The machine made Belgian tapestry on the back of this seat equates well with the quite awful gilding which has possibly been barbarously added to a quite good walnut frame. However, the combination is difficult to swallow.

Early twentieth century ∗

538 (right) A very square and sturdy frame with fairly deep husk carving. The quality of the upholstery, however, is better than the frame itself.

c.1900 ∗

539 The fine quality carved and gilt frame of this chair is almost up to the very high standard of the eighteenth century Gobelins upholstery which is still in excellent condition.

The frame late 1870s ✻

540 Another not very well gilt chair in deteriorating condition. The frames have some life in them, especially with the acanthus on the arm terminals and supports, which is especially nice where the supporting columns at the back lead into the arm.

c.1900 ✻

541 A much weaker chair of similar design without such attention to detail. The frame is painted a nondescript dull grey with the highlights rather garishly picked out in gold.

c.1900 ✻

542 A similar example; the frame is white painted, also picked out in gold. There is much more work in the carved trophy on the top-rail and the *chapeau gendarme* finials are a much more discreet decoration than the previous chair's ripening pomegranates.

c.1880

543 A perfect example of tassels and silk. The rosewood frame and gadrooned legs are typical of English furniture of the same period. The long fringes are a perfect example of the need for over decoration and upholstery. The handle at the top is very convenient to enable the chair to be easily moved around the room which, by the middle of the century, would be so cluttered that there would be little room to move around. An unusual chair and rather smart and comfortable.

1840s

544 A parcel-gilt *bois noirci* armchair of 'transitional' style that compares with the 'Louis XV' chair, no.516. The shape is a little contrived and has none of the flow of the Louis XV style chair. These ebonised and gilt chairs are comparatively rare and although this one is ungainly it has good, restrained upholstery. The construction of the arm supports and leg capitals is most extraordinary — as if two different craftsmen have set out to make the same chair, one the arms, the other the legs and both wanted to carve a *patera*.

c.1860

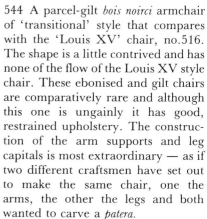

545 A poor quality child's armchair in picture frame gold paint on a beech frame. The idea is inspired by a design by Le Bouteiller reproduced in illustration no.581. This little chair has a cheap Swiss musical box under the seat which insists on playing whenever the chair is sat on.

Third quarter of the nineteenth century

546 A fascinating chair from the French Gothic revival, the ebonised frame has white painted bird finials and the pierced back is extremely delicate. The legs have a very Puginesque — the English Gothic 'reformer' — feel. The upholsteries do not belong. A rare and unusual chair in need of much restoration but a little ungainly.

1830-1840

SEAT FURNITURE — Empire Armchairs

547 Strictly speaking an interpretation of a late Directoire chair from about 1800. Veneered in well figured satin birch with light and decorative burrs, it was sold by Krieger whose label it bears. A handsome chair but the mounts are too thin as often happened with this late nineteenth century 'Empire revival' furniture. The seat covers are appalling.

c.1900 ∗

The Empire style was popularly revived for a period of almost forty years from the 1880s but with little of the former glory and quality of the Napoleonic furniture.

548 A handsome but surely uncomfortable *fauteuil de bureau* looking directly back to designs of c.1805. All the mounts are of a sub-standard quality — the lion's head arm terminals look painfully impaled.

c.1890

549 Presumably a French reproduction of an Empire chair but bearing a label of a Dutch firm, P.J. Mesker. The fact that it is a paper label leads one to the dangerous conclusion that it is simply a retailer's label — there is nothing strikingly Dutch about the chair, although the proportions are a little heavy. Past record suggests that a maker would affix a more permanent stamp or ivorine label. However, the precedent of the eighteenth century English makers using, albeit rarely, a paper label throws this theory open to criticism.

1880-1900 ∗

550 Another variation of the same type of chair. The very badly cast sphinxes' heads are capped by the gilt-brass *patera* which find their way on most pieces of late nineteenth century Empire revival furniture. The sphinxes' numb, cold feet have been almost fused together they are so badly cast. The embossed velvet upholstery is in keeping with the style of the chair.

c.1900 ∗

SEAT FURNITURE — Louis XV and Louis XVI fauteuils à l'oreilles

The fauteuil à l'oreilles *is a charming name for a wing armchair. These comfortable deeply padded chairs originated in the 1670s and by the middle of the eighteenth century had become completely upholstered at the side, shielding the sitter from draught, or from the heat of the fire.*

551 This wing armchair or *bergère* with the addition of wings is a copy of the style at the middle of the eighteenth century. The traditional carving is not very deep but the modern upholstery is inviting.

c.1900 *

552 A very similar shape but less inviting. The attention to the little detailed carving is only a token gesture — the apron being especially weak. The whole chair is too 'sit up and beg' to be confused with an eighteenth century version and the gilding must be the worst example so far.

Early twentieth century

553 and 554 These two chairs, although wing chairs, should really be called *'en confessionnal'*. This name developed in the late seventeenth century when these chairs were first popularised at Versailles. They are the early versions of the winged *bergère* and it was a logical conclusion for the *menuisiers* to expand their trade by extending the upholstered wing to the sides as in the two previous examples. The wings hid the sitter's face — ideal for a cosy fireside confessional! 553 is taken from the 1740s and 554 from the 1770s. The latter is extremely provincial in origin, the rather clumsy shape and crude carving on an oak frame coupled with heavy legs are the indications. It is very unusual to find these chairs with adjustable backs — a type of early Parker Knoll recliner that allows the sitter to stretch out completely — a *bergère à transformation*.

Both late nineteenth century *

SEAT FURNITURE — Louis XV and Louis XVI Bergères

An indication of the usages for different styles of revival furniture in their respective rooms is emerging. The comfortable shapes of the Louis XV style and even the more formal Louis XVI style were ideal for the nineteenth century drawing room. The severe outlines of Empire chairs with only the seats or padding on the arms upholstered, based more along the lines of the traditional English dining chair (introduced into France just before the Empire), were eminently suitable for the formal late nineteenth century dining room.

556 A much less exciting example which is really just an ordinary *fauteuil* with the arms filled in. The carving is not very good — nor the gilding.

Early twentieth century

555 A very comfortable small *bergère* with perhaps too much emphasis on the squab cushion. The depth of the cushion is unnecessary as it gives too much comfort for the chair with its tiny padded arms. Once again traditional carving of marguerites. The upholsterer has to be very careful with the material on the curved back which can shrink and become stretched rather like a drum.

1880s ∗

557 The shape is very similar to the previous example. The acanthus carving is quite bold and rather unusual. The little boy depicted on the back appears to be watering yet more flowers to decorate yet more chair frames. This chair was almost certainly part of a suite.

c.1900 ∗

558 This white painted armchair is extremely well made, copying the very early Louis XVI period. Unfortunately the white painting is not original and is wearing badly, with the colour of the chair frame beginning to show through. A comfortable chair but one in which the excessive construction, especially to the back, gives rise to loose joints which are expensive to repair as the upholstery must in most cases be removed.

1870s

The bergère *in many cases was included in the eighteenth century drawing room suite which could stretch to twenty pieces. These sets were popular in the late nineteenth century but did not usually contain so many pieces.*

559 A Régence style armchair with tiny wings which would hardly do their job at all. The carving on the frame, although deep, is quite ghastly. The apron especially looks like an amorphous mass of seaweed and does not match the top-rail at all. The gilding to boot is of very poor quality. The distorted male masks at the knees look as though they are shouting for help.

c.1900

560 A small comfortable *bergère* but with only average carving. The ball arm terminals are unusually plain. The finials flanking the top-rail look totally spurious.

c.1900

561 A fine and handsome chair embodying all the qualities of the very best Louis XVI neo-classical furniture. The rarity of original chairs is such that the onlooker must automatically presume that the chair is a copy until he is persuaded otherwise. The proud female heads have been discreetly draped and are so finely carved that they appear to be portraits. Thankfully they are not hard sphinx-like faces but more likely of a young French girl who unwittingly walked daily past the carver's workshop. An exceptional chair. A copy of a *bergère* by J.B.C. Sené delivered in 1788 for Marie Antoinette's *cabinet de toilette* at Saint-Cloud.

1870s ✳

562 A low chair or *chauffeuse* in Louis XVI style. The proportions are simply reduced from an armchair and consequently look slightly wrong. These small chairs were used to be drawn up to a fire, hence their name. They were often part of the larger suites of furniture. The necessity to overdecorate is seen on the weak and unnecessary finials.

c.1880

563 This charming small chair can be used as a *chauffeuse* but is a delight for children. It is almost certainly going to be used by a small dog or cat for its own personal use.

1880s-1900

564 This tiny provincial beechwood chair is certainly only intended for a child. The reductions in proportion again make the chair slightly ungainly, the legs appearing almost too big. A delight for children to use.

c.1900

565 The size of this *bergère* is midway between a full sized chair and a child's chair. The dark walnut frame is elegantly moulded and well carved. The expensive *moiré* silk upholstery should suit most tastes.

1890s

566 Another low *bergère* or *chauffeuse* of beechwood carved in a provincial manner. Like the beechwood child's chair illustrated above it is badly wormed. Worm is a major enemy of beech and, although once detected it can be stopped effectively with modern chemicals, the framework of the chair is left riddled with holes and may be badly weakened.

1860s

568 A Régence style side chair highly carved with *roçaille*. The carving is typical of the late nineteenth century. A useful and comparatively comfortable chair if used at a dining table.

1890s

567 A good example of muddled late sixteenth century 'Henri Deux' design. This small walnut chair — intended for use as a dining chair — is of finely carved walnut embodying Gothic and Renaissance motifs. The addition of a squab cushion with tassels of course would be a necessity for the unfortunate diner.

1860s

570 A rosewood chair, well made but unsure whether it is directly copying the Louis XV period or a straight forward mid-nineteenth century balloon back chair. A comfortable looking design. There is something almost Gothic about the triple arch at the bottom of the back support which possibly helps to date the chair. Rare in sets but possibly originally one of six.

c.1840

569 Strictly a copy of the 1750s, this little chair is well carved with marguerites in walnut. Rarely seen in sets and it would be difficult to collect even a harlequin set, that is a set made up of individual pairs of similar chairs.

c.1900

571 An elegant Louis XVI style chair with well proportioned *chapeau gendarme* finials. The white painted frame is parcel-gilt and becoming badly chipped.

1870s

573 A small and unusual giltwood *voyeuse* copying the style popular in the late 1770s. This type of chair was not often made in the nineteenth century in the exact style of the previous century and would normally only be made when completing a large suite of drawing-room furniture. The *voyeuse* was used, not as popularly imagined for watching cock fighting, but for watching the eternal card games of the period. For the most part the *voyeur* would sit at an angle to the side of the chair leaning one elbow on the top-rail and not with his legs spread either side of the chair back as was the custom with an eighteenth century English cock-fighting chair — which was certainly not intended for a lady.

1860s *

572 The elegance of this chair is accentuated by the well fluted twist turned legs which were a speciality of Jean-Baptiste Sené in the early 1780s. Once again the gilding is becoming chipped on this light and easily portable chair.

1870s *

574 A fine walnut side chair with the addition of a much lighter burr walnut banding around the padded back and apron — a technique not used in the eighteenth century. The discreet bronze doré mounts set off the colour of the woods.

c.1900

575 A plain beechwood chair carved with a *guilloché* banding. The whole effect is very plain and unobtrusive and many of these simple side chairs were made.

1900-1920

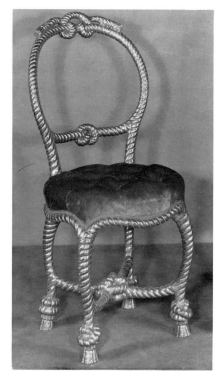

576 This wonderful side chair is one of a pair attributed to A-M-E Fournier who exhibited chairs at the 1867 Exposition Universelle. A stool by the same maker is illustrated on page 210. This mad design of interlaced ropework with a figure of eight knot forming the splat and a treacherous slip knot at the top-rail epitomises the passion for upholstery and plastic forms of the third quarter of the nineteenth century. The designer has based his invention on a standard balloon back chair but taken the desire for everything to be upholstered one stage further by imitating the ropework used for holding curtains and drapes and making it into an amusing and rather satisfying chair frame.

c.1860

577 This low, button backed *crapaud* became all the rage in the upholstery period spanning the third quarter of the nineteenth century. The deep buttoning is very plush and comfortable and the fringes add to the sumptuous feeling. It is difficult to imagine how ghastly the turning of the legs must be to need such dense covering. Notice how the upholsterer has cleverly divided the fringe by inserting intermittent larger twisted cords.

1860s

578 An extraordinary chair, possibly an early form of upholstered 'K9'. It is intended to be used as a gentleman's *voyeuse* and comfort has been taken to its busy heights with the addition of a back. The supports to the arm rest and legs, hidden by the copious amount of fringing, are fluted in typical Louis XVI style. This type of chair is rare and although not of much practical use today it is very amusing.

1860s

579 French or English? A difficult question to solve. The tapestry covers are from Aubusson and are indisputedly French but the frame is made of oak and has a similarity to the simple Gothic revival designs of A.W.N. Pugin in the middle of the nineteenth century. There was of course nothing to stop an English householder from covering or re-covering his English chairs in French upholstery — the mixture is bizarre and eclectic — mixing a tapestry style from the eighteenth century with a frame inspired by the fifteenth century. The effect however is surprisingly attractive. In conclusion it must be presumed that the chair is English.

1850s

580 This unusual side chair is an example of the French retort by the middle of the nineteenth century to the mass of Chinese export lacquer and *lac burgauté* — the mother-of-pearl inlay that was imitated in England on *papier mâché* furniture. The shape is taken from that of a standard balloon back chair and the addition of turned stretchers is novel but ungainly and surely unnecessary. At a distance and without looking at the simple gilt chinoiserie decoration this chair could be indeed taken for an English *papier mâché* chair.

c.1850

581 This small chair is taken from the *Album de l'Industrie et des Arts utiles* by Le Bouteiller, rue de la Bourse, No.1 à Paris. The catalogue, produced in the 1830s, is full of inventive upholstered chairs of all shapes and sizes. The photograph of this chair has been included as it is similar to many thousands of small chairs produced in England and France during the second half of the nineteenth century. The design is a basis for many small gilt chairs which are commonly hired out for functions, notably for the more important auctions of the world's largest auction house.

583 The climax of the Industrial Revolution — an amusing and unusual hooped iron chair, presumably originally made for a Parisian park. The neat modern button upholstery has been added to give the chair some semblance of comfort. The small pad feet could easily be set into the ground and the two pierced irons on the back stretcher were presumably for attaching the chair to a railing.

Third quarter nineteenth century

582 This good quality kingwood and tulipwood banded side chair is loosely based on the Transitional style. The well chiselled and good quality mounts are discreet and aid the colourful decoration of the woods.

c.1900

SEAT FURNITURE
Régence and Louis XV Settees

584 The companion piece to no.502 on page 181. The cartouche flanked by birds' heads on the back has wonderful strength and vigour and it recalls similar shapes on the front of Louis XIV side cabinets. The frolicking *putti* have conquered wild animals of both land and sea. The seat covers are, unfortunately, badly worn.

c.1880 *

587 A great deal of faith in strength of construction has been placed by the original frame maker of this settee. The absence of one or two extra legs to support the frame under the front of the long apron is an impressive and typically nineteenth century technique. It does not, however, make the frame any the more endearing — the upholstered back is far too big for the seat and lack of legs — the quite well carved top-rail is too thin and restrained and not in keeping with the apron and well scrolled arms. The tired upholstery is full of tired cherubs.

c.1900

The settee was made in all the popular Louis styles and was an integral part of the multi-piece drawing room suite. Upholstery varied enormously but the most popular was that in a traditional eighteenth century style with the soft hues of colours that are so attractive to the modern eye, but originally were extremely bright and garish with very strong vivid colours.

585 A carved and gilt frame of only average quality and designed without flair. The upholstery is a typical portrayal of a fondly imagined eighteenth century rustic scene, with the inevitable 'boy meets girl' routine.

1890s

586 The companion to no.513. The eighteenth century tapestry is full of life with an interesting study of wild birds.

1860s *

588 A very strong Régence style moulded frame. The movement of waves can be felt along the top-rail, although they are interwoven with boldly carved acanthus leaves. A generous shape. The frame has an easily removable drop-in seat and toggled back.

c.1880

589 This *'bergère'* settee has almost developed wings at the upholstered sides. The effect is of more comfort in that it can be sat in rather than, more formally, on. The carving is a little uninspired.

c.1900 ✽

590 This white painted and parcel-gilt frame has definite wings at the sides. The sitter(s) are protected from draughts — not on their legs, and the whole atmosphere is more intimate. This shape is simply an extension of the wing armchair.

1890s ✽

591 The good quality polished walnut frame is here spoilt slightly by a dumpy shape — a less satisfactory extension of the wing armchair. The general restraint of the carver is very noticeable and the scroll from the conventional padded arms to the equally conventional cabriole leg has a naturalistic feel which must be, unconsciously, infected by the new art nouveau freedom of shape.

c.1900

592 The small size and uncomplicated shape make this type of settee very popular — mainly for bedrooms or alcoves. They are also useful as an extra drawing room seat, for two close friends, that can be drawn up at a moment's notice. The deeply sprung seat is very comfortable. The carving is good and quite deep, especially on the top-rail.

c.1900

The air of formality of these chairs and settees, especially the more severe Louis XVI style as opposed to the Louis XV style, suggests a restricted use for the modern home. It is a natural choice for anyone setting up home to concentrate on more comfortable modern upholstered pieces. A second room or a more formal drawing room is the ideal place for the French revival styles. The 'sit up and beg' seats were not designed for lounging in front of a television but for polite and genteel conversation — or for the side chairs to be drawn around a table for the inevitable game of cards.

593 Another settee with excellent upholstery — altogether very comfortable. The frame is not of a particularly high standard of workmanship but the condition and size are a plus.

c.1900 *

594 This settee is part of the suite of which the armchair is illustrated on page 187, no.526. Once again the carving is far better than another identical chair, no.524. A similar suite is in the Henry E. Huntingdon Library, San Marino, California.

Late 1890s *

595 A poor quality, rather boring, settee but quite comfortable with the squab cushion and the three matching small cushions. Here the upholsterer's art has triumphed over the frame makers. The frame, however, has never been gilt — just left in its natural beechwood state which makes it more attractive to some eyes. At least there is not the continuous worry of chipped gilding.

c.1900 *

SEAT FURNITURE — Louis XVI Settees

596 The very good upholstery and deep carving are let down by the weakly designed and thin frame. How much better the overall effect would be if the size of the frame was on a larger, thicker scale. Nevertheless a richly decorated settee.

1880s ✱

598 Once again the quite good depth of carving is let down by a weakly designed frame that could never be mistaken for a Louis XVI original. The overall effect is left lifeless. However, the upholstery is highly decorative.

1900-1920

It is quite possible to repair the highly decorative upholstery commonly found on this type of French drawing room furniture, be it eighteenth century or later work. However the repair work, if it is to be executed to the high standard that the original work deserves, is lengthy, highly skilled and consequently expensive.

597 The overall effect is extremely severe but upon closer inspection the high quality is evident. The high gloss ebonised beechwood frame is highlighted by the contrast of good quality *bronze doré* mounts which are well chiselled and generously, but discreetly, applied. Somehow the blandness of the upholstery spoils the rather magnificent effect of the frame.

c.1880 ✱

599 A companion settee to the armchair on page 191, no.539. The eighteenth century Gobelins upholstery rather dominates the frame which in itself is of a high standard for this type of revival. The slightly earlier date of the frame compared with most of the other examples is in line with the better and more elaborate carving. As the century drew to a close the carving, generally speaking, became worse.

The frame late 1870s ✱

600 A good size and shape with attractive upholstery, let down by the frame which is totally mechanical in feeling.

c.1900 *

601 More rams' heads and altogether quite deep carving. The ribbon tied flowers and trophies on the top-rail are somewhat over-exuberant and far too big in proportion to the rest of the frame.

1920s

602 An example of the worst frame making that was produced in the larger mass-producing firms in Paris. Many metres of this sub-standard beechwood framing must have been produced to the horror of the Faubourg Saint-Antoine.

Early twentieth century

603 French Gothic not at its best. This settee, strictly speaking a hall bench, is unusually made of oak which was not common practice during the nineteenth century for seat furniture as it had been during Louis XV's reign. The overall effect is very heavy, without the lightness and delicacy of the French inlaid Gothic stringing often seen on otherwise plain Empire or Biedermeier forms. The big finials are top heavy — the small finials far too small and out of proportion with the heavy lancet arches. Nevertheless Gothic pieces are very sought-after and hard to find.

1840s

During the 1750s Madame de Pompadour had her bedroom redecorated in the newly popularised Turkish manner. The adherence to Turkey was only slight and anything from Arabia was generously included in this exotic fashion. During this period of informality and unashamed luxury and comfort the sultane *developed with its deep sides and plush feathered cushions.*

604 The generous Louis XV style frame is an exact replica of the period c.1760. The comfortable intentions of this copy have been let down by a thin squab cushion comparable to mattresses in third rate Paris hotels. The cylindrical bolsters look rock hard and most uninviting — once again a similarity to French hotel pillows is called to mind! The frame is dull but loosely carved.

1880-1920 *

605 How much more inviting this example looks. Big 'squidgey' cushions make all the difference. The frame looks sturdy if not a little too much so.

1900-1920

606 The incurved sides almost envelop the sitter(s). This seat has the novel addition of a box spring mattress and doubtless would make an excellent bed for the unexpected guest. The framework is massive — the original intention of the *sultane* was that it should stand against the wall and not be moved. This example needs no wall to keep the frame sturdy and certainly would be difficult to move in a hurry. The style is imitating the Transitional era.

c.1890

607 The carving on the top-rail is almost in full relief, the flowerheads could almost be picked. Each end is carved with boldly scrolled acanthus, the bottom of the frame is poor with short, stubby legs.

1880s

608 The battered remnants of this Louis XV style frame are heavy and somewhat overawed by the bulk of the stiff and uninviting upholstery. Almost certainly there should have been a carved wooden cresting to the top which has been abandoned during re-upholstery.

1860s

609 The calico has become dirty and stained but it should be a comparatively easy job for an upholsterer to cover this centre seat. The carved cresting gives cohesion to the overall design and the gilding is in good condition and of good quality.

1870s

610 A very similar frame but of lesser quality finish. The carving is almost identical and quite possibly was from the same workshops. However, this beechwood frame has simply been painted white to cut down on the initial cost. Frames of this light, painted colour became dirty quite quickly and can soon look shabby but they are very elegant and restrained in good condition.

1870s

611 A rare example of a metamorphic centre settee in walnut. It closely follows the mid-nineteenth century French interpretation of the Louis XV style. There are two long settees or *canapés* and a *bergère* at either end. All four pieces are simply clipped together with steel latches. Very useful if one needs to clear a room for a reception and arrange the seats around the room. However, too large for most houses.

1860s

612 A *duchesse-brisée* in two parts only, made up as a very comfortable *bergère* and a rather awkward and useless 'long footstool', especially when separated from the chair. The frame has a simple, clean and elegant line.

1850s ✳

The duchesse *or* duchesse-brisée *became popular in the 1750s in the new drive for comfort inspired by the French court at Versailles. The* duchesse *is essentially a day bed with one end taller than the other — an armchair and a low chauffeuse joined together by a stool or tabouret. They are seen fixed together as a simple* duchesse *or in two or three parts called a* duchesse-brisée. *They were very popular in the eighteenth century but a little too casual for the more formal idea of comfort required in the nineteenth century. A few examples were made in the second half of the nineteenth century, mainly as part of a larger 'Louis' suite.*

613 Like an unsure ballet dancer on her first night, this *duchesse* appears to be standing on its *pointes* as if uncertain of which direction to hop. It is a good job that the seat is all one piece and not *'brisée'* as one would be left with the feeling that it was about to separate. The whole outline is too stiff and inhibited to be confused with an original example.

c.1900 ✳

614 (above) *Brisée* in three parts imitating the Louis XVI style. The stiffly designed frame is cheaply made and gilt with the worst quality gold paint. It is, however, a good example of a three part *duchesse* with two quite sensible armchairs and a stool which is small enough to move around a room as required.

c.1900

615 (right) Halfway between a *duchesse* and a *méridienne* which became popular at the beginning of the nineteenth century but should have overscrolled ends, with or without a back support. The upholstery on this example will need a lot of refurbishing, the tired frame needs cleaning and the gilding needs considerable retouching.

1900-1910 ✳

SEAT FURNITURE — Stools

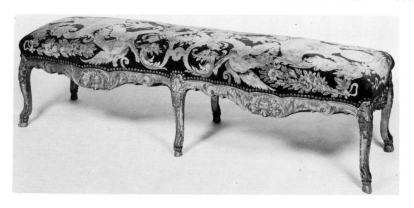

616 This elegant stool is a late nineteenth century frame with Royal Savonnerie upholstery from the Louis XV period. The upholstery is worth many times the value of the frame. However the frame is quite sympathetically carved with bold trailing acanthus and scalloped cartouches. The feet terminate in that wonderfully French foot known as *pieds de biche*. These long stools were commonly made in large sets with a drawing room suite.

The frame c.1890 *
The upholstery 1730s

617 Empire revival at its worst. The quality of some of the tremendously popular Empire revival furniture of the late nineteenth and early twentieth centuries was in many cases the worst ever applied to the furniture industry. The heavy drop-in seat is applied with modern machine made silks. The frieze is applied with mounts of the poorest quality which are repeated on almost every item of 'Empire' furniture of this period. The winged lion mask mounts are dreadful and in this case are now secured by several large screws of completely the wrong type. The boldly hipped legs, which must have required a considerable amount of wood, are let down by the *sabots* which are plainly a size too big — a good example of the maker ordering his mounts from a supplier and not getting the measurements correct.

c.1900

618 The rope-twist stool frame designed by A-M-E Fournier that inspired the Baccarat glass factory to imitate the rope-twist in glass seats. This stool compares to the side chair no.576 attributed to the same designer. A similar stool is in the Château de Compiègne. A wonderful example of nineteenth century virtuosity.

c.1860

619 An unusual stool in finely carved giltwood in direct Louis XIV style. The frame might be a little overdecorated for the small legs. This type of stool originally developed from the *tabouret en 'X'* which had a removable top and a folding frame.

c.1850

620 The Grand Cabinet de la Reine at Saint-Cloud was supplied with two of these *tabourets de pied* which serve a useful purpose for both human feet and man's best friend. The originals were made by Claude Sené in 1788, having firstly been modelled in wax.

c.1860

Cane seats have been popular since the seventeenth century in most furniture producing countries. In France split cane was extensively used for the more everyday furniture and chairs and enjoyed tremendous popularity during the nineteenth century. Many thousands of small occasional chairs designed by Le Bouteiller in the 1830s, such as illustration 581, have seats of natural fibres such as cane, rattan or rush seating. The light framed beechwood side chair with many uses and a cane back or seat, or both, became the archetypal French chair and was of a surprisingly robust nature but very definitely was intended as a cheaper form of furniture.

621 A small Louis XV style armchair most commonly used as a desk chair. The frame meekly follows eighteenth century principles. This one is gilt.

c.1900

622 Another desk chair, made, unusually for the nineteenth century, in oak. The feet are too sit up and beg for comfort and would normally be half an inch shorter on an eighteenth century model. The 'double caned' sides are a plus, a feature that is always popular.

Early twentieth century

623 A vigorous parcel-gilt beechwood *bergère*, the gilding making an elegant highlight. The back and sides are double-caned but the seat is upholstered. The front legs are spread uncomfortably wide.

c.1900

624 This restrained chair was from a very good quality set of eighteen. Once again there is a small amount of parcel-gilding to heighten the carving. A light but sturdy chair.

c.1900

625 A regal child's chair with the family crest carved on the top-rail. As so often happens, the reduction in size from an adult piece to a child's results in awkward proportions.

1860s

626 The double caning on this small *canapé* gives a very pretty and light effect. The carving is deep and profuse but a little crude.

1880s ∗

627 No amount of parcel-gilding can obviate the uncomfortable shape of the back support with its odd central cartouche.

c.1900

628 Can you spot the lot number ticket? It leads the eye to the unnecessarily thick apron which spoils the proportion of the settee. The carving is gilt onto white paint. A sturdy seat but hardly elegant.

1880s

629 A cheaply made settee but still with double-caning. The inverted breakfront seat is a novelty but would enable a female sitter to use the seat without creasing a voluminous dress too much. The top-rail is similarly dipped and carved with a pathetic gesture of marguerites.

1900s

630 The unusual combination of tulipwood crossbanding onto an oak frame is an attractive feature, in this case added to with token foliate gilt-bronze mounts. The low 'wings' on the side chair have been incorporated for strength but spoil the lightness of design.

Early twentieth century

The craft traditions of weaving split cane are being revived on a large scale and it is now not too difficult to find craftsmen who will renew cane panels or repair old damaged panels. In the larger urban areas weavers can often be seen applying their art on street corners during the summer months. Many evening classes now teach cane weaving and it has become a popular domestic pastime. It also has a distinct economic advantage as damaged cane furniture can be bought relatively cheaply.

631 A fine example of the wood carver's art perhaps but hardly suitable on a cane *duchesse*. The woven baskets of summer flowers joining the sweeps of the back are a delightful touch. The legs appear too thin to support the weight of carving but the overall effect is bound to be popular.

c.1900

632 Rattan, split cane, bamboo and wicker are incorporated in this garden seat made by Perret Viebert in Paris. Few of these chairs survive although they were made in large numbers. The design is somewhat novel with contrasting colours for added decorative effect.

c.1890

633 A triumph of wicker-work! This delightful chair is of a type that became popular in France during the mid years of the reign of Napoleon III in the craze for light and naturalism. The 'twist turning' on the legs is typically French but the numerous clusters of 'bobbins' are most unusual. The pockets at the top of each leg would be most suitable for stirrup cups. Many chairs of this type were made both in French and American factories.

1860-1900

STANDS

The centre stand or gaine was a much used decorative feature in France for displaying large Sèvres vases or decorative pieces of sculpture.

634 A very heavy but grand *gaine* signed on the metalwork by F. Linke. The quality of both the woodwork and the *bronze doré* mounts is unquestionable. All the flowers and leaves appear to be still growing and the lion masks at the capital of each corner have pelts, tails and all, casually hanging down the sides. They really do appear to hang and are not stiffly cast. If the width was reduced by one third they would be very elegant indeed but it seems to be built to take the weight of the largest imaginable bronze.

c.1905

634   635   636

635 The elegance of the Charles X period is captured in this mahogany and *bronze doré* three shelf centre stand. Unfortunately the swans appear to be only just winning the battle of the bulge of the inverted cabriole supports. A very useful and rather rare example.

c.1830

637 Another bulge, this time held back by caryatids. The bronzes on this stand are of varying quality with the acanthus and *sabots* being finely chiselled, the masks and female figures are an inferior quality gilt-brass. This type of stand was made in quite large quantities during the last twenty years of the nineteenth century.

638 Inferior quality and design of a very late rococo revival influence. There is no attempt to quarter-veneer and the ebullience of previous examples is lost.

1890s

639 This one is intended to stand against the wall. The decoration is of fine quality although somewhat restrained in an attempt to emulate Louis XVI motifs. None of the *bronze doré* trespasses out of its designated area leaving the whole effect rather stiff.

c.1870

636 One of a pair of very fine quality porcelain mounted *torchères* after a design by Bellangé. The original models are in the Royal Collection at Windsor Castle. The period of the design is Louis XVIII but the spirit is still that of forty years earlier during the reign of Louis XVI. The combination of first class quality painted porcelain and *bronze doré* is stunning and when cleaned they will be difficult pieces not to admire.

c.1830

637   638   639

TABLES — Louis XV Card Tables

The card table, in the form that it is seen in France in the nineteenth century, is normally an adaptation of the card-console table that became so popular in England during the second half of the eighteenth century and reappeared in France during the eclectic period in the middle of the nineteenth century. Later on developed the 'envelope' card table that so typifies the Edwardian period. Instead of the complicated idea of a gateleg supporting the flap the nineteenth century designers developed the idea of a hinged swivelling top, opening to expose the writing surface and uncovering the well for storing playing cards and counters in the process.

640 The top is held by a strong gilt-bronze banding and the good quality of the metalwork is consistent throughout. The restrained constrasting marquetry veneers are finely inlaid. Altogether a useful, well-made table.

1880-1900

641 A very fine quality marquetry card table of a similar decoration to the secretaires on page 123. The decoration may be a little fussy for some tastes. The mounts hardly do justice to the marquetry. The deeply recessed 'egg and dart' gilt-bronze moulding around the top is more typical of English furniture. French tables would normally be expected to have an applied moulding around the edge.

1850s

642 and 643 Another very fine quality table, even more elaborate than the previous example. The detail of the top is far more profuse and even more intricate. Notice the banding applied to the edge rather than recessed as in the previous table.

1850s

644 A similar card table but with far less decoration than the previous examples. The join of the top can now clearly be seen facing the onlooker so that when folded and turned around against the wall this line will be at the back.

1860s

645 A similar table to 640 showing beautifully inlaid tulipwood flowers with a grain running at a contrasting angle to the main ground. With the flap lifted at this angle the top may now be turned to swivel flat and rest on the frieze. The top has good solid brass bandings but poor mounts at the knees.

c.1900

646 A poor quality console card table, so named because they can be set flush against the wall when not in use. The diamond trellis is almost too restrained — even the machine that cut it must have been tired at the time.

1900-1920

647 Kingwood and rosewood combine to form the ground for the marquetry of stiff flowers. The overall colour is very dark and the insignificant mounts have become very dull.

1890s

648 Possibly even worse than the last, with token mounts and marquetry with little figuring in the veneer.

1900-1920

649 A dull mahogany table of the 'envelope' type. However, it is very well made which seems to be a consistent factor with these small and convenient card tables. The mounts are very small by French standards but beautifully chiselled.

The four triangular flaps of the envelope card table fold towards the middle. If one corner of the top is swivelled to one side one of the central points of one triangle will lift up enough for the flaps to be opened manually.

c.1900

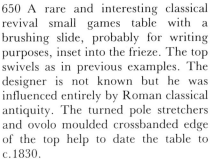

650 A rare and interesting classical revival small games table with a brushing slide, probably for writing purposes, inset into the frieze. The top swivels as in previous examples. The designer is not known but he was influenced entirely by Roman classical antiquity. The turned pole stretchers and ovolo moulded crossbanded edge of the top help to date the table to c.1830.

652 A typical product of the 1880s. A rosewood version of a card table, vaguely identifiable as in the Louis XVI style from the fluted tapering legs.

c.1880

651 Another mahogany envelope card table in Louis XVI style, this time with the addition of a frieze drawer rather than a well. The lock is signed in characteristic fashion by Paul Sormani and it also bears an English retailer's label. The *bronze doré* mounts are of exceptional quality.

1880-1900

Few rooms today are large enough to accommodate a centre table which is purely a decorative feature and more commonly seen nowadays with no other burden than the weight of a few magazines in an entrance hall or waiting room. During the Louis XIV period the centre table was normally very similar to and sometimes en suite with a pier or console table in the same room and was merely decorated on all four sides to stand free and not against the wall.

653 More a piece of sculpture than furniture, this massive and heavy table embodies Louis XIV and XV principles. The two *putti* holding the central cartouche are almost carved in full relief and the two on the massive flower-filled urn can be viewed from either side. The lower two are picking summer flowers so that the others can drape the cartouche with swags. The badly carved caryatids have turned their backs on all this frivolity. The design is muddled but the slab of white marble let in to the top is the final catastrophe. How much better a large marble top overhanging the edge would have looked.

1850s

654 The massive *brèche violette* marble at least is in proportion with the rest of the table. The frieze is strangely plain and the apron and stretcher have been carved with Régence 'C' scrolls and added to an architectural table of forty years earlier in style. Not a happy marriage, with the central stretcher and urn appearing too small for the proportions of the table.

c.1860

655 A much plainer table in Louis XV style. The rising stretchers and matching scrolls in the frieze at least give a sense of movement that is continued with the serpentine marble top. A good solid working table with comparatively few small carved pieces that will chip off over the years.

1880s

656 Quite the worst table of them all. Someone has sensibly raided the five circular porcelain plaques originally inset in the top and discarded the table which must be quite useless for any practical purpose. The fact that it is a low table is its only blessing — the best thing would be to remove the top giving it a plain surface to be used as a modern coffee table. The central boss on the stretcher was probably originally designed to have a thick baluster column which in this case has been rendered unnecessary and replaced by an urn.

1880s

657 The luxury and plainness of gently figured veneered rosewood is an unusual feature of the Louis XIV revival. Restraint has not been allowed on the legs which are profusely carved with flowers and the X stretcher, with its boring heavy urn, appears to have been made from a rococo meccano set.

c.1850

659 Nobody would pretend that this table, or the next, are from the Louis XV period but that is how they would be named in nineteenth century catalogues. The marquetry is good quality but not the very best. At least the mounts appear to fit the knees of the cabriole legs and have one or two extra well chiselled marguerites. This shape is more commonly seen on boulle tables.

1850s

658 A Louis XV style version, this time in walnut but with rather delicate carving on the frieze and stretcher. A useful and light table that could be used as an occasional writing table if necessary.

1850s

660 A much plainer version of the same table with veneers and marquetry set in opposing directions to heighten their decorative effect. The mounts are not very good quality and are rather skimpy. There is little practical use for a table of this type which does not even have a drawer, although the mount on the centre of the apron would suggest that it was intended as a handle.

c.1860

661 A beautifully executed table emulating the Régence style of Charles Cressent, signed by its late nineteenth century maker François Linke. The mounts are of an extremely high standard and the carefree laughing faces of the female terms are characteristic of his work. The winged cherub's head is rather uncharacteristic but is repeated on the next table. The kingwood veneers are extremely well chosen with the grain running in an unusual parallel fashion of light and dark striations. The marble top looks like a modern Spanish replacement and does little justice to the rest of the table.

1890s

662 Another absolutely identical table with even the same choice of veneers. However, the mounts and wood need a good clean but at least the table retains its original marble top. The bronzes are also signed by Linke.

1890s

663 A much plainer table incorporating the acanthus clasped scallop shell which is so commonly associated with the work of Linke. However the mounts, apart from this central one, are far too restrained for his exuberant work. Note how the graining on the kingwood veneer has none of the straightness of the previous two tables.

1890s

664 A much heavier table with a misplaced attempt at asymmetrical rococo foliage applied to the frieze and legs. The veneers are well done and the top quarter veneered, but altogether not a very inspiring table.

1880-1900 ✱

665 The frieze panels of marquetry could fit almost any other similar table and must be the standard production of one particular workshop. There is a considerable amount of veneer missing at the end of the table in view. How much nicer the legs would look if they had not been mounted. A light and easy-to-move-around table but once again without a drawer.

c.1880

666 The marquetry is one stage worse than that on the previous table. The flowers are totally uninspired and look as though they have been picked long ago and are wilting rather quickly. Once again the marquetry panels are of a standard size and this has left a very wide 'banding' around the frieze.

c.1900

667 The addition of a drawer has deepened the frieze which is now out of proportion and makes the table look rather heavy. It is incredible that with such a deep drawer it was not fitted with a writing slide. The mounts on the drawer and frieze make little attempt to frame each section and are applied in an unfeeling way. Good eighteenth century mounts would creep right into every available corner.

1880s

668 A good quality kingwood centre table. The marquetry is technically well cut but the drawing is poorly executed. However, the profuse decoration on the top is very unusual and colourful.

c.1870

669 (right) A very fine quality mahogany octagonal table that is very similar to the work of Paul Sormani. For once the proportions of the urn match the rest of the table. The chiselling throughout is very finely and painstakingly executed. An elegant table perhaps but not particularly useful.

1870s

670 (left) An elegant centre table veneered with a dark radiating mahogany top and on gilt-brass ringed supports. The table is itself inspired by Adam Weisweiler from the 1780s. These tables are very elegant and, as long as the legs are kept tight, are strong and remain solid without too much attention.

1870s *

671 (below) This circular table bears a signature that purported to be Linke's. Certainly his workshops had produced similar tables but the quality and exuberance are not that of this particular maker and the signature bears none of the normal flow and strength of Linke's. It is just possible that this was a late copy made in his workshops after his death in the late 1930s but the table is impossible to date accurately.

Early twentieth century

672 and 673 An extremely finely made and elegant octagonal table by Alfred Beurdeley. The mounts are beautifully chiselled. However, the incense burner on the stretchers appears to be belching out rather too much smoke — even so it is a very bold *ciseleur* who attempts to portray smoke in *bronze doré*. There is a button operated drawer in the frieze for containing knick-knacks. The top is beautifully painted with a slightly earlier gouache from the Louis XVIII period of squirrels feeding from vases of flowers.

c.1870

674 An exceptionally fine quality *bronze doré* table with a porphyry top inspired by a table in the Wallace Collection attributed to Gouthière. The casting and chiselling are a fine example of the fact that the nineteenth century bronze worker was capable of producing metalwork to at least the standard of, if not better than, his eighteenth century forebear. The ewer is in a similar vein but not added into the value of the table.

c.1870

675 A very stylish table after a model by Adam Weisweiler. The chestnut, well figured veneer is exquisite but an odd contrast to the mahogany toupie feet.

c.1850

676 A mahogany table with good quality applied mounts of the tassel and drape variety with a central plaque cast in low relief with *putti* that was used by so many of the Paris makers during the third quarter of the nineteenth century. Both the flower-filled ribbon-tied drapes and the rams are to be found on other pieces of furniture, especially in the *bureau plat* section.

1860s

677 A very poor quality but small table with those terrible gilt-bronze beadings down the legs which always pull away, as in this case, as well as a certain amount of veneer. There is little inspiration in the design of this mock Louis XVI piece.

1880s

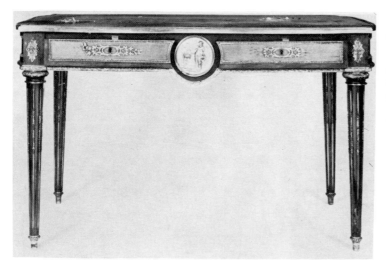

678 A very average quality satinwood centre table in a weak pastiche of the Louis XVI style. Although quite well made it has little sparkle or originality but nevertheless an unobtrusive, useful table.

1880s

679 A good mahogany and *bois satiné* centre table in typical Louis XVI style, well made and sophisticated. The parquetry trellis has an almost 3-D effect.

c.1880

680 An eclectic mixture of a Louis XV style serpentine table top on the tapering fluted legs of the Louis XVI period. The main part of the table is ebonised pearwood with a wide marquetry border on the top. The fluting has been gilt which is cheaper than inserting brass channels. Obviously the urn was so spectacular that it had to be removed.

1860s

681 Martin Carlin made tables of a very similar shape in the 1780s but would not have been pleased to see the final result of this fussy example. The marquetry top is prolifically inlaid and the woodwork generally is of quite good quality. Note that the top of the legs underneath the wide knop taper very quickly inwards which gives a much more elegant effect than the heavier graduated taper on the previous table. The hour-glass stretcher is in this instance rather elegant.

1870s

A very exotic purple heart meuble d'appui *with fine quality* bronze doré *mounts. The central plaque of Juno rising amongst clouds from the fire, held by peacock feathers, is signed 'Emile Guillemin'. It is made by the copper electrotype process and is not cast in sand or by the lost wax process as are normal* bronze doré *mounts. The exotic shape and decoration of this cabinet give it an almost certain attribution to Diehl who was an extraordinary and highly independent maker, a paltry selection of whose other work still survives, examples of which are illustrated on pages 153, 177 and 228.*

Dated 1867

The epitome of the Marie Antoinette revival of François Linke, signed on the gilt bronze mounts. The large bronze doré *plaque represents Diana as the Huntress and the jasper medallions in Wedgwood style are of the three Graces. This fine quality screen combines the best marquetry metalwork and a finely executed Aubusson panel with chubby pink skinned* putti *and cherubs busying themselves with the task of helping Cupid shoot arrows at the heart shaped target. The flanking panels are beautifully executed in coloured woods.*

c.1900

TABLES — Louis XVI Centre Tables by Alfred Beurdeley

The six centre tables on this and the next page were all made by Alfred Beurdeley et Fils, all stamped with the firm's marque au fer. *They give a fine example of the range of this firm's work which was always executed to the very highest standards. Some pieces are signed in the bronze by Beurdeley but the* marque au fer *is more common — most of the bronzes are marked on the underside, with a BY (illustrated in the maker's list).*

683 An exceptionally fine centre table with a porphyry top which contrasts with the breathtaking foliate mounts on the frieze. The whole of this table is in bronze which was often a feature of the Beurdeley firm's work. The urn by itself on the stretcher is a jewel of craftsmanship. Note the rather silly little drape with tassels below the urn — an unnecessary concession to the great vogue for upholstery in the 1880s.

1880s

682 Another version of the delightful little dressing table supplied by Weisweiler for Marie Antoinette in 1785. Two other versions by Dasson and Millet are illustrated and compared on page 135. There is little difference in the quality of all three tables.

c.1880

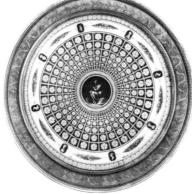

684 Here Beurdeley has concentrated on the marquetry top which is finely and inventively inlaid with a Cupid and doves amongst highly coloured scrolling foliage. All the mounts are of very fine quality even to the rather unusual bead bandings that outline the whole of the underframe and legs like the lights on Blackpool Tower. Inspired by a metamorphic table by Riesener of 1778.

c.1880 *

685 and 686 As on 672 and 673 Beurdeley has used an earlier gouache panel from the Louis XVIII period for the top of this beautifully inlaid centre table in *bois de citron.* Several tables by other makers have been seen incorporating these earlier panels which was obviously a popular pastime and certainly the effects are first class.

1870s

687 A fascinating exercise in craftsmanship by the firm of Beurdeley. This firm was capable of producing this type of work in bronze and indeed normally would be expected to produce such a complex gilt table in metal. In fact this one is made entirely of giltwood and is an extraordinary tribute to the art of the wood carver. The attention to detail is minute. The *guilloché* beaded banding on the frieze is almost carved in full relief in keeping with the twin tailed mermaids and *putti* and vase of flowers on the stretcher. The legs of the table were perhaps inspired by the maker, R. Dubois, but this is, in fact, a copy of a table in the Louvre stamped 'G. Jacob'.

c.1880

688 This is an interesting piece by Beurdeley and the style suggests that it was one of the firm's earlier works. The father, Louis-Auguste-Alfred Beurdeley, was born in 1808 and therefore it is quite feasible for him to have made such a table in this handsome Louis Philippe style of the 1830s or perhaps as late as 1840. The style is in keeping with the continued Empire forms and delicious contrast between fine mercurial gilding and well figured deep red mahogany.

1840s

689 This very unusual small table is directly influenced by the Moorish style and has a very Italianate feel. The octagonal legs and stretcher are clad in mother-of-pearl under a top of green onyx. The niches at the top of each leg are flanked by outset ivory columns. Somehow for this table to have been made in Italy one would have expected it to be more exuberant although the nationality is by no means certain.

1880-1900

690 A very handsome ebony veneered table closely based on English Regency examples. It bears the *marque au fer* of 'Maison le Marchant, A. Levoine'. The effect of the geometric gilt beading on the drawers is quite stunning and even the outset corners are acceptable but it is a pity that the turned finials were considered a necessary extra decoration to this unusual table. The Bramah type locks give an indication as to the possible date. They are not seen much after the middle of the nineteenth century but of course could have been added from another table.

1840s

691 An elegant mahogany veneered table by the art nouveau designer Louis Majorelle. The shape and form anticipate modern post-war furniture but the naturalistic moulding is typical of the art nouveau period. Majorelle always applied very finely cast and chiselled brightly coloured *bronze doré* mounts in a very restrained way to his furniture, giving a delicious contrast of colours.

1900-1905

692 Charles-Guillaume Diehl is responsible for this extraordinary Gallic centre table. The whole design is certainly very bold and inventive with very good quality *bronze doré* mounts lavishly applied with a marquetry top and platform. It is surprising how rarely Greek motifs were inlaid into nineteenth century French furniture considering how every educated person had a deep understanding of Greek mythology. A bizarre and rare piece that at some stage has had mounts added to the outset feet which have been recently removed.

1860s

693 A fitting end to the once elegant French *table au milieu*. Made entirely of gilt-bronze, this exuberant table, with a top that appears to have been taken from a design for a *surtout de table,* has no less than thirty-five frolicking and dancing naked *putti.* These infant revellers make it very difficult indeed to use the mirrored table top for any practical purpose. The boldly scrolling double 'C' legs are out of proportion to the rest of the table. In an attempt to make the whole table stay together the maker has had to hang limp swags of flowers, which were probably bought by weight from another maker, and joined the heavy legs together with a cheap metal banding. The dating of this unhappy piece of furniture is difficult.

1870-1900

694 A wood carver's dream. The carver would have had to select a well seasoned section of beechwood over 30cm wide to carve the scrolls underneath the female heads from the same section that the squashed fish heads are carved to a width of 6cm. In many cases the carver would 'cheat' by adding the scrolling wings but in this case they are of the same one piece of wood. The spirit of the Louis XIV style is there but far too over-elaborated, with an unsatisfactory conclusion to the upturned urn on the stretcher. The top is good quality marble parquetry.

c.1850

695 A far more restrained pier table influenced by the designs of Le Brun from the third quarter of the seventeenth century. Parts of the decoration are quite light in feeling. The interlaced strapwork effect on the frieze is done by building up a hardened surface of whiting which is then carved and gilt, i.e. a gilt-gesso. The stretcher looks strong enough and massive enough to hold the largest urn imaginable but the carver has decided to leave this surface relatively unadorned.

c.1850 ✶

696 A very weak interpretation of a mixture of baroque and rococo motifs. The workmanship is good with all the pierced scroll carved out of wood rather than plaster.

c.1900

697 A severe and very dry interpretation of the most formal architectural style of the Louis XIV era. Like 700 on the next page this pier table originally had a mirror inset into the back. Very few pier tables and pier mirrors made together during this period are still together as for some considerable time the mirrors have been far more popular than the tables and the latter have always tended to be discarded. The decoration of the legs and frieze is very restrained and there is a certain Englishness about the design.

1870s

698 A very fussy console table in the full bloom of the rococo revival. The vegetation hanging from the overloaded apron has almost reached the flowers growing profusely upwards from the scallop shell in the centre of the stretcher. To own a table such as this would necessitate green fingers and plenty of greenfly spray. A wonderful tribute to the woodcarver's art but an impossible piece to dust — pieces of gilding and carving would always be falling off only to be hoovered up.

1850s

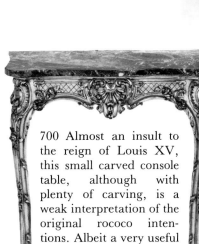

700 Almost an insult to the reign of Louis XV, this small carved console table, although with plenty of carving, is a weak interpretation of the original rococo intentions. Albeit a very useful item for a small hall.

Early twentieth century

699 This type of table can easily be imagined with its original matching mirror and there is an indent in the white marble top to accept one. This is the form of rococo most popular in England with its bold and comparatively unfussy outline. Many of the large houses built around Clapham Common in Louis XIV *château* style were originally furnished with these large mirrored tables during the 1870s and 1880s. It is difficult to be certain as to the exact origin of manufacture, France or England.

1870s

701 A plain beechwood console, well carved and nicely restrained. The central scrolled carving of the apron is a good example of asymmetry.

c.1900

702 An oddity originally intended for use as a console table with two added back supports. It is unusual to see a console veneered in kingwood and even more so to see added porcelain plaques with a rich green 'Sèvres' border. The mounts are not very good quality, the urn very French but far too small to be an effective decorative feature. This is the type of porcelain mounted furniture that was often made by English craftsmen in the 'Louis' taste but this one is definitely from south of the channel.

c.1860

703 A well-made pier table in nicely figured kingwood with restrained well chiselled mounts. The thinness and simplicity of the woodwork is matched by the restraint of the mounts and the small heavily gadrooned and typically French urn and cover is in exactly the right proportion for the rest of the table. It is so lifelike that one is tempted to lift the lid to see if there is anything inside.

1860s

704 An elegant Louis XVI style *console desserte* in the style of Weisweiller which should have a marble top. Both metalwork and woodwork are finished to a very high standard. Note once again the ever present tassel and drape banding on the shelf.

Late 1870s ✱

705 This *console desserte* of satinwood is exquisitely finished with finely cast and chiselled foliate mounts and the two tiers have a parquetry trellis. Each side of the frieze flanking the central drawer has a neatly concealed button operated swivel drawer. The tables are copied from a pair by C.C. Saunier in the 1770s. A little fussy perhaps, but very rare.

1860s ✱

706 A semi-circular side or console table, very well made in mahogany and finished in fine quality metalwork. The feathered and leaf capitals are very unusual and the twist turned legs give a very solid and strong appearance.

1840s

707 A badly made gilt beechwood console that could have been made anywhere in Europe but is always considered French as it is from France that the style, in this case Louis XVI, originated. There is little to commend this type of factory-made poor quality furniture although it has a certain use in a narrow hallway.

Early twentieth century

708 This Louis XVI style console table is very similar in shape and form to that of 697. Only the decoration has changed and become lighter and more frivolous and the addition of an urn on the stretcher is a blessing. Here the difference between legs of the Louis XIV and Louis XVI period can be directly compared. The wide square tapering legs of the earlier period and the bulbous capitals are generally heavier in appearance than the fluted legs of the Louis XVI period. This table distinguishes itself from English examples of the same period of the nineteenth century by the lightness of decoration and casual interlacing of the husks on the legs and also the strand of leaves on the stretcher that goes up behind the urn and comes down in front of it. In England almost certainly the leaves would have stiffly grown up to meet the handles and not have been so casually draped.

1870s

709 A finely made *console desserte* in the Louis XVI style with a beautifully executed parquetry trellis. The frieze contains a long drawer applied with the well chiselled factory made husk banding. Only the sides let the proportions of this piece down. The fluted tapering legs and turned *toupie* feet are just a little bit heavy in proportion to the remainder. This console bears the stamp of Grohé Frères reproduced in the makers' list.

1870s

SMALL TABLES — Tables ambulant without drawers

The idea behind the table ambulant is to have a small, convenient occasional table that can easily be moved around a room to suit the needs of the visitor. They can be used as small wine tables or for lamps and displaying objets de vertu.

There is a considerable variation in the strict definition of the myriad of small tables, not least in French catalogues, that were made throughout the eighteenth and nineteenth centuries but it is hoped that this book gives an accurate and logical sequence to the more commonly seen varieties.

710 A dull and poorly made table with a comformingly inlaid top and platform. The mounts are very poor quality. A cheap and inexpensive table but very light and useful.

c.1900

711 Almost large enough to be called a centre table, this is far better made. The segmental veneering on the top is always a plus factor. The legs look unfinished without *sabots* and the acanthus mount surmounting the stretcher is either a replacement for a lost urn or a spurious afterthought.

c.1900

712 The crab-like leaf-clasped shell motif is immediately recognisable as the 'trade mark' of Linke and the mounts bear his signature. The workmanship does not appear, from the photograph, to have the quality normally attributed to the Linke workshops. Unfortunately this table was not available for inspection.

1920s

713 The segmental veneers help this little table, but only just. The parquetry trellis on the frieze looks just as it should not — like a panel of individual squares joined together. Very average quality.

c.1900

714 Another quite large table but not too heavy to move around. The plain Spanish *brocatelle* marble top is useful for standing wine glasses or as a *table à café*.

c.1900

715 Useful but nasty. The mounts are quite good quality, let down by the cheap stained poplar? woodwork. A tall table, really only useful as a stand for a bronze or a piece of porcelain and therefore would often be erroneously called a *guéridon* (*q.v.*).

Early twentieth century

716 An eclectic version of a *table à canapé* inspired by the English sofa table. This variation has four flaps instead of the English two. A small, light table to place beside a chair although the flaps can have little practical application. Poor quality with terrible machine-made marquetry.

Early twentieth century
(and many are even later)

717 An uninspired example of French mass-produced furniture. This small *table à canapé* is *bois noirci* with thuyawood bandings. Described as 'Louis XVI' in the manufacturer's catalogues but obviously far removed.

c.1860

718 A mixture between an *étagère* and a *guéridon* but by definition a *table ambulant*. The very dark mahogany contrasts with the good quality mounts with a 'money pattern' leading from the rams' heads to the *pieds de biche*. Useful and elegant.

1870s

719 A well-made table identical to one recorded as being made by Henri Dasson but this example was not signed. In the Louis XVI style of Gouthière with a Spanish *brocatelle* marble top and fine amboyna veneers. The simulated bamboo legs are an unusual and exotic feature.

c.1880 ✱
but also made c.1840

720 This is a copy of a table in the Musée des Arts Décoratifs, Paris. It is made entirely of *bronze doré* with two tiers of *verde antico* marble. The bronze is in a very dirty state but should clean easily with a mild mixture of ammonia and water. An elegant form of table in Louis XVI style.

1870s ✱

721 Again entirely *bronze doré* with a marble top in a very similar style to no.718. These bronze tables are very popular and are almost indestructible.

1870s

722 Once again entirely made of metal with a green marble top, the legs of this table are in blue *tôle peinte*. The metalwork is good quality but the construction rather thin and will need constant tightening to stop it shaking, rendering it useless for a wine glass.

c.1880

724 The lacquer panels and fluted tapering legs imitate the 1780s and the stretcher is in the style of Adam Weisweiler. The lacquer panels are Japanese with fine quality raised gilded decoration. The top will need a glass protection for the table to be useful. The whole thing looks a little out of proportion and rather shaky.

c.1880

723 A fine quality *bronze doré* table with a *tôle peinte* frieze. Although the metalwork is dull it will clean very easily. This table is of the highest quality and surprisingly was not signed. It is typical of the better workshops such as Beurdeley and Dasson.

1870s

725 A poor quality mahogany table in Empire style. Most of the mounts look like afterthoughts and no attempt has even been made to undercut the feet into the base of the legs to give them some plausibility. The marble top is *verde antico*.

Early twentieth century

726 A set of *tables cigognes* in satinwood with burred trestle supports. This type of table was directly inspired by late eighteenth century English examples and the fad for anglomania.

1830s

727 A turned pearwood table, the legs simulating bamboo and gilt. The two tiers are decorated to simulate Chinese lacquer and the top one is in poor, almost irreparable, condition. There was tremendous popularity for this type of aesthetic decoration from the late 1850s onwards.

1860s

728 Almost a *guéridon,* this *bois noirci* table is inset with a poor quality pottery, rather than a porcelain, panel. The fluting and incised lines in Louis XVI style are gilt to give a contrasting colour but the effect is dull and eclectic. The shallow dipped top would make it most unsuitable for constant use.

1870s

729 This beautifully made ivory inlaid table could quite possibly be Italian. The ivory is inlaid in a fine Renaissance style and the ivory stringing and collars on the legs give a refined feeling.

Late 1860s

SMALL TABLES — Later tables ambulant

730 A good example of the early form of naturalistic plant forms of the first phase of art nouveau. The top of the table is signed 'L. Majorelle, Nancy'. An amusing table, quite well made but with little inspiration behind it, relying heavily on eighteenth century designs for the form of the table — only the decoration is in a new art nouveau style. However, useful and becoming rare.

1890s

731 A marquetry table by Gallé that is taken in form from a nest of tables popularised a hundred years before. The shape is pleasing with sturdy well-made legs anticipating the traditions of the English Cotswold School. The top is inlaid with the Gallé 'signature'.

c.1900

732 A highly inventive and original table by Ferrier. The marquetry top depicts the Mont Saint-Michel. The legs are inlaid with stylised 'Renaissance' necklaces and brooches. Although the form of this table is fairly standard the designer has attempted to ensure, quite successfully, that every form of the decoration is new and inventive in execution.

1900s

733 A delightful attempt at naturalism. The tripod legs are all hand finished to give a planished effect. The top lily leaf is carved with insects and two birds are splashing around the lower leaf. The style and design are certainly original but the use of such an awkward table is limited.

c.1890

734 These small easily movable tables sometimes have one or more frieze drawers. The circular marble top makes the table ideal for serving drinks or coffee. The quality of the marble and kingwood veneers is very good but with rather ordinary token gilt bronze mounts.

c.1900

735 A very weak and poorly made piece. The parquetry top is simply cut by machine and has little depth to it. The mounts are restrained but not good quality.

1880s

Modern rooms lend themselves to these small, light occasional tables.

736 The patination of the kingwood veneers is of a nice faded colour. The marquetry of flowers is quite individual but not finely executed. The brass gallery on such a low table is probably more of a hindrance than a help. This table has two opposing frieze drawers.

c.1880

737 A much better quality table with free flowing flowers cast in almost full relief.

1880s

738 The tiers are inlaid with a flowerhead trellis and once again we see the tassel and drape banding that seems to have been used in huge quantities in the third quarter of the nineteenth century. The legs have been rather neglected and the whole effect is a light table rather shoddily made. Note how the drape above the left hand side of the frieze drawer is cut to fit in a very arbitrary way.

1870s

739 A better quality table with a *brocatelle* marble top. The drawer on these tables is sometimes fitted with a writing compartment. The table vaguely emulates the Transitional style.

c.1900 *

740 The shape and decoration of this kidney table conforms with the next. The top gallery is the same and the fluted legs inlaid with husks are very similar. However the quality is superior and the kingwood parquetry decoration more popular than the dull mahogany.

1880s

741 Both the metalwork and the mahogany veneers on this kidney shaped table are of very poor quality. The whole table looks out of proportion and rather sad.

1880s

SMALL TABLES — Transitional Louis XVI tables ambulant with drawers

742 Many of these small tables were inlaid in the fashionable late eighteenth century style with gouache panels painted with important buildings and monuments. Some, like this table, incorporated early panels into late nineteenth century tables. The quality of this is quite high with a very good interlaced monogram on the platform.

1860s

743 A very fine quality *table à café* with a Sèvres panel painted with birds within a *rose pompadour* ground. Apart from the mounts the only other decorative effect is from the well chosen tulipwood veneers. This piece is directly imitating the Transitional style and, like the table above, sometimes incorporates eighteenth century porcelain but not in this case.

1860

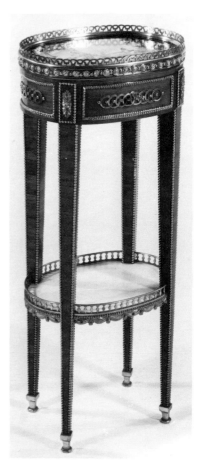

744 (right) Another finely made *table à café* the porcelain top painted with soldiers and camp followers with a *bleu-du-roi* border. A variation of the tassel and drape mount can be seen underneath the platform. The carcass is not of the same good quality as the Sèvres panel.

c.1860

745 (left) Yet more tassel and drape underneath the platform. The woodwork is a delicate light maple with Japanese lacquer panels. The drawer is operated by a brass button hidden underneath the frieze — springing open when touched.

1870s

746 In Louis XV style of soundly made but average quality. The top looks as if it should lift to reveal a fitted well but instead there is a plain frieze drawer.

c.1860

747 The legs of this appallingly made table are braced to stand the weight of a tea cup as anything heavier would not be supported. The wood veneers and mounts are of the cheapest quality and the designs a ridiculous imitation of Louis XV styles.

1860s

748 This thuyawood veneered table could almost be considered a *table au milieu*. It is an honest nineteenth century piece with only a token gesture to the Louis XVI period. It therefore has an acceptable and honest quality but is not particularly well made.

c.1870

749 A very well-made *bois de citron* parquetry table with beautifully shaded veneers and finely executed inlay. The proportions are early Louis XVI but the large platform, wider than the top, and outset tapering legs spoil the overall balance.

1860s

A very fine Meissen porcelain and ebony veneered cabinet made purely as a decorative item. The very good quality solid porcelain panels on the four doors are painted on both sides with portrait panels after the painter N. Largillierre and harbour scenes after J.B. Weenix. The drawers are painted with numerous tavern scenes after David Teniers the Younger. In this instance the carcass is well finished with an ebony veneer but only veneered on to a pine carcass, which is hardly substantial enough for such a magnificent amount of porcelain. The metalwork is poor and care has been taken not to draw the eye away from the panels, which have the familiar Meissen crossed sword marks. The back of the cabinet bears a red wax seal stamped 'st. Dresden'. A similar cabinet was exhibited at the Paris International Exhibition in 1878 by Mr. William Oppenheim, an agent for the royal factory at Dresden.

Late 1870s

750 A very plain *table bouillotte* with a brushing slide at either side and a drawer in each of the other two sides. The mahogany veneers are dull and poor quality. This type of plain French furniture fits into most decorative schemes unobtrusively.

c.1900 ∗

751 A poor quality table, probably of provincial manufacture. The spirit of the segmental veneers and marquetry is fine but the execution poor. The legs have been left too plain and heavy for the top.

1870s

752 Another *table bouillotte* but of much smaller, more nineteenth century proportions than 750. The top has been segmentally veneered in well-figured mahogany of the 'fiddle-back' type. Once again there are the two compulsory slides and two short drawers.

c.1900

753 The top of this table has a baize-lined inner section. The flowerhead *guilloché* frieze is of only average quality. The legs have been cleverly inlaid to simulate fluting by the insertion of a band of light *bois de citron* and a conforming band of ebonised pearwood.

1860s

SMALL TABLES — Tables en Chiffonnière

The table en chiffonnière became a popular form of light, easily portable table with one or more short drawers, in the second half of the eighteenth century. Suitable for the drawing room or beside a bed, they are extremely popular today although their use as 'chests of drawers', as their name implies, is limited. Most nineteenth century examples are in the late Louis XV and Transitional styles.

754 (right) This table is oval and the veneering is good quality with simulated fluted pilasters. The mounts are poor quality and those at the top of each leg are very similar to the next example. The legs curve inwards a little too much, making the main body of the table appear top-heavy. How unnecessary the elaborately shaped apron with its dreadful leaf cast mounts is to the overall design.

1870s

755 A tulipwood table of exaggerated kidney shape of only average quality. The style of handle is similar to Dutch eighteenth century examples and the general uncomfortable shape coupled with the sparse crudely cast mounts suggests a provincial nature.

1870s

756 The serpentine form of this table is more unusual. The whole table is inlaid crudely but attractively with birds, flowers and follies. At least the maker has not attempted to overdecorate by using poor quality mounts.

c.1870

757 Once again much better quality without the unnecessary use of too many mounts. The top is oval with a kidney shaped platform which in this instance works well. The platform is inlaid with an inkwell, quill pen and manuscript — decorations more commonly found on similar tables fitted with a writing drawer called a *table à écrire*.

1870s ∗

758 and 759 These two are both almost identical to the previous example, all inlaid with the same devices on the platform. Notice that the devices are reversed on illustration 759 — this is the work of the *ébéniste,* not a reversed negative. The gallery on 758 is very unsatisfactory with a crude join in the centre above the drawers.

Both 1870s ✳

760 Another similar example to the previous three but rather tired and a lot of chipped marquetry veneer.

1870s

761 The kidney shape is generally lighter and more attractive than the mixture in the previous examples. The marquetry on the top and platform is of casually abandoned ewers of wine amongst sprays of flowers.

1880s

762 A well-made table in finely figured kingwood with contrasting crossbanding. The mounts, however, do not fit particularly well and let down the finish of the *ébéniste*. This is an unusual form but rather elegant and useful. Note the poor condition of the lifting veneers on the platform stretcher which, although not difficult to re-glue, ought to be done professionally to ensure that they do not keep lifting.

1860s

763 The designer of this kidney shaped table must have made several with a platform stretcher but forgot to change the shape and proportions of the cabriole legs when this was designed without. Normally a table without any stretcher or platform is far lighter-looking and more elegant but the thin pinched-in lower section of the legs needs something to hold the piece together. Good use is made of contrasting veneers and there is a considerable amount of work in the dark foliate banding.

1870s

764 (right) The long drawer of this table suggests that it may have been designed to have a fitted writing drawer but although the top is heavily ink stained there is no evidence of it ever having fitments. The legs are a little spindly and even with the added strength of the platform the table would always be slightly shaky.

1880s

765 A pretty table in the Transitional style of Topino. The mounts are good quality but somehow the female heads on the top of the acanthus capitals seem rather unnecessary and over elaborate.

1860s

248

766 A very elegant small table that should really have a fitted writing drawer. The drawer in this case is on the other side, a fact overlooked by the photographer. The thin high hipped legs have well fitting mounts — the acanthus *sabots* are most unusual as they stop short of the feet. A light table with many uses and easily portable.

c.1860

767 Another small and mobile table that would normally be expected to incorporate a fitted writing drawer as a *table à écrire*. This is similar to a Louis XVI example by M.G. Cramer who made several similar examples as *tables à écrire* in the 1770s. This good quality nineteenth century example was made by Grohé, a fine Paris maker an example of whose work has recently been purchased by the Victoria and Albert Museum. The little button feet are novel and certainly should not wear out.

1850s ✳

768 Halfway between a side table and a card table this *table en chiffonnière* is intended to stand against a wall and is so badly made that it needs a wall for support. Both the marquetry and mounts are 'token' only. A useful table made by the *'tôleurs'* of Paris.

c.1880

769 A *demi-lune* table in Louis XVI style probably intended for use as a writing table but without a fitted drawer or a writing surface. The marquetry and mounts are dull and the construction of the interior of the drawers is shoddy. It would be difficult to know where to place such a table in a room.

1870s

SMALL TABLES — Louis XV Nécessaires

The small nécessaire à ouvrage *was an ideal metamorphic item for the drawing room. If a visitor was suddenly and unexpectedly presented, the seamstress or embroiderer could quickly put all her sewing into the well of the sewing table, which could then be used as an occasional table. The quality of these ladies' work tables was invariably high as they were inevitably drawing room show pieces.*

770 This table is inlaid with opposing veneers of kingwood with silhouette marquetry of flowers. The construction is very sturdy but as is so often the case, the mounts appear to be ill-fitting and not up to the quality of the woodwork.

1850s

771 Unusually for French furniture, this piece is veneered in satinwood. It is quite possibly an English example with the restrained porcelain plaques and rather bolder mounts that have been more individually tailored for the table and water-gilt. A very fine quality table, once again of sturdy construction and in this instance with a leather lined top for writing the occasional *billet doux*. Unfortunately it was not possible to inspect this table in the flesh. Could it have traces of an Edwards and Roberts stamp?

1850s

772 (left) The whole surface of this table is veneered with a honey/red tortoiseshell and elaborately applied with well fitting chiselled mounts with leaves appearing to grow in and out of the strapwork in a three dimensional effect. The top, however, is rather awkward as it has a very irregular surface of marquetry veneers with a recessed mirror panel and is then applied with even more bronze mounts. A very unusual piece and highly decorative.

c.1850

773 (right) An average quality table but with considerable attention to detail. The proportions of the top are a little unwieldy but at least this allows the well to be capacious.

c.1880

774 This extraordinary little work table has been made to the very highest standards, the concave frieze has been inlaid in brass boulle marquetry like an overdecorated wedding cake. Although the brasswork is mechanical the design and finish are extremely good quality, especially in the swirling stringing around the apron and legs. Unfortunately the *bronze doré* acanthus clasped *pieds de biche* are outset so much that it would be easy to tread on the leg and break it. However, a rare and attractive table.

Mid-nineteenth century

775 This painted 'Vernis Martin' table is at the other end of the scale. The paintwork is very sketchy and badly applied and is now deteriorating rapidly. The lid is of a rather novel trefoil form.

c.1900

776 Cube parquetry is always an effective decoration although in this case a little too dazzling in the smaller sections of the top. The main veneer is rosewood. The legs have been applied with gilt-metal beading as an added decoration which is coming away in several places and always catches on clothes in this state. A mechanically made not very good quality piece.

c.1880

777 A fine quality table in kingwood with average marquetry, well executed but badly drawn. Note the extra scrolls of acanthus on the frieze.

c.1860

SMALL TABLES — Jewellery Cabinets

778 An exquisitely made tulipwood and purpleheart jewel casket with painted Sèvres panels of flowers. The top is hinged and lifts upwards and the front falls *à abattant*. A pretty interpretation of the Louis XV style.

1840s *

779 Another very similar example with an unusual painted panel of birds.

1840s *

780 (left) A well figured burr walnut jewel cabinet quite possibly of English origin, although this example had been fitted with a French double lock and once again there is a gallery of tassel and drape.

1860s

781 (right) A very finely made jewellery cabinet in Transitional style with a painted scene of soldiers relaxing at camp. The mounts are beautifully finished and chased and there is a lovely touch of the two tassels hanging below the keyhole, one slightly longer than the other.

c.1860

782 A severely handsome tulipwood and parquetry jewellery-cum-dresssing table with a mirror in the lid. One drawer is fitted for jewellery below a writing slide. The mounts are finished to a very high standard and are exceptionally bold where they lead from the capitals to the *sabots*.

1870s

784 A badly designed jewellery box on stand with a poorly painted enamel plaque of a cherub. The box can be lifted off and stored in a safe place leaving a useful bedside table during the night.

1880s

783 This small cabinet is a *table de chevet* to go beside a bed. It has been converted for jewellery and watches that can be guarded during the night by their jealous owner. The complex parquetry trellis is rather unusual but a little monotonous. Note how the top section cuts off the head of the flowers and the bottom section cuts off the stalks — a sure sign of mechanical marquetry.

1870s

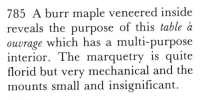

785 A burr maple veneered inside reveals the purpose of this *table à ouvrage* which has a multi-purpose interior. The marquetry is quite florid but very mechanical and the mounts small and insignificant.

1870s

786 This well meaning *nécessaire à ouvrage* is a very good, standard shape let down by terrible marquetry which has been stamped out regardless of what the finished item was to be and regardless of the size of the area to be decorated. The walnut veneer has a striking black grain which would have been sufficient decoration for most palates. The mounts, it almost goes without saying, are terrible.

c.1860

788 The unusual combination of oak, elm and rosewood confuses the origins of this Louis XVI style table. The style is French but the crude yet enjoyable marquetry has none of the normal French sophistication. The inlay is a naïve but charming romantic tale of an Oriental discoverer. Probably made in Northern France or Belgium.

1880s

787 The kingwood veneers of this dull table are inlaid with token sprays of flowers in a contrasting veneer. The top hinges upwards and the drawer — there is only one, the lower one being a dummy opening with the top drawer — slides out. The restrained mounts need a good cleaning — which must be done when they have been taken off the carcass.

c.1880 *

789 This amboyna veneered table has the engraved name and address of Paul Sormani on the lockplate. His work certainly does vary wildly from the fine to the indifferent and this small *table à ouvrage* is of the latter type and not one of his *meubles de luxe*. The Louis XVI legs from the 1780s which these are imitating are spoilt by the narrow turning at the top and the wide, in this case, dipped brass collar.

1860s

790 A good honest quality *table à ouvrage* by Tahan, quarter-veneered in tulipwood. The eclectic mixture of Louis XIV gadrooned knops and Louis XVI tapering circular legs works surprisingly well.

1860s

791 A well made but rather solid version of a Transitional model by J.F. Oeben. Everything looks rather lumpy and the marquetry strapwork, although intricate, is very stiff, as are the mounts. The rams' heads have wide staring eyes that are poorly chiselled giving the effect of myxomatosis.

c.1910 *

SMALL TABLES — Louis XV/Louis XVI Vide-poches

The vide-poche *is essentially a gentleman's dressing table. It is a marvellous idea to have a small movable piece of furniture into which one can literally tip the contents of one's pockets after a long day. One imagines the eighteenth century gentleman carefully placing his gold and enamelled watch and chain on to the table with two or three golden coins and a silk handkerchief alongside. Many of the eighteenth century examples also incorporated a fitted writing drawer for that last-minute letter.*

792 A fine quality *vide-poche* in late Louis XV style. The kingwood veneer is cross-banded and applied with well detailed foliate mounts. This table doubles as a *table à écrire* as the fitted drawer contains a writing slide.

1890s

793 Another elegant, good quality piece with the maker's stamp of G. Durand. His veneers are always chosen with care and although his furniture is normally dark mahogany the feeling is never one of dullness, more a regal formality. His mounts are always of superb quality. This table is based on a design by J.H. Riesener whose work was so admired during his lifetime by Marie Antoinette and by all the revival designers of the nineteenth century.

1850s *

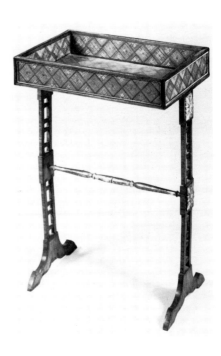

794 The contrast of the fine quality mahogany veneer with the *bronze doré* mounts is highly sophisticated. The best type of *meuble de luxe* by a fine but unknown Paris maker.

1870s *

795 (right) A spindly version of the Louis XVI style. This type of trestle support was nevertheless very popular. Possibly a provinicial copy of a period piece.

1870s

TABLES — Guéridons, Porcelain Mounted Tables

The incorporation of porcelain panels into French furniture was a highly popular pastime amongst several major ébénistes in the second half of the eighteenth century. Martin Carlin was one of the most famous and the dealers Poirier et Daguerre specialised in porcelain mounted furniture in the 1760-1780 period. Porcelain mounted furniture became very popular again during the reign of Louis XVIII and all the best pieces are attributed to Alexandre-Louis Bellangé who flourished in the second quarter of the nineteenth century. Three fine examples of his work are now at Windsor Castle. With the vast commercial output of the second half of the nineteenth century, the quality of not only the porcelain but the carcass varies enormously, especially on the very popular Napoleon III centre tables reproduced on this page.

796 Beautifully hand painted Sèvres mounts on good quality tulipwood veneers make this one of the top quality centre tables. The couple in the central panel are playing backgammon in a garden. The stands of these tables are invariably ebonised wood with *bronze doré* supports.

c.1870

799 This smaller circular table is fairly common, the porcelain held by engraved brass mounts. It is important to check that the ceramic content is in fact porcelain and not pottery as the latter is far less valuable.

1870s

797 and 798 The oval top is rather uncommon, with the added interest of family scenes in the panels divided by royal portraits. The base shown in illustration 798 is typical of the period and these tables are unashamedly Napoleon III, not attempting to copy an earlier style.

c.1870

800 This is the worst possible quality of both metalwork and pottery with transfer printed decoration. The rather wispy portrait of the girl in the centre is typical of the late nineteenth century and is almost photographic.

1890s

801 Most of these tables have a poor quality turned *bois noirci* centre column. This rare example is held by a rickety porcelain centre stem painted with flowers on a beautiful pastel blue ground. The quality throughout of both metalwork and porcelain is very high but the decoration and the rather cluttered and unnecessary swags of chains leave a lot to be desired. There is little one can do with a table of this type but to stand it in a room well out of the way of children or dogs and it certainly is not possible to find an even surface to stand anything on the top.

1860s

802 The frame of this table is gilt-bronze, in this instance with a pottery top bearing the artist's signature 'Picard'. At least the shallow bowl has a more practical use than the previous example and the strong tripod framework is far more sturdy.

1860s

803(below) This is the revival of the interest in Napoleon that became fashionable from c.1880 onwards. Napoleon himself is portrayed in the centre panel with important marshalls and ladies of his court around the outside. The base reflects more the Charles X period than the Empire period, underlined by the burnished *bronze doré* swans. The winged victories on each side of the concave triangular pedestal are an imitation of the work of Thomire. This is an unusual example of this type of centre table or *guéridon,* although again for decorative rather than practical use.

1880s

804 (right) Another example, the top painted with Louis XVI and his court with very bold corbel supports. The quality of the rest of the woodwork, however, in keeping with most of these tables, is very poor. As a general rule of thumb, if the top is pottery the metalwork and woodwork will not be as good a quality as the combination with a porcelain top. This example is porcelain but of the lowest quality. The top is signed by the artist, C. Rochette.

c.1880

TABLES — Guéridons

805 The quality of the metalwork is fit for an Emperor. This *verde antico* marble and bronze table bears a crowned 'N' mark and the stamp 'Tuil' in a *marque au fer,* and most probably was made for Napoleon III for the Tuileries. The overall effect is massive and although only 69.5cm wide, it is impossible for one person to move it unaided. The design is an early indication of the return to the early nineteenth century style that became popular in France, also in the rest of Europe, in the guise of the Biedermeier and Regency styles during the last quarter of the nineteenth century. This table is a little too massive even for the masculine Empire style. The feet are out of proportion with the table itself and the concave sided triangular base is far too large. Somehow even the swags of flowers are too stiff. However, a very rare table of exceptional quality.

c.1865

807 (below) This eclectic mixture of early eighteenth century forms is cast from good quality dipped brass and not mercury gilt *bronze doré.* The hand chiselling has been well finished but the overall effect is of a very bright brassy colour. The bright green malachite top is good quality hardstone veneer from Russia and makes a strong decorative contrast with the metalwork. The design of the support with its baby faced cherubs is novel but how much lighter the whole effect would have been without the base, which is surely not needed for strength.

Last quarter nineteenth century

806 More a piece of sculpture than furniture. The carved wood monkeys and caryatids lead to distraught looking lion masks which rest on bearded satyr masks who are having to put up with having their ears pulled by frolicking *putti.* The whole weight of carving rests on the backs of three complaining tortoises. This tall stand is unusually high, approximately 150cm. The carving is an exceptional example of a type of revived Régence style. Napoleon III at its best.

1860s

808 (right) Very mechanical gilt-bronze but nevertheless decorative and useful, the casting is typical of French foundries under the Second Empire and later. An interesting sign of quality is that great attention has been paid to each of the caryatids' faces, each one a portrait of a different girl. Here the theory often discussed at length by students of the fine arts is partly proved. French carvers and bronze modellers invariably model the exposed but delicate parts of the female anatomy pointing out quite dramatically sideways — whilst the English carver keeps everything looking more or less straight ahead. A useful rule of thumb when deciding the nationality of a piece!

1870s

810 (right) A very rare copy of a Louis XVI *serviteur-fidèle* with a top platform of finely painted Sèvres porcelain that is adjustable for height. A novel arrangement based on the principles of the English tripod table and dumbwaiter, which is why these tables are sometimes erroneously called *serviteurs-muets*.

1870s *

809 (above) A beautiful rosewood example of the Charles X Gothic revival. This is a period always much loved by furniture dealers, decorators and specialists but one that has only within the last year or so become popular on a wider basis. In keeping with this particular Gothic revival the form and shape of this occasional table is standard for the period and indeed compares with English Regency shapes. Only the decoration is 'Gothic' — the stringing and the attention to the details of the frieze and lunettes attached rather spuriously to the column. Unfortunately it is not possible to see the delicate holly interlaced stringing on the top.

Late 1820s

811 A humble but very useful article of furniture bearing the stamp of Lacroix of Nice (reproduced in retailers' list). The walnut top is inlaid with a rustic scene in keeping with this very provincial piece.

Nice was still a part of the Italian state of Genoa until 1860 which makes establishing the true nationality of Niçoise furniture a little hazardous.

1860s

812 Another example of the early nineteenth century Gothic. This large *guéridon à abattant,* so named because the top tips up enabling the table to be left out of the way in a corner of the room when not in use, would mainly be used as an informal supper table. The twelve sided top is unusually complex — more than eight sides is rare. Once again the form is based on current early nineteenth century examples, only the decoration being Gothic.

Late 1820s

813 A bronze base cast in the 'antique' Roman style that first became popular after important archaeological discoveries in the third quarter of the eighteenth century. The tripod support has a twist-turned centre column which is difficult to see in the photograph. The specimen marble top is attractively coloured with the added bonus of an inlaid marble chess-board. It is essential to count the number of squares if one is buying such a table to play chess on, as not all have the required eight squares and chess with only one rook is a difficult game! Not a very inspiring design. These marble tops are now becoming rare. The marbles in this instance are Devonian, on a French base.

c.1880

814 A puzzler. The marble top is edged with malachite but not the tight swirling veined malachite that is normally associated with Russia, but the late Congolese variety. The base and column are English/European influenced but with an almost aesthetic decoration of flowers. The workmanship is almost certainly Indian but the nationality of the European patron remains a mystery. A rare and highly decorative table.

1840s

815 A large table big enough for eight people to sit at. The top is veneered in ebony with a delicate marquetry of flowers. The massive gilt-metal dolphins are rather tinny in comparison with the rest of the workmanship. Tables of this type were not really made to sit at — and there is certainly nowhere to put one's feet in safety. Dolphins became a very popular feature from the early years of the nineteenth century.

c.1840

816 A good quality table in a vague imitation of what would have been considered the Louis XIV style with Louis XVI marquetry. Also intended for use as a centre table and not for dining. The outset supports are a sensible feature to give the large top support but the design of the base is very messy. The centre column is exactly the same as those used on the porcelain mounted centre tables on page 256 and is far more in proportion.

c.1880

817 A *bois noirci* and thuyawood *table à pliante* shown open and closed. This one is of a very inferior quality, although surprisingly inset with a plaque from the house of Giroux, see illustration of stamp in retailer's list. The flimsy and rather awkward design of the support suggests that it would be very unsafe for a substantial amount of tea and cakes.

1850s

818 Simply a useful grey and green painted *étagère* of rather nondescript origins.

c.1900

821 A centre table, occasional table, *table ambulant* or possibly even a bird bath? There is no specific use for this decorative painted porcelain table veneered in kingwood. The top is hung with an unrecorded attachment of tassels and drapes. Hardly a satisfactory piece of furniture but a popular piece nevertheless.

c.1860

819 The exaggerated moulded walnut curves of this folio or music rack give it an almost naturalistic art nouveau look. Louis XV would have turned in his grave. However, very useful.

1920s

820 An unpretentious small mahogany music rack that does not try to copy, only to make itself useful with fairly good well chiselled mounts that look back to Louis XVI.

Early twentieth century

TABLE DISPLAY CABINETS — Louis XV

The smaller table display cabinets are an excellent investment for the collector with only a limited area to display a collection of small objects, netsuke, coins or an assorted display of knick-knacks. The contents can be easily seen and displayed and examined in some detail without having to be removed by the inquisitive. Their main disadvantage is that the top surface does not make a very satisfactory table top and that to stand anything on the top permanently not only hinders viewing but becomes in the way if the top has to be opened. The most useful have glazed sides as well as a glazed top but, by the very nature of their purpose, there is rarely a drawer to keep boxes, stands and the accoutrements that go with the collection.

823 A small *guéridon* display table of cartouche shape. A useful and mobile cabinet, quite well made but let down by the stretcher, which it would look far lighter and more elegant without.

c.1880

822 The grandest of them all. A very fine quality cabinet of unusual proportions but with an enormous display capacity. The gilt-bronze mounts are of very good quality and are well chiselled. The kingwood veneers are strikingly marked and highly decorative. The large serpentine glass lid looks terrifying to open but is in fact a standard side panel from an upright vitrine and so not too difficult to replace. A very rare cabinet ideal for a permanent shop fitting or for the collector with plenty of room.

1860s

824 The size is a little deceptive and at three feet wide this cabinet would need careful placing in a small room. Note how the leaves meander over the glass surface as with the previous cabinet. The good quality gilding and veneer are difficult to see on this dull photograph but the table does need professional cleaning. The glass sides would probably have to be specially made if damaged.

1880s

825 A pretty hideous black lump of a cabinet that would have been a little better if it had stuck to its original purpose of a writing desk. In fact this one had not been converted from a writing surface to a glazed display surface although it would be a very simple operation to do so. Tassels and drapes have crept back into the gallery mounts. A capacious and useful piece but with a limited market.

c.1860

827 (right) A very weak table both in design and construction. The mounts are poor and totally unadventurous and the marquetry could be on any other piece of furniture without the need for adaptation. A cheaply made piece whose only real advantage is its usefulness.

1890s

826 A striking kingwood veneered table of unusual almost Régence inspiration. The drawers are simulated and only there for show. The gadrooned mount applied *over* the rim of the top suggests that the table might be of English manufacture but closer inspection only resulted in an indecisive conclusion.

c.1860

828 A japanned display table which is an unusual decorative feature in France. The corners are badly painted with gilt diaper flowerhead spandrels on to a dull red ground.

c.1900

829 A table of similar proportions but the addition of the platform stretcher makes it look heavier. At least the spray of flowers is more elaborate and better finished than the table above and the banding of the top is also inlaid. The extra 'reversed longbow' at the centre of the longest sections of the frieze is just enough to give a feeling of lightness that the previous table does not have, even without a stretcher. These small touches, if correctly done, can make all the difference to the overall finished look of a piece but if overdone can ruin it.

1880s

TABLE DISPLAY CABINETS — Louis XVI

830 and 831 Two *vide poches* in the style of J-H Riesener in the manner popular in the late 1780s. Both have been simply converted to glazed tops and make very effective display tables. Variations on this type of table can be seen on page 255, some incorporate a drawer in the frieze with a fitted writing surface. The plainness of the first example is lessened by the jasper plaques made to imitate Wedgwood — some, but only the very best, are actually Wedgwood and all will be called Wedgwood by the unthinking or the unscrupulous. Both are beautifully made but the parquetry trellis and exquisite mounts on the second example make it the more popular.

Both 1860s ✷

832 Veneered luxuriously in ebony with painted glass side panels simulating lapis-lazuli, this elegant table is severe but made to the finest standards. Very few French pieces were veneered in ebony, most of the makers being able to satisfy their undiscerning clients with the much cheaper ebonised softwoods — the *bois noirci* is normally ebonised pearwood.

c.1870 ✷

833 The last throes of Louis XVI's reign produced this shape of table and the severe limited and plain decoration is from the Directorate period immediately after the Revolution. The quality of this nineteenth century example does not do justice to the very high standards that were applied to the making of furniture which at this time had reached a peak. How plain the stretcher looks without a good gutsy urn.

c.1900

835 A brass table with bevelled glazed panels and shelf. This little table is an obviously nineteenth century piece vaguely following the Louis XVI style with an hourglass stretcher in the style of Adam Weisweiler. From the mid-nineteenth century onwards there was a great vogue for producing highly ornamental metal furniture. A comparatively rare piece that is almost guaranteed to wobble.

1880s

834 A handsome ebonised display table, the fluting gilt and not inset with brass fillets as happens frequently. A plain table and one that can be used for display purposes without the eye being led away by an over fussy piece of functional furniture. The heaviness suggests a Germanic origin but heaviness alone is not enough to determine the nationality.

c.1880

836 One of a pair of good quality display tables by Henri Dasson. The fluted tapering legs have unusual scrolled ionic capitals of gilt-bronze. The appearance is slightly heavy for Dasson's work and the mounts are not of the high quality normally expected from his workshops. However, the signature is genuine. Possibly Dasson knew that he was dealing with a client who would take a long time to pay and built in an 'interest rate' by applying cheaper mounts?

Dated 1886

838 The form of 836 (above) has been effectively boxed in to make a convenient, fairly capacious, centre display unit in mahogany.

c.1880

837 An elegant combination of mahogany and turned brass, based on a table by Riesener made for Marie-Antoinette, which is now in the Louvre. The legs are inset with brass fillets.

c.1870

MINIATURE DISPLAY CABINETS

839 A rather sweet little table cabinet for *bijouterie* and *vertu* of the type with poor quality mounts and 'Vernis Martin' decoration popular at the end of the nineteenth century in a revived rococo taste. Unfortunately the reduction in size from a larger cabinet has rendered the proportions rather dumpy. However, fairly rare and rather sought after. Approximately 40cm high.

c.1900

840 A miniature sedan chair not suitable for conversion into a phone booth but a useful jewellery cabinet in a style popular at the turn of the century. It is interesting to see that the original *brancards* or carrying poles are still present. The condition of this one is rather poor.

c.1900

841 Another turn of the century revival of early rococo scrolls producing a very dumpily shaped display cabinet with a glass top, the sides veneered in red tortoiseshell.

c.1900

842 A *bureau à cylindre* reduced to a width of 40cm and given a glazed cylinder is inevitably going to have rather odd proportions. The top half is from the Transitional period of the eighteenth century and the base from the rococo period and the marriage is an uneasy one.

c.1900

VARIOUS

843 This rococo wall panel was made to fit over a door. The decoration is plaster and therefore is far less valuable than a more sturdy carved wood example. The musical trophy is placed over a mirror. Unfortunately the panelled construction of the back is opening up and beginning to damage the decoration.

1880s

844 This *meuble d'appui* is a rather dumpy table cabinet for storing jewellery and other personal effects. The inlay is very mechanical and the mounts of very ordinary quality. The proportions have not been well reduced to the height of 50cm.

c.1880

845 A rare example of a porcelain-inlaid quarter-veneered kingwood panel. This was a speciality of Maison Rivart, (see retailers' list and photograph of label). Very few pieces of furniture have survived inlaid with this delicate and brittle porcelain in gentle pastel colours.

c.1880

846 A *repoussé* gilt brass copy of a twelfth century reliquary casket adapted for the purposes of a display cabinet. The shape and design are flawless — only the converted use is questionable. Approximately 50cm wide.

Second half nineteenth century ✱

847 A leather bound casket firmly clasped by brass strapwork with *champlevé* enamel decoration. A nineteenth century imagination of a form believed to have been used in the romantic past but with a very definite practical use for the travelling *bourgeoisie*.

c.1870

848 The beautiful red hues of the kingwood and tulipwood cube parquetry cannot be reproduced in black and white. This unusual travelling writing box has an engraved lockplate with the maker's name of Peret. Very heavy to carry around today and not of practical use.

c.1860

849 This desk cabinet or *cartonnier* was made by Paul Sormani, (see retailers' list). The framework is of veneered kingwood with gilt-tooled leather lined drawers of a form that was very popular in the eighteenth century. Placed on a desk, the shape would appear far more plausible. Not useful for today's purposes.

1860s

850 (right) A far less serious *cartonnier* than the last, although the principle of the drawers being useful as 'filing cabinets' is the same. Many *cartonniers* have a clock in the cresting and some, a timepiece only so that there is no annoying chime to disturb the writer. The naked *bronze doré putti* is determined to undo the ribbon which keeps the clock face in place. The candlesticks had a very practical use when the piece was made but over the years the arms have become bent making candles hazardous to use.

c.1870

851 (above) The most outrageous of them all. An oversize copy of a mid-eighteenth century sedan chair, laid to rest on a tall carved platform. This lumbering giant is tailor-made for the perfect telephone booth. A piece of this size would need a very large room to house it.

Third quarter nineteenth century

VERNIS MARTIN

The Martin Brothers became highly fashionable 'interior decorators' in the middle of the eighteenth century. One of their principle commissions was to decorate some of the Petits Appartements at Versailles. The brothers also decorated the apartments of the Dauphine at Versailles in 1749. Their novel 'lacquer' work rapidly became all the rage in terms of decoration, not only for rooms, but also for furniture. The prepared surfaces were carefully painted with contemporary decorative scenes, characteristically with romantic garden arbours and baleful young couples, shepherdesses and heavenly goings-on in the styles of Watteau and Boucher. The effect was given an 'antique' finish by carefully leaving an exaggerated craquelure *to simulate the pattern that had developed on paintings from earlier centuries where the paint had dried and cracked leaving rings in a spider's web fashion which become more noticeable depending on age. The whole effect was then lacquered over, giving a resilient glazed surface. Gold dust that had been incorporated in the background imitated the Japanese* nashiji *and* tamakie *grounds that had become so popular in the late seventeenth and early eighteenth century in the whole of Europe, not only France. Unlike most paintings, the furniture was not applied with a canvas and then decorated, the painting was applied directly on to the carefully sized ground.*

The technique was so popular in the latter half of the eighteenth century that many small objects were made, decorative boxes, wine vessels and a wide range of small household objects. Perhaps the finest collection of these can be seen at Scone Palace.

The last thirty years of the nineteenth century saw a tremendous vogue for an imitation of the technique, by the turn of the century most of the Paris makers, large and small, were making 'Vernis Martin' furniture. Many European countries are making Vernis Martin furniture today, more especially Spain and Portugal. The most popular form is in the style of the imaginary vitrine *of the Louis XV period. The turn of the century Vernis Martin was invariably in the Louis XV style with occasional forays into the Louis XVI. Gone was the sophisticated varnished painted decoration of the eighteenth century, which was often simply restricted to a delicate trellis or swirling ribbons. The full fury of a late romantic ideal was unleashed on the decorated panels with the wistful couples who invariably had nothing better to do than to be wooed by the gardener or spend their time on a swing. The panels were often very poorly painted and even these were signed by real or imaginary artists about whom little is known today. Many panels are cleverly disguised varnished prints, especially the more recent examples although generally speaking, the better the cabinet work, the better the painting.*

852 Neither Louis XIV nor his grandson would recognise this *meuble d'hauter d'appui* but it is from their reigns that the inspiration has come. This large cabinet is very well made but the whole effect is let down by the unnecessary raised centre section — a flat top would be more acceptable today. The one wide centre door reduces the interior to occasional use, the door being too wide for constant opening unless the owner has a very large room.
1890s

853 This *bureau à cylindre* has a standard lower section that turns up fairly frequently. It is unusual, however, to see the addition of an upper section. The addition will add 'value' in terms of expense to buy but will not necessarily make it more desirable in real terms than the two similar desks on the next page. The quality is acceptable without being high — the mahogany veneers are a beautiful rich red which is a definite plus.

c.1900

854 A *meuble d'appui* painted to soothe the owner with a pastoral scene in a mock eighteenth century style. The young gardener boy is picking fruit for two maidens that can only be described as the sisters of Cinderella. The generous mounts are well chiselled and are used to frame the door, overlapping the kingwood banding of the carcass. The Vernis Martin panel is signed 'Crozet'.

Early twentieth century

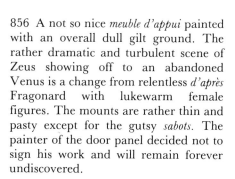

855 A highly ornate, fine quality example. For a change the mounts dominate the painting of a celestial beauty attended by cherubs. The asymmetry of the mounts is delightful. The broken reed clusters on each capital of the outset 'legs' are almost certainly the trade mark of an as yet unidentified maker. The general quality is not as good as that of the masters, Linke or Zwiener, but on a par with Mercier Frères who were exhibiting at the beginning of this century.

c.1905

856 A not so nice *meuble d'appui* painted with an overall dull gilt ground. The rather dramatic and turbulent scene of Zeus showing off to an abandoned Venus is a change from relentless *d'après* Fragonard with lukewarm female figures. The mounts are rather thin and pasty except for the gutsy *sabots*. The painter of the door panel decided not to sign his work and will remain forever undiscovered.

c.1900

857 A very pasty commode but an unusual piece rarely chosen for the adornment of Vernis Martin. The river landscape painted on the side panel is typical of the endless oil on canvas paintings of dreary birch tree forests so popular at the turn of the century. This is a good example of mounts and decoration that have been unthinkingly applied to an item of furniture from 'stock' rather than designed specifically to complement the shape of the piece.

1900s

858 Disappointingly this exotic shape is only a cupboard but ripe for conversion into a drinks cabinet. If the long painted door had concealed a fall-front secretaire it would have been less practical — although it lends itself to being paired with a matching desk. Unfortunately the vogue for making matched pairs had dwindled by the latter part of the nineteenth century and so we have only this single cabinet of a dramatically tapering form. The veneers, mounts and construction are of first class quality with none of the meanness associated with later examples.

1860s

859 Machine cut marquetry, mainly applied with mean mounts but at least an attempt to inlay the sides which bow out in a bold swagger with a far better outline than the poor finish suggests. Secretaires are uncommon with Vernis Martin panels.

c.1910

860 A beautifully finished *bonheur-du-jour* designed in a vigorous Louis XV inspired shape with the pull-out slide in the frieze. The varnished panel is too heavily *'craquelured'* for most tastes — the result of an over-eager but contemporary attempt to give an appearance of antiquity. The mounts, veneers and carcass are of the finest quality and the design is unusual.

c.1880

861 An example of the rare Louis XVI style incorporating Vernis Martin panels. The flat top surface has inevitably become badly worn and scratched. The shape is restrained but the quality poor. The setting out of the legs, however slight, spoils the original sophisticated line.

1870s

862, 863 and 864 Three identical bureaux to all intents and purposes in a watered-down Louis XV style that hardly does justice to the original theories of Nicolas Pineau or Charles Cressent. The form is exactly the same in all cases with variation in the mounts and the quality of the veneers, no.862 being the best, with a darker rosewood and slightly more gutsy mounts. The drawer, cylinder and flap mounts are the same on 863 and 864. This, however, is no proof that they were made by the same manufacturer, the mounts possibly being ordered from a central supplier.

All early twentieth century

865 This *bureau à cylindre* is in the Louis XVI style and is very unusual for French furniture, being veneered in satinwood. The form is identical to the next desk except that the fluted legs, cylinder supports and fluted drawer dividers do not have brass fillets. Apart from the wood the quality is poor.

c.1900

866 A far more lustrous decoration contrasts with the very dark mahogany. The brass fillets add to a vertical line which gives an elegant effect. The decoration on to a gilt ground is more reminiscent of the eighteenth century. A well made piece.

c.1900

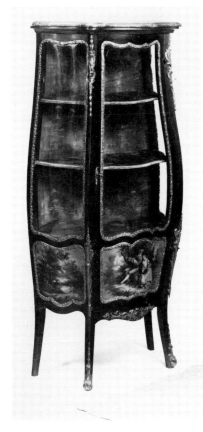

867 Like the pot-bellied fat hero of a dozen comedies this vitrine's bowed form has a certain appeal, if only for its eccentricity. The boldly shaped swelling sides would be more appropriate when the shelves are stuffed full of porcelain and *objets de vertu*. A good solid cabinet of unusual form but of the all too common average quality.

c.1890

868 Here the pot belly has sagged to the knees producing a large cabinet that has surprisingly little display space but a cavernous cupboard space below. Full marks to the brave designer whose efforts have been ably captured by the manufacturer. The whole surface is decorated with all kinds of heavenly goings-on painted on to a varnished gilt ground. A rare example that would be keenly sought after by collectors.

1890s

869 Another fairly unusual type of cabinet but far less exciting than the previous two. The proportions are just wrong rather than exaggerated, the legs being far from satisfactory. However the cabinet is well made, with rosewood veneers.

1890s

870 The serpentine door and sides are the only qualities that redeem this unadventurous vitrine. The mounts are unexciting with a gesture of asymmetry to the cresting.

1900s

The glazed serpentine doors and sides of these cabinets are quite thin and care must be taken if the cabinet is to be moved. They can be fairly easily replaced by the bigger glass suppliers but they are expensive. The thick plated glass shelves can be easily chipped at the edges by their metal supports.

872 The casting of the restrained asymmetric cresting is of a much higher standard than usual for this type of cabinet and the whole appearance is of a well-made cabinet with moiré silk linings. The top and bottom of all the glazed panels are curved, which obviously would cost more to make initially, and gives a more finished appearance.

1890s

871 The pierced mounts are an unusual feature on the door and sides but are very cheaply cast. The rosewood veneer is strikingly marked but the overall effect is not one of exceptional quality. The interior is damask lined which, in this case, was a contemporary lining.

c.1910

873 *Craquelure* at its best. The whole ground is painted in a true speckled gilt Vernis Martin gold with heavily accentuated imitation cracks and crazing. Even the pictures on the sides of the cabinet are crazed, making them almost impossible to see. The mounts, which are almost unnecessary on such a decorated piece, have been kept to a minimum and can hardly be distinguished against the background.

c.1910

874 A horrible example, in this case originally painted with an off-white finish. Many cabinets were supplied painted and many have been painted at a later date to fit in with the decor of a room. Many cabinets have a similar appearance where the rosewood or kingwood veneers have been bleached by the sun, or made in the 1920s and 1930s 'and bleached to match the fashionable light-coloured dining room suites. The flat top looks almost unfinished but has the singular advantage that an object can be displayed on the top. To match the flat top the tops of the glass have been left straight and only the bottom of each panel is concave.

Early twentieth century

VERNIS MARTIN — Louis XV/Transitional Cabinets

875 More crazy paving but in this case restricted to the front panel only and 'artistically' placed in one corner so as not to spoil the decorative panel. The quality of both the mounts and tulipwood is high, with the added bonus of delicate, but machined marquetry flowers giving a sumptuous feeling.

1890s

876 Plain and practical, at least the pseudo Transitional/Louis XVI outline does not shout from the other side of the room. In comparison with the previous examples, however, this vitrine is almost boring!

c.1900

877 and 878 Two 'Transitional' vitrines of widely varying qualities. Both have identical tassel and drape bandings hanging from the gallery and the same glorified Vitruvian scroll and pendant flowers applied to the frieze. The comparison stops there. The first cabinet has a far more luxurious finish with concave and convex side panels as opposed to plain concave panels on the latter, which is veneered in the thinnest and cheapest mahogany available. Both have velvet-lined wood shelves giving a heavier feeling than glass shelves.

Both early twentieth century

VERNIS MARTIN — Two door Vitrines

The larger cabinets are very capacious and imposing, varying considerably in quality. They have a guaranteed popularity amongst both dealers and collectors.

880 Mirror mirror on the wall .... Certainly the most majestic Vernis Martin vitrine of them all. Well made with good quality kingwood veneers and five panels of couples cavorting in garden settings. The mounts, almost inevitably on this type of furniture, are a little disappointing.

1890s

879 An exotic decorated cabinet that is rarely seen today. To complete the effect of the porcelain inside the cabinet, there should be three large figures or a clock garniture on the three flat tops. By no means suitable for every taste but if it appeals you will have to save up to buy such a piece, for it provides a painting, a drinks cabinet, two showcases and three display stands all in one item of furniture and the carpet underneath can still be hoovered!

1880-1900

881 Three painted panels below the glass with the added bonus of an arched cresting panel of heavenly cherubs, holding swags of roses, presumably picked from the gardens painted below, for the wistful figures dreaming of their loved ones. A good quality piece without the majesty of the previous example.

1890s

882 Once again five painted panels with sumptuous concave and convex curves with exaggerated buttresses flanking the door, headed by very ugly female heads. The maker obviously decided against a flat top very much at the last minute and added the small cresting.

c.1900

883 A well finished piece with restrained details and mounts. The sides are not glazed, which is a very uncommon feature, but highly decorative with the striking kingwood veneers.

1890s

884 A very similar cabinet with glazed sides. Once again the choice of the more expensive well-figured veneer makes all the difference to the overall effect.

1890s

885 A more unusual shape with good dark veneers spoilt by the too fussy leafy mounts. This particular shape was a very popular one for Spanish and Portuguese makers and these two countries are still producing a similar type of 'French' vitrine today.

Early twentieth century

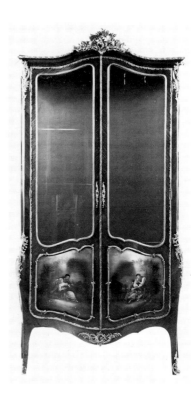

886 The flat-fronted glass ensures that there is little or no reflection of light so that the objects displayed inside the cabinet are clearly visible. There is also a sensible large amount of display area.

c.1900

887 The sides have matching painted panels to the doors and the outset cabriole legs are actually separate attachments and are consequently 'pierced' behind the knees. The tall legs give a much more sophisticated idea of design but add approximately another 45cm to the height. See how the light from the photographer's equipment has reflected against the upper part of the doors. A normal electric light would not have this intensity but could spoil the view of the interior display. For some, as yet unexplained, reason the pierced cabriole leg Vernis Martin vitrines are often of beech or pearwood painted to simulate rosewood. They could possibly all be supplied by the same maker.

c.1900

889 (below) A 'transitional' vitrine ideal for an antique shop or for a collector who simply wants a decorative piece to show off a large amount of porcelain or whatever. The shelves are wide (one is missing in this photograph) and the broadly canted sides give far more visibility. The quality of the mounts and the rosewood veneer is average.

c.1910

888 (above) A quite large five panel cabinet but of mediocre quality. The mounts are far too small, especially the cresting, and are mass-produced and nasty.

c.1910

890 This elegant sophisticated cabinet, interpreting the best features of the Louis XVI style, is made to the highest standards of workmanship and would normally be expected to be signed. Dasson especially would have approved of the finely cast and beautifully chiselled mounts contrasting against the rather chocolate coloured veneers of mahogany. The Vernis Martin panel is unobtrusive but still quite decorative. The frieze has a central drawer flanked by two spring operated quadrant drawers. A large cabinet, too big for most modern homes and one that was unlikely to have been made in great numbers, it would be surprising to find more than five to ten of this design and quality, and even that may be an overestimate.

Late 1870s

VITRINES — Louis XIV

891 A very unusual example of a display cabinet that was almost certainly originally intended to be a book cabinet. The mounts are elaborately cast and chiselled to the very highest quality of finish. The three panels are an exceptional example of small enamel plaques which are rarely attached to French furniture, of the type more commonly found on the very best carriage clocks. The feet are massive pieces of *bronze doré*. The cabinet work was signed by an unrecorded maker, A.H. Sauvrezy, Paris. The green marble top and enamel plaques suggest a late nineteenth century date which contradicts the mounts on the frieze and the ornate chiselling but there is no suggestion that the cabinet has been altered.

1880-1900

892 This cabinet is of a typical form commonly known as a *credenza,* which strictly speaking is a buffet or sideboard. This example is a cross between a *meuble d'appui* and a vitrine. The display capacity of this type of cabinet is limited. The incongruous bevelled glazed mirror hardly appears to belong to the central door and on such an exotically mounted cabinet is probably a replacement for a large porcelain panel. The feet are quite terrible and are far too small for the overall proportions. The outset columns flanking the central door are the size of a column used as a plant stand and it is quite exceptional to see them mounted on a piece of furniture complete with their composite capitals.

1860s

894 A vitrine proper with a raised central cresting for displaying a bronze or other large object. The straight sides and glass are practical and there is an enormous amount of showing space. A very well made piece.

1880s

893 A much smaller and more restrained cabinet with the unusual feature of a glazed display top. The canted sides allow far easier viewing and give a light appearance to the whole piece. The mounts are rather fussy and probably quite spurious on the apron.

1860s

895 An extraordinary decorated cabinet with bronze and gilt-bronze plaques cast in low relief, the outset columns cast with numerous individual figures. The whole effect looks as though it has had an upper section of the frieze added to the centre section with a lower glazed display section sandwiched in as an afterthought and put on the first set of legs that were available — in this case legs in the Louis XIV style. A very messy hotch-potch that would be very useful if one's porcelain collection was of an indifferent quality or with many repairs, as the viewer would spend his time looking at the extraordinary cabinet.

1860-1880

896 A finely carved giltwood vitrine inspired adaptation of the Régence style. The deep and crisp carving has to be admired and it frames a large cabinet, not interrupting the display area in the slightest.

1880s

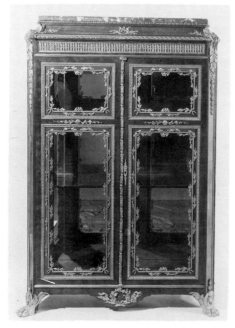

898 A well made cabinet but slightly lumpy in overall proportion. The fine quality mounts are comparatively restrained and contrast well with the kingwood veneer. The cabinet has an inset galleried marble top which is always indicative of French origin. An unusual feature is that all the display areas are concave.

1880s

897 (above) An ugly and fussy cabinet surprisingly bearing the signature of F. Linke. The quality is typical of this maker but the fussiness far more finicky than his normal style. The interwoven berried leaves around the glazed panels would normally be far bolder from Linke's hand. Not very satisfactory as an overall design and one has a feeling that it would be necessary to peer in as one does with a shop window to view anything displayed inside.

c.1910

899 An ungainly and large piece in kingwood with mediocre gilt-bronze mounts. It is simply two display cabinets joined together with a cupboard in between. Very useful if you have the space. The clock movement by Le Roy is so very small for such a large cabinet and the tiny marble top is an extraordinary gesture.

c.1880

900 An unusual small marquetry display cabinet. Unusual for two reasons. Firstly that it is on a stand and secondly that the stand contains a small secretaire drawer. The standard of workmanship is not particularly high, with poor quality machine-cut marquetry. However, it is a fairly attractive and useful cabinet/desk with clean elegant lines.

c.1880

901 and 902 Two exquisitely made kingwood and *bronze doré* vitrines in a mock Louis XV/Transitional style that are to all intents and purposes identical and certainly by the same manufacturer. The only difference can just be made out in the graining of the veneers which can never be matched exactly. The quality and style are of a type often attributed to Linke, an attribution made more and more frequently as his work becomes scarce. It would not be surprising to find one of these pieces mysteriously developing a signature on the mounts. A lot of Linke's mounts had a number below his initials cast into the back of the metalwork; certainly this was common after 1900. Unfortunately it would be impossible to strip all the mounts off such a piece in the vain hope of finding his signature. Cabinets of this quality were made by many Paris makers, especially Mercier Frères.

1880-1920

903 Another exotically shaped display cabinet with a writing drawer in the frieze. The obvious advantage of this cabinet with its four shaped glazed sides is that it can stand in the middle of a room and its contents can be viewed from any angle. It would be a bold person to use such a cabinet for writing letters and the slide was probably intended originally for standing objects on while the display was being arranged.

1860s

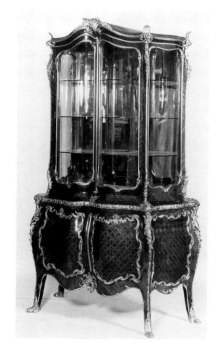

904 A large and elaborate cabinet with good quality mounts, although not finished to the highest of French late nineteenth century standards. Such an elaborate cabinet is certainly rare and unusual. The deep *bombé* cupboards are very useful for storing items not to be displayed and cases of those items on display.

1860s

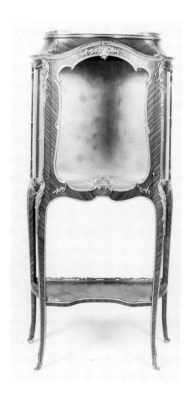

905 (left) The crab-like acanthus leaves surrounding a shell are the 'hallmark' of François Linke, a hallmark underlined by the superb quality of both the mounts and the cabinet work of this elegant vitrine. One of the mounts on this piece is in fact signed 'F. Linke', characteristically on the right hand side, at eye level, but on the opposite side to an onlooker looking dead on to the cabinet. Even if one is not drawn to French furniture of this eclectic period, it would be wrong not to stop and admire the quality of the workmanship which can be seen even from a photograph.

c.1900

906 (right) From the sublime to the ridiculous. This poorly made free standing cabinet, of exactly the same period as the last, has only one redeeming feature, in that it has a bevel-glazed panel in its roof to let the maximum amount of light as possible on to the objects displayed. Therefore, hopefully, the onlooker will not be tempted to look at the cabinet but only at the well-lit display.

c.1900

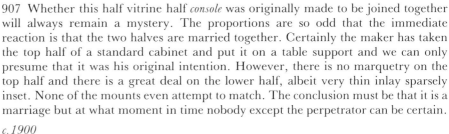

907 Whether this half vitrine half *console* was originally made to be joined together will always remain a mystery. The proportions are so odd that the immediate reaction is that the two halves are married together. Certainly the maker has taken the top half of a standard cabinet and put it on a table support and we can only presume that it was his original intention. However, there is no marquetry on the top half and there is a great deal on the lower half, albeit very thin inlay sparsely inset. None of the mounts even attempt to match. The conclusion must be that it is a marriage but at what moment in time nobody except the perpetrator can be certain.

c.1900

908 One of the most magnificent pieces of furniture to be made in the nineteenth century. This enormous vitrine was perhaps the *chef-d'oeuvre* of its maker, François Linke. Made in the last few months of the nineteenth century, it was exhibited to an astonished public at the 1900 Exposition Universelle. It stands over twelve feet high and, with the large *bronze doré* figures cast in relief, is as much an exercise in sculpture as a piece of cabinet work. The *putti* at the top have been teaching geography and architecture to the young un-dressed girl who straddles the cresting, while two enormous *espagnolettes* flank the central doors, one with an artist's palette, the other composing poetry. At the base of the door a two-tailed merman is uncomfortably placed into the story, with a naturalistic tree growing from just above his head up to the cresting. An extremely fine quality piece of the very best exhibition standard and a salute to two centuries of the cabinet maker's and the *bronzier's* art.

c.1900

909 There are no excuses for this piece, which is a poor imitation of the Louis XV style and is in the same low category as the cabinet above. The top half is simply the same as a Vernis Martin vitrine, no. 877. The mounts are identical and the cabinet has been reduced in height to sit on the tall thin (as opposed to slender) cabriole legs.

Early twentieth century

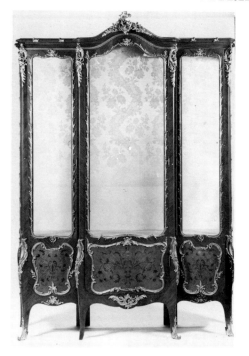

910 (left) The marquetry is far less adventurous on this large cabinet. Somehow the proportions are too tall and there is not enough emphasis in the lower panels to carry off the height. If the panels were *bombé* which, of course, would have made it far more expensive to make, then the proportions would have been more satisfactory.

1890s

911 (right) A fairly small and useful vitrine with two good chased gilt-bronze swags, one triple swag at the top and a large and individual cluster on the rather clumsy cartouche at the base of the door. How small and unnecessary the other mounts seem in comparison with the main decoration which is designed for the piece and not ordered by weight to fit any piece at random.

1890s

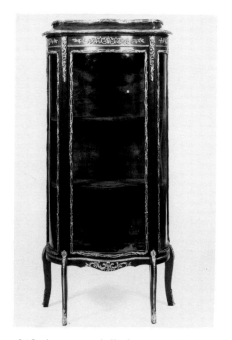

913 A double door vitrine considered 'good' in quality compared with other examples but not of the high standard possible during the closing years of the nineteenth century. The marquetry of flowers is free and is co-ordinated with the rather unusual mounts.

1890s

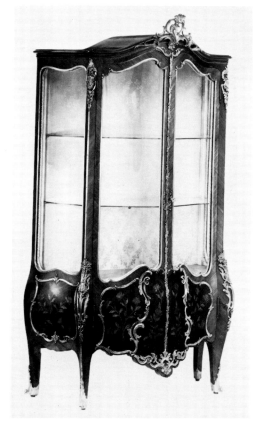

912 A very dull but practical cabinet which compares with the Dutch cabinets on page 462. The pierced mounts are the same shape and are of the same poor quality. The legs are more typically French, however, but this cabinet's origins are by no means certain.

1890s

By the turn of the last century marble was becoming comparatively expensive as labour and transport costs began to rise — after the Great War these costs escalated. Marble was cut thinner and more and more was exported from Spanish rather than Italian and French quarries. It is difficult and expensive to replace an earlier thick marble today. Therefore, unless the marble is a later replacement the thickness is an arbitrary guide to the possible date of a piece of furniture.

914 The large capacious cupboard door renders half of this cabinet useless for display purposes. The doors for the glazed part of the cabinet are at either end, a feature seen fairly frequently where there is a large central door. The quality of the 'oyster'-veneered parquetry and the bold mounts is good but the overall appearance is a little heavy.

1870s

915 This is really a *demi-lune commode*, the design of which has been adapted to incorporate two convex display cabinets. The tall legs are a typical feature of the Transitional style. A useful and small piece — probably ideal in a small dining room as a sideboard.

c.1880

916 (left) A well made neatly designed marquetry vitrine, in this case lacking its marble top. The baskets of flowers inlaid into the lower panels of the doors look slightly odd at such a casual angle. The Vitruvian scroll in the frieze looks so much nicer in marquetry than the equivalent in brightly gilt-bronze.

1890s

917 (right) Another good quality cabinet with pretty ribbon-tied swags of flowers. The mounts are an addition to the overall decoration rather than an unnecessary hindrance and are both restrained and adequate.

1890s

918 A handsome mahogany and tulipwood *demi-lune* vitrine. Note the flowerhead *guilloché* banding on the frieze which is similar to the one on the *demi-lune commode* on the previous page — only this one does not have a pierced band and the finish of the earlier example. The plaque is jasperware in imitation of Wedgwood and portrays a lovestruck young maiden inelegantly helping Cupid to string his bow.

c.1910

919 A well made and practical small vitrine that is entirely functional, the decoration being discreet and taking second place.

c.1890

920 (left) The magic hand of the Linke workshops can just be discerned in the fine quality mounts and parquetry trellis. Not a very inspiring design, probably made in the twentieth century when his pieces, in many cases, took on a rather heavy look.

c.1910

921 (right) Good quality mounts applied to a lightly figured *acajou moucheté* ground. Much attention has been given to the detail of the mounts on the legs and lower door panel and those above eye level have been neglected, although they are still well made. Once again silk floral damask is the popular choice for the contemporary interior lining.

c.1910

922 A *meuble d'appui* in a mixed Louis XIV and XVI style that quite possibly was originally made with a solid panelled centre door that was altered soon after it was made. The central bevel-glazed panel does not match the two plain glass convex panels and the stringing on the central shelves consists of only one band whereas in the sides it is two. The maker would almost certainly have matched the stringing, and balanced the shelves if he had intended the whole cabinet to have been glazed. A rather heavy item of furniture, in foreboding and unpopular black with weak mounts.

c.1870

923 An interesting cabinet or *bibliothèque* with a drawer above the *tambour* lower cupboard. An applied paper label on the back bears the inscription 'Made by P. Sormani, Paris, for Geo. A. Glazener & Co., N.Y.'. The thin rather poor quality veneers do not match the better mounts and it is possible that this cabinet was in fact made late in the nineteenth century by Sormani's widow who, in a fascinating French tradition of cabinet making going back to the eighteenth century, continued her husband's business for many years. It is also an interesting insight into the export of French furniture abroad at this time. Home-made American furniture in the French style was often very poorly made and poorly designed and all the smarter shops, as in Europe, wanted the kudos of retailing real French furniture.

1880s

924 (left) An uneventful, practical cabinet, probably made as a shop fitting but perfectly at home in the average living room. It does its job of displaying its wares without any pretensions to artistic merit itself. Indeed, after some of the previous examples this one looks decidedly boring.

c.1910

925 (right) A Louis XVI equivalent of 914 but with a glazed central door making it infinitely more desirable. Not quite the same fine quality mounts, however, except for the frieze where the mounts are the same as several other pieces in the French section of this book.

c.1880

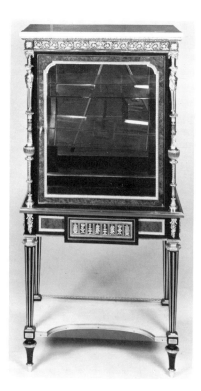

926 Fine veneers of amboyna and mahogany combine with exquisitely chiselled *bronze doré* mounts on this little vitrine by Henri Dasson in a fine and innovative pastiche of the Louis XVI style. His work is almost invariably of the highest quality, especially the mounts which in this case, on the outset columns, reflect the influence of Gouthière.

Dated 1882

927 A large vitrine or *bibliothèque,* this time with the *marque au fer* of Alfred Beurdeley. The fine mahogany veneers are sparingly applied with well chiselled mounts. This is a copy of a cabinet in the Ministry of Finance, Paris made a hundred years earlier.

c.1880 ✱

928 A display cabinet on a stand with tall legs has a certain elegance but so much of the potential storage space is lost. In this case the whole design is completely spoilt by such a weak and badly shaped stretcher with its imitation of an Irish silver potato ring in the centre. Imagine the cabinet without the stretcher and it would look a lot better. It is of course quite possible that the stretcher was added later upon the whim of a one time owner as it cannot possibly be functional or essential to the overall strength of the legs. Otherwise a very finely made and finished cabinet and also rather unusual.

1880s

929 Once again the elegance is spoilt by not only the platform stretcher which is probably essential to the strength of the legs but by the vast expanse of quarter-veneered kingwood used as a backboard. The mounts and veneers are of good quality and the piece is signed 'V'tor Raulin, 226 Bd. St. Germain'. Unfortunately the method of signature was not recorded.

1880s

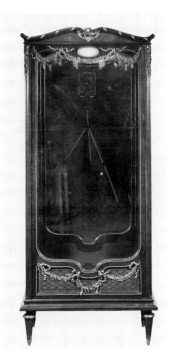

930 Many pieces of French and English furniture have a similar serpentine cresting to this cabinet but very few are so obviously in the shape of a longbow — Cupid's favourite weapon for ensnaring innocent young maidens. The overhanging ends give an almost Chinese effect and look rather incongruous. If the bow had been larger and bolder it would be more effective. The generous swags of ribbon-tied flowers are well cast and chiselled and are a better quality than the veneers. The unusually shaped door has a matching shaped and bevelled mirror to reflect the items on display. The cost of replacing this mirror today would be prohibitive. The moulded apron above the fluted *toupie* feet is rather dull and unnecessary.

c.1900

931 A fine quality small vitrine with a mirrored back and adjustable brass shelf racks with 'keyhole' pegs that became popular from the late 1880s onwards. Note how much more elegant the slightly longer *toupie* feet are than those in the previous example.

1890s

932 A much more mechanical cabinet but quite small and useful. Once again the swags of flowers are well cast but the rest of the metalwork is of a very average quality as are the parquetry kingwood veneers.

c.1910

933 Another nice quality cabinet with a jasper plaque, in this case depicting a young innocent actually stealing Cupid's bow — she will surely fall victim to one of his arrows if he ever retrieves it. The decoration is mixed Louis XVI and Transitional style.

1890-1910

VITRINES — Louis XVI and later

935 A very standard earlier cabinet that is commonly seen of both French and English manufacture. Many have a solid cupboard door and are in better, well figured veneers. In this case the door was originally glazed although many have been altered at a later date. If they have been altered to a glazed cabinet they often have a very strange look to the door, very stark, unbalanced and unfinished. It is very difficult to change the function of a piece of furniture, however small the change is, without spoiling the line, even if the line is not good in the first place. The *bois noirci* finish is tired and of poor quality on this example and the mounts slapped on without feeling. The added luxury of the transfer printed porcelain panels is the only salvation.

1860s

934 A very watered-down Louis XVI design, with the unusual feature of two long drawers for stands and boxes. This type of factory made furniture has little to commend it except that it is practical and soundly made, if not of an exceptional quality.

1910-1920

936 A neo-Gothic shrine cabinet, hardly suitable for display purposes. Made of carved oak in true Gothic tradition, this was probably made for a private shrine in a provincial area. It has none of the sophistication of the limited Paris Gothic which in itself was only a decorative Gothic. A heavy cabinet with limited use and of a design that A.W.N. Pugin would not have approved of.

Mid-nineteenth century

937 More Gothic, probably intended for a shop fitting. The carving is crisp and good quality. It is unusual to see exposed dovetails on French cabinet work but this later nineteenth century piece is influenced by the English Arts and Crafts Movement with its love for down-to-earth practical furniture and functional design.

Late nineteenth century, possibly c.1900

WALL CABINETS AND BRACKETS

938 A carved walnut corner bracket incorporating Louis XV scrolls, flower heads and masks. It is difficult to believe that this has not been made up from sections of another piece of furniture but it constitutes a useful and decorative item.

Third quarter nineteenth century

939 This ugly face is one from a set of four extraordinarily fine quality wall brackets with the very best mercury gilded bronze by Henri Dasson. The signature is reproduced in the retailers list. It is unfortunate that the choice of a grotesque bacchic male mask spoils what might have been a pretty effect.

Dated 1879

940 A weak and muddled wall cupboard with two shelves in front of a mirror for displaying porcelain. Traditional veneering has been used but the mounts are far too weak and totally uninspired. Very useful.

c.1870

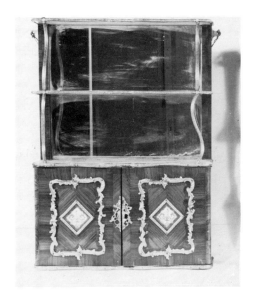

941 The same applies to this hanging cabinet which is one of a pair.

c.1870

942 An impressive example of Rupert Carabin's work. A large and very individual walnut *bibliothèque* — how hard it would be to concentrate in a study or library filled with furniture of this type. Carabin's work is exceptionally rare and this, coupled with its faintly erotic design, makes it extremely difficult to value. This inspired furniture was always made entirely by Carabin himself — adding considerably to its interest.

c.1890

A fine Renaissance revival side cabinet. The execution is very similar to that of the better Paris makers, notably Alfred Beurdeley, who made a similar cabinet for the 1878 Paris Exhibition. However, the comparative lack of attention to the carcass, which is walnut, suggests that the cabinet was in fact made in Italy, quite probably in Milan or Turin. One would normally expect a French cabinet to be veneered on to an oak ground with the highest possible standards of cabinet work. The whole piece is encrusted with various 'jewels' of precious and semi-precious stones. A highly decorative but not particularly useful piece of furniture of a quality as good as that produced by most Italian towns in the nineteenth century, apart from the exceptional piece by Gatti illustrated in colour on page 159.

c.1880

DETAILS
A Fake Cabinet

This page gives an interesting insight into the types of problems that auctioneers, museum experts and dealers are constantly faced with. This selection of amateur photographs of a pair of *meubles d'appui* was sent in for identification and valuation. As is invariably the case, initially one colour 'polaroid' photograph was sent in for identification. This is normally quite sufficient but in this instance it was not possible to be 100% sure from an indifferent photograph and so detail photographs were asked for, as the cabinets were not available for inspection. The confusing factor was that, with the 'polaroid' photograph, a note said 'stamped Cressent J.M.E.'. Any piece of furniture stamped 'Cressent' is enough to throw furniture lovers into instant alternating fits of joy and tears, and turn him or her into a quivering wreck, unable to analyse the evidence presented before him. The sight of a pair of cabinets by Cressent demands the utmost control of the type only displayed by such masters of the art as Mr. Cyril Boggis, the mythical furniture dealer from the Kings Road, Chelsea, who as The (Bogus) Reverend Cyril Winnington Boggis, President of the Society for the Preservation of Rare Furniture, in association with the Victoria and Albert Museum, wormed his way into many a home in Roald Dahl's famous story 'Parson's Pleasure'!

With the advantage of these black and white photographs the quality, or lack of it, can be readily ascertained. The front view in figure H shows very weak and thin mounts with marquetry panels that are typical of the standard of the average Paris maker at the turn of the last century, not of one of the greatest eighteenth century makers. Cressent was appointed *ébéniste* to the Regent and was responsible for leading the slightly heavy style of the Régence period into the full bloom of the *rocaille*. He sculpted his own furniture mounts and, although the mounts on this cabinet are very much in his style they do not have the vigour of the second quarter of the eighteenth century, nor the vitality of Cressent's fine veneering and spectacular mounts. This cabinet and its companion piece are probably good pieces made during the period 1880-1900 which, either at the time of manufacture or very slightly later, were made to look earlier and were stamped with the bogus marks. There was a great craze for making furniture in the exact manner of our forefathers at this time, in all countries, antiquing them to give a well-worn look. Possibly these cabinets were made genuinely as 'old reproductions' with no intent to deceive and the fake marks were added at a later date. Certainly upon closer inspection the cabinets are quite plainly nineteenth century.

Figure A. A bogus stamp of *fleur-de-lys* trying to persuade us that the cabinet was made for the Royal Palace. Note the convincing looking dowels or wooden pins (*goujons*) at the bottom of the photograph. These wooden pegs, often called trennels in England (from tree nails) were used in the eighteenth century on most pieces of French furniture, especially in chair joints. The advantage was that these wooden joints allowed more movement in the wood as the atmosphere changed and oak, as used in this carcass, tends to rust iron nails.

Figure B. A genuine eighteenth century dowel, used this time on a walnut commode from the same Régence period as the cabinets purport to be from. Note that the pin sticks out slightly from the carcass — a good sign. Also there is a considerable build-up of polish and dirt around the pin over the years. This of course could easily be applied to a later piece of furniture. In the case of the previous illustration there should not be any polish as it is the back of the cabinet but there is not even a speck of dirt.

Figure C. A detail of the *fleurs-de-lys* stamp and the maker's stamp. Cressent rarely stamped his furniture and this stamp is not recorded by him. It is also unlikely that a Royal piece, as this is purporting to be, would bear the maker's stamp if it was a genuine eighteenth century piece. At least the stamp is in a feasible place for the intended period — on the top edge, underneath the marble. Eighteenth century furniture was often stamped more than once, in various places, but this is the most common place. The nineteenth century makers, using a *marque au fer* rather than a stamp, tended to put their name neatly and symmetrically on the back or the underneath. The 'J.M.' is supposed to be the 'J.M.E.' that the master craftsmen were obliged to add to their stamp to accord with Guild regulations. The *Corporation des Menuisiers-Ebénistes* required these stamps from 1743 until the collapse of the Guilds during the Revolution. The construction of this top corner is wrong for a supposed eighteenth century piece. It should be far sturdier, without the incised dowel lines on the left or the open tenon in the middle. Both leading edges should be held by hidden tenons with the head of the dowel showing at each corner.

Figure D. The poor little English stool from the mid-nineteenth century is being made to take all the weight of the cabinet as a photographer's prop! In this general photograph of the top, the top left corner as we look at the photograph is the one with the bogus stamps illustrated in Figure C. The back corners are not substantial enough for an eighteenth century cabinet, or commode. Almost invariably the corners would be dowelled. So would the centre muntin or crossbar. The panels would also be made up from several planks of wood and not thin wide boards as on this piece.

Figure E. The back, with its panelled boards of 'old oak', almost in keeping with the rough planking that would have been used at the correct time in the 1740s when the cabinet purports to have been made. Certainly rough boarding of oak has been used as was common practice in the eighteenth century, almost regardless of the quality, however good, of the 'visible parts'. This roughly made back would never have been allowed by the better Paris makers of the second half of the nineteenth century, unless they were consciously trying to 'fake'. Also the side supports should be dowelled.

Figure F. The underside, which at this angle is quite convincing. The legs look terrible with their huge mounts which dwarf them like goloshes. The apron would have probably been more undercut to give a better feeling of lightness when viewed from the front. It is also unlikely to have been made from one large piece — the bow of the apron would normally have been made separately and added on.

Figure G. An open view of the cabinet showing the intentional appalling finish of the interior. No nineteenth century cabinet would have been finished like this. Although eighteenth century French furniture was less well finished there would have been much more effort to have finished the *visible* part of the oak carcass of the interior to a far higher standard. The quarter-veneered doors would have been crossbanded on the inside and Cressent would have found it difficult to have resisted a marquetry scroll or two. The dip where the closed doors meet should be ironed out and, at best, cut out halfway to match a similar half recess on the larger door.

Figure H. The overall effect is very weak in terms of mounts, marquetry and the lack of lustre and depth to the veneers. The features are certainly plausible for Cressent and have the same feeling for shape as the *commode Cressent*.

These three photographs show quite clearly the three stages of locking that are unique to French locks. The drawer is open in the first illustration, in the second the key has been turned once and the locking plate or tongue protrudes halfway, enough to lock the drawer and for the key to be extracted. The third photograph illustrates the final stage, with the locking tongue thrown completely for the extra security that the French require. Of course these locks may have been replaced on a piece of French furniture that now lives in another country so this guide, like all other rules of thumb, should be used cautiously and with care.

 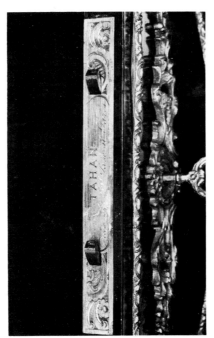 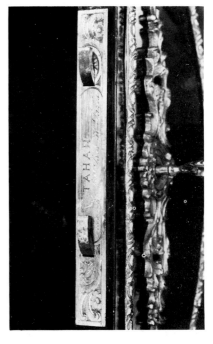

Another three, showing the three stages on a lock that holds the lid and locks it on a flat top table, in this case a small work table by Tahan, his engraved signature can be clearly seen. The lock throws the tongue out halfway, which in this case is hardly enough to do more than hold the lid closed. The extra turn of the key throws the curious curled tongue right out, locking the lid securely.

These two illustrations are of an eighteenth century lock from a period Louis XIV boulle desk. It is laboriously cut out from a steel plate. As with all the French locks from the eighteenth century onwards, the tongue moves twice to securely lock. These photographs show the lock half out. The second notch can just be seen halfway down the long tongue. How simple the mechanism is! Note the hand filed bevelling around the edges of the visible part of the lock and how the steel has rusted over nearly three hundred years.

In France another important distinction from England in construction is the long locking plates used for cupboard doors. This method appears to be used exclusively in France, whereas in most other furniture making countries a cupboard door is held by a small drawer lock in the middle of the door. The quality of the bolts varies from country to country but not the practice. In France nothing is taken to chance and a double lock is used that travels from the top of the door to the bottom, locking firmly into the carcass at both ends. The other door is often not bolted at all but simply held by the main lock. c.1880.

A brass equivalent from the third quarter of the nineteenth century. The lock does not fit as well as an English lock would be expected to. However, obviously the lock has been taken out at some stage as the screws are replacements, being far too small. The added plate probably means that a new key had to be cut, using a deeper barrel. This may be the reason that the lock was removed in the first place.

Dovetails

A very crude eighteenth century detail of the dovetails on the side of a drawer c.1770. The walnut drawer front and dovetails are all made out of a solid piece. This was rarely done in either the eighteenth or the nineteenth century unless the wood used was in plentiful local supply. Labour was cheaper than materials and therefore employers would prefer to spend longer making an oak drawer front to contain the dovetails, veneering in the wood fashionable at the time. The use of solid walnut as late as the 1770s suggests that the commode, from which this drawer was taken, is a provincial piece. This is borne out by the very cheap and nasty pine drawer linings. Note the incised lines left by the marking gauge when the depth of the dovetails was marked out. Also note the very slight indication of the saw marks that go a millimetre too far on two of the pine bottom edges of the two top dovetails.

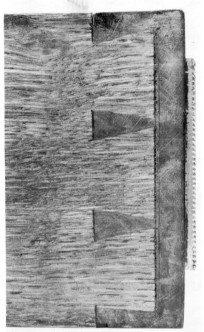

An oak-lined drawer with mahogany dovetails and a *very* thin veneer of ebony, barely visible on the outer edge. On only one dovetail has the hand of the carpenter allowed the saw line to nick the drawer side. c.1870.

Once again three dovetails with a complicated lower pin to receive the running board at the bottom of the drawer and to provide a leading edge to act as a handle to pull the drawer out — there is no lock or other handle. The drawer front and sides are oak with a thin veneer of mahogany just visible. 1870s.

A very poorly made English drawer from a *bonheur du jour* with Staffordshire plaques in the traditional Sèvres style. The two centre pins are very English, in between the two outer lapped dovetails. French drawers are *more likely* to have three lapped dovetails i.e. only one centre pin but this is a dangerous rule of thumb and, as always, other evidence must be used as well to decide nationality. 1870s.

A fairly crude drawer seen from the corner at the back of the drawer. The wood used is cedar which is not common for French drawer linings, being normally associated with English cabinet making during the period 1780-1860. Note how the drawer runner is an integral part of the side of the drawer and not pinned on with glue and nails as so often happened in England during the early part of the nineteenth century. The lapped joints of the dovetails on this drawer are not a very good fit — there is far too much air for the comfort of an English craftsman. However, by the interior standards on French carcasses this is quite good. Some care has been taken to chamfer off the corner which allows the drawer to slide in more easily if completely removed for any reason. c.1880

A shocking example of drawer making. At least the runners are part of the side of the drawer and not separate. Look at the top dovetail — where the back leading edge has been rounded off no attempt has been made to allow for the fit of the top dovetail. The sides of the drawer have not been trimmed to allow them to act as stops rather than putting in small blocks inside the carcass to stop the drawer sliding in too far. The bottom panel is a thin piece of cheap oak which, as can clearly be seen, has been stained on the top and bottom. A machine made drawer c.1880.

An unusual view of the bottom of a drawer made in England by the French firm of Mellier & Co. who had a large percentage of their furniture made in Paris and sent over to England for retailing. The medullary rays of the oak can clearly be seen. Note the English technique of having two pins between the two outer pins of the dovetails. The high quality of finish of this unusual drawer is accentuated by the rounded lower edge with a separate, applied rail added to the curve of the bottom of the drawer. The effect is very luxurious. Note that the crossgrained oak drawer lining is held at the end by a neatly countersunk screw. This was also a practice in Paris in the second half of the nineteenth century but in France the screws were rarely so neatly countersunk — if at all. See illustrations on the next page. c.1880.

This is an English, machine-made drawer made in the third quarter of the twentieth century. The 'dovetails' have literally been stamped out — cut out would be an exaggeration. They are round, which in itself is a novelty, and barely fit their· recesses at the back of the drawer. Very crude indeed and not doing their job correctly as they will allow dust to work into the drawer. The bottom panel is made of a very cheap softwood applied on either side with excruciatingly thin veneers of African mahogany or sapele — in fact the modern *ébéniste's* plywood! 1970s.

Various

Two illustrations of French drawer pins. They are very slightly larger than most English equivalents and are only countersunk to the exact depth of the head of the screw, not slightly recessed as on the English drawer on the previous page. 1880-1900.

The corner of a small *meuble d'appui* made by the firm of Beurdeley. It is a detail of the right hand front underneath the marble top. The two countersunk screws are not tapered as tap and die has been used to thread into the gilt-brass moulding, holding it into position underneath the marble. The large square hand-cut nut with bevelled edges holds the bronze column that stands out from the sides of the cabinet. The nut is incredibly even for a hand-made one. The later machine-made ones are normally hexagonal — especially the later twentieth century variety. The single screw, countersunk flat into the oak carcass, holds the top of the carcass to the sides — it would have been constructed in a very different way in the eighteenth century as figure D on page 295 clearly shows, albeit on a fake cabinet. To save excess wastage the outset circular corner has been applied where it runs with the grain, glued on. At the sides where the corner is cut out from the solid *against* the grain the

corner is a part of the main plank. This is for the simple economic reason that it is more expensive to cut from a wider plank — as the wider the plank the more costly the timber. Although a long plank is also costly it is not as expensive to buy the length as it is to buy the width. The proportion of the width of a tree to its height means of necessity that width is more valuable. c.1880.

The back of the same *meuble d'appui* viewed at the top left hand corner. The dovetails are made very evenly but not made by machine. Once again an eighteenth century cabinet would have two large sections of wood meeting at this angle, which would be pegged together. Figure E on page 295 gives an impression of what an eighteenth century corner should be like, although on the fake piece there are no dowels.

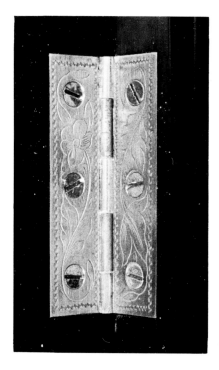

(left) An engraved gilt-brass hinge for a lady's work table. As the hinge will be clearly seen every time the user of the table opens the lid a certain amount of care has been taken to decorate it. The engraving is not very good but is at least done by hand. The swirling border is so standard that it is probable that this was done when the shape of the hinge was stamped out and not engraved later. 1850s.

(right) The lockplate on the same lady's work table showing the engraving, which must be by the same hand.

A section of a marquetry trellis that has been cut by hand. In this instance the flowerheads have been let into the veneered ground and the two lines of stringing of the diamond grid have been cut into the flowers. For each diamond lozenge there are therefore eleven pieces of wood that make up the decoration, including the four borders. The centre of each flower is a separate piece of wood. The cross hatching and the black tendrils have been etched on with a sharp point and filled in with a stain. It is important to look carefully at marquetry panels to ensure that they are in fact marquetry and not incised. On this illustration it can be quite clearly seen that the grain of each individual piece goes in all sorts of directions denoting that there are several pieces of wood let in. Some of the finest 'marquetry' is not inlay at all but incising and a careful look will ascertain whether or not the grain is all running in the same direction, interrupted by incising. c.1880.

A pair of brass nuts used to hold two pieces of gilt-bronze metalwork together. Each has been individually hand made — very precisely made at that. Note how the hand threaded bolts taper at the ends — a 'rounding off' that is a sure sign of hand work. 1860s.

A section of the complicated turning of a traditional Breton cabinet. In the provincial districts of France, which all had their own local characteristics, the traditional styles carried on for many years, from the eighteenth to the nineteenth century and later. In many areas the constructional methods were the same as they had been for many years. Some of the larger provincial workshops started to employ the use of machinery but for the numerous small firms and owner/occupier workshops machinery was a luxury that few could afford. A steam-driven lathe would be used to make the hundreds of tiny balusters and double balusters that identify these Breton cupboards. Almost certainly there would be a small local maker of the turned parts which could be bought by the *menuisier* who would make the comparatively simple carcass in his own workshop.

A view of the inside of an English drawer showing the quarter moulding or cockbeading that distinguishes England from all other furniture making countries. It was first used in the late eighteenth century but became common after the turn of the nineteenth century. The interior of the drawer is very well finished and stained evenly. The addition of the cockbeading is also an indication of a high standard of finish, making the drawer very strong with fewer crevices to hide dust. 1880s.

A *marque au fer* of Napoleon III with a crowned N in brackets. The additional lettering is from a separate stamp and presumably means that this particular piece of royal furniture was at the Tuileries.

The crowned initials of Louis-Philippe branded on to the underside edge of a seat rail. Below that is the inventory mark for the Château Eu.

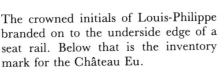

A stencil from a London retailer on the underside of a seat rail of a set of late nineteenth century Louis XV style giltwood chairs. The chairs are believed to be French and this *marque au pochoir* was presumably added in London.

'FRANGLAIS'

By the middle of the nineteenth century national borders had ceased to be a barrier to furniture styles. The political and economic troubles in Paris resulted in many cabinet makers fleeing Paris for London. In London there proved to be an insatiable demand for the French style and anything of French design was a guaranteed success. Of course the reverse was the case in Paris where the very *chic* wished to purchase high quality goods of English design and manufacture.

This, coupled by the new internationalism of the 'Universal Exhibitions' and the corresponding cross-flow of ideas, led to a singular confusion as to the nationality of various items of furniture. Is a piece French designed but executed by English craftsmen French or English? — is a piece French designed and built but bearing an English trade label? The combinations and possibilities are numerous.

The ever present French double lock is almost always the best giveaway as to the origin of a piece in doubt — a feature never employed elsewhere. The French lock turns clockwise to lock — the English anti-clockwise. The English lock is fully bolted with one turn but the French lock traditionally has to turn twice for the locking pins to be fully home. The first turn effectively locks the piece but it must be turned a second time for maximum security. This principle is the same on the long locking bar that is commonly employed on French and Continental furniture on cupboard doors. The lock, inset an inch or two into the inside leading edge of the door, travels the complete height of the door (see illustration on page 298). In England small inset bolts are normally used.

The English lock is nearly always conveniently stamped with the maker's name, but it is important to be able to distinguish a genuine French piece with a Victorian lock added at some unspecified time in the nineteenth century when, for example, the original set of keys had been lost. Some French provincial locks and also those of other Continental countries, especially Germany and Italy, are made of very light brass, the whole effect being much less substantial than the English versions. The pins in, for example, the lid of a box are round whereas the English version is almost inevitably square or rectangular with a hook rather than a round hole through the pin. English 'mechanical' metalwork is invariably more robust.

French, and again Continental — especially Italian and Iberian Peninsula — hinges are some-times set on the outside of the carcass. The pin of the hinge can clearly be seen on the outside and in fact is a decorative feature (see illustration on page 302). The screws are concealed on the inside of the door and the pins have small turned metal knops and finials at the top and bottom.

Normally speaking the interior metalwork will not be to such a high standard, but this differential becomes less and less apparent as the century progresses. It is always important to expect the exception to every rule, especially if the rule is one of thumb. It is quite common to see a perfectly good piece of honest French make that has lived in England for the last one hundred years to have a replacement English lock — often stamped 'secure lever', or a large English cup caster by Cope and Collinson.

The overall form and line of French pieces was far more restrained than the excesses of England. However, the marquetry of French cabinet work is more ebullient than that of the English. One sees therefore a classical, quite restrained item of French manufacture inlaid with the excesses of the period. This is also typical of the porcelain mounts used commonly on French and English cabinets during the '60s and '70s. In France the porcelain panel, profusely painted or transfer printed with abundant swags and baskets of flowers, will be a large and obvious decorative feature. The English equivalent is smaller and more often of an inferior quality, with perhaps several panels trying to compete with only one on the French piece. If in doubt an obvious check is to gently prise the gilt banding holding the mount away from the carcass, and take out the panel. This should enable a porcelain connoisseur to establish the origin of the porcelain, if it cannot be done from the front. Of course this does not prove the nationality, but an architectural piece with a single lock and a Minton plaque (commonly used in England for furniture mounts) is unlikely to be French, or from any other manufacturing nation.

The eighteenth century French guild requirements were no longer obligatory in the nineteenth century and so today we do not have the convenience of most pieces being stamped with a *marque au fer* or *marque au pochoir*. Numerous items of good quality 'Franglais' furniture made in England during the third quarter of the century were stamped with the name of the maker or retailer (more often than not the same firm).

Unfortunately unscrupulous dealers in the past have gently planed off these stencils, repolishing the new surface and selling the piece as French, which would have meant, certainly in the past, a higher retail or auction price. Today the auction houses are slowly becoming more discerning and are able to spot the English piece and are brave enough to catalogue it as such. Previously a buyer would have been prepared to pay more for a 'French' item and the vendor, if he described it as anything other than French, would have been thought of as stupid!

Ignorance is bliss for many and it can be extremely difficult to convince a vendor that his item of cherished Louis furniture is in fact not French but of good honest English origin and in today's more enlightened market possibly even more valuable for being so.

The planing off of a surface is made all the more easy as the English cabinet maker or retailer did not normally use any other mark of identification than the 'stencil' stamp — the equivalent of the French *marque au pochoir* rather than the brand or *marque au fer*, which went much deeper into the surface of the wood. The light stencil was often conveniently on the top of a main drawer of the article of furniture and it was a very easy matter to remove the drawer, rest it on a bench, and lightly plane the leading edge. There was no construction involved, nor any need for the services of a skilled man.

Drawer linings on a considerable number of the English examples have a quarter moulding of dust or cock-beading on the inside. This is a traditional English method of finishing a drawer in the nineteenth century, generally considered to have been first used in the late eighteenth or early nineteenth century. See detail illustration on page 303. The detail is taken from a drawer on a Louis XV *bureau plat* illustration no.954 by Mellier & Co. London. It would have been all too easy to plane off the maker's stamp which is a very light stencil mark on the top of the drawers, see page 317. However, the use of cock-beading would normally be a giveaway that the piece was English.

Generally speaking the dovetails and drawer linings of French and English pieces are very similar in the second half of the century, whether the joints are machine cut or sawn by hand. It is very easy to see the difference in a modern English drawer lining on a Louis XV *bureau plat* illustrated on page 300. The dovetails hardly fit their crudely stamped out recesses and there is certainly no pretence of a fine dust free joint.

Both countries use one or more small screws at the far underside end of a drawer, see page 301. This would normally be considered English but since the high mechanisation of the late nineteenth century, this feature is also seen on French drawers.

Edwards and Roberts were arguably the leading makers of 'Franglais' furniture whose excellent work suffered most from this 'Euro-market' treatment but, as in all cases, there are thankfully other ways of identifying the true nationality. On the rare occasions that a *marque au fer* is seen it is on pieces handled by the nineteenth century retailer and dealer, Edward Holmes Baldock. His iron brand mark is seen occasionally on various, usually small to medium sized, pieces of furniture mostly of the porcelain mounted type. The stamp, simply using his initials with the added luxury of a full stop either side of the 'H' is reproduced on page 317. His furniture is normally, but not categorically, of French rather than English make. Baldock was an active figure at the great nineteenth century auctions, buying important eighteenth century pieces from the Watson Taylor Collection at Erlestoke Park near Devizes in 1832. One cannot, therefore, assume that a piece with his *marque* is automatically nineteenth century.

There are several pieces of eighteenth century style French furniture made at the turn of this century by Gillows of Lancaster at Temple Newsam House near Leeds. Like most English makers, the quality and standard of the Gillows craftsmen's work is beyond reproach. A small parquetry *table de chevet* had been for some years included in the Jones Collection of seventeenth and eighteenth century Continental furniture until recent years when a bill for the piece was found from Donald Ross in the 1860s. The newly discovered Victorian copy was hastily removed to the nineteenth century English galleries where it now stands as a tribute to the finest English cabinet work and to the Louis XVI revival.

English furniture catalogues of the period contain many drawings of 'French' furniture, especially cabinets. Few of the more exotic cabinets appear to have survived and quite possibly many were never executed. Many of the cabinets in G.W. Yapp's catalogue were copied directly from the exhibition catalogues that he helped to compile and are thus merely images of French design of the preceding decades. Therefore, on finding such an item of furniture in real life, one could not automatically presume the nationality from the catalogue but would have to look at the construction in detail. Even the work of John Braund and Henry Lawford in the 1850s, at first glance totally French, does not have the same freedom of movement as the French originals and is far more clumsy in proportion.

The passion for other countries' furniture styles was not simply limited to France. Hamptons of Pall Mall were advertising Italian Renaissance style chairs in their catalogues at the beginning of the

This illustration is a wonderful insight into the English trade during the period of expansion in the 1830s. The industrial revolution was an established phenomenon that was quickening its pace every decade, trade was buoyant and, at last, there was peace in Europe. England still hankered after French taste and all things French, just as much as the French hankered after the English styles.

The spelling is an inspired mixture of French and English — an early example of 'Franglais'. Boulle is spelt in the popular English early nineteenth century fashion, 'marquetrie' is spelt in Englishman's French and, as for the spelling of one of France's most important cabinet makers 'Resner' for Riesener!

The prospectus talks about porcelain mounted furniture and also Boulle and Louis XIV revivals as well as Louis XVI by implication. These are early signs of the revivals that were all the rage in France and England during the 1830s. It is a pity that the manufacturer's name is so incomplete.

twentieth century, in elaborate Florentine and Venetian styles for between £2 and £4 each. Hamptons, Hindley and Wilkinson and many others offered a considerable amount of varied Renaissance furniture in their catalogues from the 1880s up to almost the beginning of the Great War. They also copied Flemish and Dutch styles from the seventeenth century. It is very difficult to distinguish from the Continental nineteenth century copies of national furniture and the prolific amount of English work. Doubtless for a long time, as in the past, the English copies of Continental styles will be sold under the heading of 'Italian' or 'Dutch'. It will need the study of many years to unravel a list of distinct differences in construction of the various nationalities, but some headway should have been made by the second edition of this book. As a general rule, the English machine made copies were made to far better standards in more expensive, well seasoned woods. The attention to detail of both the outside finish and the interior drawer linings and carcass work was much higher, English craftsmanship reigning supreme.

It is interesting to note that when Arthur Hayden published his book *Chats on Old Furniture* (Fisher Unwin, 1907) he used photographs lent by Messrs. Waring to illustrate examples of period French furniture that were in French museums. It is safe to presume that these photographs are in fact of French eighteenth century style furniture made or imported

by Warings in the early part of the twentieth century.

Every self respecting businessman in the English furniture trade during the second half of the nineteenth century was designing 'French' furniture and publishing these designs in his catalogues. Louis XV and XVI drawing room seat furniture would have the upholstery woven specially in the French factories at Aubusson and Beauvais. For firms such as Mellier and Co. this was done as a matter of course and without difficulty with the company's French connections. Mellier appears to have made many such suites in England, often using the company's identification stamp, revealed when the 'French' chairs are re-upholstered. The Renaissance had become popular after the great interest in this style at the Exposition Universelle in Paris of 1878 and the Louis XVI style, fostered by the Empress Eugénie in Paris, had arrived in England with a vengeance when the English firm of Jackson and Graham carried off one of the gold medals for furniture in that class during the 1855 Paris Exhibition. James Schoolbred, a prolific but only average quality maker of the Tottenham Court Road, illustrated many items in the Louis styles in his numerous catalogues. Undoubtedly such a large firm secured many orders for such furniture but little has been identified to date. This is a little puzzling as Schoolbred frequently stamped his furniture. Like many German and Belgian firms, could he have exploited the crisis in the French furniture industry in Paris in the 1880s and exported a lot of his French style furniture to France? If so, he may have decided to be tactful and not use his stamp for fear of inciting the anger of the Paris trade. This of course is speculation, but may prove to be an indication of events as more research is done into this fascinating period.

Certainly more pieces in the French and Continental style that appear on the British market must be of English manufacture than commonly supposed. Although the adventurous British must have brought back an infinite number of pieces from their Grand Tours, many more people must have been content to purchase Continental style furniture from British shops as a reminder. A huge quantity of this type of furniture must have been made to satisfy a wide and cosmopolitan demand. Surely the British furniture trade must be responsible for far more 'Continental' furniture than normally appreciated but in the absence of order books and detailed production numbers, definite answers are not yet possible.

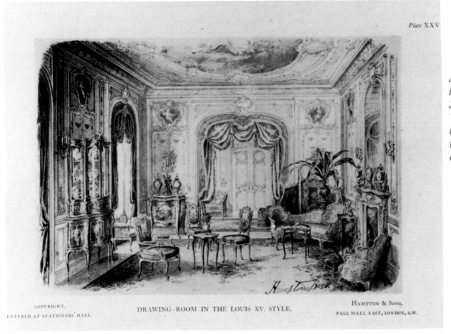

Plate XXV.

COPYRIGHT.
ENTERED AT STATIONERS' HALL.

DRAWING-ROOM IN THE LOUIS XV. STYLE.

HAMPTON & SONS,
PALL MALL EAST, LONDON, S.W.

A page from one of the many catalogues of the retailers and makers, Hampton & Sons, at the end of the nineteenth century. They were supplying complete rooms in all the revival styles, even in the latter part of the century. The origin of the furniture, if ordered, is open to discussion.

A page from a Hampton's catalogue with photographs, as opposed to line engravings, of items actually in stock. Louis XV, Transitional and Louis XVI are illustrated together. An interesting aspect is the prices marked in the catalogue. They are, from left to right, 20 guineas, 13 guineas, 19 guineas, 15 guineas and 19 guineas.

HAMPTON & SONS.

LOUIS XV. & XVI. CABINETS.

No. 476.
Mahogany Louis XVI. shaped front Cabinet, with open shelves, chased & gilt mounts. 13 Guineas.

No. 478.
Louis XVI. Show-case Cabinet, in mahogany, with chased & gilt mounts. 15 Guineas.

[No. 475.
Fine Marqueterie Louis XV. Cabinet, with gilt bronze mounts. 20 Guineas.

No. 477.
Louis XVI. semi-circular Show-case Cabinet, in mahogany, with Vernis Martin panels & chased and gilt mounts. 19 Guineas.

No. 479.
Louis XV. shaped front Show-case Cabinet, inlaid & enriched with chased gilt mounts. 19 Guineas.

HAMPTON & SONS,
PALL MALL EAST AND COCKSPUR STREET, CHARING CROSS, LONDON, S.W.

ALL GOODS CARRIAGE PAID—SEE PREFACE   EVERY ARTICLE IN CATALOGUE PHOTOGRAPHED FROM STOCK.

ENGLISH CABINETS

943 This solemn English breakfront cabinet is inset with fine quality *pietre dure* panels set with precious and semi-precious stones, including lapis-lazuli. The camel and the cow at the bottom of the centre door are very unusual instances of animals in this media. The panels are, of course, Italian, from Florence. The Italian method of hard stone inlay is explained on page 496, showing how it differentiated from traditional Derbyshire stone marquetry. The possible explanation for this cabinet, very much in the French style, is that the panels were simply exported to England. However they are so unusual that a connoisseur, or a dealer on holiday, may have purchased them on his Grand Tour and had them set into the cabinet. A magnificent and highly important cabinet at the Victoria and Albert Museum was made for just the same purpose.

1860s

944 The insipid Minton plaques are the first clue as to the English origins of this small cabinet. The paper label of 'Wilkinson & Son, 8 Old Bond Street, 10257' is another clue but by no means a firm pointer to nationality. Many such firms imported Paris made furniture, some even appear to have changed the locks and added English locks, which confuses the issue almost to the point of exasperation. The 'floating' mounts and plaques and the well-figured walnut grain are very English, as is the polite and discreet marquetry. The quarter-veneered kingwood pilasters are 'borrowed' from France.

1860s

945 and 946 Two glazed cabinets, unfortunately called 'credenzas' by those with an uncertain knowlege of Italian. Both have a very similar outline with slightly more swagger to 946. Again the quarter-veneering is very

French in style and became far more common in England after the 1851 Exhibition. The dipped serpentine doors are an English feature, following the lines of a magnificent upright burr-walnut piano that was a great hit at Crystal Palace. The heavily figured walnut on 946 is a very English feature that the French did not really try to emulate — their equivalent was thuyawood from the Atlas mountains in Morocco.

c.1860

The flat-fronted cabinets, either absolutely flat or breakfront — inverted or otherwise, were normally made in France with the extremely irritating habit of having only one centre door, leaving one to grope around to the right or left for anything hidden. Several cabinets of this type that are definitely of French manufacture have been seen with conversions, sometimes crude, to make the two side panels into doors. The addition of English locks and hardware underlines the English irritation at this cross-channel practice and the imported French models have been 'improved'.

948 There is a general feel about this side cabinet that is very similar to an Italian cabinet at the Bethnal Green Museum — the museum's example, of far better quality and very differently finished, has the same strong 'neo-classical' feel with similar rather upright proportions.

Late 1860s

947 A quite well made small — remember small is beautiful in the furniture world — cabinet with well figured woods but very stiff mechanical marquetry. There is a very Dutch feel about the inlay.

1860s

949 If there are bad points about some French nineteenth century furniture there are at least as many in the English equivalent. This ebony-veneered uninspiring cabinet defies serious comment. There are many of them about and they are certainly useful.

1870s

950 An absolutely magnificent cabinet with fine quality English porcelain plaques. The well balanced design and profusion of plaques is typically English — so is the soft colour of the 'water-gilding' on the mounts. A fine example of craftmanship with a decoration and design that, certainly in the flesh, has to be admired.

c.1860

951 The marquetry compares to the style of 948 but is better executed and designed. The egg and dart water-gilt moulding *underneath* the top, itself wooden, in well-figured wood is very English, so is the wood veneered top as opposed to marble. A very good small cabinet, unusually decorated and becoming rare.

1850s

ENGLISH DESKS

There were several great firms of furniture makers in England during the second half of the nineteenth century. Only a few of them ever marked or stamped their furniture in any way. The most common method is the plain block capital stamp — the equivalent of the term estampille. *The bigger English firms are Edwards and Roberts, Howard and Sons, Gillows and Johnstone and Jeanes. One or two of the Arts and Crafts makers also employed the stamp, especially the makers of aesthetic and ebonised furniture from the late 1860s onwards, such as Henry Ogden and William Watt.*

952 Once again the typical English hallmark of delightfully figured burr-walnut. This type of very well made furniture will always be referred to as 'the little French desk' and so, of course, it is — in design only. The fine quality of the metalwork, more especially the hinges and locks, is normally far better than the average French equivalent. Certainly the very best French furniture of the nineteenth century has superb metalwork but on average England wins hands down. This is the English equivalent of a *bureau en pente* — more commonly called a *bureau de dame,* with an English accent. Note the curvacious little *bombé* swell at the sides.

1850s

953 An even more sophisticated example, appealing to a different taste. Superbly made with exquisite marquetry. It is not known who made this first class article. It is very sad that the modesty of the English nature did not allow the practice of trade labels to develop or that there were not the guild requirements that encouraged the practice of maker's stamps as in France. The true maker of this piece will probably never be discovered.

c. 1850

954 A typically French *bureau plat* made by the French-run London firm, Mellier and Co. of 60 Margaret Street. The style is unmistakably French and it is not possible to identify the country of manufacture without detailed inspection. Mellier in this instance used an English style light stamp on the top of one drawer. The interior finish of the drawers, the cockbeading and the dovetails is readily identified as English. Almost certainly the mounts were from Paris. It would be fascinating to know who did what in their workshops in London and exactly where their materials came from. However, on a piece so finely made does it really matter?

1865-1880 ∗

955 A fine small desk or *bureau plat* inlaid in a very similar manner to 953. The centre part is inlaid with well-figured walnut in the English manner. This makes it slightly impractical as a writing desk but on such a good example this should not be too important.

1850s

956 Externally a very well made large desk — made in Brighton during the 1970s. In many ways this modern English copy is better than many of the late nineteenth century French equivalents. The style is that of France in the second quarter of the eighteenth century. A detail photograph is illustrated on page 300, where it is compared to earlier drawers from France.

1970s *

958 A well made desk with good quality marquetry. The locks on this desk are stamped by the English firm of Cope and Collinson. This in itself is not a true indication that a piece of furniture is English but if the drawers are clean and the locks appear to be original then one may start looking for other clues of the English origin. Remember an English owner losing the key to his French desk will have the locks changed by an English locksmith to readily available English lever locks. Nice well-cast water-gilt mounts on this piece.

1860s

It is more than likely that over the years English locks have been removed from the drawers of English nineteenth century furniture in the French style and that they have been replaced with French double locks to make them appear French, which in the past would have made them more saleable and more expensive. However, the quality of the English workmanship is appreciated these days and the prices would be comparable, so it is less likely to happen now.

957 Another desk from a similar but not the same stable. The metalwork is very poorly cast with little detail and little attention to the features of the faces of the *espagnolettes*. The colour of the mounts is very 'brassy' indeed. The legs on both these examples are very heavy, far heavier than would be allowed in the eighteenth or nineteenth centuries.

1970s *

959 The casters — or castors, the spelling is interchangeable but more frequently with an 'o' in old trade catalogues — are typically English but these could have easily been added. However, many English pieces during the middle years of the century had casters, a feature not as common in France.

1860s

A very ungainly oak sideboard which was originally one of a pair bought by King Oscar II of Sweden in 1901 for the Royal Collection. The exact place of manufacture is unknown and many theories point to Germany. However, the rather odd proportions, combined with the vase of flowers which is a very Scandinavian feature imported from France, and with the apparently very late date of execution in this muddled baroque style suggest that it was perhaps made in Stockholm and therefore would be a much more logical acquisition for the Swedish king.

1880-1900

Hindley and Wilkinson, Gillows, and Wright and Mansfield made exact copies of French furniture and by the turn of the century the opening of the Wallace Collection, coupled with the opening of the Jones Collection in 1883, the reproduction of fine quality French furniture had become all the rage. Pauline Agius in British Furniture 1880-1915 *quotes from a Gillows Catalogue that ". . . the work is carried out in Paris, either at our own Factory or by ébénistes of the highest reputation. . . The work is often done by descendants of those who worked on the famous originals." Sales talk or fact? Certainly a possibility, but there may have been a misinterpretation by the Gillows Public Relations man of 1900!*

960 and 961 Two *bonheurs-du-jour,* both in a very similar style. The latter was made in some numbers. The porcelain plaques are from Staffordshire in both cases and the locks are English. Note the English castors on 958. Interestingly enough both are veneered with thuya from the Atlas mountains, not a firm indicator that a piece must be French but if the veneers can be obtained from Morocco the mounts can be brought from France. The *guilloché* mounts are the same in both cases, one inset with plaques. The design of the former is very uncertain and rather spindly.

Both 1870s

If Gillows were making French reproduction furniture in Paris for the English market could they have been making the carcass, veneering it and polishing it in Paris and then shipping over to England the unfinished article? The fragile porcelain mounts, the mirrors and even the mounts and locks could have then easily been added in the English workshops — there would then be less risk of breakage to the fragile parts during shipping — an interesting thought but the subject of another book and hours of fascinating research.

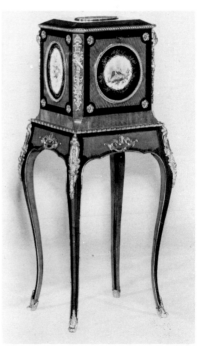

962 (left) A beautifully made *bonheur-du-jour* in the Louis XVI style with the familiar porcelain mounted *guilloché* bandings. The exceptional quality of the drawer linings and interior finish is typical in its English thoroughness and craftsmanship.

c.1880 or later?

963 (right) Another exquisitely made English piece, this time a jewel cabinet with a writing slide in the frieze drawer. The porcelain plaques are English, so is the lock. It would be easy to cut a recess for the usually larger French locks to 'convert' this to being 'French'.

1860-1880 or later?

VARIOUS

965 (right) The style is very similar. All the mounts look English except for the 'tassel and drape' banding on the upper section. The egg and dart moulding along the edge of the writing surface is a repeated English feature.

1860s

964 This porcelain mounted table has lost its top half, which probably consisted of a superstructure with open shelves and more 'apple green' plaques in the Sèvres style. It bears the initials E.H.B. for Edward Holmes Baldock, the collector and dealer referred to in the 'Franglais' introduction. In this instance it is difficult to be sure of the exact nationality of the table, the plaques were definitely English but the mounts, especially the brass moulding around the top, are very French. Could Baldock have been importing carcasses into England and having them finished in this country?

1860s

966 It is easy to simply call this type of marble top 'Italian' and the matter ends there. The English stoneworkers made many marble tops and there was a thriving industry in Torquay and Derbyshire. Loudon reported on the state of the marble industry as early as 1833, describing how it was going over to steam power. The English craftsmen copied the Florentine styles and techniques. This large slab is veneered with a large cross-section of Devonian marbles with a black surround from Ashburton in Derbyshire, suggesting that the Torquay samples were assembled in the Midlands. The base, in a florid Italian style, was made long after the table top.

The marble *mid-nineteenth century*

967 A well made kingwood vitrine bearing the maker's stamp 'Mellier & Co, 60 Margaret Street W. London', illustrated in the French retailer's list. The whole feeling of this piece is French and it is difficult to accept that it was made in England. It seems much more likely that it was made by Mellier in Paris and exported — the stamp could easily have been put on by the maker in Paris prior to its export. The interpretation of the Louis XV style is inventive but elegant. The galleried platform stretcher is a French feature, also the plain moulded gilt mounts clasping the edge of the apron and the crestings. Not, however, a cut and dried case.

1880s

968 An English version of the very common oak chair in the Flemish 'seventeenth century style'. These chairs were made in large numbers and are one of the few sets made in a satisfactory style. They survive today in large numbers and can often be found in sets of six side chairs and two armchairs, making them highly sought after. Of course this style is almost as much English as Dutch, as the Dutch immigrant craftsman made this an indigenous 'English' style — improved of course by the early Victorians. Note the eclectic Elizabethan influence to the strapwork on the back.

1850s

970 (left) Louis XVI? or a nineteenth century French copy from one of the Paris *ébénistes*? No, a satinwood and marquetry occasional table by Donald Ross, made in London in the 1860s. For many years an identical table stood proudly in the Jones Collection in the Victoria and Albert Museum as an original French eighteenth century table. It was only in the last few years that documentary evidence was found proving the English origins.

1860s *

969 A dotted marquetry trellis on a satinwood ground by Donald Ross possibly made for Edwards and Roberts.

1860s

971 (right) One of a pair of pedestals for displaying bronzes or porcelain. The decoration is incised and gilt in the more common English style, most French *ateliers* would have preferred to inlay a brass decoration if the purse strings allowed. As always, the porcelain plaques are the giveaway — they are from the Minton factory.

1880s

972 Donald Ross made many pieces including desks, side tables and a *bonheur-du-jour* in this Louis XVI style with a dotted marquetry trellis in the manner of the eighteenth century maker J.B. Sené. At first they look French, until one looks at the brassy water-gilt quality of the mounts and the very English interior construction.

1860s

973 A giltwood window seat upholstered with Aubusson tapestry which was presumably made directly to order. The treatment of the cabriole legs and the carving in general is far heavier than it would have been in Paris — there is an almost Germanic feel to the execution of the woodwork. There were many German, Polish and Russian workmen in the London furniture trade during the latter years of the nineteenth century which might possibly account for this influence. A highly decorative piece of furniture and although not very useful, very popular for bedrooms.

1880-1900

974 An extremely poorly made *bureau en pente* in the Louis XV style. This is the epitome of the worst possible machine-made production of the Louis revivals made not in France, nor England but in New York. Various Paris firms were supplying the American trade with furniture varying from first class to the third rate but most American 'direct copies' appear to have been poor quality. The carcass is cheaply made of plywood with the thinnest veneers.

Early twentieth century

A label found loose in one of the drawers of the bureau illustrated above. The eccentric form of the settee is typical of the badly proportioned line engravings often reproduced in trade catalogues. The style of the chairs and the settee suggests the style of as long ago as the 1850s. However, these labels would be used by firms for many years and were not always redesigned as fashions changed. The label did not appear to have ever been attached to the bureau above but is probably contemporary.

975 (left) Another problem piece. The shape and proportions of this unusual desk are English. Although heavily scuffed, the carcass is very good quality pine. It is therefore unlikely to be Italian, which is the first country that springs to mind. The decoration is reminiscent of the Italian *pastiglia* technique — a type of carved gesso. The romantic Gothic armour of rather languid footsoldiers posing awkwardly is simply an imaginative attempt at recreating the Middle Ages and is not accurate to a particular period or country.

c.1850

Details

The *marque au fer* of Edward Holmes Baldock, the English dealer and collector who was so prominent in the middle of the nineteenth century, stamping imported contemporary French pieces as well as eighteenth century furniture that he handled.

A close-up of a standard English lock — neatly stamped 'Patent' — they are often conveniently stamped 'English Lever' as well, which helps to identify the nationality.

The stamp of Mellier & Co. who took over the London business of Monbro. English manufacturers normally use a stamp as opposed to a fire brand. Unfortunately the use of a stamp, even with the addition of 'London', does not prove that the piece was made in England, some may have been imported from Paris.

The two separate stamps give Mellier's address.

GERMANY AUSTRIA AND SWITZERLAND

GERMANY AND AUSTRO-HUNGARY

The combined states of Germany and the large Austro-Hungarian Empire produced between them a vast quantity of furniture comparable to the production achieved in France or in England during the second half of the nineteenth century. Like the rest of the manufacturing European nations, Germany and Austria produced a wide range of furniture from the very best quality to the worst, cheaply made examples and from the highly exotic to the most mundane designs.

The nineteenth century was important, both politically and economically, for the German speaking nations. The Congress of Vienna in 1815 had established for the first time a German Confederation of thirty-nine states including Austria, Prussia and Bavaria, by far the three largest and most important. The Hapsburg Empire of Austro-Hungary had spread eastwards and south to the Balkans and Italy.

Insurrection in Paris against Bourbon rule saw sympathetic rumblings in Germany in 1830 that were bitterly quashed by Metternich who wanted to see economic growth under an authoritarian government, not a democratic one.

The mid-1840s saw a severe economic recession combined with a recession in the new and rapidly emerging industrial might of the German states. Once again it was the stimulation of political unrest from Paris that sparked off a series of revolutions in Germany and Austria in 1848. The worst troubles were in Vienna, the heart of traditional thinking and fashion and a major city in the manufacture of furniture. The restoration of the German Confederation in 1850 saw a welcome return to capitalism, economic growth and political certainty. From now on the German states were able to concentrate on a vast expansion of the sizzling industrial potential that had been held back by political strife.

The Seven Weeks War between Austria and Prussia in 1866 brought the northern states into the limelight and saw the waning of the Austro-Hungarian Empire as a political force. The predominance of power that Vienna had enjoyed for over fifty years was now to be wielded by Berlin. The final sealing of a unified Germany was the Franco-Prussian War of 1870 which brought the nationalistic tendencies in Germany to a head and amalgamated north and south in a common effort against France, the unwitting and weak aggressor. Before the Franco-Prussian War some 12,000 to 15,000 furniture workers from various German towns had been working in the Paris furniture trade, but afterwards many of them returned to Germany, taking with them many of the skills and fashions of the French trade, to the great and everlasting advantage of Germany and to the detriment of France. The dreams of the deposed Bismarck were realised and the dawn of the Second Reich spread a light over the might of German industry.

The main centres of manufacture and production in the 1830s were in the capital cities of Vienna, Berlin, Frankfurt and Munich, but numerous other smaller cities and towns were making their own furniture to satisfy a huge and ever-growing demand. This demand was as great in the country regions and traditional painted and carved Alpine furniture continued to be made in quantity by local craftsmen.

The furniture of the Germanic states was for a large part of the nineteenth century influenced by

English styles, traditions and tastes. Once the long Napoleonic Wars had ended there remained a Germany devastated by the war with little chance of building up its economies to anything like the previous prosperity, for there was little left for the ordinary man in the street to apply his industries to. With 'victory' over the French there was nothing left of the previous economic stability as everything had been thrown into and soaked up by the war. Politically, the story was very much the same. Political unrest had come about not only because of the war which had brought widespread deprivation, but also because of the upheavals of war with its far-reaching social consequences. Even in Paris the defeat of 1815 had not brought about quite the same catastrophic consequences, the furniture trade had continued and social unrest had at least a common cause in defeat. The Germanic nations had no comfort in their shared victory with England. The population of England, although forced to mark time for a short while, soon recovered its poise and the economy, combined with political stability and unity, surged ahead with a lively, inventive and encouraged trading situation converse to that of Germany.

This stimulation, in furniture as well as trade generally, was a major influence in Germany and Austria. English technical know-how and expertise was to play a major part in Germany at the end of the nineteenth century, partly through influences learnt by Hermann Muthesius who studied English Architecture from 1896 to 1903 at the German Embassy in London and who, in turn, was a great influence in the German Modern Movement, along with Richard Riemerschmid, Peter Behrens and Walter Gropius, from the Werkbund to the Staatliches Bauhaus, opened as a major creative centre for the whole of Europe in 1919 as a school of art and of arts and crafts.

The first stage in reconstruction came from the middle classes who subconsciously developed their own nationalistic style, playing an at first latent part in unification. Much has been written on the style that now is identified as a nationalistic theme and typifies the taste of the middle to the eastern part of Europe, spanning the whole of the second quarter of the nineteenth century.

This Biedermeier style was born out of the swansong of the Napoleonic style, the Empire. The influence of neo-classicism had been the all pervading style from its slow and uncertain introduction into the various Germanic courts in the late 1760s and early 1770s. Karl Friedrich Schinkel was one of the great architects and furniture designers who stamped out Prussian neo-classical taste in the 1820s mixing it, for the first time, with practicality, comfort and, in keeping with other European nations' developing romantic tastes, smatterings of gothicism, with charming effect.

Biedermeier in its purest form is a short-lived style restricted to the years immediately after the war ended in 1815, until approximately 1830. However, its influences were to be felt long after this time, to be revived alongside the Modern Movement at the end of the century. The name of Biedermeier was conjured up retrospectively, with the benefit of hindsight. The true Biedermeier style is summed up by its name. 'Meier' is a very common name in German speaking countries and epitomises the ordinary man in the street. 'Bieder' is a word synonymous with plainness. The two names together summarise the definition of this important style which was the style of the ordinary man. Furniture at this time was essentially middle-class, made by the numerous small craftsmen in towns throughout the German states. It was made in an unpretentious manner, without frills and elaborate decoration, reflecting the austerity of the times.

Court furniture was only made in limited quantities, the era of elaborate overdecoration and overspending of wealth gleaned from taxes was temporarily over. The northern or Hanseatic towns were making use of the large quantities of comparatively cheap mahogany imported from the West Indies and the Americas and, with their close trading ties with England, followed the English style with almost copy-book accuracy. English cabinet making was regarded as the finest in the world at the time, influencing the northern cabinet makers of Hamburg, Bremen, Lübeck and Altona. Altona was in Danish hands until 1864 and was an important centre of furniture, both for manufacture and for export to the ready markets of Scandinavia and England.

The southern towns, especially Vienna, Munich and the whole of Bavaria, Berlin, Mainz and even as far as Zagreb and Budapest were the home of this middle-class style. The style is best identified by the use of indigenous woods, walnut, birch, cherry-wood, poplar, pear and occasionally maple. The figured woods were to be the sole decorative effect, relying on the soft colours and decorative burrs of the veneers rather than fussy bronze work. Thus local craftsmen were able to make furniture in a fashionable style without having to buy in expensive and frivolous mounts and rare and costly samples of veneer that had to travel halfway across the world and then the length of the Rhine. Certain styles and pattern books became established, such as the designs of Wölfer and Mercker from Leipzig. These, combined with the well-tried and well-known designs of Percier and Fontaine's Paris publications a generation before, were enough to inspire the local craftsmen who were obliged to pass out from their apprenticeships with a piece of their own design. In most cases these designs were local derivations of the above and relied heavily on the traditional styles of neo-classicism from the time of Louis XVI in France, mixed with the Empire.

Carcass work throughout the German-speaking states is normally comparatively poor, with the possible exception of the northern towns. Pine was used almost exclusively, again with the exception of the north which drew some inspiration from England and the Dutch cabinet makers who, in the main, used oak for the carcass, at least for drawer linings. The plain mahogany furniture from the north during the period from the 1820s to the 1840s, whether it was made from oak or deal planking, often shows signs of the veneer buckling in line with the carcass planks on the larger flat, plain surfaces. This can happen on any furniture of similar construction but appears to be a more common tendency in the coastal regions than elsewhere. Certainly the local craftsmen were bent on emulating the sophisticated English techniques but possibly they did not have quite the technical know-how to make such a sturdy framework.

The plainness of the furniture was matched by the lack of extravagant mounts. Where it was necessary to use mounts for handles, escutcheons or feet, they were made of pressed or stamped-out brass in a similar fashion to the work in the Low Countries but without the familiar Dutch *repoussé* decorative effect.

The combination of warm veneers, simple construction and an everyday, practical design was the essence of the Biedermeier style, which, apart from the hiccough that was about to dominate the next fifty to seventy years is, essentially, the hallmark of good German design and the first sign of a nationalistic style. In a sense, this style represented the last throes of local furniture that was hand-made and, to a certain extent, designed by craftsmen, in the old traditions of cabinet making. The coming domination of mass-production in factories was to overturn these standards at a time when the progressive reformers in the major manufacturing nations of Europe were desperately trying to preach a return to the old standards lost by the machine several generations before.

The end of the Biedermeier period coincided with another revolution that was progressing at different speeds and at different times throughout the rest of Europe. In Germany the great period of the revivals was to start in the 1830s, a period that coincided with the era of machinery and pattern books on a large scale. Both pattern books and machinery had been familiar in France and England since the latter years of the eighteenth century. Sheraton's *Drawing Book* had been translated into German in 1794, Percier and Fontaine's *Recueil* had been readily available during the early Biedermeier period. By the late 1820s the circular saw, the band saw, steam driven planes and veneering machines were becoming more familiar in the larger German speaking towns and, slowly but surely, by the middle of the century the larger workshops were all using a combination of machine power and hand craftsmanship.

The rococo revival became more and more popular as the 1830s progressed, marking the final end of the pure Biedermeier. A Mainz cabinet maker, Wilhelm Kimbel, published the *Journal für Möbelschreiner und Tapezierer* which set the trend for the rococo and by the 1840s this magazine, alongside others, was publishing designs in all the by now familiar revival styles. Rococo was to be mixed with the baroque and Gothic with the Renaissance in a fanfare of romanticism. Vienna was the main host to the rococo. This traditional city had also been a major centre for the previous long reign of neo-classicism but readily accepted the traditional rococo style which its cabinet makers had held on to for so long in the eighteenth century. As late as the 1770s German craftsmen were only tacitly applying neo-classical motifs to rococo forms and to many makers and buyers alike the Second Rococo was a welcome return to traditional ideals interrupted by war, political dissent, economic hardship and neo-classicism.

The early *Zweites Rokoko* was merely an application of plastic rococo forms to the Biedermeier shapes. The slightest curve would grow an acanthus scroll. The popular Rhinish table support of three dolphin legs lent itself to rococo exaggeration, plain surfaces were applied with carved wood or composite sawdust foliage and chair backs began to follow the Paris and London fashion, becoming sculpted with accentuated waisted balloon backs — especially in and around Prague. The rococo style that had for so long been regarded as base and tasteless in the Germanic nations soon found a ready market amongst the middle classes. At first, the *Zweites Rokoko* was a watered-down version of the full extravagance of the style but it soon developed its own vigorous forms.

Romantischer Historismus had been an underlying trend even in the eighteenth century but by the arrival of the Second Rococo had become all important. Great attention had been paid to the idea of the informal English country garden in the eighteenth century, with its grottoes, ruins and Gothic elegance. Throughout the latter part of the eighteenth century there had been numerous magazines published in Germany encouraging the English ideals. These ideals were the basis of the return to the rococo.

The rococo exuberance was a style that never died, continuing throughout the second half of the nineteenth century. It was the main source of decoration in many of the great houses. In the mid-1870s the Schloss Linderhof was decorated with complete furnishings in rococo porcelain. Console tables and mirrors of fine quality Meissen porcelain were modelled in bright colours, typifying the very worst excesses of the new rococo.

The large firm of Carl Leistler & Sohn, founded in 1794 by the father, Mathias, was given the important and prestigious commission of redecorating the Liechtenstein Palace, which took from 1842 to 1847 to complete. This Viennese firm was responsible for some of the finest furniture in the second half of the nineteenth century. One of their finest creations was purchased by the British Government, a great patron of the European arts, especially German, from the Great Exhibition of 1851. Leistler was very fond of the use of lime which suited his firm's speciality for carving (following the true traditions of Grinling Gibbons in England in the late seventeenth century).

A strongly designed interpretation of the French mid-eighteenth century rococo was to continue in Germany for many years. Julius Hoffmann, Anton Pössenbacher and Adolf Seder (who designed porcelain furniture for the Schloss Linderhof) all continued this tradition in a bold and distinctive manner that set it apart from French designs which were rarely able to compete with the outrages of the German makers who gave this fluid style a sense of strength and purpose. Hoffmann was designing exotic examples of the rococo in the mid-1880s for the Schloss Herrenchiemsee with an assurance of style that combined the Italian sense of frivolity and architectural shape with the best of French detail and a solid overall feel that becomes identifiable as German. Julius Zwiener, another great maker in this style, went full circle and designed furniture in a very full Louis XV style for Wilhelm II in Berlin. This furniture — a bedroom suite — was exhibited in Paris in 1900 and sits alongside the work of the Czech maker and designer who moved from Germany to Paris — François Linke. Both men had a similar distinctive style of bold cartouches and the finest execution and craftsmanship available. Another stylish maker in the rococo manner was

Ludwig Hesse who, in the 1860s, was making furniture directly in the Potsdam tradition of the Spindler brothers in the style of the 1760s.

Furniture and architecture for Ludwig II of Bavaria was an important indication as to the predominant tastes of the era. Ludwig I had employed the architect Leo von Klenze, who later was to become such an influence in Russia but whose designs too closely reflected the Empire style and the immediate past for the likes of Ludwig II. Berlin of the 1860s still had a strong monarchical system but fashion was more readily and quickly disseminated by this time and the excess of the second Ludwig became a model for the rest of Bavaria.

The introduction of the International and local exhibitions, which by the middle of the century were annual events in parts of Europe, combined with the greater use of the telegraph and the railways, helped to develop Germany's furniture industry rapidly after its comparatively slow start. Europe was by now united by the railways and the telegraph and the huge population boom, with increased prosperity by the middle of the century, had increased the demand for furniture out of all proportion compared with localised craftsmanship immediately after the Napoleonic wars.

Germany's industry was by now reliant on machinery to keep production up to unprecedented levels. Machine carving had been developed at the expense of the Biedermeier style with its later rococo additions which lent themselves to these new techniques. As elsewhere in Europe, upholstery had almost completely taken over the art of furniture making by the 1850s and became one of the few arts applied to the science of furniture that still required considerable handwork. The large furniture and retail department stores helped to encourage this growth and the feeling and demand for comfort. By 1862 there was free trade between Prussia and France — freedom to trade between the various German states had been permissible since the end of the Napoleonic Wars. This, combined with the unprecedented improvement in communications, stimulated trade beyond the dreams of the rapidly emerging large firms who had an ever increasing middle-class market to sell to. What was more important commercially was that these middle-class markets were susceptible to suggestions and, unlike the previous major patrons, the German princes, did not dictate their demands to the suppliers. Patronage had its price in the sense of a restriction on the scope and variety of styles that any one patron could want. The untutored masses of the Germanic speaking peoples were easy game for the worst eclectic excesses of the hundreds of new designers and manufacturing firms. They had the money to buy and were not averse to the cheapness of mass-produced furniture or a mixture of styles. The only credentials were that the styles reflected the glories of past centuries, everything was to be steeped in romanticism and to be a pastiche of the past. It was as a reaction to this morass of indiscriminate design and manufacture that such organisations as the Munich Verein Zur Ausbildung der Gwerbe was founded as early as 1851 — the year of the Great Exhibition. The architect Gottfried Semper, whose Dresden Gallery and the Dresden Opera had been high points of the Germanic Gothic revival in the 1830s to 1850s, was amongst the first to reconcile the fusing together of technology and the industrial arts. The concept of *Kunstgewerbe* was born at an early period in Germany but did not manifest itself as a useful code of conduct until the 1890s when a definite reaction, achieving positive results against the mass-produced eclecticism, became a driving force in Germany and Austria. Imitation and pastiche were the order of the day — imitation had become synonymous with innovation in the minds of the designers.

The mixture of styles brought into Germany in the second quarter of the century confused the purity of the Biedermeier. Pierre Antoine Ledoux de la Mesangère's *Collection de Meubles et Objets de goût*, Henry Shaw's *Specimens of Ancient Furniture* and the teachings of Augustus Welby Northmore Pugin were all major influences in the spread of the mixture of styles in Germany, influencing Kimbel and Alexander Heideloff. The Gothic revival had first manifested itself as a simple and pure form of decoration on established Biedermeier forms continuing the gothicism of the late eighteenth century. Marius Wölfer and Friederich Mercker's journal of the late 1830s promoted not only the rococo but the Renaissance, the Gothic and the baroque styles in their revived forms. Karl Friedrich Schinkel had designed buildings in the early Gothic revival style alongside the work of Semper. Like the early forms of rococo, Gothic was essentially at first a style and decoration of application, especially in northern Germany. Joseph Mayer produced engravings in a total Gothic style in 1839, more in line with the work of Pugin in England. Franz Xavier Fortner during the same period, J.F. von Racknitz, also in Munich and, to a limited extent, von Klenze, were designing a light but complete style of Gothic in the 1830s and 1840s which with its heavy tracery and quatrefoils began to develop its own forms of furniture as distinct from Gothic art applied to established shapes. The Vienna firm of Leistler produced their masterpiece in lime for the 1851 Crystal Palace Exhibition at the zenith of the romantic Gothic period in England but continuing in Germany with the fine panelling for the Munich Rathaus in the 1880s, long after the style had given way in England and France to the continuation of the rococo and the bombardment of the baroque and Renaissance. This magnificent exhibition piece was designed by Bernardo de Bernardis and carved by Franz Maler and Anton Ritter von Fernkorn. In the intervening years of the third quarter of the century rooms were built and furnished in a heavy late Gothic manner, the main span of Gothic *per se* continuing from the late 1830s to the First World War.

The earliest signs of a revival in baroque and late mannerist forms are to be found in the design books of the 1840s. There does not appear to be a great deal of furniture produced in these styles in this decade, it is not until the late 1840s and the 1850s that the Germanic Jacobean revival manifested itself in the furniture of the large commercial firms. Copies of early seventeenth century baroque German furniture began to appear and some of the old huge cabinets or *wrangelschrank* were renovated and altered at this time leaving many pieces to confuse the expert of today, with old metalwork and new veneers and small alterations here and there to many pieces. There was a great interest in the past and there was no shortage of seventeenth century furniture to use as a yardstick or to adapt to the new lifestyle. The designer C.F.H. Palmbeck made exquisite examples of furniture in this style in the 1850s, treating it with new eyes, creating a genuine seventeenth century revival style whereas Wilhelm Kimbel was producing his own version of the late sixteenth and early seventeenth century styles in a manner copied direct from England.

Large quantities of chairs, in long sets for use at the dining table, were made in various seventeenth century styles. There were vague copies of the Louis XV style and also Charles II style chairs with their Huguenot influence. The lazy twist-turned column was used as a support at every conceivable occasion on chairs, screens, beds and tables. Salzburg was a popular centre for the spindly Elizabethan style but many centres of manufacture made this type of furniture, most of it directly influenced from England, encouraged not only by the international exhibitions but by the associations formed by the Prince Consort whose interest in the applied arts stimulated not only England's bursting productivity but acted as a catalyst to Germany who, by the third quarter of the century, was beginning to feel her strength in the furniture industry. Baroque forms

Decoration eines Schlafzimmers mit zwei Betten.

A sumptuous engraving from a mid-nineteenth century Berlin trade catalogue showing the fashionable love of copious upholstery. The room is completely divided by a carved pelmet hung with a lambrequin and tassels. The designer's intention is for the curtains to be untied so as to completely seal off the sleeping area from the dressing area with the two fringed tasselled button upholstered chairs. The two beds have the type of crestings that were popular in northern Germany and Holland and are not too different from the style of furniture that became popular in the United States of America in the 1870s — a style that may well have been imported from Germany.

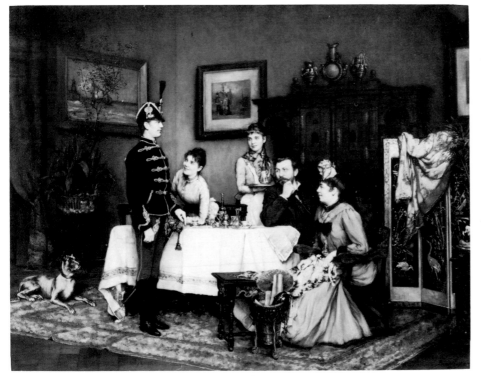

A typically romantic interior scene so loved by nineteenth century artists. This painting is of a young Austrian cadet in his new uniform by the artist Gyula Baschi and dated 1889. In the foreground there is a cane or wicker work basket and a similar cane or wicker jardinière by the doorway on the left. The large cupboard in the background is of an architectural Renaissance revival form in a style that dominated most of Europe for the last twenty years of the nineteenth century. The mother is sitting in an Italian Renaissance style Savonarola X framed arm chair. Behind her is a Chinese embroidered screen of the type that was imported into Europe in vast numbers from the 1870s onwards.

were not used as widely as the Renaissance in the Germanic nineteenth century revivals. Apart from applied decoration to small pieces of furniture it was mainly reserved for the large cupboards, beds and sideboards which were to be made from the earliest days of the baroque revival in the 1840s to the demise of the popularity of this style which was not until the end of the century. Vienna, one of the largest manufacturing cities with a large middle-class population to absorb the various styles, was a major source of the later baroque pieces, which were made to very high standards by machine. There was not, however, any geographical restriction to the baroque taste which was to become mixed with the Renaissance revival in a confusing and muddling way when the Renaissance became the dominating and almost engulfing style from the 1870s right through to the second quarter of the twentieth century. The King, Ludwig II of Bavaria, who was to see his fantasies created in the decorative arts with the extraordinary Peacock Throne by Anton Pössenbacher at Linderhof in 1877, had nine years earlier decorated part of his railroad car in the baroque style. One car was a total festivity of neo-baroque, another a rococo fantasy in a similar vein to his bedroom at Linderhof.

The Renaissance revival took a firm hold during the 1870s and was to be the dominating style for the next forty to fifty years. Encouraged by the success of the Vienna World Exhibition of 1873, the Neudeutsche Renaissance began to filter its influence throughout Germany and the Austro-Hungarian Empire. The powerful new feeling of national unity, stirred by Bismarck, deepened the already nostalgic air of historical romanticism in Germany and designers and manufacturers began to look back to the golden years of the Renaissance for inspiration. The Renaissance and early mannerist styles immediately before the Thirty Years War in 1618 were the zenith of German cabinet making and marquetry. In Augsburg it was all too easy for the nineteenth century designers to turn to the style of the earlier magnificent Augsburg cabinets. The city had always maintained a quite large furniture industry, as had Nuremburg deep in Bavaria. The department store of Bestelmeier was to produce catalogues of its wide range of furniture and other goods, as it had done since the second quarter of the century, in various styles with many neo-Renaissance designs and products.

The very early seeds of the Renaissance revival had taken hold, like most of the other revival styles, with the interest in the many old castles from different periods of German history. The Danube and the Rhine and the forests of Bavaria were the sites of many early Gothic, Medieval and Renaissance castles that had fallen into sad disrepair. The stabilising political and economic situation had increased the interest in *Historismus* and many old castles were to be restored in a distinctive nineteenth century revivalist style. In 1816 the political figure, von Stein, commissioned the architect Claudius von Lassaul to rebuild the Renaissance tower at Nassau — Lassaul later rebuilt Stolzenfels in a Puginesque Gothic style. These early seeds were not to take root in popular demand for some considerable time.

Franz Xavier Fortner had experimented with highly eclectic Renaissance designs for Ludwig I in 1840 and some of the many Viennese makers were producing highly refined pieces in this style in the 'fifties. By the 1860s turned spindles and balusters had begun to appear on chair backs and galleries of desks in a style more conscious of Louis XIII of France than of the true spendours of the early sixteenth century German Renaissance of Dürer and the Younger Holbein. By 1874 the Todesco Palace in Vienna had been decorated in a free Renaissance style with ceilings and wall panels of lightly carved foliage, birds and female figures using a nineteenth century interpretation of the work of Heinrich Aldegrever and of Peter Flötner whose designs in the early sixteenth century had done so much to spread the gospel of the Renaissance in Germany. Vienna remained the largest centre for the ever popular neo-Renaissance furniture but other cities such as Cologne, Karlsrühe and Frankfurt were by this time large scale furniture manufacturing cities, producing mass-produced furniture and design catalogues of their own. The Todesco Palace was a neo-Renaissance paradise and an example for many other makers to follow. The marquetry traditions of the sixteenth century were readily revived in this new surge of nationalism and many fine pieces were made in the Renaissance style, inlaid with fine details of various woods and a certain amount of engraved ivory marquetry similar to the work of the Milanese craftsmen working at the same time but with a far superior finish and technique to that of Italy. At first some of the German pieces look similar to the Italian but after inspection the superiority of German craftsmanship can be easily spotted. C.F.H. Palmbeck of Hamburg and O.B. Friedrich were two makers who were among the best in this field, spanning the last thirty years of the century.

The French styles never had a great influence in later German nineteenth century furniture. The heyday for French design had been the eighteenth century and most of the German revivals looked back to the origins of the various styles in Germany and Austria rather than directly to France. The drawings of Percier and Fontaine and la Mesangère had helped to spread the word of the Empire in the Germanic states and certain German pattern and design books illustrated French styles, such as the *Berliner Möbel Journal,* but the strict execution of these designs appears to be limited. Certainly, there is an abundance of rococo throughout the second half of the century — there is also evidence of German furniture made in the style of André-Charles Boulle during the late 1840s and early 1850s, but the Louis XV style was in the main restricted to chairs designed in the International manner with moulded balloon backs and cabriole legs. Neo-classicism had survived in the hands of the architect Alexis de Chateauneuf and others in Hamburg into the 1830s but was not the driving force that it was to become under the Empress Eugénie's France.

The Louis XVI style was rarely in evidence, appearing on the English market as neo-classical and in France during the 1860s at a time when Germany was still experimenting with baroque forms that led straight into the new Renaissance and the revolution of the arts and crafts.

The 1880s brought electric generators which could now be afforded in even the smallest workshops who were able to take advantage of the use of power saws, milling machines, planes, lathes and drills. This brought down the price of furniture and enabled even the smallest towns to produce more to satisfy the ever increasing demands. German and Austrian furniture production had now reached a stage at least on a par with France and England after a slow start in the second quarter of the century. German craftsmen had set up businesses in Paris in the 1880s. Linke and Zwiener, like the best cabinet makers in Paris in the eighteenth century, were both from Germany.

By the time of the strikes in the suffering Paris furniture industry in 1882 Germany was poised and well able to supply the French population with the furniture that it constantly required. The frontiers from Stuttgart were open to trade and the German manufacturers were able to supply well-made furniture, mainly in the Renaissance style, to fill the void created by the lack of production during the Paris strike. Of course the French considered all foreign production inferior to their own but it did have the distinct advantage of being cheaper, thus foreign trade, especially that of Germany, found a ready and eager market. The German stores had representatives combing the thirsty Paris retail and wholesale outlets bringing with them highly sophisticated marketing techniques and photograph albums of their various furniture wares. Records show that prices of imported goods, possibly not quite as well made in detail but just as useful and well finished, could be purchased at three-fifths of the price of a Paris-made object. The German factories had been established more recently than the traditional French workshops and were running on modern, cost effective lines. German workmen were not divided so rigidly into categories of the various woodworking trades and, apart from seniority and responsibility, they were not earning even as much as half the wages of their French counterparts.

Every European country that had established itself as a major manufacturing nation developed its own eccentricities. The Hamburg firm of H.F.C. Rampendahl had supplied horn and antler furniture to the Crystal Palace Exhibition in London in 1851. There must have been several German firms making these exotic and uncomfortable looking settees, chairs and stools from antlers and other locally hunted horns. Even imported moose and ibex horn was used in the morbid quest for the exotic. Seat furniture was completely formed by the spread of sometimes massive horns, leaving the genteel sitter suspended on the intervening upholstery. The Great Exhibition catalogue illustrates a line engraving of a secretaire writing cabinet by Rampendahl with the traditional horn carved cameos as mounts and ornament and a fine pair of antlers as a rather unnecessary cresting. This naturalistic furniture which admirably suited the tastes of the great hunting families from the north to Vienna is seen as a passing phase in the development of German furniture and its zenith does not seem to have lasted longer than the decade of the 1850s, although less important pieces continued to be made for some years.

The myriad of porcelain factories in and around Dresden were supplying mounts for the furniture trade in quantity, mainly in the form of decorative painted plaques in the Sèvres manner, much as the various Staffordshire factories produced plaques for English neo-classical revival furniture. Meissen itself is responsible for the large cabinets made in the late 1870s, richly mounted with finely painted porcelain plaques and figures in a mixed neo-classical and late mannerist style. The carcass of the furniture was uncharacteristically poorly made with exceptionally thin veneers, using the cheapest pine framework. The purchaser was to look only at the fine and highly decorative colourful porcelain and not the vessel that housed it. Several of these large cabinets were shown at the Paris Exhibition of 1878 by an agent for the Meissen factory, a Mr. Oppenheimer. The porcelain factories were anxious to show off their furniture making virtuosity and produced lavishly mounted cabinets with porcelain legs and supports encrusted with *putti* held together with iron bars for stability. The architect Adolf Seder seemed at home with his frivolous rococo designs in any material and his porcelain console tables are a triumph of technological achievement from the Meissen factory.

The enamellers of Vienna were to produce their own masterpieces in the form of furniture and were not solely content with Renaissance revival polychrome enamel table pieces. Several types of enamel mounted furniture were made, one of the most common but most dramatic being the large Louis XIII influenced writing bureaux. However, they also made various cabinets on stands to house collections of rare gems, *vertu* and assorted treasures. The mint condition of many of these cabinets suggests that they were mainly purchased as showpieces and not put to any practical purpose. Like the porcelain mounted pieces the carcasses were very poorly made and were probably commissioned by the various enamelling concerns from small local tradesmen to be executed as cheaply as possible. They date from the late 1870s until the immediate pre-war years of the twentieth century and are probably often much later then generally supposed.

Michael Thonet was another brilliant example of genius combined with eccentricity. Thonet will always be remembered for his bentwood furniture which has established his name as a household institution in most countries of the world. His first attempts at furniture making were even more intriguing than the eventual success of the Thonet Brothers. Thonet started a furniture workshop in his home town of Boppard am Rhein at the age of twenty-three, experimenting with steaming wood to suitable shapes for furniture. The process of bending wood by steam was well established in the German shipbuilding industry, the system being developed to machine power by an Englishman, Major Trew, in Brunswick in 1750. At first the Thonet pieces were restricted to chairs and from approximately the mid-1830s several chairs survive in laminated wood by Thonet. These chairs were somewhat staid and conventional in design, although they had a rococo freedom of interpretation and were extremely fluid. Mostly they are constructed of several strips of walnut glued together and bent into the required shapes for arms, legs and splats. These techniques were common enough in Germany and Austria at the time but Thonet eventually perfected a process for bending whole sections of wood, normally birch, into shapes suitable for the framework of furniture. Beechwood as well as birch was used and was firstly

boiled before it could be bent into shape after being clamped into iron moulds. This process, developed around 1850, was the basis for cheap mass-production and had the distinct advantage that the boiling and bending increased the pliability of the wood and made it very strong. In 1842 Thonet was awarded an exclusive licence to produce his bentwood furniture for the Austro-Hungarian Empire. This vast market was to be a springboard for Thonet who was rapidly able to fulfil his original aims and go into mass-production on a scale unprecedented in furniture making, or even in the entire manufacturing world. From chairs he designed tables, hat stands and a whole range of ,domestic and commercial furniture for factories and restaurants. His factories literally made millions of pieces of furniture, much of which was exported throughout the world in kit form to be assembled in the retailing country. The simple original ideas of a basic Biedermeier design were thus carried through-out the commerical world and Thonet chairs with their refined rococo curves became a standard form that was used by the twentieth century modernists such as Le Corbusier, who took Thonet's simple designs from cheap bentwoods into tubular steel.

One of the most interesting Thonet designs is a lobed circular centre table with intricate bentwood supports in true Thonet style but elaborately mounted with gilt-bronze acanthus and armorial devices and inlaid with a finely executed parquetry trellis. This table, exhibited at Crystal Palace in 1851, displays a remarkable style that raises Thonet as a designer and furniture maker far above that of a mass-producer. After the various patents had expired there were several imitators of the Thonet technique, such as Fischer and the firm of J. & J. Kohn, all who labelled or branded their furniture in a similar manner to the Thonet Brothers.

John Henry Belter, a cabinet maker trained to his profession in Württemberg, became one of the most important influences in American furniture after he emigrated in the 1840s. Belter took to the thirsty American market the art of laminating woods into a plywood which was then steamed and bent into shape in a manner similar to that used by Michael Thonet and to laminated furniture produced by Chapuis in Belgium.

In an era of nostalgic revivals it is not surprising to see that essentially Germanic style, the Biedermeier, being re-incarnated at the end of the nineteenth century. Indeed it is possible that this nationalistic, elegant fashion never really left the minds of German designers but was only clouded by the years of eclecticism that intervened between its demise and its revival. Once an energetic and highly productive

A photograph taken c.1900 of a study in central Germany. The furniture is almost all Italian — note the large carved Florentine mirror and Murano glass chandelier. The room is full of various schools of painting, Chinese porcelain and Caucasian, Persian and Turkeman rugs. There is little evidence of the nineteenth century except for the fitted cupboard and the barely discernible stylised floral frieze around the room.

Another photograph of c.1900 taken of a room in Berlin decorated in the eighteenth century Adam revival style that became popular in England from the 1860s onwards and, to a limited extent, in Germany slightly later. Once again the room is full of a mixture of furniture with a set of four very English looking dining chairs but a strangely proportioned oval backed chair at the piano. On the right there is a large day bed with a little table en chiffonnière *from France.*

Germany began to shake off the horrors of mass-produced romantic furniture of the International Style her designers began to recreate an elegant, severely classical new Biedermeier. In the last few years of the century this style enjoyed a wide popular appeal alongside the designs of the modernists. Bruno Schmitz, Franz Stuck, Rudolf Schröder and Martin Dülfer were designing elegant furniture that had much in common with the Modern Movement but could not quite throw off the old style. Helbig and Haiger were to create the old Biedermeier style faithfully in a manner that was to encourage many designers, especially from Vienna, where Biedermeier had had its home in the second quarter of the century. In the first few years of the new century many of these designers were able to produce traditional furniture in an elegant style alongside the modernists with an eye open to developing ideas. The importance of the Biedermeier style on the modernists of Germany and Austria is often overlooked but, combined with the English progressive reformers' ideas, it is a main root of modern design.

The feelings and hostility to the doctrine of total upholstery that became the plague of the progressive designers throughout Europe was felt strongly in Germany. There was a feeling that the decorative arts should emerge from architecture and in turn compliment it but total upholstery had ousted any such concepts from the mass-producers.

There had been an Arts and Crafts Exhibition in Munich in 1876 and several museums had been inaugurated under the influence laid down by Prince Albert in the Victoria and Albert Museum for the teaching of the arts and the continuation of crafts techniques. The *Osterreichische Museum für Kunst und Industrie* was opened in Vienna in 1863, the *Bayerisches Nationalmuseum* opened in Munich in 1867 and the *Hamburgisches Museum für Kunst und Gwerbe* in 1877. These museums enabled the designers to look back on the achievements to date and at this time a great deal of influence began to be felt from the English progressive designers.

From the strong and powerful Germanic form of the Gothic adapted, in many cases, from Pugin's designs, architects such as Georg Hauberrisser of Munich began to look at the watered-down style of William Burges in a medieval reform style in the 1880s. By the 1890s crenellated mixed Gothic and medieval forms were becoming commonplace in the larger towns, after designs by the English architects. Neuschwanstein Castle was revamped in the mixed styles of William Morris and Burne-Jones, with certain rooms in an amalgamated medieval and romanesque fashion and a Gothic bedroom inspired by the ideas of Pugin. Even the English purists were to have their ideas adapted. Art nouveau, a term that was unintentionally coined by the Hamburg dealer Samuel Bing when naming his Paris shop, had not touched Germany and Austria in the same way that it had affected France and Belgium. The Belgian artist and designer Henry van de Velde had found a sympathetic audience in Dresden for his pure linear furniture without cluttered ornament and from 1897 he worked in Germany in an almost exclusive style. His work was to influence Otto Eckmann, whose somewhat heavier style continued with van de Velde's into the twentieth century. Alongside the languid art nouveau forms developed a short-lived style which, like certain parts of Scandinavia, looked back to the early Viking days. Basic early forms of furniture were simply incised with runic knots and decoration, which Georg Hauberrisser readily adapted, as did the architect Gustav Fischer and, surprisingly, Richard Riemerschmid of Munich. Riemerschmid was soon to break away from this limited traditional style and to become a driving force in the relationship of art to industry that laid down the principles of the Modern Movement that still dictate the forms of furniture today. Riemerschmid had experimented, rather unsuccessfully, with the designs of the Glasgow designer George Walton but by 1899 he had developed one of the strongest designs of the time with his simple oak chair, that was far superior to his other normally contrived designs and combined functionalism with the ability to mass-produce. Riemerschmid experimented with wood, using it to achieve decorative effect in a similar way to the Biedermeier craftsmen eighty years before him. The natural effects of wood had been exploited by August Endell and Hermann Obrist in the last three years of the nineteenth century. Obrist had been designing art nouveau textiles since 1893 and, with Endell, formed a powerful lobby for art nouveau in Munich. Endell's Elvira Photographic Studio of 1898 went a long way in its abstract façade of plant forms to free the new *jugendstil,* a term coined from a critical art magazine *Jugend,* founded in 1896.

Another Munich designer, Bernhard Pankok, developed a powerful art nouveau style, incorporating marquetry and various veneers into exotic forms, often asymmetrically designed but, in some cases, his designs appear to be contrived, merely trying to consciously adapt traditional shapes of furniture to fit new ideas. With the possible exception of Endell, Munich stood apart from the linear forms of art nouveau that were developing in Vienna.

Influenced by the Glasgow architect and designer

Charles Rennie Mackintosh the Vienna Sezession developed its own peculiar style of art nouveau forms reacting against the powerful plant forms of Munich and Paris. Otto Wagner, his pupil Joseph Olbrich, Josef Hoffmann, and even the Thonet firm were to carry their own Austrian art nouveau into the twentieth century, helping to lay down positive roots of European functionalism. The Sezession was a group of Austrian artists whose building by Olbrich, built from 1898 to 1899, became the focal point of Austrian progressive design. Numerous other Viennese designers were active in this Sezessionist style, an important contributor being Adolf Loos, who was opposed to ornament of any kind on furniture. Hans Christiansen, Hermann Billing and Bruno Paul were German designers who began to reconcile the work of Vienna with that of Germany with their linear furniture which had little ornamentation and distinctly elegant lines. Inspired by the lead of the English Arts and Crafts designers, Muthesius had brought back to Germany a need for elegant simplicity. Muthesius and the director of the Hamburg gallery, Alfred Lichtwark, preached this new style of purity combined with functionalism that became known as *Sachlichkeit,* the password for German design in the new era of the twentieth century.

A glimpse into a room at the Paris Exposition Universelle of 1900. Erected by the Vereinigte Werkstätte of Munich, the whole style of this room setting is one of art nouveau and naturalism but with a strength and conviction rarely found in France at the same time. The ceiling is especially bold, the architectural details flowing into the frieze in a unified way.

German Cabinet Makers, Designers and Retailers

ABBT, Johann (fl.1830). Austro-Hungarian cabinet maker.

ALBERTY, J., Professor (fl.1850s). Exhibited a carved frame designed by Stüler (q.v.) for the 1851 Exhibition.

BARTH, Adam & Stephan (fl.1850s). Makers of Würzburg Renaissance style furniture.

BEER, Franz (fl.1860). Architect. Mannerist revival doorway in Schloss Frauenberg, Hurboken?

BEHRENS, Peter (1868-1940). Modernist designer and innovator.

BELTER, John Henry (1804-1863). Born in Württemberg. Cabinet maker who introduced laminates to the United States of America.

BEMBE, Philipp Anton (fl.1835-1845). Mainz maker of English Regency style and Biedermeier plain furniture. Set up his own furniture factory in 1835.

BERNARDIS, Bernardo de (1807-1868). Austro-Hungarian designer in Gothic style. Exhibited bronze lamp at 1851 Exhibition cast by the foundry of Prince of Salns, Vienna.

BESTELMEIR (mid-nineteenth century). A large department store producing furniture catalogues.

BING, Samuel. Hamburg art dealer who founded shop in Paris called 'L'Art Nouveau'.

BORGEMANN, Karl (fl.1890s). Hanover Gothic designer.

BORMANN. Unidentified bronze founder. (See illustration on page 333.)

BROCHIER, Franz. Munich. Architectural baroque.

BROMEIS, Johann Konrad (fl.1835-1840). Very heavy late Empire style.

BRUGGEMAN, H. (fl. early twentieth century). Exhibited at Liège 1905.

BURKLEIN, Friederich (fl.c.1850). Munich architect and furniture maker carved Biedermeier.

BUSEK, Peter (fl.1860s). Naturalistic furniture maker who worked with Pruvot (q.v.). Mannerist pieces.

CHATEAUNEUF, Alexis de (1799-1853). Hamburg architect who built Neuer Jungfernsteig in Hamburg and Schloss Fierhagen, Holstein. Empire 1825/35. Also Angelica Kaufmann revival style.

DANHAUSER, Josef (fl.1800-1838). Prolific interior designer and manufacturer from Württemberg. Danhauser also had a huge factory in Vienna producing a wide range of goods. Died 1830, his son continued the business.

DEVORECKY, Damien (fl.c.1860). Architect. Mannerist revival doorway in Schloss Frauenberg, Hurboken?. See Franz Beer (q.v.).

DOPMEYER, Karl (fl.c.1890). Hanover. Medieval.

DUBELL, Heinrich (fl.mid-1850s). Vienna Louis XV revival of fine quality.

DURM, Joseph (fl.c.1880). Fine quality late Renaissance carved pieces.

ECKMANN, Otto (1865-1902). Berlin. Watered-down version of van de Velde (q.v.).

EINHOLZER, A. (fl.1830s). Vienna. William IV style designer and maker.

ENDELL, August (1871-1925). Munich artist. Exponent of art nouveau, also Chinese and traditional shapes. Plain Liberty-like forms decorated with seaweed, as was his Elvira Photographic Studio 1897-98. Some forms similar to Hoffmann (q.v.).

ERNOT, Franz (fl.1830-1840). Vienna decorative stove maker.

FARAGO, Edmund (fl.c.1900). An Hungarian designer who designed in green stained oak for the Musée Commercial Royal Hongrois in 1900. Also worked in green stained ash. A stained poplar cabinet designed by Farago was made by Kantor Thomas.

FEIGEL, Franz (fl.1830). Austro-Hungarian furniture manufacturer.

FELDSCHAFER, Rudolf (fl.mid-1890s). Vienna. Late mannerist architectural furniture.

FENNER, Franz (fl.1830). Austro-Hungarian cabinet-maker.

FERSTER, Heinrich von (fl.1880s). Vienna. Eclectic Louis XIV.

FISCHELL, D-G (fl. early twentieth century). 12 Wipplingerstrasse, Vienna. Exhibited Liège 1905.

FISCHER, Adolf (fl.c.1900). Mixed medieval and Gothic forms with runic tracery.

FISCHER, Karl (fl.mid-1850s). Architect. Mannerist and medieval pieces of fine quality.

FORTNER, Franz Xavier (1798-1877). A Munich fancy cabinet maker who produced fine marquetry in Charles X Empire Style and heavy Gothic for Schloss Stolzenfels.

FRIEDRICH, O.B. (fl.1870s-1890s). Dresden manufacturer. Brass labels engraved 'Kunst & Luxusmöbel Fabrik von O.B. Friedrich Hofheforant, Dresden'. Ivory inlaid pieces in seventeenth century style. (See illustration)

GEDON, Lorenz (fl.mid-1870s). Munich. Mannerist. Mixed Renaissance and baroque.

GEYER, Johann N. (fl.1835-1840). Late Biedermeier/rococo *bois*.

GLINK, Leonhard (fl.c.1835). Gothic style.

GOSER, Felix. Patented machine for stamping wood, 1828.

GOTTHILF, Ernst von (fl.1900-1905). Vienna. Eclectic Louis XV.

GRASSEL, Hans. Munich. Incised carving in a runic style derivative of formalised William Morris foliage for Munich State Archives.

GRISEBACH, Hans (fl.mid-1880s). Berlin. Mannerist.

GROPIUS. Berlin. Garton Pierre frame at Great Exhibition 1851.

GROPIUS, Walter (1883-1969). Important modernist architect.

HAGEN von Erfurt. Normal North German secretaire of walnut profusely carved in the Great Exhibition style 1851.

HAIGER, Charles (fl.c.1900). Munich Biedermeier revival.

HANSEN, Theophil (fl.c.1880). Vienna. Mannerist and baroque pieces. Classical revival. Also for Schloss Hernstein.

HARTMANN & Sohne, J.G. Vienna. Papers.

HASE, Conrad Wilhelm (fl.mid-1850s). Runic influenced furniture.

HAUBERRISSER, Georg (fl.1880s and 1890s). Munich. Designer and maker. Medieval style of William Burges. Also runic carved pieces 1890s.

HEIDELOFF, Carl A. (fl.1840-1842). Nuremberg. Architect. Stylised Gothic for Schloss Lichtenstein. Designer in Greek and Gothic styles 1830s.

HELBIG, Henry (fl.c.1900). Munich Biedermeier revival.

HELD, C. (c.1900). Baden-Baden, intarsia water fountain provided for local Spa.

HELLER, von B.K. (fl.1850). Nuremberg. Gothic.

HEMCKER, Wilhelm (1802-1874). Bremen designer and cabinet maker.

HERDTLE, Hermann (fl.1890s). Vienna. Fine quality mannerist pieces.

HERTEL, Johann (fl.c.1830). Viennese furniture maker.

HERWEGEN, Peter (fl.c.1883). Munich. Gothic medieval shrine for Schloss Neuschwanstein.

HESSE, Ludwig (fl.1860). 'Regency' revival.

HIMMELHEBER, Heinrich (fl.1840-1858). Maker Biedermeier Gothic style.

HOFFMANN, Joseph (1870-1955). Vienna. Helped found Wiener Werkstätte near Dresden 1903. Functionalist, reacted against art nouveau.

HOFFMANN, Julius. Munich. Exquisite Régence revival incorporating Vernis Martin panels mid-1880s. Also romanesque, baroque and rococo styles.

HOFFMEISTER & Co. Thomas (fl.1851). Saxe-Coburg. Mixed Gothic and Renaissance style 1851. Fine carving. 1851 Great Exhibition chair in Victoria and Albert Museum.

HOFFMEISTER, Thomas (fl.mid-nineteenth century). Exhibited a carved oak figure at Crystal Palace in 1851 and an intricate carved oak Gothic armchair in name of Hoffmeister & Behrens. From Coburg.

HUBSCH, Heinrich. Empire.

HYRTZ, J. (fl.c.1838). Interiors.

KACHEL, Georg (fl.c.1870). Louis XIII style.

KACHEL, Gustav (c.1870). Carved baroque furniture similar to English Warwick School.

KAYSER & GROSSHEIN. Berlin retailers (interiors).

KIMBEL, Wilhelm (1786-1869) (fl. late 1830s to mid-1840s). Mainz designer. Gothic, Louis XIII revival and rococo. Trained in Vienna.

KITSCHELT, August. Vienna. Lime wood chair in rococo style Great Exhibition 1851. Also centre table comparable to Thonet's design.

KLENZE, Leo von (fl.1820-1840). Worked in Munich for Ludwig I of Bavaria. Frivolous Empire, Biedermeier and Gothic styles. Designed for the Residenz and the Hermitage.

KNUSSMANN, Friedrich (fl.1840). Mainz. Heavy wooded.

KNUSSMANN, Johan Wolfgang (1766-1840). Mainz workshops founded in eighteenth century continued to 1874.

KOCHLIN, Karl (fl.mid-1880s). Vienna. Late mannerist.

KOHN, J. & J. (fl. late nineteenth and early twentieth century). A producer of bentwood furniture in Poland.

KRAMER, Joseph (fl.c.1851). Architect. Designed incredible Gothic cabinet with Bernardis (q.v.) made by Leistler & Sohn, now in Victoria and Albert Museum.

KROGER, Franz (fl.c.1849). Vienna. Fine quality seventeenth century style hardstone cabinet.

LASSAUL, Johann Claudius von (fl.c.1816-1830). Architect. Folksy Gothic. Free but heavy style. Schloss Rheinstein and Nassau Tower.

LAUR, Josef (fl.c.1860). Designer/maker, late Gothic style, for Schloss Sigmaingen.

LAVES, Georg, Ludwig (fl.1830s). Hanover. Gilt and painted furniture in Empire style.

LECHTER, Melchiar (fl.mid-1890s). Münster. Medieval forms with runic carving.

LEISTLER, Carl & Sohn (fl.1842-1847). Vienna first class quality manufacturer. Plant stands, chairs, interiors. Redecorated Liechtenstein Palace 1842-47 in rococo style. 1851 Great Exhibition. Highly varied designs.

LOOS, Adolf (1870-1933). Vienna. Modernist designer influenced by W.A.S. Benson.

LOOSE, Herman (fl.1890s). Hamburg. Pictorial marquetry work and carving.

LOVINSON, Louis and Siegfried. Berlin. Exhibited 1867 Paris carved pieces in loose Gothic and also Jacobethan styles.

LUDWIG, Bernhard (fl.1870s). Vienna. Fine Renaissance marquetry on architectural form.

MANN, Johann (fl.1846-1848). Maker to A.W.N. Pugin designs for Gothic hall and furniture in Schloss Rozmberg (Rosenberg). Also mid-seventeenth century style.

MAYER, Joseph (fl.1830s). Munich. Gothic designer.

MEISSNER, Paul (fl.mid-1890s). Frankfurt. Gothic forms with runic carving.

MERCKER, Friederich, Wilhelm (fl.1830s). Leipzig designer. Exotic designs in 'Arab' Moorish and Chinese taste.

MICHEL, Franz (fl.1880s). Vienna. Dutch style floral marquetry. Also mannerist.

MOHRMANN, Karl (fl.c.1890). Hanover. Gothic and medieval, also stylised runic carving.

MONTEFORTE, Alexander Wielmans von (fl.1875-1881). Vienna. Renaissance furniture.

MOSER, Kolo (fl. early 1900s). Vienna. Sezession.

MUTHESIUS, Hermann (1861-1927). Architect and important contributor to the Modern Movement.

NIEDERHOFER, Christian (fl.mid-1850s). Maker of plain north German style.

NIEDERHOFER, Philip (fl.1880s). Frankfurt/Saxe-Coburg. Inlaid mannerist.

OBRIST, Hermann (1863-1927). Munich artist; exponent of art nouveau. Well carved traditional shapes with naturalistic decoration.

OLBRICH, Joseph (1867-1908). Functionalist reacted against art nouveau in the 1890s. Designed Villa Friedmann at Hinterbrühl, Villa Stift, Hohe Wate.

OPPENHEIMER. Meissen agent exhibited Paris in 1878.

OPPIER, Edwin (fl.c.1866). Hanover. Heavy medieval furniture. Light marquetry. Bookcase in Schloss Marienburg.

OREANS, Robert (fl.1900). Karlsruhe. Highly individual designs with carving mixture of runic and Aztec.

ORLEY, Michael (fl.mid-1870s). Vienna. Baroque style.

ORTLEPP, Friederich (fl. early twentieth century). Exhibited at Liège 1905.

PALLENBERG, Heinrich (fl.mid-1870s). Cologne. Early mannerist.

PALLENBERG, Jacob (fl.mid-1870s). Cologne. Early mannerist.

PALMBECK, C.F.H. Hamburg maker of marquetry in the 1850s. Exhibited at Crystal Palace 1875?

PANKOK, Bernhard (fl.1897). Munich and Stuttgart. Moulded sinuous forms after van de Velde (q.v.), also functional art nouveau.

PATATSCHNY, Chr. (fl.1843). Vienna furniture.

PERRON, Philipp (fl.1870s). Munich. Very fine carving and gilding crescent style.

PERSIUS, Ludwig (fl. late 1860s). Berlin. Gothic/medieval furniture.

POSSENBACHER, Anton & Joseph (mid-nineteenth century to 1870s). Munich. Very fine quality French style pieces of lots of ormolu rococo mounts. Comparable to Zwiener (q.v.). Anton Possenbacher made Peacock Throne for Ludwig II.

POSSENBACHER & EHKENGUT. Panel makers at Neuschwanstein Castle.

PRUVOT, Joseph (fl.1847-1862). Gothic dining room and library furniture at Schloss Sychrou.

RAAB, Johann, Valentin. Frankfurt. Very Italian Empire style. 1818-53. Furnished Wurzburg Residenz 1799-1853.

RACKNITZ, Joseph Friedrich von (fl.c.1835). Gothic revival style.

RAMPENDAHL, H.F.C. (fl.c.1851). Designer of Horn furniture. Exhibited at Crystal Palace.

REIMANN, Johann. Biedermeier.

REISCH, Anton (fl.mid.1840s). Vienna cabinet maker. Baroque revival.

RIEMERSCHMID, Richard (fl.1890s). Munich. Early work of runic form developed into very strong style especially chairs using grain of indigenous woods following simple naturalistic forms.

RITTMEISTER (fl.1851). Munich. Tassels.

ROHRS, Friederich (fl.1820-1850). Furniture factory in Austria founded 1834.

SAUERMANN, Heinrich (fl.1890-1895). Stylised mannerist.

SCHERER, Dominik (fl.1830-1840). Vienna. Chandeliers.

SCHINKEL, Karl Friedrich. An important architect/designer from Berlin. Plain formal Empire/Biedermeier compare to Charles X marquetry work. Schloss Charlottenshoff, Neues Palais. Designed fireplace cast in bronze by Fegell of Berlin after Thorbaldsen for 1851 Great Exhibition.

SCHMIDT, Friedrich von (fl.1880s). Vienna. Gothic.

SCHMIDT, Karl (1873-1948). Furniture workshop in Dresden 1898. Influenced by England at first.

SCHMIDT-RUMPF, Ludwig (fl.1830s). Frankfurt designer. Late Empire.

SCHMITZ, Bruno (fl.c.1905). Berlin. Biedermeier revival.

SCHOTTLE, Georg (fl.1890s). Stuttgart. Light painted pine Japanese style.

SCHOYERER, Anton (fl.1890s). Aesthetic movement of a type popularised in England in early 1870s. Also Renaissance.

SEDER, Adolf (fl.1870s). Munich. Very fine carving and gilding. Crescent style. Worked with T. Hansen (q.v.).

SEITZ & SEIDL, Gabriel. Interior designers and execution.

STORK, Joseph (fl.1870s and 1880s). Vienna. Fine Renaissance and Adam marquetry work on seventeenth century shapes. Highly eclectic furniture. Massive 'renaroque'.

STOVESANDT, Gustav. Karlsruhe. A massive architectural carved wood 'baroque' sideboard at Paris Exhibition 1887.

STUCK, Frans (fl.1900). Munich Biedermeier/neo-classical revival, thin attenuated lines.

STULER, August (fl.1850s and 1860s). Berlin designer for Great Exhibition 1851. Sculptural furniture.

THONET, Michael, Gebruder. Vienna. Father of furniture mass-production of bentwood. Also designed neo-baroque forms. Geometric marquetry work mounted with ormolu. Assembly plants throughout the world and showrooms in Bistritz, Karitschan, Hallenkau, Wsetin (Movaria), Ugrocz (Hungary), Nowo-Radonsk in Russia as well as Paris and America. Boasted manufacture without the use of glue. Worked with Leistler (q.v.).

TISCHLER, Ludwig (fl.c.1872). Architect in Vienna. Light baroque carved interior.

TRENTSENSKY. Vienna 1843 interior.

TURPE, A. Dresden cabinet maker in early baroque forms. Ebony cabinet with pear carved reliefs at Paris Exhibition 1867.

A typical German, completely enclosed, lock by Türpe.

UNGEWITTER, G.G. von (fl.1850s). Leipzig designer. Pugin-like Gothic.

VELDE, Henri van de. Brussels architect/artist working and teaching in Germany and Zurich. Settled in Germany 1899. Professor at School of Decorative Arts at Weimar. Sinuous and strong. Designed a mixture of plain art nouveau forms with English Arts and Crafts construction and simplicity. Also cane and rattan furniture.

VETTER, Johann Wilhelm (fl.1835-1844). Cabinet maker. Neuwied. Plain wood style. Some very strong Gothic furniture. (Oval stamp 'J.W. VETTER IN NEUWIED'.)

VOIT, John Henry (1804-1863). Munich designer born in Württemberg, became a state cabinet maker.

WAGNER, Otto (1841-1918). Functionalist. Early reaction to art nouveau.

WENZ, Gerhard (fl.1840). Neuwied. Plain mahogany cabinet maker.

WENZEL, J.H. (fl.1870s). Frankfurt. Louis XVI revival.

WESSICKEN, Joseph. Salzburg. Gothic, traditional baroque style, also plain mahogany, also Louis XIII, copies A.W.N. Pugin for Schloss Anit, late 1840s. Also

straight copies for third quarter seventeenth century baroque.

WETTLI, Bene. Whitewood carved writing desk in individual naturalistic style with animals and attendants. 1851 Exhibition.

WHITTHAUER, Fr. (fl.1836). Vienna. See Franz Ernot.

WILD, Karl (fl.1849-1853). Maker Regensburg. Late Gothic style.

WINGELMULLER, Georg (fl.1846-1848). Gothic staircase in Schloss Eisgrub.

WIRTH, Gebruder. Swiss carvers and furniture makers. Exhibited at Paris in 1867 in a Renaissance and Tudor revival style.

WOLFER, Marius (fl.1830s). Furniture designer in Quedlinburg and Leipzig. Biedermeier and Gothic styles at same time.

WURFEL & Co. (fl.c.1880). Viennese makers in the mannerist style.

ZIEGLER & WEBER (fl.mid-1870s). Makers of good quality Renaissance.

ZWIENER, Julius von (fl. late nineteenth century). Berlin. Important fine quality pieces in Régence and rococo styles. Fine ormolu and marquetry work. His work is very similar to that of his contemporary E. Zwiener of Paris. Further research would hope to prove that they are of the same family.

The following are recorded as furniture manufacturers from Budapest exhibiting at the 1905 Liège Exhibition.

GELB, M. & Sons.

KARAY, Jules.

STEINBACH, Gabor.

THELK, A.

The crudely engraved signature of an unknown maker of an ormolu mount on one of a pair of fine and large German porcelain vases.

Terms

Ankleidespiegel. Psyché or cheval glass. Also *Stehspiegel.*
Anrichte. Dresser, sideboard.
Arbeitstisch. Work table.
Aufsatzmöbel. Cabinet on chest.

Bett. Bed.
Bücheretagere. Open bookshelf.
Bücherschrank. Bookcase.

Coiffeuse. Flat top dressing table (French).
Couvertrahmen. A wooden framed cover for a bed, decoratively upholstered, to cover the bed during the day.

Eckkastel. Floor standing corner cabinet.
Elkschrank. Floor standing corner cabinet.
Etagère. A series of flat, open shelves (French).

Fufssefsel. Upholstered chair or stool.

Garderoben. Dwarf cupboards.
Glasschrank. A cabinet with a vitrine above cupboards.
Globustischen. A globe shaped work table on stand from the Biedermeier period.

Himmelbett. Bed with canopy.

Kamin. Fireplace.
Kasten. Cabinet or wardrobe (two doors).
Klapptisch. Gateleg table/tip-top table.
Kommode. Low cabinet with doors or drawers.
Konsoltischen. Console table.
Konsolschrank. Side cabinet.

Lehnstuhl. Armchair.
Lesetisch. Reading table.
Liege-sofa. Day bed.

Nächtischen. Bedside table.

Ofenschrim. Pole screen.

Patentsekretär. A small light reading or writing table used as a shield against the fire.

Papierkorb. Ornate waste-paper basket.
Pultschreibtisch. Bureau.

Rollschreibtisch. Cylinder bureau.
Ruhebett. Chaise longue.

Schatzbehälter. Strongbox.
Schränk. Cabinet.
Schreibschrank. Bureau cabinet.
Schreibtisch. Writing desk.
Sekretär. Bureau.
Sevante. A side cabinet with a serving shelf for the dining room.
Sitzmobël. Chair.
Sitzbank. Settee.
Spieltisch. Card table.
Ständer. Pot stand.
Standuhr. Longcase clock.
Stehpult. Adjustable reading or writing table.
Stehspiegel. Psyché or cheval glass. Also *Ankleidespiegel.*
Stuhl. Small chair or stool.

Tellerbord. Plate or pot rack.
Tellerbordschrank. Dresser.
Tische. Table.
Toilettentisch. Toilet table.
Truhe. Blanket chest.

Uberbauschrank. A dresser with a, usually tall, superstructure.

Wandkastl. Wall cabinet.
Wiege. Cradle.
Wrangelschrank. A cupboard or cabinet. Originally a small highly inlaid Augsburg cabinet taken from the city during the Thirty Years War by the Swedish soldier Count Wrangel.

Zeichentish. Drawing table.

976 A poorly made porcelain mounted small writing box with painted panels in the Sèvres style but made in the Dresden area. The ebony veneered framework is not well finished and is veneered on to a pine carcass. The box is reminiscent of the style of the early seventeenth century and the panels are in the French mid-eighteenth century manner.

c.1880

977 A small carved walnut box in a very florid style that is quite similar to Italian ornament. The shape however is typically Germanic with its exaggerated forms. The *putti* carved on the lid are too restrained to be Italian. Thousands of these small carved fruitwood pieces were made, especially in the tourist areas.

c.1900

798 A Meissen mounted sewing box in the same vein as the cabinets on the following page. Once again the very carefully painted porcelain panels are in the mid-eighteenth century style of the Sèvres factory. Most of these 'furniture' pieces with German porcelain mounts are mounted with genuine Meissen pieces, many have the familiar crossed sword mark in underglaze blue on the reverse. Although the porcelain world is full of Dresden copies of Meissen, it appears that the German porcelain-mounted pieces are furnished with some of the best quality porcelain available at the time from the Meissen factory itself. The inside of the box is delightfully coloured, the tulipwood veneered lids, imitating French veneering, still have their original bright red/brown colour.

c.1880

979 An imposing German mahogany linen press of fine architectural proportions, a little too big, however, for most people today which limits the market — making this type of furniture cheaper for those who, in theory, are most able to afford it, those with large imposing houses! The overall taste is Biedermeier with the natural decoration of the quarter-veneered door panels using flame figured wood. The shape conforms to English linen presses of the George III period (1760-1820) except for the triangular pediment. The pediment, however, does conform to the grandest designs of Robert Adam. The gadrooned feet are very stylised and have a feeling of late Empire and are quite often seen on German furniture of this period.

c.1830

CABINETS — Porcelain Mounted

980 To most eyes a hideous monstrosity of anaemic coloured porcelain. This type of Meissen cabinet, sometimes with a writing drawer in the frieze, was made in the Meissen area as a triumph of German cabinet making — from the viewpoint of the porcelain manufacturers anyway. The carcasses, or what there was of them, were always very thinly veneered in ebony on to a cheap, normally pine, ground. The colours of the porcelain vary from hues of emerald green through to light blue and fleshy pink tones for the *putti* and other figures that liberally decorate the base. They were obviously made purely as decorative items and not intended for use. Condition is all important and if any of the little figures or flowers are badly damaged then a considerable amount of the value is lost. In most cases these cabinets are meant to stand against the wall and are not decorated at the back. The strength of the porcelain legs, trestles and pole stretcher is a brilliant technical feat.

1880s

983 (below) One of a pair of enamel mounted Vienna columns. Large cabinets were also made in this style, usually with a writing flap, see colour plate on page 142. As with the porcelain mounted pieces, the carcasses were poorly made and thinly veneered in ebony, yet the enamelling on thin copper plaques is well executed and highly decorative, contrasting considerably with the black framework.

c.1900

981 This style is the most common of the porcelain mounted pieces from the Meissen factory. The painted panels are either predominantly emerald green in decoration or light blue — the green normally being slightly more popular and unusual. Once again the construction of the actual furniture is extremely poor, the maker concentrating solely on the porcelain. The tall columns and legs are made up from numerous pieces of porcelain held together with the aid of a long iron rod.

1880s

982 A photograph of an almost identical Meissen mounted cabinet to the one shown in colour on page 244. In this case the doors are shown open giving an indication of the extraordinary quality and attention to detail of the interior. All four of the main cupboard doors are painted on either side. The central section of the upper part has a 'secret' revolving section showing four different sets of panels, small figures of the seasons and a mirrored niche. In the frieze there is a pull-out slide with a large painted oval porcelain panel. Again, a decorative piece with little practical use.

1880s

CABINETS

984 A cabinet inspired by the English Arts and Crafts Movement or more correctly the medieval revival of the 1860s whose champion, William Burges, had considerable influence in Germany. This cabinet is rather poorly made with a cheap softwood carcass. The decoration of the panels is effective simply by pen and ink staining with painted highlights and flowerheads. There is a considerable influence in the interlaced strapwork and foliate incised carving of the framework from early Viking and Scandinavian decoration. This runic decoration became popular in Scandinavia and possibly in northern Germany towards the end of the nineteenth century. This cabinet compares to the work of Ludwig Persius of Berlin working in the 1860s.

c.1890

985 An eclectic version of Bavarian early seventeenth century baroque. The decorations are inlaid with copper, ivory and pewter that were popular in the Brunswick area throughout the late seventeenth and early eighteenth century. The baroque columns are almost overpowering and dominate the whole piece of furniture which is angled to fit in the corner of a room. The carcass is quite well made and veneered in walnut. How similar the four small turned finials above the twist turned columns on the cupboard doors are to English decoration of the 1850s and 1860s.

Second half nineteenth century

986 A very elegant cabinet in the late Empire style, delightfully veneered in a beautifully figured golden coloured Hungarian ash which was used to good effect in the Germanic countries and occasionally in England. The style is Biedermeier and is a fine example of how the Biedermeier taste relies essentially on the natural decoration of the wood but was unable to shrug off dominating Empire forms.

1830s

987 A fine example of the German 'Arts and Crafts' Movement, albeit somewhat later than its English counterparts. The form is eclectic in the extreme, with Gothic decoration on a Renaissance shape. Well made, in walnut, by a competent factory.

c.1890

988 A very uninspired small corner cabinet in well figured walnut veneers which, as in England, were used considerably in Germany in the nineteenth century. It is difficult to accept that this cupboard started life in exactly this shape but upon detailed inspection there were no signs of alteration visible. The light rococo mounts, of poor quality, are typical of the German rococo which was usually interpreted by thin trailing scrolls and flowers.

c.1900

989 (right) The individual use of a very wide walnut crossbanding can be seen on both this tall corner cabinet and on 988. It is a common feature of German furniture in the style of the mid-eighteenth century, especially around the area of Bamberg. Once again the proportions look most odd but there is no evidence of any alteration. The mounts are virtually a waste of time and are even more spindly than the worst examples of French decoration. The legs are extraordinarily heavy, unnecessarily so.

c.1900

990 (left) Once again a similar technique of veneering has been used and also spindly rococo mounts. This cabinet was presumably intended for use in the bedroom, possibly as a gentleman's cabinet. The severe architectural cornice is reminiscent of the second quarter of the eighteenth century in the Dresden area. Not very well made but nice veneers which will make up for design and construction errors.

Third quarter nineteenth century

991 (right) A distinctly odd looking small cabinet whose entire purpose in life was to save the panels of late sixteenth century south German marquetry, normally associated with the area around Ulm. This marquetry was always finished to extremely high standards but often seems to have been removed from its original setting, which was normally in over-large pieces of furniture suitable for only the largest palaces and inserted into small convenient sizes. A pair of Ulm marquetry cabinets are now in the Victoria & Albert Museum in the English section, as they were incorporated into small cabinets in the French manner in the 1770s. Unfortunately, no such lucky fate was predetermined for these panels which have been incorporated into a cross between an early radiogram and the legs of a commode stool.

Made up mid-nineteenth century

992, 993 and 994 These three cabinets are all of very similar construction. They are ebony veneered on to a soft carcass and designed in a very severe geometric form that is highly effective. Considerable dramatic impact is obtained by the contrast of the severity of the ebony with brass mounts, doors and fluting. The outside cabinets are almost identical and must have come from the same source; only the lower part of the legs appears to be different. No.992 with English type white ceramic castors, no.994 with French style *toupie* feet. All three cabinets are entirely functional — there is nothing to take the eye away from the display on the inside.

All 1880-1900

995 A very plain mahogany cabinet with small amount of reel and baluster moulding. It is the epitome of later Biedermeier furniture that became progressively more and more decorated towards the middle of the nineteenth century.

1840s

996 An unusual mixture of Gothic and early baroque forms, veneered in ebony. It is rather effective but the main dramatic impact is the extraordinary self tapering cabinet which, like the previous cabinets, would certainly give maximum visibility to the graduated display of objects. This is a good example of the German desire to create extraordinary shapes even if beauty sometimes has to be sacrificed.

1840-1880

997 The rather bulbous *bombé* form of this cabinet is nearly always ascribed to Germany with her love of eccentric shapes. The mounts are not very good quality but on the apron at least they are more robust than normal on nineteenth century German furniture. The *bombé* cresting is a mixture between Vienna and Venice, between which two towns there was a constant cross-flow of ideas and cross influences which greatly affected the whole of southern Germany, Austria and northern Italy, giving the entire area a distinct style of its own but making it extremely difficult to pin down the exact origin of any particular piece of furniture, especially in the eclectic period of the nineteenth century.

1860-1890

998 A very similar shape but without the cornice. The top is marble in a very French style and even the hinges are outset with very French-looking finials. The marquetry decoration of the sides and the courting couple on the front door are not of the quality and execution normally associated with France and the mounts lack the vitality of the Paris makers. It is unusual for the German cabinet makers to quarter-veneer furniture in kingwood. Possibly this cabinet was made in a provincial district between the disputed borders of Germany and France.

1860-1890

999 A detail photograph showing clearly the outset hinge that was in common usage in France, Spain and Italy and also southern parts of Germany. The crude carcass and construction immediately make one think that this corner cabinet is mid-eighteenth century but quality is no indication of period. Many of the pieces made in southern Germany and northern Italy during the second half of the nineteenth century were made in this rather cavalier fashion. It is not entirely certain whether this cabinet is from the very southern areas of Germany or from northern Italy. Unfortunately, man-made borders were not enough to limit styles and design of cabinet making and therefore the exact origin is not always clear-cut.

1860-1890

1000 An example of what was to develop in Vienna in the early twentieth century. This walnut cabinet has contrasting rosewood panels and pilasters, traditional enough woods but the style and date is entirely Modernist, the highly individual style which grew out of the influence of Mackintosh and the combination of art and industry that was the hallmark of the Wiener Werkstätte.

1910-1920

CHAIRS — antler

1001 A fine pair of antler chairs that are hardly comfortable enough to be called armchairs — the sitter would have to sit very carefully with his or her arms placed on his or her knees to avoid being spiked. Most antler chairs are made entirely of antlers and it is very unusual to see the oak framework with its well modelled legs and hooves imitating those of a deer. Apart from the legs the base is a simple chair base with a button upholstered drop-in seat.

Third quarter nineteenth century

1002 This little chair is the height of naturalism with its asymmetric 'rococo' antlers. The padded button-upholstered seat is adjustable for use at a piano. It is fascinating to ponder upon the probable design of a matching piano. To our modern tastes a chair like this would hardly be comfortable but at least the piano student would learn to sit bolt upright. Possibly this is the German equivalent of the child's correction chair!

Third quarter nineteenth century

1003 A far more comfortable looking example of antler furniture in a similar style to that of the maker Rampendahl of Hamburg who exhibited at the Great Exhibition. The whole framework is carefully made of various types of antlers and deeply padded for comfort. Only the legs spoil the design in their attempt to continue the theme of the antlers. The seat rail has been carefully veneered with antler horn with a carved central horn panel of a gentleman and his dog resting on their expedition through a dark Germanic forest. These carvings have a lot in common with cameos.

Third quarter nineteenth century

1004 A very unusual horn and horn veneered centre table based on the mid-nineteenth century English loo table. Chairs are more commonly seen. The maker is not certain but almost without doubt it would have been by C.F.H. Rampendahl of Hamburg.

1860s

1005 Another pair of exotic side chairs combining the mid-nineteenth century love of naturalism with the growing demand for pneumatic upholstery. This pair of chairs have a certain amount in common with earlier Biedermeier styles and are of the same overall shape as the pair of fan chairs illustrated on the next page. The wide front legs would be ideal for tripping up passers-by. Had they been as controlled as the backs, the whole effect would have been more elegant and more practical.

Third quarter nineteenth century

1006 Here great effect has been made of a complete spread of a magnificent stag's antlers which forms the entire apron and legs without the need for any other supports. The chairs are not quite a pair although obviously made by the same maker. Of course it would be extremely difficult, if not impossible, to find an exactly matching pair of antlers. The back of the chair on the left has been constructed with metal brackets to help form the splats. The two scrolling metal 'shepherd's crooks' on the front of the left hand chair underneath the apron look like the antennae of a weird and wonderful crustacean and this has obviously been done to protect the sitter from injury.

Third quarter nineteenth century

CHAIRS — 'Empire'/Biedermeier

1007 A delightful pair of fan back chairs in fruitwood, made probably in Vienna for use in the vast Austro-Hungarian empire. The lightness of the wood and simple decoration is a delightful version of the simple Biedermeier style. Although the finish is nothing like as good as the better French or English chairmaker's work, a great deal of skill has been used in the making of the fans which combine realism with a certain amount of strength — an extremely unusual pair of chairs.

1830s

1008 A highly original interpretation of the Empire style but in its revived form of the latter part of the nineteenth century. The apron and legs have none of the quality or attention to detail of the upper part. There is a certain similarity and lightness of style with the previous two fan chairs. The sphinxes are ebonised and parcel gilt with thumb cut headbands and chokers in the Venetian style. The overall style of the chair is a fairly sophisticated form that was popular in Vienna and right across the width of the Austro-Hungarian empire.

1880-1900

1009 Another highly simplified fruitwood chair in the early nineteenth century Austro-Hungarian style with much in common with the pair of fan chairs illustrated on the previous page. From the seat downwards the style is almost identical. The absence of a splat denotes a highly simplified construction and obviously this chair could have been made very cheaply by any chairmaker or modest carpenter in any part of the outback of the Empire.

Second quarter nineteenth century

1010 A severe elm armchair in the early nineteenth century style, probably from north Germany. There was a strong English influence in this part of Germany due to the close proximity, trade and political affiliation during the Napoleonic wars. This chair is a later reproduction of the earlier style and made somewhat crudely by a provincial craftsman.

Second half nineteenth century

1011 and 1012 Two Empire revival side chairs, both of a very similar style. Their exact origin is uncertain although they are closely based on Louis Philippe decoration and the mixture between Empire and Biedermeier. The style is similar to that of the popular *fauteuil à gondole.* Note the almost identical legs on both chairs.

1880-1900 in the style of the 1840s

1014 (right) A bentwood folding armchair ideal for campaign purposes. The style is very much that of Michael Thonet but the frame does not bear his label or stamp. There is a simplicity about the style and framework of this chair which suggests an early feeling. The upholstery arms are attached in a very sympathetic and novel manner. If the nineteenth century had been allowed to progress along the clarity of thought and style that this chair suggests the era would not have obtained the reputation of 'eclectic mess' which so bedevils it even in today's more enlightened thinking.

c.1850

1013 A finely figured birchwood rocking chair. This type of veneer — or, as in many cases, solid wood sections — was very popular throughout Europe during the period of the Biedermeier era. Satin-birch with its multiple burrs was one of the *bois clairs* which were so popularly used as a natural decoration. Here a favourite Empire feature of the swan is used as the arm terminal. For some reason the angle of the rockers is very steep, so much so that it would be very difficult to relax.

Late 1830s to early 1840s

1015 An ash armchair with a huge overstuffed seat but otherwise in a standard Biedermeier form that typifies the Austro-Hungarian sense of style during the modestly un-adventurous second quarter of the nineteenth century. Note the little fans halfway down the back supports, a feature which occurs frequently in Vienna.

1830s

1016 (above right) A small side chair in a similar style, highlighted only by the simple but effective ebony stringing. The back is a familiar 'balloon' shape but with a delightful sweep at the cross-bar.

1830s

1017 An 'X' frame stool in a fairly vigorous style that is difficult to identify but is similar to styles that were developing in Germany. The northern part of Germany, as in Denmark, favoured the mixture of gilding and mahogany but the style of the giltwood carving owes much to Venice and Florence. Is that a small 'fan' creeping into the join of the arms and the legs?

Second quarter of the nineteenth century

1018 Once again of uncertain nationality but in the true manner of cataloguers all over the world if it's heavy and ungainly and you are uncertain of the origins, call it German. Certainly the interpretation of the rams' heads in the carving is of provincial German origin, vaguely in the style of the early 1700s. The highly detailed back is of eighteenth century Spanish leather that was probably once used as wall covering. The wood used is walnut which again does not give a particularly clear idea of origin.

c.1900

1019 A heavy, rather squat, style that suggests a Germanic influence. Certainly the architectural cornice with its elaborate broken swan-neck cresting suggests the swaggering style of southern Germany and Saxony. Somebody has had a great time with the upholstery. Note that the 'C' scrolls and fish scales of the walnut legs have been parcel-gilt.

Mid-nineteenth century

1020 A painted and parcel-gilt side chair with a considerable amount in common with Danish furniture — possibly this chair is from the northern part of Germany or even Denmark. The style is basically Louis XV in its rather cosy but heavy mid-nineteenth century interpretation, even down to the trailing flowers.

Mid-nineteenth century

1021 Another fairly heavy interpretation of mid-eighteenth century rococo with a very slight hint of asymmetry in the cresting. The rococo style is not as exuberant as the eighteenth century rococo that became especially precocious in the Berlin court. Both the seat and the chair-back come out easily for re-upholstery, not a common nineteenth century feature.

Mid-nineteenth century

1022 A comfortable looking *bergère* in very poor quality walnut with parcel-gilt decoration and highlights. Like the previous chair it is based on mid-eighteenth century style but the interpretation is much heavier in both overall design and the carving. The legs of German rococo chairs always seem to be too heavy or alternatively too squat.

Mid-nineteenth century

1023 A tenuous rococo design. The shape of this 'corner' armchair suggests that it was made as a desk chair. The carving has a lot in common with the Italian nineteenth century rococo. Certainly there are many features that would suggest this is in fact an Italian chair, namely the style of carving, especially of the laughing masks at the knees and the rather weak incised decoration on the apron.

c.1900

1024 This little walnut child's chair is based on the French *fauteuil à gondole* but like most pieces of furniture made for children the proportions are incorrectly reduced giving a very squat overall feeling. This is heightened by the necessity of a base to raise the chair to adult table height. However, rather charming and certainly becoming difficult to find. The graining of the walnut is quite black in places resembling rose-wood and the small dotted decoration resembles the English practice of inlaying mother-of-pearl roundles into rosewood at the same period.

c.1840

1025 One of the many thousands of balloon-back chairs made throughout Europe. The frame is comparatively light and note how the back is waisted in a much more accentuated fashion than an English version of the same chair. Once again this chair could have north Italian origins.

Mid-nineteenth century

1026 and 1027 These two chairs are from a common stock which was made from southern Germany through Austria into Switzerland and it is difficult to narrow down the identification any further. As always there are rather naïve inlaid panels on the backs and the solid seats of Alpine hunting scenes. The small side chair is carved with a spray of edelweiss which is not enough to automatically label it Swiss. Compare to a similar chair no.1101.

c.1900

1028 An extremely fine pair of dining chairs made of solid ebony inlaid with engraved ivory grotesque animals and foliage. The style is very similar to that of Milanese engraved ivory inlay but the heavy baroque overall design is typically German. The crestings are pierced and carved with a visored helmet above a vacant cartouche. The finish of these chairs is impeccable, made to a far better standard than the Italian equivalent.

1860s

1029 A pair of very elegant armchairs in the heavy Germanic Gothic style. It is a pity that the execution is just a little bit dumpy — the legs especially. The arms and thickly sprung seats have a lot in common with the Flemish 'Jacobethan' chairs so popular in the second half of the nineteenth century. The Renaissance style baluster supports to the back look a little incongruous. The Gothic tracery is very thick and heavy. German Gothic was influenced by the English architect A.W.N. Pugin but his forms were all too often made heavier, mixed with the English Strawberry Hill Gothic that was so very light and attenuated during the 1770s.

c.1840

1030 A common or garden Thonet chair from the turn of the century but with quite pleasing shapes at the back. The solid panelled scallop shell seat is normally a later feature.

c.1900

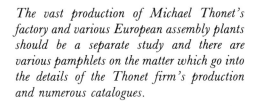

The vast production of Michael Thonet's factory and various European assembly plants should be a separate study and there are various pamphlets on the matter which go into the details of the Thonet firm's production and numerous catalogues.

1031 (left) A more unusual chair also by Thonet with an extremely elegant frame but strangely reverting to the fluted tapering legs of the Louis XVI style. The cane seat is more typical in mid-nineteenth century Thonet chairs.

c.1900

1032 Again the tall back which became popular towards the end of the nineteenth century and a very simple overall outline with a stamped 'crocodile skin' seat.

c.1900

1033 A most ungainly chair, not of bentwood but in similar vein, now with a replaced plywood seat. The underside of the seat is stamped with an indistinct Polish factory mark.

Early twentieth century

1034 The famous and much copied Thonet rocking chair which was first exhibited in England at Crystal Palace in 1851. The complex scroll work of the sides has a light and elegant feel and shows the design of a highly individual mind. Compare this chair to the folding chair no.1014.

Third quarter nineteenth century

PIANOS

1035 The elegant simplicity of Viennese design looking back to the early nineteenth century and Biedermeier forms and use of contrasting veneers. The satinwood is extremely straight grained — a cheaper variety that was imported in large quantities into Europe from the Dutch East Indies in the nineteenth century. This is a good example of the revival of early nineteenth century forms towards the end of the century.

1890s

1036 A wonderful mid-nineteenth century baroque extravaganza with beautifully figured walnut veneers carefully chosen and expertly applied to the continuously moving and rolling shapes. The upper part has an amusing 'human face' look about it. The legs are extraordinary in their immensity with their generous and profuse bunches of fruit and flowers. The look of this exotic and extraordinary shape is one of fecundity that even the most outrageous rococo shapes of the second quarter of the eighteenth century could not capture. The piano looks as though it is about to take off in a hurry. Surprisingly, a piano in a similar theme was exhibited by an English maker in 1851 at the Crystal Palace but there was little of the natural outrageousness of this example. A masterpiece of cabinet making and, for its originality, a masterpiece in design. At this period a piano may well still have a wooden frame which reduces its interest to a would-be piano player. The iron frames are stronger and are not liable to warp and therefore keep in tune. It would be difficult to imagine the purchaser of this piano actually having the nerve to sit down and play it. The piano bears the initials V.R. and N.E. and was reputedly a wedding present from Queen Victoria to Napoleon III and Eugénie in 1853. The maker is not recorded but could Prince Albert have commissioned it from Germany?

1850s

1037 A honey coloured Hungarian ash settee in the late Empire style with simple ebonised stringing. The shape is similar to the large Danish and Scandinavian settees of the same period.

1830s

1038 The heavy Gothic features of this oak hall seat have a lot in common with English gothicism but the overall effect is too heavy. The mixture of baroque columns with Gothic finials was a common eclectic mistake that spoils the purity of much nineteenth century Gothic revival. The languid gentleman asleep in the niche is as yet unidentified. The two attendants flanking him look decidedly uncomfortable in comparison.

Mid-nineteenth century

1039

1041

1040

1039, 1040 and 1041 The German love of heavy rococo forms (note the similarity in shape of the walnut piano no.1036 to the top-rail of the settee no.1039) did not do away with their feeling the need for comfort. Although the first of these settees looks hard and unrelenting, its shape *looks* comfortable and has an overall feeling of warmth and generosity. It is not so formal as to inhibit the sitter from putting his feet up. No.1040 is almost Italian in the sculptural effect of the carving which is very finely executed. Certainly pieces of this type would dominate a room and be vastly expensive to upholster. They are in mahogany which is quite generously figured; an indication of the love of natural woods in the second quarter of the nineteenth century.

1039 *1830-1840*
1040 *c.1850*
1041 *1840s*

1042 A cast iron garden bench that appears in English, French, German and American catalogues and could have been made in any one of these countries. The Gothic styling, however, is a little more complicated than would normally be allowed in England and has a Germanic interpretation in this rather severe feeling of what is normally a very light style. This type of furniture is continuously being re-cast and is difficult to date but it is important to differentiate between a nineteenth century version and a modern version. Conceivably American.

Mid-nineteenth century

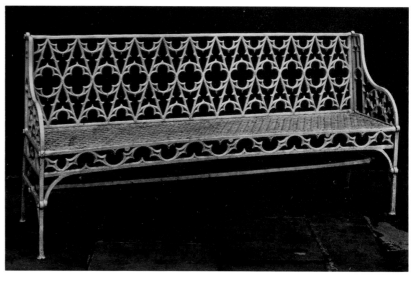

CHAIRS — upholstered

The following four photographs are all from the Berliner Möbel Journal and they show upholstered furniture designed by various hands. They all demonstrate the need for 'pneumatic bliss' and the love of upholstery, tassels and fringes. It some cases the designs were so literally interpreted by plagiarising cabinet makers and upholsterers that the proportions of the finished article had the rather naïve feeling that some of the drawings create.

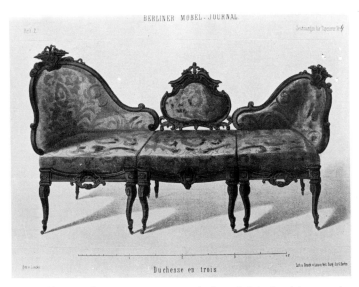

An Italianate three part settee or *duchesse brisée*. In this case the German retailer has given it a French name.

Here upholstery has almost completely taken over but where the woodwork peeps through it is baroque, which adds to the 'comfortable' feeling.

In a wonderful mixture of German and French this has been entitled a 'Fauteuil und Fufssefsel'. The feeling once again is of an international French style, imitating the *duchesse brisée*.

A simple armchair but with elaborately overscrolled side supports. Heaven help the joiner who tried to make such a chair on so spindly a set of legs. The decorative upholstery resembles that of the second quarter of the eighteenth century except, of course, the tassels and fringes.

COMMODES

1043 A poorly made walnut small chest of drawers in a weak interpretation of the mid-eighteenth century style. Once again the style has much in common with the northern part of Italy. The light rococo marquetry however is of the 'constructivist' type popular in the states of southern Germany. That is the 'C' scrolls and flowers are all very solidly joined together and appear to have been built up rather than to have just grown as in other countries. Also, German decoration often has a 'shell' in some part of its rococo decoration, usually at the top, as in this case.

c.1860

1044 A mediocre inverted breakfront commode in the shape of an exaggerated longbow. The wide crossbanding is a repeated Germanic feature. The mounts are vigorously thought out but made very insubstantially.

Late nineteenth century

1045 The veneers are very similar, as is the crossbanding, the overall shape is slightly less exaggerated than the previous chest. There must have been thousands of these small walnut commodes made after the popular style of the 1760s. Many have the little stand — a feature also common to Denmark.

Late nineteenth century

1046 A toilet or dressing table with a great deal in common with the Spanish Empire style known as the Fernandino style. This one is thought to have been made in Germany or Austria where the Empire forms were to remain popular for many years. The swan motif and the parcel-gilding are also repeated in Spain, together with the pure white marble top. However, the overall feel is more reminiscent of Vienna whose large Empire was to influence and be influenced by many independent sources.

1825-1835

1047

1048

1050

1049

1047, 1048, 1049 and 1050 A selection of walnut bedroom furniture in a similar style, once again with the very familiar wide German crossbandings, in this instance carefully chosen to give a chequered effect. The five drawer tall commode has an upper shelf supported by two poor quality Dresden figures. All four pieces have very spindly cheaply gilt-brass rococo mounts which hold the crudely painted enamel plaques decorated with romantic couples. Some of the handles are identical. Of course nos. 1047 and 1048 are from the same suite but no. 1050 is not, yet its handles are the same. All these pieces are mass-produced factory-made articles that are simply a commercial way of filling houses with the types of furniture that yo-yoed up and down in popularity throughout the second half of the nineteenth century.

All c.1900

1052 An elm table in a simple seventeenth century style with a tip top. Once again it is difficult to know whether this was intended as a copy or made in a traditional provincial style.

c.1830

1051 A large pine cupboard in an architectural mid-eighteenth century style that is still very provincial and has not caught up with the Empire although there is a glance at neo-classicism.

c.1835

1053 A painted pine hall or kitchen chair of very simple form with little pretence at elegant design but with a very definite naïve charm.

c.1835

1054 A huge carved and decorated cupboard in the same style as the cupboard from Bayern illustrated at the beginning of this page. The imposing baroque carving is weakly supported by the bending columns. What a monster but even so, sure to be very popular.

1830s

1055 A simple painted commode with a 'marbled' decoration. The shape is ostensibly late eighteenth century but the execution much later.

c.1840 *

1056 A marvellous bed painted with rustic charm and naïvety. It is interesting to see the simulated drapery on the head and footboard.

c.1830

1057 A Schwabian painted cradle. The lightness of the decoration is not unlike that popular in Italy in the mid-eighteenth century. Once again the style of this provincial piece looks back fifty to eighty years, making it extremely difficult to date.

1830s

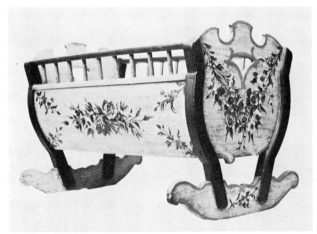

1058 A rustic rush seated chair that is found in various forms throughout England and the rest of Europe from the period 1750 to 1850. Once again this type of chair is very difficult indeed to date. The turning at the top of the back supports and the top of the spindles is very distinctive but does not appear to be a regional indication as it is not often seen on any other furniture from the Hamburg area.

1840s

1059 The theme of the 'marbled' decoration with naïve rustic scenes is a familiar German feature on provincial furniture. The shaped panels on the cupboard doors are repeated again and again on these German provincial *armoires*.

Dated 1838

TABLES — tripod

1060 and 1061 Although by no means identical, these two lady's work tables are drawn from the same inspiration. There must have been many designs like the one below from the *Berliner Möbel Journal* which intended this one to be executed in palissandre. The table below is made in veneered mahogany, with well-figured wood. The cushion frieze is a common Germanic feature. The lock pins will be round and not very good quality.

The design and the table 1840s

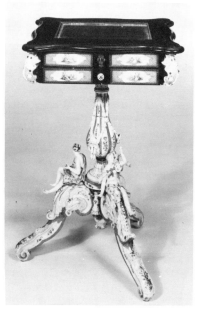

1062 and 1063 Two examples of Meissen mounted furniture in the same theme as cabinet no.980. The top of no.1062 is very like the top of an Italian table on page 434, which itself appears to draw its inspiration from England in the second quarter of the eighteenth century. The heavy baluster support is out of proportion but at least the child figures do not stick out as vulnerably as the two larger figures on the other table. The Meissen factory also made porcelain chandeliers in a similar vein. The little table on the right is a display table — how difficult it would be to focus on the display with the gaudy colours of the base. These small tables seem to survive in fewer quantities than their larger brothers, the cabinets. At least the cabinets are almost immovable whilst small tripods can be moved easily and become liable to damage.

Both 1880s

1064 An ebonised centre table with a tip top painted overall with gilt flowers. It is poorly made with uninspired proportions. The complicated tripod support has flat sides in keeping with the more eastern European countries.

1840s

1065 (above) A finely made large breakfast table in well figured walnut with good scrolling marquetry. The marquetry around the edge has a certain similarity with Dutch marquetry. The similarity disappears with the centre spray of flowers. This type of table is certainly very handsome and practical, appealing to a wide range of tastes.

Late 1850s

1066 A quite horrible example of antler furniture. This small occasional table was obviously made up from someone's trophies of an East African safari. It is not quite as bad as elephant's foot waste paper baskets, but almost.

Third quarter nineteenth century

1067 The peace and quiet of an early eighteenth century reproduction form in various panels of figured walnut joined by ebonised strapwork. The heavy cross stretchers must surely be totally unnecessary on such a bulky table and are an extraordinary hangover of the late seventeenth century style in a nineteenth century reproduction. The general feeling of this table is that of Saxony. It is good and solid but without drawers, an all too common and frustrating feature of this type of table throughout Europe.

Second half nineteenth century ✳

1068 A fine centre table in Empire style in light Hungarian ash with ebony stringing. The shape is similar to an English sofa table but without the adjustable end flaps. It is a pity that the maker has joined the columns together at the half way stage and felt it necessary to use such wide scrolled trestle supports, which upset the rather elegant clean lines. The slightly raised pole stretcher with its flat footbar is a novelty. It certainly appears that the table was intended for occasional use as a writing table.

1830s

1069 Nineteenth century naturalism taken to its logical (?) conclusions. This root work garden table is made entirely of cast iron and is the height of sophisticated rustic furniture. Cleverly the designer has been sensible with the multiple pierced top, allowing the rain to drain away quickly on such a vulnerable metal that rusts easily — of course a tray would be needed to make any use of the table. The base has a lot in common with the antler chairs illustrated on pages 341 and 342, which is one of the reasons for identifying this table as German although it appeared in various European catalogues.

Third quarter nineteenth century

1070 This is the German interpretation of the Louis XV era. The top swivels and is baize lined for playing cards. The ebonised softwood decoration contrasts all too boldly with the kingwood veneers which are quarter veneered in the French style. This is a typical example of Germanic overdressing. If only the apron was not so heavy and the legs had not been extended by just one scroll too many, the overall feeling would be far more satisfactory.

1850s

1071 and 1072 An extremely unusual bureau cabinet veneered in walnut and with copious painted decoration. This is the ultimate in Germanic design, recalling the splendours of the baroque period with a little Renaissance thrown in in the upper columns. The whole decoration consists of very well fed naked cupids, cherubs and *putti* picking grapes and hanging abundant swags of flowers. The inside of the upper cupboard doors is decorated with two innocent cupids each holding a plaque inscribed in German. How difficult it would be to work and concentrate with all the goings-on of this cabinet. However, a finely made example of the German baroque revival and very rare.

Dated 1862

A dramatic indication of the possibilities of malachite in furniture. This Russian table is beautifully made with fine quality ormolu, albeit a little naïvely cast with grotesque chimera. The malachite is well figured but does not have the tight swirling cloud figuration normally associated with Russian malachite. However, the provenance of this table suggests that it was originally made in Russia with the malachite veneer. There is a certain amount of work being done in Paris and New York on plain "Russian" pieces adding malachite veneer of the Congolese variety. A highly decorative table and very rare.

Mid-nineteenth century

1073, 1074 and 1075 An exquisitely made *bureau rognon*. All the small drawers in the frieze and upper part operate from six push buttons hidden in the central cupboard. The style of the marquetry is that of the finest work of the mid-eighteenth century but on a plainly nineteenth century base. The profuse inlay is finely executed in various woods and baroque mother-of-pearl and ivory. This is the type of work popular in Augsburg which continued to make high quality marquetry furniture from the seventeenth century right through into the middle of the nineteenth century. The almost identical table was partially constructed from the writing cabinet of a mid-eighteenth century bureau bookcase and was bought by the Baron Meyer Rothschild when forming his collection, even before he built his famous Mentmore Towers. This type of profuse marquetry became popular in Germany and in France in the revival of boulle work in the second quarter of the nineteenth century. The German craftsman was certainly capable of producing the very best marquetry. The profuse decoration is comparable to some of the furniture made by Abraham and David Roentgen in the mid-eighteenth century but in a far more fussy style.

1830s

WRITING DESKS

1076 An ugly interpretation of the mid-eighteenth century style with rococo constructivist decoration. Once again the veneers are walnut. The shape, as so often happens with German furniture, appears to be trying to be different for the sake of difference. A poorly made desk with little to recommend it except for its small size and practical use.

1860s

1077 A fall front secretaire in the style of mid-eighteenth century France, again with a complicated asymmetrical rococo decoration, in which every flower and every tendril has been carefully joined together to form a solid construction. The German cabinet makers certainly gave themselves a difficult task with the undulating sides, which in this case are of a triple *bombé* pattern.

1860s

1078 A tambour fronted writing desk with a pull-out writing drawer decorated completely in parquetry and copying willingly, if not faithfully, the French Transitional style. It would be easy to imagine that this piece of furniture was made in France but the proportions are too ungainly and the curious inverted breakfront form which is consistent from top to bottom is an unnecessary Germanic architectural feature.

1880s *

1079 An elegant small *bureau en pente* bearing the arms of Princess Mathilde. The style is that of Louis XVI with the fluted tapering legs but the upper part is really a box that has just simply been placed on a convenient set of legs. However, the kingwood veneering and tulipwood banding are of fine quality. Certainly the Viennese (?) cabinet maker who made this small desk was trying to copy the up-to-the-minute French *Louis Seize* revival.

1860s

WRITING CABINETS/SECRETAIRES

1080 and 1081 Two very similar *secretaires à abattant* in a style that was popular in northern Germany and in Holland. Certainly the concave and convex drawers are a Germanic feature (which is repeated on the little worktable and its companion design nos. 1060 and 1061). The extra decoration is a Germanic rather than a Dutch feature and the baroque twist-turned columns on no.1081 are also German.

1840s

1082 An extraordinary example of a secretaire that goes back to the decorative features of the large seventeenth century German cupboards which have various styles, the most amusing being 'Hamburger Schapp'. Great effect has been made of the contrast between the black walnut veneers and the burr walnut panelling. The normal effect and shape of the burrs can clearly be seen on the writing flap. The ebonised mouldings contrasting with the walnut have a lot in common with American furniture from the Grand Rapids area. This American style may well have been imported by German immigrant craftsmen.

1870s

1083 Another example of plain but well figured mahogany similar to nos. 1080 and 1081. However, the use of a pair of cupboard doors in the lower part, rather than drawers, will make this less popular.

1840s

1084 and 1085 A very finely finished burr-maple veneered pedestal writing desk that doubles as a dressing table. Certainly it was intended as a dressing table but is more likely to be given pride of place as a desk at today's prices. The brass and pewter marquetry is inlaid with stunning precision — all beautifully engraved. The detail photograph gives some impression of this technical skill that was perfected by the German craftsmen in the sixteenth century. The crest is that of the Rothschilds engraved with the family motto *Concordia Integras Industria,* which might well have been the maxim for the workshop which was able to produce such an excellent piece of furniture.

c.1840

1086 An extraordinary and curious writing desk. The slatted front falls downwards and away to form a writing surface. The carved walnut has small flowers in a German/Austrian style but there is no clear pointer as to the true origins of this unusual desk. At first glance it looks art nouveau but there is none of the decoration normally associated with this period, only earlier features. The almost elegant front legs have swan's head terminals in a clear interpretation of the popular Empire motif common to most of Europe. The brass pierced hinges and escutcheon have a practical Gothic/medieval simplicity. A very unusual piece which remains at present a mystery.

Late 1870s

1087 A return to simple baroque forms of the period c.1700. The twist turned columns are a permanent German feature even in the nineteenth century. The walnut veneers with their wide banding are a characteristic feature. The only problem with this particular type of desk with its very shallow kneehole is that it is very difficult to use effectively, regardless of the size of the user. There is nowhere to stretch the legs and the sitter's knees would always be in the way of the lower drawer.

1900-1920 *

VARIOUS

1088 Another unusual writing desk after a design by Danhauser in the form of a pedestal. The curious shape leads one to imagine that it was possibly intended for use as a clerk's desk for a butler or servant. The two flaps fold inwards and the hinged main flap then conceals the drawers. Quite possibly this was one of a pair, each with a clock or bronze or other ornament. Perhaps if this was intended for a hall it might have been used, standing, to finish the address of a letter or a last minute note. Clearly the style is very similar to the English Edwardian period with a cheap straight grained Dutch East Indies satinwood and ebony stringing.

c.1900

1089 A photograph of one fold of an exuberant three-fold rococo screen with parcel-gilt walnut carving. Once again each piece of the rococo carving is carefully interlaced and constructed with other pieces giving it a feeling of strength and solidity, notwithstanding the lightness of the decoration. The needlework is mid-eighteenth century on silk and in this case only adds to the riot of scrolls. Could be French.

c.1860

1090 A German equivalent of the English Warwick school that became popular in both countries during the late 1840s. Certainly game had featured in baroque carvings throughout northern Europe in the very late seventeenth century but was never so morbidly executed as in Germany and England at the height of the Exhibition Era in the mid-nineteenth century. The Austrian firm Carl Leistler of Vienna made large amounts of similar carved furniture but it is uncertain whether the inspiration originated in Germany or England.

1850s

1091 and 1092 A considerable quantity of these carved bear hat, coat and umbrella stands must have been made in southern Germany and Austria during the second half of the nineteenth century, attracting home as well as overseas buyers. Most, like these two, are made in several pieces, not from one piece of wood. The bears are always quite well carved but the remainder, the tree and the rock work, nearly always are rather crude using heavy dark stained woods although sometimes best quality pine is used. The one on the right with a barometer is certainly a novelty.

Late nineteenth century

1093 An oak side chair that sums up the most stylish achievements of the later German art nouveau or *jugendstil*. This powerful design is by a furniture maker and designer from Munich, Richard Riemerschmid. Designed almost at the end of the nineteenth century, it was a beacon of the Modernist Movement of the twentieth century, incorporating flowing lines of reserved plant form with strength, style and, above all, functionalism. The design was just a one-off streak of genius from a man who had earlier been interested in the German Arts and Crafts style and within two or three years, with one or two possible exceptions, he was designing modern-looking furniture based on pedantic traditional ideas.

Designed 1898, exhibited in Paris 1900

1094 An interesting nest of four beechwood quartetto tables by the Thonet brothers. The attenuated form and stylised plant form on the splats of the largest table show how closely Thonet followed the Vienna *Sezession,* with its elegant designs and almost Glasgow School feel.

c.1900

SWITZERLAND

1096 A glove box of very similar export form. It is amazing that the pheasants' tails have survived. The whole form is very similar indeed to the previous box, especially in the detail of the stippled ground for the applied decoration. In both cases the carved game groups on the top are applied separately and were probably made by one particular craftsman secluded in an isolated chalet.

c.1900

1095 A small Swiss carved walnut cigar box that was made in large quantities for a greedy and adventurous tourist industry. Swiss pieces are invariably carved with edelweiss and hung with fruit or game in a very Austrian manner. Although the overall effect is quite good, the quality is never very high. The carver always appears to be aiming for quantity rather than quality.

c.1900

1097 and 1098 These are detail photographs of the lock on the last illustration. Note that a round locking pin goes into a typically Continental round hole and the pin itself is held by a bar inside the lock once the key is turned. English locks never have a pierced locking hole — the locking section is always cut out of the pin from one side. This type of lock is common to Germany, Austria and Switzerland throughout the nineteenth century.

1099 A rocking chair of uncertain origins made for two children but with the added amusing provision that a toddler can sit facing either way in the middle held firmly by the surrounding bars between the stylised leaves. A robustly made and very unusual rocking chair that was probably made for a special commission. It could have been made anywhere in central Europe.

Mid-nineteenth century

1100 A rare example of Swiss furniture, carved in fruitwood with oak leaves and spring flowers. The carving is done on a stippled 'sanded' ground not unlike the English mirrors of the George II period. The writing surface is made up of a simple parquetry. Although the overall style is the dominant Louis XV form, the decoration and execution are at least individual.

1890s

1101 A very crudely carved hall chair in walnut closely following Austrian and Swiss traditions with a certain amount of Italian influence thrown in for good measure in the legs. The etched decoration on the back and seat panels depicts a hunter leaning precariously on the edge of an alpine rock and a solid cow is portrayed on the seat.

c.1900

1102 This detail photograph shows the extraordinary construction of this chair. The back supports have large square pegs which go right through the seat. The supports in turn are held by large square tapering pegs. The iron bar has been added at a later date for extra strength to one of the legs.

1103, 1104 and 1105 An unusual and good example of a Swiss carved walnut armchair, once again with the familiar edelweiss which in this instance is quite boldly carved, especially round the pierced splat. The central splat and seat have that very weak incised decoration which is so commonly found on late nineteenth century Swiss furniture. The two detail photographs show not only the carving of the edelweiss and the popular incised and stippled decoration at the top of the splat but also how susceptible walnut is to woodworm, with which this chair is riddled.

c. 1900

SPAIN

Spain, torn by war during the eighteenth century, had been influenced by both France and England. However, the interpretation of furniture designs always retained an individual character and style, albeit nearly always incorporating a definite Italian influence.

It was not until almost the last quarter of the nineteenth century that Spain finally threw off the Fernandino style. A distinctive style, in Directoire and Empire shapes, the Fernandino resulted in an amalgam of heavy, rather contrived forms richly adorned with bronze mounts and carved gesso work. Workmanship was often indifferent. Walnut tended not to be used as much as in previous centuries but poplar was in considerable use for chair making, as it was easy to turn and stain. Rosewood was in plentiful supply from South American colonies and became highly popular. Mahogany, however, continued to be most in demand, as its supply too was readily available from Spain's colonies.

Together with Italy, romantic ideals led to a revival of Gothic forms during the 1830s, which prevailed with only slight effect alongside the Fernandino style.

Spain began to look back at this time to the eighteenth century both at home and in France and an eclectic mixture of motifs and shapes started to dominate design by the middle of the century. Gilt baroque forms adorned with *putti* and flowers often carved in almost full relief were cultivated as a direct reaction to the severe forms of the Fernandino style. The Fernandino style had itself pointed the way to a baroque revival in that the Spanish craftsman, like his Italian counterpart, found it difficult to resist incorporating sculptural forms into furniture design. There was no shortage of skilled carvers or gilders and few later Fernandino pieces are to be seen without a purely decorative piece of carved gilding or flamboyant giltwood leg supporting an otherwise severe desk or chair.

This baroque extravagance takes its name, 'Isabellino', from Queen Isabella, whose reign neatly straddled the middle of the century. A fine example of Spanish iron furniture by Tomas de Megne of Madrid was exhibited at the Great Exhibition in London, 1855. Traditional ironwork was the mainstay of the Spanish craftsman's art at this time, the small work of Placido Zuloaga (fl.1851-1890) being possibly its greatest exponent.

The strengthening of the Spanish economy after the civil war of 1868-1875 allowed time to reflect back to the purely Spanish styles of the sixteenth and seventeenth centuries. Traditional *vargueños* or fall front writing cabinets on trestle tables, the legs joined by a wrought iron ringed hoop and turned chairs with embossed leather upholstery, derived from the *sillón de fraileros* or monk's chair, were copied by the hundred. The *vargueño* and *papeleira*, simply an open cabinet on a trestle or twist-turned stand, were made by traditional methods using traditional tools popular during the sixteenth century. Indeed, in many districts neither the tools nor styles had been changed considerably during the last three hundred years. Consequently, many pieces of cabinet work in Hispano-Flemish style are exceedingly difficult to date as the same softwood linings, heavy crude iron locks and large dovetails were still being used and are invariably copied today.

For the most part, Spanish furniture of the nineteenth century was a weak and crudely executed reflection of past glories of the Empire. A notable exception to this is furniture made for the Court of Isabella II. A bedroom suite supplied to her c.1850 and now at the Palacio de Aranjuez is an example of a wonderfully overdone Louis XV style profusely inlaid with flowers, the exaggerated proportions in a style only imagined in the English design catalogues of Henry Lawford but rarely executed. In fact, the proportions are so exaggerated that one is forced to believe that the execution was naïvely copied directly from a design book. Needless to say, the Spanish love of sculpture ruled the day and the bed is covered in huge gilt-bronze vases of flowers in full relief.

A popular revived theme was the Churrigueresque style, named after a leading architect of the seventeenth century. Many flat plain table tops with hooped and knopped iron supports were made in a cunningly 'early' style in the late nineteenth and early twentieth centuries.

Antonio Gaudi y Coronet (1852-1926) was the architectural genius who almost single-handedly brought Spain from the nineteenth into the twentieth century. Only Lluis Domènech y Montaner (1850-1923), whose most important work was at the beginning of the twentieth century, can begin to be compared with Gaudi. Gaudi's novel and ferocious work was mainly reflected in his architecture, especially the stunning Church of the Sagrada Familia built between 1883 and 1926. Influenced by the teachings of John Ruskin in England and the architectural practices of Viollet-le-Duc in France, Gaudi's furniture was first seen at the Casa Vicens built between 1878 and 1880. Even the sparkling originality of Gaudi, however, seemed to falter and some of his furniture designs of the latter part of the century are of a disappointingly conventional form, only relieved by the application of vigorous wrought-iron decoration. Barcelona stood alone representing modern development of style at the end of the century in Spain. This purely Catalan equivalent of art nouveau was termed simply the *Stile Modernista* or *Arte joren* and was an important contribution to the Moorish influence which overtook that of the Japanese style in northern Europe at the turn of the century. Spain and Portugal inadvertently contributed to the English Arts and Crafts Movement when C.R. Ashbee, architect and designer and founder of the Guild of Handicraft, started to design adventurous desks and cabinets on stands whose form was taken directly from the sixteenth century *vargueño*.

PORTUGAL

England, France and Germany influenced Portuguese taste and ideas during the early part of the century. England had close trade ties with Portugal and the crushing occupation of Napoleon left a dominant Empire style that was employed throughout most of Europe. German design had a surprising impact on fashion and, unlike other southern European countries, the Biedermeier style enjoyed a certain popularity.

Simultaneously Spain and Portugal had developed an Isabellino or neo-baroque style, although Portugal never quite inherited the love of gilding and carving of free standing figures as in Spain or Italy. The art of carving was far more restrained, developed along northern European lines. The dominant use of imported South American, mainly Brazilian, woods such as jacaranda or pausanto allowed free crisp carving of these hard but easy to work woods.

At the accession of Carlos I in 1889, the strong influence of Queen Maria II's consort, King Ferdinand, encouraged a revival of earlier styles copied faithfully, much as in Spain and Italy at the same period. Fostered by the International Exhibition in Oporto in 1865, the Louis styles embodying the principles of Louis XIV or baroque furniture were manufactured at this time for wealthy patrons.

Portugal's tendency was to look back to seventeenth and eighteenth century forms rather than to the troubled times of the sixteenth century with their heavy French influence in carving, from which period surprisingly little remains. The seventeenth century *contador* — long tables with elaborately turned and knopped legs, traditional canopy beds and furniture of the Donna Maria style of a hundred years earlier, began to dominate Portuguese furnishings, interspersed with the ubiquitous tub and button-upholstered chairs and the sense of comfort necessitated by the dominant influences from northern Europe.

This is an interesting room with its curved walls lined with purpose built cases for a collection of fans and is fitted with comfortable button-upholstered benches. The fire screen is an example of the sculptural excesses of the Spanish furniture maker in a very heavy rococo style c.1860.

The nineteenth century love of tassels and upholstery has even covered up the naked door to match the window curtains. Note the sharp angle of the mirrors on the right hand wall. The large boulle centre table in the middle of the room is French c.1860 and looks to be an impressive and very unusual example — not a type seen on the international market. It is flanked by two jardinières in a matching style — an impressive and rare suite. The set of armchairs around the room are white painted with gilt carved decoration in the Isabellino style.

This rather severe and dark gentlemen's smoking room is furnished with mahogany furniture in the late Empire style known as Fernandino. The guéridon with its dolphin supports is much heavier than French or Italian examples. All the proportions are excessive, even the scrolled arms of the chairs. The settee looks as though it is probably German.

A delightfully light and airy bedroom with Moorish arches supported on composite columns. The chairs, pillars and dressing table are very cheaply made and white painted with gilt decoration. The wardrobe on the right is vaguely in a Louis XVI style and probably dates to c.1900. The beds also are probably early twentieth century.

Terms

A madeiras vistas. Leather upholstery attached to back rails of chairs.
Araña. Chandelier.
Arcon. Chest, flat topped.
Armario. Cupboard.

Cadeiras de vestir. Chair cover (brocade).
Cama de Bilros (Port.). Turned frame canopy bed.
Cofre. Arched coffer.
Consola. Self supporting side table.
Contador (Port.). Panelled cabinet on stand.

Doiradinha (Port.). Painted chair.

Fernandino. Empire style till c.1850.

Guadamecil. Coloured leather, esp. Cordora.
Isabellino. Baroque style of mid-nineteenth century.

Leito a inglesa (Port.). Dual purpose bed/settee.

Manufactura real. Royal workshop founded in mid-eighteenth century.
Mesa. Table.
Morillos. Fire dogs.
Mudéjar. Geometric mouldings and intarsia introduced by Moors comparable to Italian *certosina* (q.v.).

Papeleira. Open fronted cabinet similar to *vargueño* (q.v.).
Pe de pincel. A scroll foot of a chair.
Pe de sapata. Portuguese claw and ball foot.
Pe enrolada. Double scrolled foot.
Pie de puente. Trestle stand.

Ratona (Port.). Low table.
Reloj. Clock.
Rinconera. Corner cupboard.
Sillón. Chair.
Sillón de cadera. 'X' frame chair.
Sillón de fraileros. Monk's chair.

Taquillon. Panelled chest often used as a cabinet stand.
Tremidos (Port.). Waved mouldings, usually ebony.

Vargueño (bargueño). Fall front cabinet.

Spain

1106 A very well made *papeleira* on stand in the traditional style of the mid-seventeenth century. The panels are engraved ivory on a red tortoiseshell ground depicting the story of Don Quixote (after Gustave Doré) and his various adventures. This is a tribute to the modern Spanish cabinet maker's art and because of the good quality workmanship would be very expensive to buy. The style of the cabinet has a lot in common with Flemish mid-seventeenth century cabinets.

Third quarter twentieth century

1107 Another *papeleira* on stand in a traditional Moorish *mudéjar* style. The base is of a type used in the first half of the sixteenth century, especially in the Catalán area. The top is decorated with coloured glass on a gilt and gesso ground. A highly complex design in a traditional manner.

Early twentieth century ✳

1108 A variation of the *sillón de fraileros*. The studded and embossed leather seat is a popular Spanish seventeenth century technique and the leatherwork is of the finest quality.

1880s ✳

1109 A most extraordinary chair. The heavy brass studding and embossed leather seat have much in common with Spanish sixteenth and seventeenth century furniture but the carving of the bird amongst grapes is most unusual — and rather crude. This chair is carved and turned in a soft walnut which is very open to attack by woodworm.

Second half nineteenth century

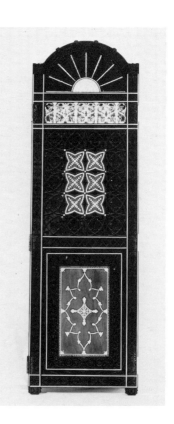

1110 (left) The heavily moulded geometric pattern of the lid of this bureau is a late influence of the Spanish *mudéjar* style but in this instance seems to have been muddled up with architectural ornament that is very popular in northern Europe. There is a very distinct cross-flow of Hispano-Flemish influence. An ugly brute by northern European taste, not very well made but certainly unusual.

Second half nineteenth century

1111 (right) A three fold screen with a delicately pierced Gothic central panel and heavily biased Indian style inlay.

Late nineteenth century

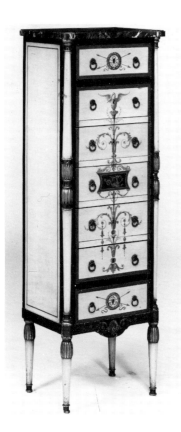

1112 A 'Napoleonic' *semanier* painted an egg-shell white with late Empire motifs. The top is simulating *verde antico* marble. There was a great vogue for white painted furniture with gilt decoration in Spain in the late eighteenth century. The gadrooning on the legs is a common feature.

Early twentieth century

1113 A reproduction commode vaguely imitating the French Louis XV style. A large amount of this type of furniture has been made in the twentieth century in Spain and is often confused with French nineteenth century furniture. The inlay is very restrained and unimaginative and the shape totally wrong for French furniture. The inlay and shape vaguely looks back to the Madrid royal workshops — the Manufactura Real — which were run by the Neapolitan Gasparini from 1768.

Third quarter twentieth century

A very fine pair of vases and a pair of tables veneered overall in fine quality malachite with tight dark veined scrolling cloud bands. It would be wrong to call this set complete. Close examination reveals that the vases are a pair and the tables are a pair but there has been no attempt to match the bronze doré of the vases with that of the bases. Although the quality is similar, none of the details match. However, they make an extremely good set. An indication of the fine but rather naïve quality of the metalwork can be seen on the colour detail on page 413.

Mid-nineteenth century

Malachite was found in quite large quantities in Russia and was used to decorate furniture and small objects of vertu in the middle of the nineteenth century.

1114 A very badly made console in mahogany with marquetry detail on the 'cushion' drawer. There is also a small drawer incorporated into the apron. The marquetry of swans was a favourite Spanish decoration from the 1820s onwards. This type of furniture is known as the 'Isabellino' style.

Second quarter nineteenth century

1115 (right) Another console in the Isabellino style with weak marquetry and the familiar heavily scrolled legs. Once again the furniture is complemented by a sculptural gilt cresting.

Second quarter nineteenth century

1116 This is a much better example of the true Isabellino style, which covered the various Louis revivals prominent in the middle of the nineteenth century. The heavy moulded decoration is a prominent Spanish feature of machine made mid-nineteenth century furniture.

1860s

1117 (left) Another version of the Isabellino style, with heavy Empire influence. The very thin marquetry can only just be made out in this photograph. The mahogany is highlighted with parcel-gilt decoration and this, combined with the carved sculptural cresting, is a hallmark of Spanish nineteenth century furniture. The wood carvers in Italy and Spain could never resist adding some sculptural improvements to veneered furniture.

Second quarter nineteenth century

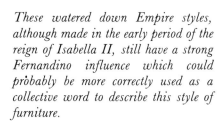

These watered down Empire styles, although made in the early period of the reign of Isabella II, still have a strong Fernandino influence which could probably be more correctly used as a collective word to describe this style of furniture.

1118 A very handsome example of the earlier Fernandino style strongly influenced by Directoire restrained decoration on an Empire form. Once again there is gilt carved decoration.

c.1830

1119 Another example of the Fernandino style almost directly comparable with the French Empire, in a shape very similar to that in Germany and Holland in the early nineteenth century. Stylistically this is c.1800 but could be up to thirty years later.

1800-1830

1120 A very poor photograph of a Louis XVI style sofa and two armchairs from a suite of six chairs, two armchairs and a sofa. The only decoration is the moulded frame and the mechanically carved miniscule floral cresting which is typical of furniture in the Alfonsino style which spanned the last quarter of the nineteenth century.

1875-1895

1121 An armchair and a side chair, also in the Alfonsino style. The fluted back supports with their exaggerated swelling are a very Spanish feature. Quite large quantities of these chairs were made in the Madrid workshops and are often of very poor quality indeed.

1880-1900

1122 Another example of the Louis XV or Isabellino style of mass-produced furniture. The frames are machine carved mahogany with that familiar thumb moulding of a peculiar heavy style that is so typically Spanish.

1860s

1124 The boldly scrolled supports can be more clearly seen in this photograph and typify the late Fernandino style. There is a very Portuguese feel about this type of bed, although the gilt carvings of billing doves, marshall trophies and addorsed terms against a mahogany background are wholly Spanish. In this case the inlay is not unlike Dutch floral marquetry.

Second quarter nineteenth century

1123 A very poor photograph of an Empire style bed in a very late Fernandino style. Once again there are heavily scrolled Empire style supports and the extraordinary shaped bedhead is surmounted by carved and gilt finials.

Second quarter nineteenth century

1125 The bed is another fine example of the Spanish late Fernandino style. It is inlaid with various woods and mother-of-pearl. Once again the huge urn cresting and sculptural decoration is a familiar feature.

Second quarter nineteenth century

1126 Once again a piece of Fernandino furniture slightly out of period and probably made at the very beginning of Isabella II's reign. The thin pure white marble top is seen again and again on Spanish bedroom furniture. The decoration of geometric stringing is unusually reserved and a noteworthy feature for identifying Spanish pieces. The turned legs look straight back to the sixteenth century and have probably been added.

1830s

Also in the same photograph are four little chairs in a traditional style but also called Isabellino. The commode is late Fernandino with a thin white marble top and the unusual inclusion of Gothic decoration. The little table on the left is Italian.

The chairs and commode: second quarter nineteenth century

Portugal

1127 A Portuguese colonial occasional table made in Goa on the western coast of India. The highly intricate almost seaweed marquetry with bone or mother-of-pearl dots suggesting eyes is a very common feature. This type of furniture is very sought after but rarely seen nowadays.

Mid-nineteenth century ✳

1128 Another highly intricate Goanese large centre table. The swan supports are also incorporated in a highly stylised form on the previous table. There is a very definite mixture of European and Indian decoration. The swan, however, is also represented in early nineteenth century Spanish furniture at the Palacio Nacional Madrid.

Second half nineteenth century

1130 A set of metamorphic library steps in a traditional English style specially commissioned for a retired English Army Officer living in Madeira. The capitals and square sections of all the joints are inlaid with heads of foxes and hounds, which must have been a bizarre experience for the lucky Madeira craftsman who was so heavily patronised to make these steps and a matching suite.

c.1850

1129 This very severe ebony cabinet has a lot in common with the early Spanish *mudéjar* style. It is a collector's cabinet with numerous drawers. The contrasting diagonal mouldings are highly effective and very unusual.

Mid-nineteenth century

ITALY

Political instability has never been a good seed-bed for industrial growth and economic strength. Italy in the nineteenth century had little left of its once prosperous economy and almost no industrial power to build up. The northern states were dominated by Austria and there was continual revolution and insurrection in all the states by the middle of the century. The unifying influence created by the leadership and military genius of Garibaldi from 1860 that was to install Victor Emanuel as King of Italy was a tenuous one and there was little to base economic recovery on. The vast majority of the population were peasant farmers producing only at subsistence level, most were illiterate. By the time unification was complete in 1870, with the capture of Rome, the other European powers were all on the way to economic superiority.

As a result the various Italian states still continued to produce furniture in a traditional manner, with the work being carried out by small workshops even in the large towns. Furniture continued to be made in the various regional styles that had been popular for some years using the same hand made techniques and skills passed down through the generations. It was not until the spell of the Renaissance revival had taken hold of the rest of Europe in a firm grip by the 1880s that Italy was stylistically on a par with the rest of the Continent, although it was never an equal industrially. Even today, Italy is a hive of small furniture workshops. These artisans are capable of producing large amounts of furniture in almost any style as faithful reproductions of the past.

Sculpture had for a long time been a prime factor in dictating the forms of Italian furniture. The zenith of this technique was reached at the Palazzo Reale, Turin, by Pelagio Pulagi in the last five years of the decade 1830-1840. However, this sculptural theme was still reflecting the French Empire style which refused to die out in the Italian states, albeit a style now mingled with a romantic form of neo-classicism.

The whole feeling of fashion was French, dominated by the Napoleon family; craftsmen, furniture mounts and designs were imported from Paris. However, by the 1840s an elaborate, more floral, Empire style developed. The work of an Anglo-Italian craftsman, Peters, made an impact at Savoy in rounding the edges of this severe style, gilding the lily possibly but new ideas were welcomed so long after the fall of Napoleon.

It was difficult for a consistent flow of ideas and designs to exist in a non-unified Italy. Each of the numerous states had its own traditional styles of furniture making and design and throughout the century it was still possible to identify regional peculiarities. The classical severity of Rome, the exuberance of the Tuscan baroque style and the circular lobed medallion so loved by the Genoese cabinet maker. Each state with its own court tended to influence local design and it was not until the third quarter of the century that Italian furniture took on the international flavour similar to the rest of Europe.

The Esposizione dei Produtti Dell'Industria Francese at Pirigi in 1844 was a climax over French domination in Italy. The Gothic had enjoyed a limited popularity since the 1820s but never achieved the refined elegant style of Charles X. The possible exception to this is a fine centre table made in Sorrento by Antonino Damorra. The top, in shape, belongs to the Gothic revival and also the column, the base is purely fifteenth century Tuscan. The straw inlay completes the eclectic feeling with free scrolling foliage not emulating Gothic motifs as one would expect.

In the 1850s an ornate Gothic room was built in the Villa Sartorio, Trieste which appears consciously to achieve a Strawberry Hill flavour but is distinctly 'Victorian' in heaviness. The Italian carver was not satisfied with the attenuated forms of the earlier Gothic revivals and inevitably their furniture lacked the essential simplicity that some of the earlier Gothic furniture had enjoyed in France.

The global search for the romantic was ever present in Italian literature and art and designers did not have to look far for inspiration. Renaissance and medieval forms were to be found in abundance and the Dantesque style became increasingly popular. Once again the Italian sculptor/carver was able to make his presence felt in the manufacture of furniture. Wonderful huge winged female caryatids adorned sideboards by Besarelli; the full glories of the Renaissance were reflected in a huge walnut cabinet by Baccetti, both Florentine carvers.

It was at this time, in the middle of the century, that the great Italian love of the fake started to dominate the revivals of furniture design. In cut-off provincial areas the placing of furniture in the various rooms had remained the same as the sparse Renaissance interiors and even by the middle of the nineteenth century furniture was still being made quite commonly, without any intent to deceive, in a style almost three hundred years old. This made it all too easy for craftsmen to produce copies which,

These two photographs both show interiors of the Palazzo Serristori in Florence.

This shows the grandiose Italian love of decorating walls and even ceilings *en grisaille with* trompe d'œil *architecture. As is common with most of Europe, the floor is made up of wooden tiles which were normally, at least by the mid-nineteenth century, strewn with Persian rugs. On the left can be seen a large rococo style mirror above a heavy Roman baroque pier table. The writing desk appears to be made up or altered from an early eighteenth century table and the chair beside it is a copy of a Flemish armchair c.1670. The two mid-seventeenth century style armchairs flanking the desk are copies, as are the three tall backed chairs around the room with their exaggerated outswept back legs in the English style and heavy turned front legs.*

A cosy corner of a large room in the same building. Note the use of the rococo screen of the 1850s with contemporary silk flowers in eighteenth century style. The screen here has a very practical use. The huge Florentine mirror is a wonderful example of the baroque revival that continued in Italy for the last fifty years of the nineteenth century. In the foreground there is a cheaply made Parisian kidney table. To the right of that there is an oval table with four supports, presumably made of walnut, with a marquetry top of a type very popular in Italy from the 1860s onwards. The three chairs in the right hand foreground are all copies of French Louis XVI chairs. The architectural features of the settee and side chair on the back wall are often repeated on the cornices of Italian furniture.

with the plentiful soft walnut timbers in everyday use, were all too easy to artificially age. Many 'faked' pieces of this genre can be found in England today, brought back by Englishmen on their Grand Tour as prized possessions and passed down through the generations as 'the genuine Italian Renaissance *cassone*', making it very difficult to persuade the owner of its dubious authenticity. This is doubtless the same in many other countries of Europe, to say nothing of the myriad of American visitors taking back 'Renaissance' and other 'treasures' after their extended tours.

Comparatively little cabinet work was executed in Italy. The lack of suitable indigenous woods and the sparsity of mechanical production meant that most pieces were made along well established traditional lines. Veneering was laid on a very soft carcass of pine, so soft in many cases that an indent can easily be made into the drawer linings with a thumbnail. Locks were crude iron working on a single lever, the lockplate often crudely cut, bending over at the sides and tapering out away from the tongue. Many southern pieces, especially in Malta, have numerous small pegs or dowells literally pinning the veneer to its soft carcass, but without forming a regular pattern.

The influence of England was quite strong throughout the middle of the century to the extent that various types of furniture were faithful copies and reproduced so that the form of Italian furniture of the international era is similar to that of England. On inspection, however, the construction and materials are quite different, Italy not achieving the high standards of carcass work so common in England and, by the middle of the century, France. A notable exception to this rule is the delightful cabinet by Gatti, inlaid in various woods to very high standards of cabinet work, see colour illustration on page 159 and black and white details on page 441. Machine production in both England and France created a need for new markets and the Italian artisan, with his passion for carving, was no match for commercial competition.

The era of the Risorgimento was one of a middle-class domination of ideals and styles. The world of Dante was revived with fond nostalgia and under his revered name an eclectic style was born.

The Venetian love of the exotic was doubtless inspired by the comparatively close proximity of the near East to this important trading port. Venice was responsible for most of the chinoiserie decoration in Italy in both the eighteenth century and in the nineteenth. The use of blackamoor figures reflects this love for the exotic. Often there were Turkish figures incorporated into Venetian and north Italian carving. It is certainly the love of the exotic which inspired the Turkish themes in European art, especially in France in the 1750s when Van Loo decorated everything *à la turque*. However, in Italy there may have been a more subtle reason for carving Turkish figures in poses of subservience and slavery. Prince Eugène of the famous and powerful House of Savoy had successfully repelled the marauding Turks from the walls of Vienna in the early eighteenth century and the dominant Turks retreated from their European strongholds.

The last half of the century saw an almost unparalleled eclecticism not in a combination of styles forming one piece of furniture but in the furnishing of rooms. Whereas in England at this time eighteenth century furniture was stored in the attic, in Italy it was on show with original Renaissance examples and with nineteenth century furniture, especially upholstered pieces, in the new vogue for comfort. Generally speaking, however, there was not the need to clutter rooms with carpets, upholstered mantelpieces and many small pieces of furniture. The warm climate lent itself to plainer rooms.

The main contradiction to this was in the ever increasing number of hotels built towards the end of the century to house visiting nobility and successful entrepreneurs from Europe and America doing their Grand Tour. An elegant sense of comfort was required whilst still retaining an airy atmosphere.

Italy is one country which appears not to have been inundated in quite the same way as the rest of Europe with the Louis Revival styles. Certainly the vast output of catalogues from France, Germany and England were readily available but the style never really developed in Italy. Likewise Italy was not affected by a socialist movement of art furniture until art nouveau became ever increasingly popular, remaining so throughout the 1920s.

A solitary spark of genius in the Renaissance revival of Italian furniture of the late 1880s was that of the inspired work of Carlo Bugatti, father of the famous car designer, Ettore and the Impressionist animal sculptor Rembrandt Bugatti. Nicknamed 'The Young Leonardo', Carlo Bugatti had an extraordinarily inventive mind. The earliest recorded furniture by Bugatti is a bedroom suite made in 1880. The highly individual flavour rests heavily on Arab taste and architectural and decorative features predominant in nearby North Africa and all the rage amongst Paris painters and sculptors. Stylised *merhabs* and attenuated columns are bound in pressed copper and there are traces of ivory inlay in a predictable Italian-Moorish style seen on so many articles of Italian furniture during the latter years of the century.

The somewhat severe lines of Bugatti's furniture before the turn of the century are relieved with long, naturalistic tendrils of flowers and leaves reminiscent of Carabin's work in Paris. As the years progressed Bugatti experimented more and more with different combinations of materials such as wood, copper, pewter, vellum and leather. All of which, except vellum, were in common enough use in North Africa and still are today. This inspired borrowing from a nearby continent finally developed into a more easily developed art nouveau style, albeit highly individual, after Bugatti moved to Paris at the beginning of the century.

The art nouveau style, commonly called *gusto floreale,* was never indigenous to Italian native design of the late nineteenth century. Italy borrowed a weak watered-down version of the art nouveau from England known as *Le Stile Liberty.* This new style had not really become popular by the end of the century but it continued in a moulded attenuated style, referred to amusingly amongst Belgian and French critics, referring to their own art, as the 'macaroni style'. Certainly this nickname would have been eminently suitable as a reference to *Le Stile Liberty* which continued for some considerable time and is amongst the worst examples of cheaply made, badly designed furniture of the commercial era, only eradicated by the bold radical designs of Gio Ponti and other post-Second World War designers.

MONARCHS

Bourbon and Austrian rule	to 1859
Victor-Emanuel II	1849-1861
	King of Sardinia
	1861-1878
	King of Italy

The above included the rule of the following States: Lombardy, Moderna, Naples, Parma, Piedmont, Romagna, Sardinia and Tuscany. Venice was ceded in 1866 and Rome occupied in 1870.

Umberto I	1878-1900
Victor Emanuel III	1900-1946

Italian Designers, Architects and Makers

ALBERTOLLI, Giocondo (fl.c.1840). Lombardy designer.

ANNON, Luigi (fl. mid-nineteenth century). Furniture designer in Renaissance style.

ANTONELLI, Giuseppe (fl.1840s). Designed and made neo-classical and neo-Gothic furniture.

ARRIGONI, Giuseppe (fl. mid-nineteenth century).

BACCETTI, Andrea (fl. third quarter nineteenth century). Florentine furniture maker and carver, see illustration no.1269. His carvings are in a highly naturalistic style loosely based on Renaissance, anticipating the freedom of movement apparent in art nouveau at the turn of the century. His signature is usually a carved script of surname and christian name followed by *Firenze*.

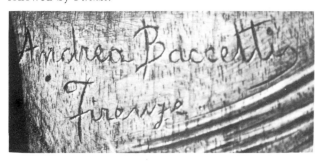

BARBETTI, Angelo (fl. third quarter nineteenth century). Siena cabinet maker and carver. Exhibited at Philadelphia Exhibition 1876. A fine walnut cabinet in sixteenth century style was exhibited at the Paris 1855 Exhibition, now at Bethnal Green Museum.

BASERGA, Giuseppe (fl.c.1900). A maker from Méda exhibiting at the 1905 Liège Exhibition.

BERTINETTI, Diego (fl. second quarter nineteenth century). Decorator working in Geneva and Turin.

BOGLIANI, Giuseppe (fl. second quarter nineteenth century). Decorator working in Geneva and Turin.

BORSATO, Giuseppe. Working in Venice in the early nineteenth century.

BRAMBILLA, Giovanni (fl. third quarter nineteenth century). Milanese(?) ivory engraver.

BUGATTI, Carlo (1856-1940). A brilliant designer at first working in a Moorish idiom. In 1888 he worked from 6 Via Castelfidardo, Milan. In later years he had premises in Paris in the rue Jeanne d'Arc in the *13ème quartier*. Became Italy's most prominent designer. In later years his business at 13 Via Marconi in Milan was taken over by the firm of De Vecchi.

CAPELLO, Gabriele (fl. second quarter nineteenth century). Decorator working in Geneva and Turin. Made classical revival furniture for the King of Sardinia in 1851.

COLLA, Giovanni (fl. second quarter nineteenth century). Decorator working in Geneva and Turin.

DAMORRA, Antonino (fl.1830s). Sorrento furniture maker working in an eclectic rococo Gothic style. Has a table in the Museo Correale, Sorrento.

DE AMICI, Angelo (fl.1860s and 1870s). Milanese cabinet maker. Exhibited a magnificent ornate and inlaid Renaissance style cabinet at the 1867 Paris Exhibition.

FANTASTICI, Agostino (fl.1820s). A Siena architect/designer working in a late Empire style.

FERRERO, G.B., also Carlo Ferrero (fl. second quarter nineteenth century). Working in Geneva and Turin for the King of Sardinia.

FONTANA, Luigi & Co. (fl. early twentieth century). A Milanese firm exhibiting at the 1905 Liège Exhibition.

FRULLINI, Luigi (fl. third quarter nineteenth century). Florentine cabinet maker, although primarily a carver working in a revived Renaissance style. His signature is usually a carved script with the full name, *Firenze* and the date. A trade label is recorded — 'Luigi Frullini, sculptore Legno Lavorante in avorie e su tutti e Legni Ouri Fabricante De mobiliti et Corneie do Ratee del su Colore Firenze Natiole del 1861 In Firenze'.

GAGGINI, Giuseppe (fl. second quarter nineteenth century). Decorator and wood carver working in Geneva and Turin.

GAJANI, Egisto. Florentine carver and gilder exhibited a profuse and finely carved mirror at the Paris 1867 Exhibition.

GATTI, Giovanni Battista (fl.1850-1880?). One of the finest ivory inlay firms of the Exhibition era, exhibiting in 1855 and 1878 in Paris to the very highest standards. Little is known at present about this maker, his few pieces are always highly praised and are well above normal Milanese standards. The Austrian Emperor and Cardinal Amant were amongst his important patrons.

GIUSEPPE, Franzoni (fl.1860s and 1870s). A Milanese carver working for De Amici (q.v.).

GIUSTI, Salvatore (fl.1830s). A Neapolitan decorator.

MANFREDINI, Luigi (fl. second quarter nineteenth century). A Lombardy founder.

MARETTI, Giovanni (fl.1850s). Published furniture designs in the middle of the century.

MARIELLONI, Diego (fl. second quarter nineteenth century). Working for the King of Sardinia in Geneva and Turin.

MEZZANZANICA, Cherubino (fl.1830s). A Milanese cabinet maker copying the commodes of Maggiolini produced in the late eighteenth century.

MIGLIORA, Alessandro (fl. second quarter nineteenth century). Stucco work possibly for the King of Sardinia.

MOGLIA, Domenico (fl.c.1840). Followed the designing work in Lombardy of Albertolli (q.v.).

MORA, Frattelli (fl. third quarter nineteenth century). Cabinet maker in Louis XV style.

NOVARO, Francesco (fl. second quarter nineteenth century). Decorator in Geneva and Turin.

OTTAIANO. Neapolitan exhibitor at the 1876 Philadelphia Exhibition.

PACETTI, Fretelli. Florentine carver and gilder in the third quarter of the nineteenth century.

PALAGI, Pelagio (fl.1830s). Produced sculptural furniture in bronze and wood in a romantic classical Empire style.

PANTALINI, Ditto & Sons (fl. mid-nineteenth century). Cabinet makers in Louis XV style.

PARRI, Francesco and Sons (fl. late nineteenth century). Premises at Via degli Elisi Num. 4. Livorno.

PETERS, Anton (fl. second quarter nineteenth century). An Anglo-Italian cabinet maker working for the wealthy House of Savoy and exerting considerable English influence on contemporary furniture.

PICCHI, Andrea. A Florentine designer/maker working in the Renaissance style, exhibited in 1867.

POGLIANI, Ferdinando (fl.1860s and 1870s). Had premises at Borgo di Porta, Vittoria N.81, Milan. Created massive architectural items of furniture with heavy baroque influence inlaid with marquetry and engraved ivory figures. See illustration no.1183.

RINALDO. Siena cabinet maker exhibiting at Philadelphia Exhibition 1876.

ROSANI Brothers (fl.1840s). Working at Brescia.

TRUCI, Emilio (fl. third quarter nineteenth century). Cabinet maker in Louis XV style.

VACCARI, Gretano. Lombardy designer and/or cabinet maker.

VISCARDI, G.B. (fl.1840s). Milanese founder.

ZANETTI, Giuseppe (fl.1840s). Neo-classical and neo-Gothic furniture.

ZUCCOLI, Luigi (fl. mid-nineteenth century).

Terms

Armardio. Tall cupboard

Armardio vetrina. Glazed cupboard.

Arte povera. A technique used to decorate furniture in the eighteenth century with paper cut-outs which were then varnished with *lacca contrafatta* (q.v.).

Attaccapanni. Hat rack (wall fitting).

Cassapanca. Hall seat.

Cassettone. Chest of drawers.

Cassone. Large chest or coffer.

Certosina. Decorative geometric inlay of small patterns, usually in ivory.

Comodino. Bedside cupboard.

Credenza. Tall side cabinet, sometimes glazed, not to be confused with English trade term for low side cabinets.

Divanetto. Small settee.

Divanetto da salone. Formal small settee.

Divanetto di linea barocca. Baroque style settee.

Divano. Settee.

Divano da centre. Centre seat.

Divano im bottito. Day bed or chaise longue.

Falegnami. Joiners.

Fioriera. Flower stand.

Inginocchiatuio. Prayer chair.

Lacca. Thin varnish or japan. Also term used for painted furniture.

Lacca contrafatta. A poor quality varnish used on *arte povera* furniture (q.v.).

Letto. Bed.

Letto a barchettone. Double ended bed with overscrolled end (similar to *Lit Bateau*).

Letto di ferro. Steel bed.

Letto di gondola. Boat shaped bed with only a dip between the headboard and footboard.

Libreria. Book case.

Mensolina. Blackamoor *torchère* from Venice in the style of Brustolon.

Mobiletto per toletta. Tall shaving stand.

Parafaville. Fire screen.

Parafucco. Fire screen.

Pietre dure. Semi-precious hardstones applied or inset into furniture. Fernandino I founded the Opificio delle Pietre Dure in 1588.

Poggiapiedi. Footstool.

Poltrona; poltroncina; poltrone. Armchair.

Poltrona da palazzo. Gilt armchair.

Poltrona da scrivania. Desk chair.

Portalegena. Coal, wood, wine(?) scuttle.

Portamusica. Canterbury.

Portego. Reception room.

Putti. Children, usually naked, without wings.

Quadratrure. *Trompe l'oeil.*

Scaffale. Set of open shelves (*étagère*).

Scagliola. A powdered selenite plaster used to imitate marble and *pietre dure* (q.v.).

Scaletta da biblioteca. Library steps.

Scrignetto. Portable writing desk or book.

Scrittoietto. Davenport.

Scrivimpiedi. Clerk's desk.

Sedia a gondola. Gondola chair popular in France.

Sedia da fumo. Smoking chair which can be sat on either way.

Sedia da ingresso. Hall seat in sixteenth century style, often wrongly named *sgabello*.

Sedia interamente dorata. Seat to be placed along a dado rail.

Sedile da ingresso. Window seat.

Sedile girevole. Small revolving piano seat.

Sediolina all'olandese. A lacquered chair gilt with foliage.

Seggiocone della nonna. Comfortable upholstered chair with open arms and waisted back.

Sgabello. Hall stool or bench, without a back.

Sgabello di corte. 'X' frame cushioned stool.

Sgabello di palazzo. Squat circular upholstered stool on four gilt legs.

Sgabello di piuma. 'X' frame stool with arms.

Sofa. Settee.

Sofa a sdraio. *See* France. *Meridienne.*

Specchiera a piede. Cheval glass on a trestle support.

Specchiera da terra. Cheval glass on plinth.

Specchierina da como. Toilet mirror.

Studio. Room containing prized books, etc.

Tavoli dei marescialli. Circular table mounted with porcelain on concave sided tripod base.

Tavolino da lavorno. Work table.

Tavolino portalavoro. Small music stand.

Tavolino portavassoio. Small table with portable tray.

Tavolo ad alette ribaltabili. Sofa table with central stand or trestle support.

Tavolo a rotelle. Sofa table.

Tavolo da centro. Centre table.

Tavolo da muro. Small console table.

Tavolo per letto. Multiple reading stand.

Tavolo portagioielli toletta. Toilet table, also *tavolino toletta.*

Toletta con specchio. Mirror top dressing table.

Trespoli. Small three-legged tables.

Trono. 'Throne' armchair.

Vetrina. Glazed display cabinet.

BEDS

1131 A familiar Italian style that is seen on various items throughout this section. This footboard is profusely inlaid with ivory geometric patterns in an overall style known as *certosina*. The inlay can be either ivory or bone, or both, and originates from north Africa and the Moors. It was originally in common use for decoration in the sixteenth century. Italian figural inlay, in this case in ivory, is often crude but always highly decorative. The two *putti* seem far too small and unimportant for their respective roundels. An effective decoration in an honest nineteenth century style eclectically copying the various influences popular in the sixteenth century.

1880s

1132 A carved walnut headboard with two small bedside cupboards, each with room for that essential ceramic article that is handy to have nearby on cold nights when there is no electric light. The restrained decoration is carved in a watered-down late Renaissance style and, although well carved, is very flat and mechanical. This factory-made Renaissance style was popular from the 1850s until well into the twentieth century.

c.1900

1133 A highly entertaining bed straight out of Disneyland. The scalloped boat shape is most unusual and follows a distinctive style that was developed in central Italy in the last twenty years of the seventeenth century. A table with a large scallop shell, thought to have been designed by Daniele Seiter in similar vein, is in the Palazzo Reale, Turin and is an early indication of the grotto style that became popular in England during the second quarter of the eighteenth century.

1900-1930

1134 Two unmistakable pieces of Carlo Bugatti furniture. The chair shows a style developed from the essentially Moorish feeling of his work exhibited at the Italian Exhibition in London in 1888. The seat and back are of vellum held by copper and brass mounts. The illegible Arabic script is inlaid in pewter. Like a great deal of this designer's work this armchair is not very well made. The design was used again for an even more exotic four-seater settee with two of these chairs supporting a central raised platform. Not for the average householder perhaps, but a very original design and very rare.

Bugatti also designed this novel bed with accompanying shelf for his sister as a wedding present. The effect is highly colourful both in inventiveness of design and the casually placed green stalks of the flowers with their red flowerheads, which contrast vividly with the black ground of the head and footboard. This is the designer's first attempt at furniture design and it is easily identifiable. Later the saw-edged architectural forms develop into the more familiar *merhab* or circular arch that was a constant feature of the more commercial Bugatti. A bizarre form and unique.

Chair c.1900
Bed c.1880

BLACKAMOORS

The first blackamoors were carved in Venice in the late seventeenth century and were freestanding pieces of the sculptor's art rather than items of furniture. They often had little practical use except as stands for vases or candelabra but were occasionally seen as supports for magnificent display cabinets and for stools. They are a derivation of the work by Domenico and Francesco Stainhart whose magnificent carvings included figures in full relief and often full size in the 1670s. The major exponent of the negro figures was Andrea Brustolon who worked in Venice from 1684 carving sculptural furniture for the major Venetian families. Blackamoors continued to be made as a Venetian speciality throughout the eighteenth and nineteenth centuries and are still being made there, in a very convincing manner, today. Their popularity has grown since the late seventeenth century and examples in good condition are highly sought after. Condition is very important as repairs are difficult and expensive. The soft pine or fruitwood carving is often of a poor quality wood that is easily damaged when knocked and great care has to be taken when moving these lacquered and painted figures.

1135 A poorly carved figure on a stand in poor condition. He looks as though he is a direct copy of a live model whose arms were aching badly. The scallop tray is too high for all but the tallest to use, indicating possibly that the stand was added later, although made at approximately the same time.

1880s

1136 (left) One of a pair of rather hermaphrodite *torchères* on painted stands to simulate porphyry. The stance is casual if not provocative. Stands are not commonly found with the figures and the added height makes for a more impressive effect.

Third quarter of the nineteenth century

1138 A useful and decorative figure with a plentiful candelabra held casually aloft. The light pastel colours, not clear in black and white, but evident when compared with the other examples on this page, are indicative of the more modern examples of the twentieth century.

Second quarter of the twentieth century

1137 (above left) A decorative *torchère*. The skirted figure shades his eyes from the bright light he is holding up. The whole figure looks dubiously effeminate and corresponds to sculptural styles in bronze throughout Europe at the end of the nineteenth century. An unusual model nevertheless.

1880-1900

1139

1140

1141

1143

1142

1139 One of a pair of very silly looking figures who look as though they are about to drop the glittering candelabra. The light pastel shades and crude carving are a giveaway as to date.

modern

1140 A wonderful and proud exotic figure copied directly from the models of the period c.1700. The head is held up high and the face carved in a disdainful manner. The exotic and bold feathers show a muddled native origin, imagined by the original designer. The cornucopia holding the lamp is very big and possibly held a bigger display of lights as it was made before electricity. The stand is modern.

Second quarter of the nineteenth century ✱

1141 One of a very fine pair of figures in first class condition. Although the figures are obviously made as a pair the value would be greatly enhanced if each was in a different pose but balanced to be shown together. The chubby negress faces have incongruous late nineteenth century coiffured hairstyles.

c.1880

1142 This female figure has black lacquered skin, an African hairstyle and a very Italian face. It portrays the image of a late seventeenth century slave, in the privileged role of a lady's attendant, holding up a looking glass. A very novel and unusual idea. The cushion that she stands on seems little dented considering her ample figure.

1890s

1143 A common type of blackamoor figure of a young negro boy standing on the prow of a gondola holding an oar. The right hand would normally be holding a lamp. The bow of the boat is inscribed *Venezia*.

c.1910

1145

1147

1146

1148

1144

1144 A very similar theme, the boy with a typical Italian Renaissance face and page boy hair-cut but with a blackened skin. The swaggering pose is spoilt by the total lack of proportion of the figure. This one is without a stand, and has lost his (removable) oar.

c.1910

1145 Another modern example included to make the reader aware of the variety of modern figures and their easily recognisable style of carving, finish and colouring. The pose is very good on this one with good attention to the flowing pantaloons and towel. The strong pastel colouring and the hard, almost aggressive, face are typical of the more recent figures. Close inspection will reveal a smooth undamaged surface and an even paint with heavily speckled gold. Age can be very deceiving with these figures but those made fifty or more years ago will almost certainly have suffered some minor damage and some repair on the bright hard black surfaces of skin.

1970s

1146 Possibly this richly dressed blackamoor, in an exotic Turkish style, is asking for his wages or pleading for mercy. However, the more likely interpretation is that this small figure, intended to be that of a very young houseboy or servant, originally held a tray and is standing in a humble pose holding the tray for his master — or mistress. The pleading eyes give a wonderful insight into the mentality of the first owner who probably expected total subservience from his servants. The tray has long gone but could easily and cheaply be replaced. An unusual figure.

1880s

1147 Yet another variation of a common theme, the various workshops producing slightly different models.

Modern

1148 The face on this wonderful figure is well carved and realistic — the effort of the poor young acrobat can clearly be seen. Unfortunately the legs are very thin and too short for the rest of the body, a point that would never be over-looked by the late seventeenth century Venetian carver. The top platform would originally have a removable tray or dish for fruit. A very rare example.

1870s

1149

1150

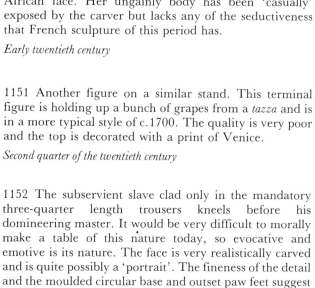

1152

1149 One of a pair of extremely ugly wall brackets. The grimacing face only too well portrays the uncomfortable posture that the carver has given this gnome-like figure which struggles to support a shelf while clinging on to the curtaining for dear life with his other hand. These are common and popular.

c.1900

1150 An unadventurous stand with a smiling central African face. Her ungainly body has been 'casually' exposed by the carver but lacks any of the seductiveness that French sculpture of this period has.

Early twentieth century

1151 Another figure on a similar stand. This terminal figure is holding up a bunch of grapes from a *tazza* and is in a more typical style of c.1700. The quality is very poor and the top is decorated with a print of Venice.

Second quarter of the twentieth century

1152 The subservient slave clad only in the mandatory three-quarter length trousers kneels before his domineering master. It would be very difficult to morally make a table of this nature today, so evocative and emotive is its nature. The face is very realistically carved and is quite possibly a 'portrait'. The fineness of the detail and the moulded circular base and outset paw feet suggest an early date.

Second quarter of the nineteenth century

1151

BOXES

1153 and 1154 A charming example of the nineteenth century Renaissance revival. This style of carving is typically Florentine and is signed 'Angiolo Cheloni Firenze'. The signature, in capitals, can just be seen inside the lid. The swan carved in relief on the lid is part of a crest and the sides are carved with birds and fruit in a free Renaissance manner. Like most of the nineteenth century Florentine carver's work, this tea caddy is in walnut.

Dated 1876

1156 An engraved ivory table cabinet (standing on a Dutch marquetry side table). The cutting of the ivory figures and leaves is crude, as is the engraving. The heavily built Diana dwarfs the terms effortlessly supporting the arch. The box is a copy of the early seventeenth century style, and made very much as a direct copy, even possibly with an intention to deceive.

1870s ∗

1157 (right) A mystery piece in the Eygptian style. The various Egyptian archaeological discoveries in the nineteenth and twentieth centuries sparked off a flood of interest in pyramids and all things Egyptian. This large box, with no apparent purpose other than decoration, has a conforming stand. Both are highly intricate but poorly and disappointingly made, although indisputably exotic. Various woods are inlaid into an ebony ground and the decoration is completed by ivory, bone, pewter and copper, with boxwood *appliqués*. It is possible that this is a 'one off' box and table made by a one man team, which would explain its individuality. The highly stylised vultures suggest a date in the 1930s and it is possible that the discovery of Tutankhamun's tomb in the 1920s sparked off this creation, although it could easily be twenty to fifty years earlier.

1880-1930

1155 More Florentine walnut carving with fat little *putti* in a very realistic sixteenth century style, playing with a necklace found in a box at their feet — suggesting that the original purpose of this box was for jewellery, although there is no provision for a key. Amusing, but nothing of the fineness of carving of the previous box.

1860s

CARVED FIGURES AND CLOCKS

1158 An extraordinary carved and painted pine group from the northern borders of Italy with heavy German/Swiss influence. It is not difficult to imagine the German carved bear hall stands, illustrated on page 367. Here a street musician is entertaining the onlookers with one monkey beating time with cymbals and another holding out his hand. This is a rare variation of the blackamoor figures but with a decidedly European bearded moustachioed face.

c.1900

1159 Another carved pine figure dressed as a page boy, with various stained woods highlighting the flesh and clothes. The tunic is carefully detailed with 'pokerwork'. Originally the boy had a plank of wood held across his knees as a tray and he is sitting on a Gothic style stool.

c.1880

1161 Another example of a carved and stained pine page boy with a decorated pokerwork tunic, quite probably from the same workshops as no.1159. His stance is quite extraordinary — perhaps pose would be a more accurate word. The long haired youth standing coquettishly holding a purse in a gloved hand would not pass without comment in today's society. The falcon is very badly carved and is as emaciated as item no. 1164.

c.1880

1160 This longcase clock has been converted into a neo-baroque exercise in sculpture with hardly any space left uncarved or unadorned. The quality varies enormously. The main strapwork leaves and terminal figures are very well carved but the applied *putti* and figure of Atlas (noticeably wearing a figleaf, a very nineteenth century prudish feature) are all less well carved and almost certainly from another workshop. It is not even out of the bounds of possibility that the figures were added at a much later date as an 'extra' decoration. The three train movement chimes the hours, half-hours and quarters and is an export from Germany.

1880s

CASSONI

The cassone *was an important part of Italian life, often being made in pairs as wedding presents, one for the bride with her coat-of-arms and one for the groom with his arms carved or incised in the gilding. The early* cassoni *were gilt, with little decoration, incorporating painted panels, like the example in illustration no.1163. Later on, by the year 1500, the decoration became progressively more profuse and sculptural and the natural colour of the walnut carcass took the place of gilding.*

1162 A large profusely carved walnut *cassone* in late sixteenth century style. The central panel has a bacchic procession carved with all kinds of revelry. The carving is far too stiff to be anything but nineteenth century but quite often Italian Renaissance revival furniture will incorporate one or more early panels. Great care must be taken to examine the detail of the panel to see if it has been incorporated into a later carcass. A large and not very useful piece.

1860-1880 ✳

1163 This Florentine gilt-wood *cassone,* in mid-fifteenth century style, does incorporate rare and valuable panels dating to c.1450 depicting the story of Achilles.

The cassone 1870s ✳

CENTRE STANDS

1164 and 1165 Two views of a carved walnut stand by Luigi Frullini. This extraordinarily mangey beast has little to commend it, carved in the form of a heavily breasted winged griffin in a crude and stiff manner. An interesting point is the asymmetry of the wizened branch growing out to the side of the stand intended to give extra support. It was presumably matched by the 'missing' pair of another stand. Although the style is similar to Frullini's the finished article has little of the guts of this carver's work. How easy it would be to carve a signature into the soft walnut.

1870s

1166 (above left) A painted and gilt column with a very lazy twist, often termed 'a Solomonic column'. The vine is being raided by a very silly looking bird.

1860-1880

1167 (above right) My favourite. This amusing and totally useless item is typical of the Florentine school of carvers working around the 1860-1890 period. They restricted most of their carving to walnut which, although a dark colour compared to 'Queen Anne walnut', acquires a mellow hue and glow over a period of a hundred years. The naturalism of this school of carving is unparalleled and represents a very early form of plant and animal life captured by the furniture maker. There appears to be little of this work outside Italy, indeed outside Florence, and although its carvers and designers have been neglected to date there is little doubt that as further research is made the Florentine school will take on an importance that, at the moment, it is not credited with. This piece is itching to be signed and compares directly with the work of Andrea Baccetti.

1870s

1168 (far left) A plain walnut stand similar to the blackamoor no. 1151, the only difference being that it is not painted and the features of the boy's face are more distinctly European.

Second quarter of the twentieth century

1169 (left) Another walnut stand or *torchère* with very heavy French influence in the *pieds de biche* and small fluted tapering stem below the musical trophy. It is difficult to be exactly sure of the true origin of this nineteenth century example but the crude incising and general lack of sophistication point more towards Italy.

1880s

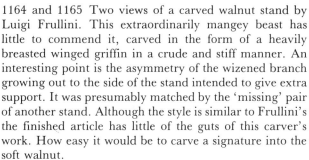

1170 and 1171 A fine steel centre table with an elaborate top painted with views of Rome. The figures in the foreground of St. Peter's Square can just be made out dressed in the fashion of the early 1830s, which helps to date the top which otherwise would seem thirty to fifty years earlier. The base is in the style of the sixteenth century and, as with all metalwork, is extremely difficult to date accurately. More modern copies of steel furniture are nearly always arc welded, a process only used since the 1940s — a useful hint in spotting a modern copy.

Second quarter nineteenth century

1172 and 1173 A beautifully inlaid Florentine mosaic panel with love-birds drinking from a silver vessel, one gazing at its reflection in the water. The lightness of form and decoration are quite unbeatable and the detail of two feathers falling lightly to the ground and peas spread to one side as food for the birds is a supreme example of the art of mosaic. The meandering Greek key and maze pattern border is beautifully executed in a 3-D effect and really does look like a continuous tall brick wall. The chased and dipped brass snake tripod is a popular feature of the early nineteenth century.

Early nineteenth century

1174 Another fine mosaic table top inlaid with views of Rome. Even the flowers and fruit that join each panel are finely executed in mosaic.

Early nineteenth century

1175 This table top incorporates exactly the same scene of birds as no.1173, but without the fine detail and not of the same quality. The small views are of Venice — a first class tourist memento — many of these poorer panels are to be found in this country brought back from the Grand Tour. The marble and malachite border is often repeated and in this case is most probably English marble from Torquay or possibly Ashburton in Derbyshire, suggesting that the bird and Venetian view panels were exported to England where they were made up into black slate table tops with Devonian marble borders.

Mid-nineteenth century

1176 and 1177 The top is inlaid with *pietre dure* in the larger, Roman style. The figures in late eighteenth century costume suggest that the mosaic work itself was later incorporated into the circular table top and placed on the unusual giltwood stand. A fine and rare table.

1820-1840

1178 and 1179 Once again the familiar design of birds at a water vessel is interpreted on this table top with large marble mosaic pieces in a comparatively crude manner, with the wide borders dominating the central pattern. The giltwood base is in early nineteenth century rococo revival style and could well be English or a recent Italian, Florentine copy. Both the gilding and the marble have been so extensively cleaned and restored that dating becomes an academic exercise.

Probably a twentieth century copy

1180 A painted table top in the style of the Florentine mosaic workers, on a black slate ground. The painting is extremely realistic, each corner with a brace of small birds shown in their natural habitat representing each of the four seasons.

Mid-nineteenth century

1181 A charming pictorial mosaic panel scattered with letters, pens, matches and even a cigar stub. The casual approach is most effective and there is a very realistic 3-D feeling aided by the clever use of shading. This top was set into an English ebonised tripod support.

Mid-nineteenth century

1182 A fine quality *pietre dure* panel inlaid with semi-precious stones. Many hundreds of panels incorporating birds in an identical style must have been made. Similar bird inlay was executed in the late seventeenth century and it is important for the collector to try to establish the difference. Look for realism and signs of wear in early stone. A similar type of Italian inlay can be seen incorporated into an English side cabinet illustrated on page 310, no.943.

Third quarter of the nineteenth century

1183 A Milanese ebony-veneered, engraved and inlaid ivory table with a label by Ferdinando Pogliani. A similar label by this maker is illustrated on page 389 but the one on this table calls Mr. Pogliani an *ebenista*. He was certainly a major Milanese producer of ivory and bone-inlaid furniture. The style of the furniture is French influenced from the late seventeenth and early eighteenth century.

1860s

1184 A very similar table almost certainly from the same Milanese stable as the last but, as is so often the case with furniture, there is no evidence to categorically prove the origin. The form is almost identical but the foliate strapwork and decoration on the frieze and legs is crude and mechanical. The top, which unfortunately is impossible to see clearly, is engraved by hand in an assured manner with a battle scene.

1860s

1185 A similar style but a poor relation to the previous example. The bold arched 'X' stretcher is more Italian and less complicated than the previous table but the ivory inlay is very poor.

1860s

1186 The top of this table is very fine quality, let down somewhat by the framework. The gaping masks on the frieze are a favourite revived motif. The trestle support with a flattened platform stretcher owes its origins to the seventeenth century but its reinstigation was due to the English influence at the beginning of the nineteenth century.

c.1870

1187 A good painted and *scagliola* marble top on a frame in the Louis XV French style. The shape and decoration is very similar to France but the handling of the decoration is carried out in a much broader, more Italian, fashion. Quite a successful and attractive piece of furniture, probably from north-west Italy.

c.1860

1188 Another seventeenth century revival table with the by now familiar emaciated winged griffin supports. The arched stretcher owes more to the rococo than the mannerism of the sides. Predictably enough made in walnut.

1860-1880s ∗

1189 A Venetian giltwood table with a *pietre dure* top of a stupified parrot. Unless these hardstone inlays are of the very best quality the animals that they portray can look very silly, normally it is their eyes that are so hard to effectively and convincingly reproduce in stone. The naturalistic supports were much favoured in Italy and reflect the mid-eighteenth century work of both Italy and England. The scroll feet and star incising on the base are a clue as to the table's Venetian origins.

1840-1880

1190 A good example of the Italian watered-down art nouveau style. The cheaply gilt surface follows the line of an ordinary oval table with a stylised decoration of flowers. The accomplished traditions of the numerous Italian carvers surely could have achieved much more than this.

1900-1920

CHAIRS

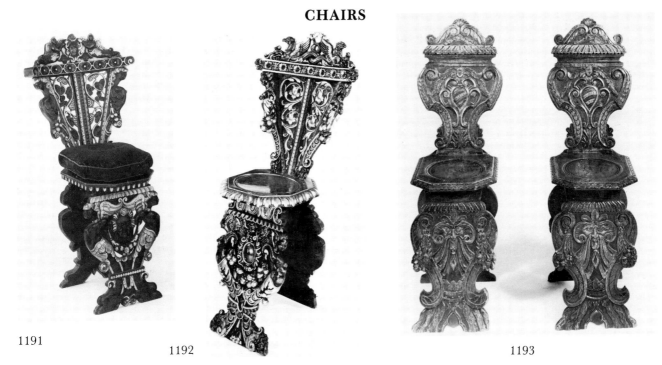

1191   1192   1193

1191, 1192 and 1193 This type of chair is commonly mis-named a *sgabello* but is in fact a development of the *sgabello* or hall seat or stool. The back was a later feature added to this type of 'stool' with boarded front and back ends. As the style changed the 'boards' became more and more elaborately decorated, carved and sometimes gilt or parcel-gilt. The logical progression was the addition of the back, carved in a similar style. These three examples of chairs all reflect, with varying degrees of success, the style of the early 1600s. As is common with Italian furniture, the best pieces are carved with the arms of the patron who ordered the pieces. No. 1193 is the least inspired example with no piercing or gilding. Both chairs from the pair in no. 1193 have been included to show the difference in detail of the carved decoration which, even in large towns, would be unlikely to be cut by machine even well into the twentieth century, and therefore lacks the symmetry of mechanical pieces.

1191   *Tuscan c. 1880*
1192   *Tuscan c. 1880*
1193   *Florentine 1880s*

1194 A finely made folding armchair that became common amongst the larger houses at the beginning of the sixteenth century. This example is in ebony with ivory inlay and is a very solid and substantial armchair despite its portability.

c. 1870

1195 The 'X' frame folding armchair was a very popular style of chair in the sixteenth century made throughout the Italian states, especially in Tuscany. This type has taken the name of 'Savonarola'. There is a far heavier type of chair, with a leather or upholstered folding seat and back, as opposed to the solid 'slatted' seat here, known as a 'Dante' chair.

c. 1900

1196 This flat armed chair is a derivative of early seventeenth century chairs from the northern part of Italy and has much in common with Spanish chairs of the same period. The inlay in this one is very similar to that of nearby Southern Germany and is a series of ivory *putti,* as always without clothes, playing ball games and with hoops. The solid frame is not relieved by upholstery and without a squab seat is most uncomfortable.

1870s

1197 (right) An ivory and engraved side or hall chair in a vague seventeenth century style with much in common with the Milanese tables on page 405. The back is engraved *Rattvick Galarne.* The severe architectural style is good but let down by the poor quality of the materials and finish.

c.1870

1198 A strange little armchair, probably from Tuscany. It looks as though it should be a folding chair but it is rigid. The cheerful goats seem to be about to leap over the back of the seat and there is certainly no lack of movement on this heavy walnut frame.

1860-1880

1199 and 1200 These two northern Italian armchairs are heavily influenced by the Moorish and Eastern styles of decoration known as *alla certosina.* This type of inlay was commonly found in the area around Pavia as well as Lombardy, especially Venice with her trade from the near east. The chair on the left is inlaid into an olivewood ground, the one on the right into walnut. Both are highly decorative which makes them popular but both are uncomfortable and would not be suitable for continual use.

Both c.1850

1201 A Venetian walnut armchair in the style of Andrea Brustolon. The style is influenced by a suite of furniture supplied by Brustolon c.1690 for the Vernier family. The asymmetric apron owes more to the middle of the eighteenth century and the base and legs are very similar to French examples of the third quarter of the seventeenth century. Altogether an eclectic mess but a bold interesting piece of furniture nevertheless.

1880-1900

1202 Once again there is influence of the widely popular sculptural style of Andrea Brustolon. The carved walnut *atlantes* appear to strain as they support the arms, resting one leg on the grimacing outset lion's head corbels. The men's heads make uncomfortable arm and hand supports but the upholstery is generous, if not overdone.

1900s

1204 A very much more restrained chair in Roman late eighteenth century style. As was common with other European chairs of the late eighteenth century the back is easily removed to attend to the upholstery, and likewise the seat. The style uses popular neo-classical decoration, the legs with imaginary ram's head capitals and a framework of flowerhead *guilloché*. This type of deeply carved gesso deteriorates rapidly and is not suitable for chairs that are going to be used more than occasionally. In the style of the 1770s.

First half of the nineteenth century

1203 A very assured Florentine gilt chair with broad and bold carving in an imposing architectural style. The sculptor, however, has been restrained more than usual and although the carving is bold there are no *putti* or wholly unnecessary features. In the style of the 1740s.

1850s *

1205 A generous armchair from northern Italy in the style of the 1760s. The feeling is now much more one that conforms to the style of the rest of Europe. By the time the original version of this chair was made Italy had ceased to become a major influence in furniture design and was drawing her inspiration from France and England. A comfortable and practical walnut chair.

1880-1900 *

On this page the influence of the sculptor has dwindled almost to nothing and any carved decoration has become restrained, giving way to the design and framework of the chair rather than overpowering it.

1206 A typical Venetian chair copying the mid-eighteenth century. The painted decoration became very popular and is still being made today in a very convincing manner. This type of painting, often very prettily executed, is called *lacca* and is always a popular style for bedrooms.

c.1900 *

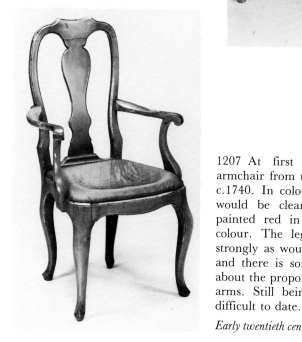

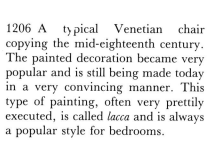

1207 At first glance an English armchair from the George II period c.1740. In colour the Italian origin would be clearer as the chair is painted red in a dull Post Office colour. The legs do not finish as strongly as would English chair legs and there is something a little odd about the proportion of the back and arms. Still being made today and difficult to date.

Early twentieth century *

1208 A weak art nouveau style incorporated on to a late eighteenth century style chair. Only the decoration makes any pretence at being late nineteenth century, except for the shell which appears from the second quarter of the eighteenth century without warning and without any apparent need or reason.

1900-1920

1209 An elegant chair of indeterminate origin. The flowing frame with its triangular section at the top of the legs suggests that the chair was made in the Genoa area. The little acanthus leaves are very Italianate. A very rare and sophisticated chair, extremely unusual with its attractive pierced frame.

1850s

1210 A giltwood stool carved in the grotto rococo style of the second quarter of the eighteenth century and probably made in Venice. The carving is very bold with broad leaves and little attention to detail, which is typical of a lot of nineteenth century Italian furniture.

1850s

1211 (left) Another very elegant and unusual giltwood chair. The tall back suggests an art nouveau influence more akin to that of Belgian furniture of the late nineteenth century. The immaculate button upholstery is modern but imitates the original style of upholstery. A mystery chair but very rare.

1880-1900

1212 A wonderful example of the late nineteenth century Egyptian and Empire revival. It is unusual to see sphinxes with wings, legs and a tail, all of which have been very amusingly and cleverly incorporated into the chair frame. There is no other woodwork showing — the two exotic animals with the added decoration of a string of pearls form the entire framework. The luxurious silk upholstery is worked with the Napoleonic bee and the overscrolled padded seat is very generous and comfortable. The frames are beechwood painted black and cream. Could it just be English?

Late 1880s

Metalwork

The highest standards of gilt bronze are obtained by mercurial gilding. This is a dangerous process that can only be done today in controlled conditions. The brass or bronze surface to be gilt is coated with a mixture of mercury and gold powder which is fused by fire. It produces a delightful dusty effect that is not bright and brash like the effect obtained by bright brass dipped, which has a very hard strong golden yellow colour. The following detailed photographs and those illustrated on page 432, are numbered in order of quality of both gilding and chiselling. The work of the *ciseleur* is very important in obtaining the highlights on the cast bronze before gilding.

1 A magnificent piece of casting equally well chiselled and gilt giving an even glow which contrasts incredibly well with the imitation flambé *porcelain. German. 1880s.*

2 Again there is a delightful contrast between the burnished gilt pierced metalwork and the green malachite veneer beneath it. This Russian metalwork is nearly always of the finest quality although the casting and design may be a little naïve. 1850s.

3 A fine section of engine turned milled banding, surrounding a drawer of plum pudding mahogany. The metalwork has been made entirely by machine but the quality of the metal and the gilding are very high. French. c.1880.

4 Through the dirt on this pattern of interlaced circles can be seen the high quality of casting, chiselling and gilding. This detail is taken from a piece of furniture by Alfred Beurdeley, one of the finest Paris makers with his own workshops for both cabinet making and for making the mounts. The delicate scrolling of the leaves is highlighted by careful hand chiselling. c.1880.

5 The casting and finishing of this Ionic capital taken from a clock is not to a very high standard but the gilding is of a quality that suggests the very best. French. 1830s.

6 A bronze doré encrier. The gilding is very flat but even and is highlighted by the hand chiselled shell work. 1860s.

7 Another example of high quality Russian metalwork with extreme care taken in the chiselling stage. In fact, the photograph is a detail of a bird's back with outstretched wings. The chiselling perhaps is rather naïve but the gilding is very good. 1850s.

8 Another example of very good quality Paris casting and gilding finished down to the very last detail. Although a little dull, once the mount is removed from the piece of furniture it will clean amazingly well with a very small drop of ammonia added to a bucket of water. A useful hint to anyone attempting this is to do it outside as the fumes are dangerous, to wear rubber gloves and always remove the metalwork from the carcass before attempting to clean it. c.1880.

9 The colour of this foliage is good and so is the chasing but the casting is a little bit naïve and nothing like the quality of the eighteenth century metalwork. This is a detail from a longcase clock by François Linke and the quality of the metalwork is not very high by Linke's standards. 1900-1920.

10 A crude but rather nice fleur de lys *finial. The gilding is good and has a very rich golden sunset colour. This type of casting and chiselling is delightful as the hand work can clearly be seen. French. 1850s.*

11 A well chiselled banding around a drawer with a kingwood and tulipwood trellis. It is well made and has good quality gilding that has rubbed in places with constant handling and polishing. French. 1860s.

12 The sabot *from a French* commode. *The casting is crude but there has been a lot of work in the hand chiselling. The colour is very poor — rather too bright with too many highlights that appear almost artificial. 1860-1880.*

(continued on page 432)

1

2

3

4

5

6

7

8

9

10

11

12

1213 Whether this or the next chair will take the prize for the most outrageous and amusing items illustrated in this book is a matter for conjecture. This giltwood and highly carved Florentine piano stool has a back formed of a detailed grimacing human mask with four ferocious eye teeth and bushy eyebrows detailed as a cartoonist would characterise a politician or famous person. Whether the grimacing face is being pulled at the weight of the musician or the music he plays will remain a mystery. A wonderful example of sculptural furniture.

1850s

1214 The two large sunflowers are reminiscent of the English love for all that is aesthetic. The exact nationality of such a chair at the moment remains a mystery but the Italian carver with his love of incorporating carving and sculpture into furniture will surely be given the credit for this extraordinary chair. The back is so weak that it would be hardly possible to sit comfortably on such a chair without the fear of going through. The paw feet are growing leaves in the highly naturalistic manner so loved by the Florentine carver. Not the sort of chair that will 'turn up' very often.

1875-1900

1215 (below) Another example of Venetian carving but this time almost in a restrained mid-eighteenth century manner. The Venetian designer loved to make outrageous furniture that was only just usable and exotic examples of this art are rare.

c.1860

1216 Once again Venice is responsible for the nautical rocking chair with dolphin arms and dolphin and seahorse supports. The style of carving, with its feeling of a grotto, is reminiscent of the second quarter of the eighteenth century in Italy. The chair frame without the rocking chair legs is often seen and is still being made today.

c.1900

1217 The Florentine carving of this armchair or *trono* is typically grandiose and almost architectural. The use of acanthus for the legs is typical and the leaves themselves form the supports and are not simply used as decoration to the legs. The arm terminals are cherubic heads looking upwards to the heavens. The arched back has a simple cartouche flanked and held by crudely carved birds with a pair of equally crude *espagnolettes*. The mid-seventeenth century revived, improved and overdone.

c.1880

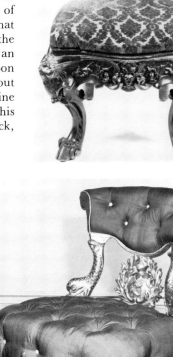

1218 A dumpy little carved walnut chair by Luigi Frullini of Florence. Frullini's art was clearly that of a carver rather than furniture designer and the proportions of this eclectic small chair are somewhat overdone. The back is reminiscent of the late eighteenth century wheelback with an eye to the mid-nineteenth century balloon back that was popular throughout Europe. In keeping with the Florentine carvers who signed their furniture, this chair is signed at the bottom of the back, clearly, on the front.

Dated 1868

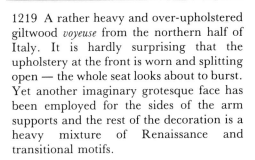

1219 A rather heavy and over-upholstered giltwood *voyeuse* from the northern half of Italy. It is hardly surprising that the upholstery at the front is worn and splitting open — the whole seat looks about to burst. Yet another imaginary grotesque face has been employed for the sides of the arm supports and the rest of the decoration is a heavy mixture of Renaissance and transitional motifs.

1860s

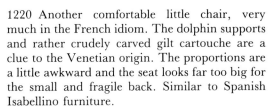

1220 Another comfortable little chair, very much in the French idiom. The dolphin supports and rather crudely carved gilt cartouche are a clue to the Venetian origin. The proportions are a little awkward and the seat looks far too big for the small and fragile back. Similar to Spanish Isabellino furniture.

1860s

CHESTS OF DRAWERS

1222 A Venetian *lacca* commode in a vague French style of the mid-eighteenth century. This type of furniture is often appallingly badly made and, like the above, difficult to date and there are many 'fakes'.

1870-1920 *

1221 A small Venetian *lacca* tall chest, one of a pair that would probably be placed on either side of a bed. Painted and carved in mid-eighteenth century style and made in such a way that the unwary find it extremely difficult to date this type of furniture accurately. The Italians would call such furniture *ottocento*, which to the northern European would suggest an eighteenth century date as all other countries look backwards when they describe a century but the Italians look forwards and would mean the nineteenth century (or 1800s).

1920s

1223 A Neapolitan commode, again copying, probably with intent to deceive, the mid-eighteenth century style and the vogue for *chinoiserie*. Another badly made piece but very popular and highly decorative.

1870-1900

1224 A Lombardy bone inlaid chest imitating the style popular c.1700. The ebonised softwood carcass is poorly made but with a very strong and unusual inverted angular breakfront. The scrolling flowerheads, cherubs and tendrils that make up the profuse inlay are fairly well executed and each piece is individually hand cut. Unfortunately this type of furniture is often so badly made that it falls apart very quickly.

c.1870 ✶

1225 Italian workshops produced a considerable quantity of similarly painted, poorly made bedroom furniture which is still made today. The style is Venetian similar to no.1222 opposite. This pinewood carcass is badly wormed — a common problem. Similar decorated pieces have been seen with the label of a certain Eugenio Pecchigle.

c.1920

1226 The gently flowing lines and slightly *bombé* form of this Liguorian commode point to a Genoese origin. The quarter-veneered marquetry and parquetry star decoration are typically Genoese and are influenced from nearby France. This example in kingwood is a late copy of a mid-eighteenth century commode.

c.1900 ✶

1227 A formal neo-classical commode from Milan, again in the late eighteenth century style of c.1790. The quarter-veneered kingwood is inset with attractively painted porcelain mounts. The ring handles with their porcelain and/or enamel plaques are a very Milanese feature.

1870s ✶

1228 An exuberant side or pier table carved in the typical broad and bold Italian manner, in this instance by Fretelli Pacetti of Florence. The massive *verde antico* marble top is as generous as the carving. There is hardly a break between the apron and the arched stretcher. The winged term supports of each leg have unusual Roman helmets and the winged, not very angelic, head at the centre of the stretcher is wearing a laurel leaf.

c.1870

1229 Another exuberant pier table, probably from Venice. The interwoven bands of trailing flowers are very similar to French mid-eighteenth century examples. The asymmetrical rococo decoration of the apron and stretcher is a little heavy and treated in a manner that would be impossible to execute in France.

1850s

1230 A small Florentine side table with the most hideous colour gilding and a thin dark black and white veined marble top. The fan-like medallion at the centre represents the outstretched wings of a griffin.

c.1900

1231 The very bold 'C' scrolls give a feeling of great width to this pier table and possibly suggest a Roman origin, although the masks and fussiness of decoration could easily be Florentine. The masks are almost as grotesque as the piano stool on page 414.

c.1860

1232 A carved walnut side table in an uninhibited Italian nineteenth century style that fondly imagined it was recreating the mid-eighteenth century. The flowerhead *guilloché* carved around the serpentine top suggests that this table was not originally designed to have a marble top and the damask lining is possibly original. Here the apron — from the eye of the camera at least — has joined the exuberant stretcher and the naked *putti* is trying to capture the leaf with his swirling cloth.

1860s

1233 Once again this side table is the work of the inspired wood carver Luigi Frullini. Every kind of horror has been incorporated into the design and carving including a bat on the apron, grotesque masks and evil looking exotic griffins on the cresting. Only the enormous winged cherubs and the delicately carved birds at either side save this piece from becoming a nightmare. At least it is totally honest in its nineteenth century origins.

Dated 1861

1234 An unusual side table taking the Venetian idea of blackamoor figures one stage further and incorporating them into table supports. The figures are rather out of proportion but great attention has been paid to the faces and the hair. Burr-maple was rarely used in Italy, and its light colour contrasts well against the black skin of the supports. The thin and out of proportion palm trees behind the figures are an amusing and very welcome addition.

1830-1850

1235 A poorly made and badly decorated red and gilt lacquer card table but nevertheless an unusual and rare form of Italian furniture. The top lifts open and swings round as in French and English examples. The heavily shawled caryatids are extremely severe and formal and deserve a far better piece of furniture.

1830-1850

1236 The mirror in this illustration is a mid-eighteenth century example, restored in the mid-nineteenth century. It stands, albeit somewhat tenuously, on a mid-nineteenth century pier table which is probably Roman in origin. The bold scrolling leaves are unusually self-assured. A very 'gutsy' table. It is interesting to note that *all* the decoration behind the mirror and table is painted in a highly convincing *trompe l'œil,* known in Italy as *quadratrure.*

The table, c.1850 ∗

1238 This neo-classical pier table and mirror are the reverse of the previous examples. The mirror is nineteenth century on a late eighteenth century table of c.1780. They harmonise quite well together but the later mirror is a little too overbearing for the elegant table. Once again the walls are painted with *quadratrure,* both the illustrations are taken in the same house.

The mirror, c.1870

1237 (right) An unadventurous rococo revival mirror from which all spirit is lacking. The sides appear to have been cut off with a sharp knife and the cresting built up from a box of spare parts. None of the life of the eighteenth century has been captured.

Early twentieth century

1239 An attenuated pier mirror and conforming *jardinière.* This unusual combination is seen occasionally in the second half of the nineteenth century and is very effective indeed when the trough is filled with flowers. Not suitable for every taste but ideal Italian hotel furniture.

1880-1900

1241 An elaborate Florentine 'mirror'. The frame is deeply carved in a fruitwood, probably limewood, which is easy to carve and takes gilding well. The foliage is so dense that it is difficult to distinguish all the features.

1860s

1240 A heavy but rather charmingly naïve mirror from northern Italy. The small sized plate could suggest that the original purpose of the frame was to hold a painting, as is so often the case with frames that are always, unthinkingly, called 'mirrors' just because there is a mirror plate. In the style of c.1700.

1860-1880 ∗

1242 Another elaborate Florentine frame with heavy and bushy acanthus leaves. It is almost as though there is a central cartouche missing from the cresting. The proportions are certainly individual.

1860s

1243 This tapering shape is typical of Venetian frames from the mid-eighteenth century and the smaller less elaborate versions of these mirrors can be extremely difficult to date as the nineteenth century examples were made in exactly the same way as the ones of a hundred years before. They are still being made and can be highly deceptive.

1870-1890 ∗

1245 North Italian or French Provincial? The very flat carving is typical of many southern French areas but the boldness of execution and broad carving is more typical of Italian carvers. A nice compromise would be to be able to say with conviction that this mirror is from the Nice area which was 'Italian' until the 1860s.

Third quarter of the nineteenth century

1244 The king of all the giltwood mirrors from Florence, this elaborate but well balanced frame is 2.18 metres high with a phoenix cresting and a dragon at either side. A huge example of the carver's art and very rare in this size.

c.1850

1246 A Murano all glass mirror applied with numerous brittle leaves and flowers in an individual style that the Murano glass-workers created. Extremely fragile but highly decorative.

1860-1880

1247 A kingwood quarter-veneered mirror with the oyster hearts that are typical of the area surrounding Genoa. An elegant mirror with a very French feeling about it.

c.1900

1248 Not a mirror of course but the type of carved and giltwood frame that is often converted to a mirror. The Gothic frame and paintings are a weak imitation of the original style and far too church-like for even dedicated Gothic lovers.

1880-1900

SCREENS/STANDS

The screen played an important and useful role in the nineteenth century and preceding centuries. The role was a multiple one and their greatest joy was that they could easily be folded and discreetly stored away in the corner of a room. In large rooms a major function was as a shield against draughts — one or more screens drawn around a fireplace created a more intimate atmosphere and acted as some form of draught excluder. It was also possible to divide up larger rooms with the arrangement of screens, allowing different functions to take place at the same time or simply cutting off the unwanted part of a large room. Many Ottoman Empire and north African mishrabeya *screens are seen in Europe. These complex screens, with an abundance of turned balusters, were employed in hotter countries to actually create a draught to cool a hot room as much as possible. Whatever its use, the screen was an essential part of a household's furniture, far more so than today when it has become almost redundant with the use of electricity. Today screens remain simply as highly decorative legacies of the past, often richly ornamented, painted and carved.*

Screens were always a popular and useful media for displaying discarded or unwanted textiles and panels and as a result often incorporate early panels in a later frame. This is especially the case with seventeenth century embossed leather wall panels, which were outdated by wallpaper and pastel paints for wall decoration in the eighteenth century. The panels were often incorporated into screens so that the earlier workmanship was not lost. It is an important point to look for these 'earlier panels' on screens, as they will make a great difference to value, especially as a panel on a screen, as opposed to a chair, for example, should be in relatively good condition.

1249 The carving is reminiscent of Luigi Frullini, illustration no.1164. A good quality piece of an individual design but quite large. So many items made for the centre of a room in the nineteenth century are too big for use in our modern small rooms.

1870s

1251 A carved walnut hall stand for coats and hats, in Renaissance style. Surprisingly, the central 'rack' was made in Italy, especially Florence in the sixteenth century. The form of this stand is typically nineteenth century. Note the emaciated griffins with large pointed breasts— a recurring feature in the nineteenth century Florentine Renaissance revival.

c.1880

1250 A very ornate and overdone three fold screen carved in Florence in the French style imitating Louis XV rococo. The silk and silver filigree floral needlework is also Italian, but from the third quarter of the eighteenth century. The rococo decoration is far too formal and stiff for France, even in the nineteenth century. The frame is very heavy compared with the carving.

1850s

SETTEES

1252 The Italian craftsman and the original designer have sought to stretch a sound French settee, based on Louis XV principles, as far as possible without going to the trouble of completely redesigning it. This was a popular Venetian sport. Large settees were needed to accommodate revellers at a ball and also had a specific function in the Venetian long room or *portego*. The rococo decoration is poorly carved and the arms have become very tenuous indeed. The carver appears to have had a final fling with the asymmetric acanthus scroll at the centre of the cresting.

Mid-nineteenth century ∗

1253 A not very inspiring product of the late nineteenth century. This poorly made settee with its weak, token carving is a 'good' example of the weakness of Italian art nouveau. It is a companion piece to armchair no.1208 and table no.1190.

1900-1920

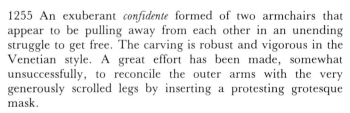

1254 There is a sophisticated air to the design of this settee that has a definite hint of French design to it. Certainly the style is French, from the transitional era, but the finish and craftsmanship, although high by Italian standards, is not good. There was a considerable French influence in Italy, especially in the north from the middle of the eighteenth century onwards and French forms were copied, often quite faithfully.

1880-1900

1255 An exuberant *confidente* formed of two armchairs that appear to be pulling away from each other in an unending struggle to get free. The carving is robust and vigorous in the Venetian style. A great effort has been made, somewhat unsuccessfully, to reconcile the outer arms with the very generously scrolled legs by inserting a protesting grotesque mask.

c.1900

SETTEES/SIDE CABINETS

1256 An outrageous hall seat known as a *cassapanca,* a development of the *cassone* that has been adapted to a seat by the simple addition of arms. This walnut showpiece has been richly and somewhat crudely inlaid with engraved ivory *putti,* or *amorini,* in a very similar style to that of southern Germany. The inevitable Italian crest is by far the most assured part of the decoration but the games and pastimes of the *putti* will keep the owner amused for hours. This type of marquetry is seen intermittently in antique shops and the salerooms and is always very popular. It compares with the mid-eighteenth century work of Johann Georg Wahl of Osthofen for the Elector Palatine.

1850-1880

1257 A brilliant ivory and coloured mosaic hall settee with a mixture of Moorish and Byzantine decoration and strange gilt Gothic finials and ogee arches, set with needlework figures. An extraordinary piece of furniture made for some unknown patron with expensive and exotic tastes but the origins remain an unsolved mystery.

c.1880

1258 (left) A poor cabinet on stand with its doors missing, also panels, mouldings and stringing. The tall legs are surprisingly heavy giving the piece a Spanish feeling.

1860-1880

1259 An exquisitely worked ivory inlaid cabinet by G.B. Gatti,, sadly without a stand. The solid ivory columns and balustrade are similar to mid-nineteenth century Indian ivory work. The fine inlay has much in common with the contemporary French Renaissance revival makers in Paris. It is a rare find to see such high quality work, to exhibition standards, from Italian craftsmen. It sets itself up above the many Milanese commercial makers who produced inferior ivory inlay.

Made for the 1878 Paris Exhibition

SIDE CABINETS

1260 A very finely inlaid Renaissance revival cabinet inlaid with ivory and set with semi-precious hardstones. This is similar to the work of the better Paris makers for the international exhibitions, but not as finely executed as the French examples. The carcass on Italian casework is never as well made as in France or England. There is not the attention to detail, the whole frame being more liable to move, splitting the almost paper-thin veneers. The inlay is far fussier than on most French examples, which have more architectural severity than Italian shapes, relying heavily on the Henri II architectural principles. This cabinet, sold in New York, bears the Guildford stamp of W. Williamson & Sons, who retailed many fine Continental pieces of furniture from c.1880-1920.

1870s

1261 A *lacca* wardrobe in typical and traditional Venetian mid-eighteenth century style. The carcass is badly made and both carver and painter have not been able to resist the temptation to over indulge in rococo motifs — taking asymmetry to its limits. The bulging shape usually occurs at either the top or the bottom of any Venetian piece of furniture that imitates, or is contemporary with, the rococo.

c.1900

1262 Italian, but fondly copying the late eighteenth century George III English style. England had a considerable but undocumented influence on Italian furniture development in the second half of the eighteenth century and the neo-classical style enjoyed a certain popularity. The poor construction of the doors can clearly be seen, although this alone is never enough to label a piece 'Italian'. The decoration is far weaker than would have been employed in England, either in the late eighteenth century or as a later copy. The central mask is especially bad.

c.1900

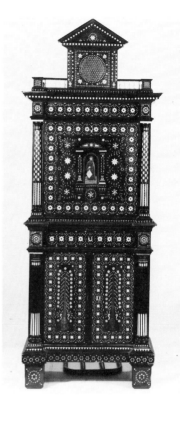

1263 (left) The extraordinary winged legs should be, by now, unmistakably Italian. All the mouldings, on the frieze, lower middle section and apron are typical Renaissance revival gadrooned and egg and dart acanthus, boldly carved and used on most pieces of Italian furniture, especially *cassoni* from c.1500 onwards. The inlay has a Persian/Indian flavour on the doors and the Moorish influence of the geometric *alla certosina* copies the style of c.1500.

1860s

1264 (right) A very similar style of inlay but no 'Renaissance' carving. The vase of flowers representing the Tree of Life is repeated six times. The portrait figure became a popular decoration in the second half of the nineteenth century. A very good quality cabinet, the ivory balustrade and inlay on a walnut ground.

1860-1880

1265 (left) The same severe Palladian cresting is applied to this cabinet, which is set with semi-precious stones and well carved ivory plaques. The plaques on these cabinets are occasionally seventeenth century and this will increase the price considerably. The severity of the base is relieved by the rather silly and very modest terms — very 'Victorian' in their bashfulness. A quite well made ebony-veneered cabinet, decorative rather than useful.

c.1860

1266 (right) Another exotic example of *alla certosina* with flowering shrubs in the lower panels. In keeping with true Muslim princples there is no representation of human or animal life. Similar geometric devices are common in Turkish and Caucasian carpets. The addition of fluted columns and obelisks gives the cabinet a more Italian feel.

1880-1900

1268 The grotesque chimera and acanthus bearded mask with its drawn in cheeks and the mouth forming the keyhole are very common Italian Renaissance revival features. This whole, fairly useless, piece is really a Florentine sculptor's dream come true, and a fine example of his art in the nineteenth century.

1870s

1267 A well finished walnut and burr-walnut open buffet or serving table. The cabinet work is better than most Florentine pieces, with more care taken over the carving. It is unusual to see the incorporation of burr walnut panels in southern European furniture, a feature that was very common in England from the 1850s.

c.1880

1269 A triumph of carved walnut signed by Andrea Baccetti from Florence. This enormous cabinet is over four metres high, one of the largest pieces of furniture to be on the open market, which of course is a problem in itself — there are few homes that can accommodate such a large piece. The heads on the door are taken from the Ghiberti door at the Baptistry in Florence, a favourite theme and source of information for Florentine carvers.

The two metre high door is a wonderful example of the naturalism of the nineteenth century Florentine carver. In a cabinet with such a severe architectural form and so inhibited by the past glories of the Renaissance, it is surprising to see such freedom in the carved flowers and lizards, snails and insects. Note the weird mask just above the urn in the detail of the door and the frog, carefully placed to one side. A detail of the signature is reproduced in the makers' list on page 388.

c.1870

1270 A Florentine cabinet imitating the style of the late sixteenth century. A poorly made piece, in walnut. The top half looks unbalanced without a pair of cupboard doors yet the lower cupboards look plain and boring compared with the normal liveliness of this period. The cresting is an ostentatious symbol of the wealthy nineteenth century patron. Note the little heads on the cornice are similar to those on the previous cupboard.

1880-1910

1271 There is a definitely Flemish feel to the doors and large heavy outset columns of the lower part. The naïve hunting scenes on the upper part are also misleading and very similar to the marquetry of southern Bavaria. The winged caryatids are a more familiar Italian feature and the cornice is a common sight on Italian furniture in the second half of the nineteenth century. It is conceivable that this oddly proportioned cabinet was made up from 'spares' but the overall impression given by the solid walnut carcass is Italian.

1880s

1272 One of a pair of unlikely shaped tall corner cabinets, crudely but amusingly inlaid with ivory hunting scenes that, once again, are very similar to Bavarian examples. The oddly proportioned tops and *bombé* lower cupboards are very effective and would be very decorative when placed in the corners of a room. They are nearly two and a half metres high and probably come from the northern tip of Italy.

1850-1870

1273 The terrible frame of this little bedside cabinet has been 'knocked up' by some back street carpenter or coffin maker, who obviously had little or no knowledge of the period but was luckily able to recognise an early seventeenth century panel with its rude little *putti* posing in rows of three, two with a strange wheelbarrow in the lower panel. Not a success. The panel will be resold and the cupboard probably discarded.

Made up early twentieth century

1274 An ivory inlaid cabinet from Milan, in the style that was common in the seventeenth century in southern Bavaria and the northern states of Italy. The squashed lion feet are an irresistible feature of Italian 'Renaissance' furniture. At least they are realistically portrayed, bearing the heavy load of the cabinet itself. The plain and simple architectural lines of the cabinet make it more suitable for present day northern European tastes than the more exotic nationalistic furniture that was produced in Italy in the nineteenth century and which is increasingly popular there today.

1870s

1275 The design of this cabinet is much more cosmopolitan and would be acceptable to a wide range of buyers. There is plenty of useful display space and the display is easy to see. The ivory stringing is in a spirited design but the foliage is very mechanical. At least there are three doors which actually open — the French have an irritating habit of incorporating only one central door in display and side cabinets, so that the user has to grope around in the sides.

1870s

1276 An *alla certosina* cabinet, finely inlaid with an overall pattern in a highly decorative manner. The columns would be especially difficult to inlay as they taper. Much better quality than most Italian pieces of the period.

1880s

1277 A highly individual small cupboard with good walnut Renaissance carving. The ram's head and finial look rather unnecessary. At first glance this strange piece looks as though it has been taken and adapted from another item of furniture, but this is not in evidence upon inspection.

c.1900

TRIPOD TABLES

1278 French or Italian? This tripod table is in walnut and olive-wood and signed 'Bailet, Nice, 25 Ponchettes', which sounds French enough but at this period Nice was still officially part of the state of Liguria. However, the quality is good with amusing scenes of contemporary life with peasants in traditional costumes, in a similar manner to that of a lot of Italian *pietre dure* panels. The sculptural lion's head, legs, and very bold entwined barley twist column are very strong Italian influences. Quite a rare and unusual table.

1850s

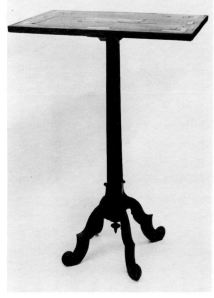

1279 A very plain ebonised occasional table with poor ivory inlaid panels on the top and a stylised 'Gothic' base. Not very good quality, or very inspiring, but useful.

1860s

1281 (left) The unusual base of this table, with its spirally carved heavy baluster and thin rather shaken looking animal heads continuing to the legs, is not a very satisfactory design. The good sectional inlay of various Roman marbles in the moulded top is what the buyer will be interested in. The underside of the top is stamped, somewhat inexplicably, 'K.E.'.

c.1860

1280 A carved and gilt table with a fine mosaic top inlaid with views of Rome. The winged griffins reappear once again and also the rather peculiar concave sided triangular foot with broadly chamfered corners, which is a very strong north Italian feature. The value, of course, is in the mosaic.

c.1870

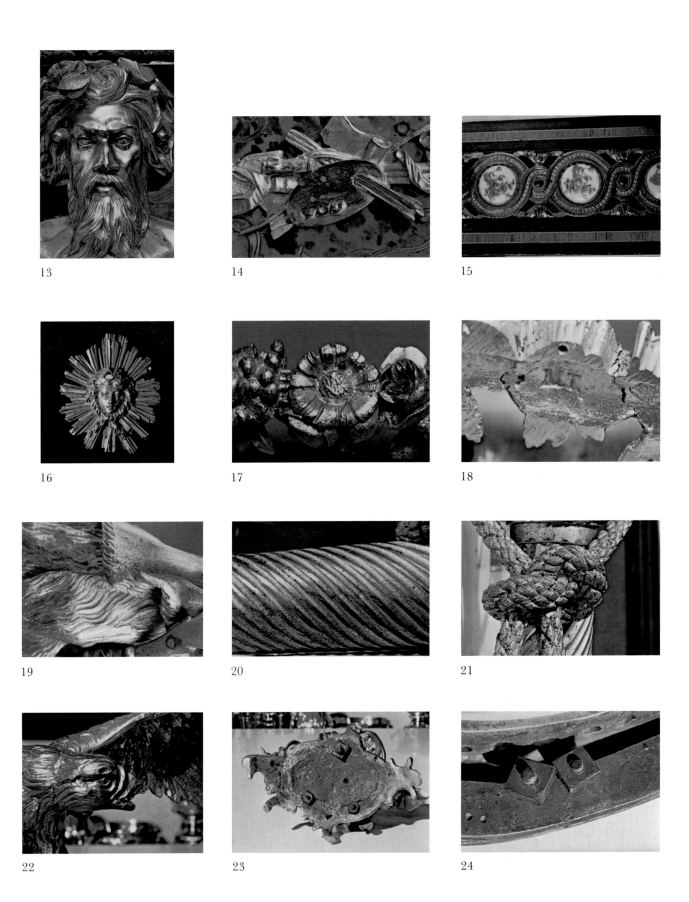

13

14

15

16

17

18

19

20

21

22

23

24

Metalwork

(continued from page 412)

13 An unusually handsome bearded mask of the type used on furniture of the Louis XIV period. Great attention has been paid to the details of the leaves, hair and beard. The face has been well modelled and is very realistic. The gilding is rather yellow and bright but the overall effect is one of quality. French. 1860s.

14 A similar colour of metalwork as the previous example but a coat of varnish, applied years ago to preserve the brightness of the gilding, makes the metalwork look dull and it has chipped on the highlights. The casting and finishing are not to a very high standard. French. 1850s.

15 This guilloché banding is English and holds a number of small enamel plaques that are, like the whole piece of furniture, made in England in the French manner. Like the milled banding no.3 on page 413 it has been run out on a machine but has none of the quality of the French example. This is not to say that the English metalworkers were not able to produce equally as good work as the French; both countries were able to produce good, bad and indifferent work. The gilding on this banding is rather poor brass dipped. 1870s.

16 This sunburst Apollo mask from a pendulum of a Viennese clock is finely cast with a lot of attention to detail, although the colour and quality of the gilding is not particularly good. 1830s.

17 This detail from a swag of flowers is extremely crude. The casting is very rough and ready and the finishing is almost non-existent. The gilding appears to have simply been dipped and is very bright and brash. Perhaps this should be considered the lowest grade of metalwork. Probably French. Early twentieth century.

18 The reverse of the previous swag showing the maker's initials M.T. cast into the back. The maker is almost certainly the founder and like many of these smaller foundries who sent their work out to the furniture makers, their names are unrecorded. The casting faults can clearly be seen around the initials. If these appear on the front, they have to be carefully filled which can be done today by arc welding. Early twentieth century.

19 The casting and finishing are very poorly done on this piece of metalwork but the colour, once cleaned, would not be too bad. French. 1870s.

20 This twist turned column showing slight entasis at one end is very finely cast and there is great strength to the uneven but tight swirling scrolls. Over the years the gilding has been partly rubbed from the top of the ridges but some of the original colour can be seen in the channels which have been stippled to give a contrasting effect. French. 1860-1880.

21 A very poor piece of casting on this rope twist that holds a tassel on to the previous column. There is none of the finishing or chiselling that the column has. French. 1860-1880.

22 The head and beak of this eagle are so poorly done that it is almost unrecognisable. Although some time has been spent on the chasing, it has none of the quality of the other items and is on a par with 17 and 18. The gilding is possibly the worst quality of all the previous examples. Probably French. Early twentieth century.

23 The underside of a small candlestick from the mid-eighteenth century in rococo style. The nuts and threads are all hand cut and the base is sand cast. To ensure that the gilding has gone right down to the edge on the outside of the base, traces of it remain on the underside, which is brown in the middle where it has not been touched. French. 1850-1880.

24 Again hand cut nuts and threads, this time from the middle of the nineteenth century. In the workshops that had not been mechanised techniques changed very little. The colour of the underside is delightful with black/red through to blue hues that contrast against the gilding that can just be seen on the edge. French. 1860s.

1282 The base of this gilt-bronze tripod table is copied from a table at the Museo Nazionale, Naples. The original was found in the Temple of Isis at Pompeii. The origin of this type of table with animal legs is from Greece but the decoration is more typically Roman in its elaboration. The top, in this instance, is more likely to be made in England, possibly Torquay or Derbyshire, with English marble made in the Italian style.

1860s

1283 The unusual combination of bronze and malachite is a strange mixture for this very solid table. The malachite, with its tightly curled growth rings, is from Russian quarries. The base looks more like a late seventeenth century andiron that has been converted into use as a table base. Could be French.

Third quarter nineteenth century

1284 The full exuberance of Florentine walnut carving is displayed in this small table of uncertain use. The well carved naked female torsoes almost begin to reflect the bizarre work of Carabin in Paris in the 1880s (q.v.). Each head is quite obviously an individual portrait. The shell that they are holding was probably intended to hold a bounteous display of fruit or food in a dining room.

1870s

1285 The bold scrolling feet of this tripod, almost growing back inside the base, are far broader than necessary for the small top which nevertheless is original. The divided top, with its grid above the painted panels of fruit, is reminiscent of the English mid-eighteenth century supper table and quite possibly a porcelain service was designed to fit into the grid to hold *hors d'oeuvres*. This would account for the wide base to ensure that the table could not be easily tipped over.

1840s

1286 A more typical Italian provincial marquetry table with a stylised star decoration inspired by the fifteenth century *certosina*. The inlay of various fruitwoods is on a walnut ground. These tables were solidly made but never of fine quality. They are simply practical pieces of furniture lacking the exotic and unnecessary sculpture incorporated into furniture made in the large towns.

1860s

1287 Another table of similar feeling. The top copies the ivory inlaid Milanese tables but uses cheaper local fruitwoods to inlay the picture of Apollo in his chariot. The multiple chequered herringbone and barber's pole bandings are typical of the Sorrento mosaic work, which has always been wrongly thought to be the origin of English Tunbridge Ware.

c.1870

1288 A fine marquetry octagonal table, the top inlaid in a much better quality than the poor carving of the base would suggest. There is considerable French influence in the base but the top is in early seventeenth century well-tried Italian styles. These tables which combine marble or various woods with a carved gilt base often look a little odd and can appear to be made up, as the contrasting materials are unusual.

1830s

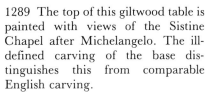

1289 The top of this giltwood table is painted with views of the Sistine Chapel after Michelangelo. The ill-defined carving of the base distinguishes this from comparable English carving.

c.1860

1290 An extremely bold example of the sculptural furniture maker's art. The young caryatids rest casually on grotesque masks, their wings helping to support the *scagliola* top. The framework of the top has a great similarity to English work of the second quarter of the nineteenth century.

c.1840

1291 The exact origin of this extremely unusual bronze and bluejohn table remains a mystery. Certainly, the French foundries were experimenting with bronze in the *chinoiserie* style and a certain amount of bluejohn was mined from northern France. The involved figure of eight knotting of the serpent-like dragons is intended to convey the knot of longevity, a favourite Chinese motif.

Third quarter nineteenth century

1292 A very handsome Italian Empire *guéridon* with a heavily black veined marble top. The table is unusually cast entirely in bronze. The applied anthemium mounts on the frieze are almost identical to similar French early nineteenth century examples. The squat leaf cast paw feet give the table the look of Horatio at the Bridge — *ils ne passeront pas!*

c.1830

1293 The intricate design of the inlaid top is like that of carefully planned parquetry floors of houses in southern Germany and northern Italy. The deep rim is interestingly inlaid with a fine band of stringing, imitating the popular stylised lotus leaf of the English William IV period — the sensitivity of the stringing recalls that of the decorated Gothic of France. The carved baluster column is perhaps unnecessarily overdecorated and fits into that heavy domed circular platform base with tiny scrolled feet that typifies furniture from the northern Italian area.

c.1840

WRITING CABINETS

1295 A nice quality heavily architectural cabinet with a much softer feel than the hardness of ebony. Cabinets such as this inlaid with walnut have a warm glow of finely grained but well coloured wood. The marquetry on this piece is even and the base for once has not been neglected. The pictorial scene of a soldier posing with a musket by a standard is rather an amusing change from allegorical heavenly figures. Note the heavy palladian overhanging cornice.

1860s

1294 A huge architectural ebony veneered writing cabinet inlaid with engraved ivory figures and *contra partie* ivory foliage. This dominant piece is not particularly well made and is far too large for most tastes. It is labelled by the firm of Ferdinando Pogliani from Milan — the label is reproduced in the makers' list. The work is typical of the 1860s and the ink inscription 'Fatto Nell'Anno 1864' is probably the actual date of manufacture.

Dated 1864

1296 Another imposing architectural Milanese piece but far too severe in both form and colour for most tastes. The ivory inlay, although of quite good quality, is restrained and the whole effect lacks the ingredients of the Italian *ottocento*.

c.1880

1297 A very crudely made and inlaid bureau in English mid-eighteenth century style from an unidentified area presumably in the northern Italian Alps. The finish of this piece hardly deserves the term cabinet work but the naïvety and rustic feel have an appeal of their own.

c.1880

1298 An exuberant rococo walnut desk with the unusual but useful incorporation of two open bookshelves on the opposing side shown in the second illustration. Few desks are ever seen with the incorporation of bookshelves. The decoration is reminiscent of Venetian mid-eighteenth century, in the extravaganza style so loved by this rich and decadent city.

1860s

1299 (left) A lacquer bureau cabinet in mid-eighteenth century Venetian style gilt with *chinoiserie*. The form is very similar to mid-eighteenth century English styles and was copied religiously throughout the nineteenth and early twentieth century in many of the major Italian cities and is often extremely difficult to pin down to an exact region. Dating is also very difficult as techniques did not change from the eighteenth century and Italian craftsmen have a knack of making even more recent pieces appear 'old'.

1900-1920

1300 (right) A poorly made bureau cabinet decorated with *arte povera*. This technique incorporated the use of prints which were glued to a painted furniture carcass to simulate marquetry in provincial areas where the expense of detailed and intricate marquetry work could not be justified. The application of printed panels could be done very cheaply by an unskilled workman. This cabinet incorporates gilt *chinoiserie* figures which are in fact painted, as well as printed panels. The style is Venetian from the middle of the eighteenth century.

1910-1920

1302 A badly made Milanese bureau in a loose imitation of the Louis XVI style. The quality of manufacture of this type of furniture has little to recommend it.

1870s

1301 A poorly made ebonised and ivory inlaid Milanese bureau in late seventeenth century Louis XIV style. Apart from the inlay, the severe architectural form of the top and the heavy legs with thin 'X' stretchers differentiate this from a French piece of furniture. The interior of such a cabinet is often very plain with very crudely made soft pine lined drawers.

1860s

1303 Again an imitation of the late seventeenth century with heavy but simplified legs of typical Italian and Spanish origin and the thin simplified scrolled stretcher also popular in the southern Mediterranean. This cabinet is better made than the previous two but with its writing slide incorporated in the drawer it is not particularly useful as a writing desk.

1860s

1304 An extremely fine and unusual inlaid ivory, tortoiseshell and mother-of-pearl writing desk of quite exceptional quality. The profuse inlay is partly in brass and copper and no surface has been left untouched. There is a definite Indian feel in not only the prodigious use of ivory but especially in the alternate ivory and ebony gadrooning of the bun feet. An exceptional cabinet that is unlikely to be seen in large numbers, quite possibly it was a one-off commission.

1840s

1305 If sculpture is not allowed to prevail in Italian furniture then architecture will immediately and automatically take over. The imposing triple arch of this cabinet is let down by the extraordinary box-like weedy legs. The maker could have had no confidence in his own cabinet making and has had to go to the extreme of adding a fifth leg in the centre to support the weight of the over imposing top. The marquetry is exceptionally fine with nicely engraved ivory panels. The cathedral-like appearance is perhaps a vague imitation of Milan cathedral. The base is in the Louis XIV style.

1850s

1306 Another good example of *alla certosina* with finely inlaid ivory, copper and pewter sixteenth century figures with an allegorical chariot group on the flap. Furniture of this type was known to have been exhibited in the Rome Exhibition of 1851 but manufacture must have continued in Milan and northern Italy for the next thirty to forty years. The elongated hermaphrodite fantasy animal supports are rather elegant and appear quite frequently on table bases.

c.1860

1307 A somewhat poor relation to the previous example. The base looks almost like an afterthought and would easily become rather unsteady and shaky. The panel on the flap is in a similar theme to the previous cabinet.

c.1870s

1308 (left) The effect of the inlay and architectural niches of this little writing desk is totally Moorish. The legs are substantial and almost too dumpy. Note that the right hand side of the balustrade is almost completely missing — the little ivory balusters will be quite expensive to have turned. There is also part of the moulding missing on one of the capitals of the legs. This is a continual problem with nineteenth century Italian furniture where the moulding and often quite large pieces of carving are simply glued on to the main carcass and never pinned. This results in the glue drying out in the changes of atmosphere and often quite large pieces become missing.

1860-1880

1309 A very large ivory inlaid tall cabinet with scenes from The Merry Wives of Windsor inlaid in copper, pewter and ivory on the door.

c.1860

These detail shots are of the amazing quality exhibition cabinet by Gatti illustrated in colour on page 159. The carcass work is of exceptionally fine quality and shows that the Italian craftsman could compete on an international scale with European craftsmen if he so desired. Every inch of the cabinet is inlaid with finely balanced marquetry in ivory and various woods and the detailed photograhs give an indication of the delicious quality of the inlay. However, there are numerous Paris and London makers who would consider even this quality to be inferior but as their work rarely, if ever, appears on the market it is difficult to test this difference in terms of market value. See date details on page 159.

MARQUETRY

This group of marquetry furniture is a very commercial and popular type of Italian furniture. It is all made in a confusing style with many similarities to South German furniture, from where it draws much inspiration. The German examples are nearly always far better executed. The hunting techniques throughout the whole area must have been very similar and not have changed much from the sixteenth century, the period that these pieces are trying to emulate, to the nineteenth century, when this furniture was made. The scenes are very similar to Bavarian hunting scenes and certainly ill-defined borders confuse the issue somewhat. Austria dominated the north of Italy and there was a constant cross-flow of the various regional styles.

1310 This *cassone* is in a vague early sixteenth century Florentine style, crossed with Roman carved decoration. The marquetry is not very good but is highly decorative. The feet are new — even nineteenth century furniture is subject to the ravages of time — the softwood feet have rotted or been ruined by worm.

1860s

1311 The ivory inlaid columns are an instantly recognisable Italian feature. The hunting scene is in a very similar vein to the previous illustration. There is a vague impression of the early Empire French *secretaire à abattant* but there the comparison must end. The Italian inlay has completely taken over from the form that the French themselves adapted from Liguria. The feet in this case are wonderful — grotesque human masks with blown out cheeks and a cork or bung stuffed in their mouths!

1860s

1312 A *cassone* that has developed into a *cassapanca* based on sixteenth century tradition. The carved leaves flanking the back of the cresting are often found on side or dining chairs. It is a pity that such a decorative item has to be so badly made. Compare with no. 1256.

1850-1880

1313 A baroque extravaganza in walnut, guaranteed to keep the user awake at night. In the centre of the headboard three *putti* are brawling while another sleeps on the footboard, serenaded by a (naked) lyre player and another *putti* holding a torch. The exuberant carving is a riot of acanthus and heavy breasted female winged caryatids with Venetian dolphins devouring the flowerhead cresting on the footboard. A rare and unusual bed, probably from Venice.

1870s

1314 A most extravagant *bombé* shape from Venice in an exact style of the second quarter of the eighteenth century. This piece was very cleverly made and it was very difficult to establish the exact date. After careful inspection the consensus of opinion was that it was one of the many late nineteenth/early twentieth century copies. The type of construction did not change at all from the eighteenth to the nineteenth century and therefore it makes cataloguing extremely difficult. Whether or not it was made with intent to deceive is a question that must remain unanswered. The eccentric late baroque shape is illustrated in *Il Mobile Veneziano del Settecento,* ed. Görlich, vol. 11, 1959, figs. CCCLXXVIII and CCCLXXXIV.

Late nineteenth/early twentieth century

DETAILS

(left) A detail of the dovetails of a drawer from a Milanese workshop. The style is very similar to other Northern European countries but the finish is not as good. Generally speaking, the further north one travels the finer the dovetails become.

1870s

(right) A view of the lock on a large Florentine *armoire*. The lock is deeply recessed into the door and made of good quality mild steel. The trefoils at the top and bottom are an elaborate feature for decorative purposes only.

1870s

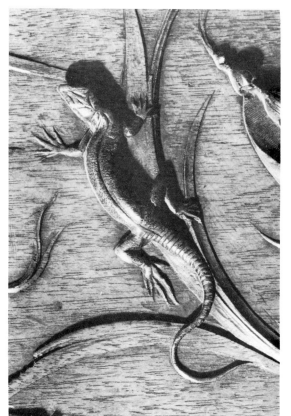

Two amusing photographs of carved animals on a walnut cabinet from Florence illustrated on page 428. It is an example of some of the best naturalistic carving by Andrea Baccetti.

1870s

444

LOW COUNTRIES

BELGIUM

On the seventh of February 1831 the National Congress, in conference in London, accepted the Constitution and a new monarchy and Belgium became a separate country.

The date conveniently coincides with the scope of this book. Belgium was founded at a time of great economic difficulty. The lands that became Belgium had suffered many years of war and played host to the greatest battle of all time, Waterloo. The policy of free commerce, founded by Frère Orban in the 1850s, steadied the economic foothold of the country and, with the help of England, Napoleon III's war of 1870 did not directly involve Belgium.

Amongst all this difficulty flourished a new romanticism and a great love for the neo-Gothic. Previously the Empire style had dominated the area of the Low Countries but this, almost without warning, disappeared to be replaced by tenuous lancet arches, cusps and crocketed finials. Oak was in abundance and in keeping with late seventeenth and eighteenth century traditions of the area, oak was used prolifically, in the solid, carved and dowelled, its forms closely connected with the style favoured by A.W.N. Pugin in England. Fine examples of this period can be found at the Château de Loppem.

The universally popular rococo revival reached Belgium in the late 'seventies and early 'eighties, not as a forerunner of the late Victorian Chippendale asymmetrical rococo popular in England and Holland during the 1890s, but as a direct form of the romantic revival popular in England in the 1840s. Moulded serpentine balloon-back chairs of vague Louis XV outline were carved with marguerites and leaves. The mahogany frames were commonly black lacquered.

Renaissance and baroque forms only enjoyed a minor popularity for the most part, with the notable exception of the mass of Tudor and Jacobean pieces decorated in a revival of carving which proliferated at the same time in England. In many cases plain seventeenth century pieces were decorated, or in some cases redecorated, by both the amateur and professional carver. Certainly by the 1880s a large number of home carvers were at work and many large sideboards were made up out of old wood and 'carved up'. The comparable work being executed in England in an identical 'Jacobethan' vein renders it extremely difficult to distinguish one nationality from the other.

Houses were filled with a 'Victorian clutter' of many small pieces of furniture imitating many

A Flemish scene by Ernest Godfrinon, a Belgian artist working in the late nineteenth century. Note that there is a thickly woven Persian runner on the floor. The wall above the panelling is decorated with embossed leather work, an influence from the time of Spanish domination of the Flemings. The cabinet in Gothic style against the back wall is typical of the work produced in and around Liège in vast numbers during the second half of the nineteenth century, all in the antique style.

styles. Directly influenced from France, the Louis revivals took their toll and much of Belgian furniture in the second half of the century was of an eclectic international style.

The *Belle Epoque* flourished cosily, unaware of the new expressionism of the art nouveau. The new industrial strength of Belgium, identified in the statue of a choirmaster in the Square du Petit Salon, Brussels in 1883, see illustration on page 458 and the founding of a Socialist party in 1885, demanded a new way of thinking and a new form of expression in art.

The Hotel Solvay, Hotel Autrique and, in 1892, Tassel's house at no. 6 rue Paul-Emile-Jansen by Victor Horta, had a tremendous impact with their new materials and attenuated forms of furniture. Horta, like Henry van de Velde, had been influenced by the work of Morris, Lewis F. Day and Walter Crane and van de Velde in turn helped to lay down the grass roots of modern German thinking, the country where his work was most appreciated. Van de Velde's own house, 'Bloemenwerf' outside Brussels, was designed in the art nouveau idiom down to the last detail, entering completely into the spirit of a new style. His obvious love of woods is similar to that of the English Arts and Crafts makers of the same period, especially the Cotswold School of Gimson. The sinuous limbs of van de Velde's furniture are at first far cleaner than the moulded, twisting forms that were to earn art nouveau its 'macaroni' image. Van de Velde, in his simple early designs in Belgium, appears to be looking directly through the naturalistic stylised plant forms that were so popular in France.

Belgian Designers, Architects and Makers

BOVY, Gustave Serrurier (1856-1910). Liègeois furniture designer and maker heavily influenced by the English Arts and Crafts movement.

CHELLENS, Louis (fl. early twentieth century). 12 quai des Charbonnages, Brussels. Exhibited a *comptoir de café* in oak at the 1905 Liège Exhibition.

DESIER, Henri (fl. early twentieth century). Exhibited a bed at the Liège 1905 Exhibition. A Brussels manufacturer.

DUVIVIER (fl. early twentieth century). 2, 4 & 7 rue Velbruck, Liège. Exhibited white painted oak furniture at the 1905 Liège Exhibition.

GOBART, E. (fl.1860s). Ghent carver and furniture maker, making late neo-Renaissance pieces highly carved and inlaid. Exhibited in Paris in 1867.

HANKAR, Paul (fl.c.1900). Art nouveau architect/designer.

HORTA, Victor (1891-1917). Major Brussels architect and furniture designer who was fundamental in laying down the principles of Belgian art nouveau. Influenced especially by the English designer Heywood Sumner.

KHNOPFF, Fernand (1858-1921). Aesthetic painter and designer in a modern style at the turn of the century in a style closer to Vienna than most of his English influenced contemporaries.

LECLERQ, Philippe (fl. early twentieth century). 72 rue Crétny, Liège. Exhibited *meubles de luxe* at the 1905 Liège Exhibition.

MAISON GILLION-CROWET. A fashionable Brussels shop exhibiting all types of art nouveau artifacts and furniture at the turn of the century.

NEUVILLE, Victor (fl. early twentieth century). A Liège furniture maker exhibiting at the 1905 Liège Exhibition.

ROSEL (fl. mid-nineteenth century). Brussels furniture maker working in a fluid French style. The only piece by this maker recorded to date by the author is in a Louis XIV style, see illustration no. 1338.

ROULE, M. (fl. mid-nineteenth century). Exhibited furniture at the 1851 Great Exhibition in Renaissance style.

SERRURIER & Cie. (fl. early twentieth century). 41 rue Henricourt, Liège. Exhibiting general furniture at the 1905 Liège Exhibition.

SMUTSEL-MONOY (fl. early twentieth century). 18 avenue Louise, Brussels. Exhibiting at the 1905 Liège Exhibition.

SOCIETE ANONYME LOUIS DE WAELE (fl. early twentieth century). 46 boulevard Leopold II, Brussels. Exhibiting at the 1905 Liège Exhibition.

SOCIETE DES VINGT. A group of influential Brussels designers holding a series of exhibitions in the modern Belgian art nouveau idiom from 1884.

VELDE, Henry van de (1863-1957). Had workshops at the rue Gray, Ettebeek. An important and influential art nouveau designer and architect whose decoration on furniture was limited mianly to purely structural work. Started working in Germany from 1897, where he was a considerable influence on the German *Jugendstil*.

WERNY—WIENAND (fl. early twentieth century). 98 rue Jean d'Outre-Meuse, Liège. Exhibited a desk at the 1905 Liège Exhibition.

HOLLAND

The French Empire style had a huge influence on Dutch furniture throughout the early years of the nineteenth century. The designs of both Percier and Fontaine, as well as La Mesangère, appealed to a wide section of the populace and their publications were avidly consulted for new ideas.

The first reaction against this formal style was, as in Germany, on the Biedermeier style. Light coloured, indigenous woods were used and although classical forms remained they were less ornamented, often using the natural grain and burr of the wood for the only decoration. This principle has now been taken an important stage further in England by modern designers such as John Makepiece.

The large factory of Matthew and William Horrix had a far reaching effect on what was available in Holland by the middle of the century. Founded in 1853, but with a few pieces dating c.1850, the firm employed two hundred and forty workers and the struggling small workshops could not compete with the Horrix Brothers' prolific and far ranging production and distribution of well illustrated catalogues.

Although Dutch furniture retains certain peculiarities of its own, the most obvious being the continued love of marquetry pieces, most of the styles are very similar to other European trends with many similarities to German furniture, albeit with a certain lightness of form influenced by France. Marquetry furniture was at its height in the seventeenth century, becoming less popular during the mid-eighteenth century. There was a tremendous influence from England, so much so that an apprentice's masterpiece had to be a copy of an English cabinet. Beautifully figured veneers of mahogany and walnut were selected to cover the *bombé* oak carcasses which lent themselves to the craze for marquetry which re-established itself after nearly two hundred years. The work of Jan Van Mekeren and other marquetry cabinet makers from Amsterdam and The Hague in the late seventeenth century was greatly admired. The period from 1880 to 1900 is that in which a vast number of good plain Dutch pieces of the period 1690-1760 were inlaid. Even plain Empire and Biedermeier pieces of the earlier part of the nineteenth century were not exempt from the expressive *marqueteurs*. Eighteenth century Dutch marquetry pieces are and have been for many years in great demand so that the prospective buyer is well advised to satisfy himself as to the exact date of the inlay. Often careful inspection will prove that the vase of flowers is too cramped or a leaf stops too close to the edge of a

A painting of a Dutch interior by Jacob Taanman, signed and dated Amsterdam 1880. It is an interesting insight from nineteenth century eyes of a seventeenth century room with a heavy Flemish dining table flanked by two mid-eighteenth century Dutch side chairs. A great play is made of the blue and white Delft tea service and vase of flowers. It is very interesting to see the small cylindrical kettle holder in mid-eighteenth century style that often appears on the market and is normally called a Dutch cellarette.

drawer or is cut in half by the crossbanding — points which no earlier craftsman would have permitted.

The great revival for marquetry which seemed to dominate Holland at the end of the nineteenth century was a nostalgic revival that many other European countries developed at the same time. In Holland there was a revival for all things Dutch and in a logical joining together of ideas the best features of earlier Dutch furniture were amalgamated into a style that is commonly seen in shops and salerooms throughout the furniture world. Vast quantities were exported to America, England and other European countries. There was no doubt that the best overall feature of Dutch craftsmanship was the marquetry which was perfected in the seventeenth century. The carefully executed baskets of flowers and exquisitely formed tulip flowerheads were the best examples of inlay of their time. However, the forms of furniture to which this art had been applied in the seventeenth century were not suitable for the nineteenth century consumer. There was little demand for the great 'showpiece' cabinets on stands from Antwerp or even the huge cupboards of the mid-nineteenth century. The popular styles of furniture at the end of the nineteenth century, as in common with most of Europe, were the well tried eighteenth century forms and it was to these that the marquetry revivalists greedily turned their lessened skills.

Oak was still used as a carcass for the better pieces although the cheap imports of pine from Russia and Canada were used in factories for the mass-produced pieces. Brasswork was generally of an average quality and handles were normally of cheap dipped brass with simple pressed *repoussé* decoration. A Dutch hinge might seem to bend with the force of the screws and never have the thickness or quality of English pieces. Towards the end of the century, however, locks and hinges throughout Europe became much more standardised and were of a more similar and higher quality.

In the vast output of the important Horrix Brothers can be seen French and German styles. A particularly elegant form of Charles X Gothic mahogany furniture was produced during the 1840s, retaining much of its French influence but often applied with yards of half-bead mouldings creating a slightly heavier form. Thonet furniture was popular from about 1870, bamboo from the 1890s. Although the *Zweites Rokoko* appears never to have been an influence in Holland, there was a great revival for the refined rococo work and asymmetry during the 1890s in a very similar vein to that of England. Rustic hat, coat and music stands, popular in England from the 1840s, appear in Dutch catalogues from 1860 onwards but the finished articles are very difficult to attribute to any individual maker.

The end of the century saw the breaking away of the progressive designers from the previous amalgam of traditional styles. The 'Arts and Crafts' sideboards of J.F. Dirks during the late 'seventies were the first visible break from the past. An art nouveau closer to that of Munich and Vienna developed, but in a half-hearted manner. Even the work of H.P. Berlage, who created the Amsterdam Stock Exchange, was designed in an English Arts and Crafts vein. The outline of a sideboard in the Stedelijk Museum in Amsterdam is almost akin to that of the English Gothic and Medieval reformers forty years before. The designs of another architect, K.P.C. de Bazel, also closely reflect an Arts and Crafts image, decorated, as is much of the Dutch 'art nouveau', with batik motifs from their Javanese colonies. Furniture design remained rather severe and formal, bearing little resemblance to the extravagant rococo themes of most of the continent of Europe. C.A. Lion Cachet was amongst the first to use the batik decoration at the turn of the century. An artist, Cachet was to found an important studio in Amsterdam with Gerrit Willem Dijsselhof who had earlier designed the Dijsselhofkamer as a house c.1890 which is Arts and Crafts in spirit and execution.

Dutch furniture, therefore, never took on recognisable art nouveau forms, although its neighbour Belgium had fostered important art nouveau designers. The turn of Holland was however soon to come in the constructivist work of Gerrit Rietveld and other members of the *de Stijl* group.

Dutch Designers, Architects and Makers

BAZEL, Karel Petrus Cornelius de (1869-1923). Architect and furniture designer first influenced by Egyptian motifs but subsequently applied batik ornament to plain rectangular furniture in the Arts and Crafts style.

BEAUSAR BROTHERS (fl. second half nineteenth century). Schiedam cabinet makers.

BERLAGE, Hendrik Petrus (1856-1934). Important architect and furniture designer whose *chef d'œuvre* was the Amsterdam Stock Exchange. Designed furniture in the new style with clear uncluttered lines at the turn of the century.

BLEESING, J.B. (fl.1870s). Amsterdam cabinet maker for Willem III.

BOER, D. (fl.1840-1890). General retailer also by appointment to Willem III.

BREYTSPRAAK, Carl (fl. early nineteenth century). Supplied a large amount of furniture in the Empire manner c.1808 to the new Royal Palace in Amsterdam.

BRUYEN EN ZOON, Frans de (fl.1885-1895). Arnhem maker and retailer supplying Louis XV style furniture including Vernis Martin.

CACHET, C.A. Lion (fl.c.1900). Furniture designer. One of the first to introduce batik ornament in Dutch design at the turn of the century.

CUEL, Joseph (fl. early nineteenth century). Upholsterer supplying furniture for the new Royal Palace at Amsterdam.

DIJSSELHOF, Gerrit Willem (1866-1924). Architect and furniture designer. His own house, the Dijsselhofkamer was furnished in a blend of Gothic medievalism heavily influenced by English Arts and Crafts. As if this was not enough some of his work, especially a glazed display cabinet, is influenced by the *Wiener Sezession*.

DIRKS, J.F. (fl.1870s). Gothic revival furniture of a watered down A.W.N. Pugin style. Also medieval revival forms reminiscent of the forms favoured by the English architect William Burges who spent his early years studying medieval buildings in Flanders.

GEFFEN, VAN DER WEEGEN, L.L. van (fl.1850-1890). Den Bosch. Retailer in Louis XVI style.

GRAAMANS, M.H.C. (fl.1850s). A Rotterdam furniture carver exhibiting at the Great Exhibition of 1851.

HACK, M.J. (fl.c.1900). Panel carver.

HAGEDOORN and Son, A.D. (fl.c.1825-1855). Rokin D 106, Amsterdam. Retailer of revival furniture especially Louis XV.

HEZEMANS, van de Heer (fl.1870s). Designer for J.F. Dirks (q.v.).

HORRIX Brothers (fl.1853-1890). The Hague, founded 1853, liquidated 1890. This was the largest and most prolific manufacturing and retailing firm throughout the second half of the nineteenth century. They supplied a wide variation of styles with a definite regard for tradition, covering a wide range of nationalities. The firm's photo archives and catalogues illustrate many pieces of French designed furniture. Much of the furniture they sold was imported.

HULST, Wed van der (fl.c.1880-1890). Premises on the Klaverstraat, Amsterdam, supplying Louis XIV and revival furniture including *jardinières*.

KAMPHUIS, J. (fl.c.1826-1880). Zwolle maker and retailer specialising in marquetry and Italian furniture.

KEMMAN, J.H.W. (fl.c.1860). Amsterdam maker exhibiting heavy, profusely carved furniture from 1859 onwards.

KUPERS and Son, J.A. (fl.c.1860). Amsterdam piano supplier.

MESKER, P.J. (fl.1880-1900?). Furniture retailer from Zutphen — labelled furniture — see Rugler (q.v.).

MUTTERS and Son, H.P. (fl.1880s). Vaktentoonstellig retailer importing all types of French wares. Exhibited at 1866 Amsterdam Exhibition with Horrix (q.v.) in Louis XVI style.

MUYSKEN (fl. third quarter nineteenth century). Cabinet maker supplying dining room furniture and chairs in Dutch Renaissance style.

NOOIJEN, L.J. (fl.1850-1880). Rotterdam furniture maker.

NORDANUS, G. (fl.c.1820). Cabinet maker from The Hague.

PANDER and Son, H. (fl.1880-1910). Retailer from The Hague selling William Morris style upholstered furniture and plain pieces in the Louis XV style.

QUIGNON (fl. mid-nineteenth century). Worked as a supplier with the Horrix brothers.

RIDDER Brothers, F. & L. (fl.1880-1900). Upholstered furniture, also cane and wicker.

RIETVELD, Gerrit (fl. early twentieth century). A member of the influential *de Stijl* group of constructivists.

RUGLER, Firm Wed. G. Ade (fl.1880-1900?). Retailer from Zutphen — labelled furniture — see Mesker (q.v.).

SCHMIDT & Co., J.D. (fl. third quarter nineteenth century). A catalogue engraver producing catalogues in Rotterdam, heavily influenced by rococo.

SIEM, D. (fl. second half nineteenth century). Engraved catalogues including massive pieces of furniture in Flemish baroque style.

STRACKE, J.T. (1817-1891). Produced late examples of Flemish baroque furniture of Jacobethan influence, mainly in oak. From 1876 he was Director of the Koninklijke School van Nuttige en Beeldende Kunsten.

TEKSTRA, H.S. (fl.1893-1914). Leeuwarden maker producing similar furniture to the above.

HOLLAND AND FLANDERS

The Antwerp Style

The Antwerp furniture makers and marquetry workers gained an enviable reputation for their intricate cabinets inlaid with tortoiseshell with a red foil backing to heighten the colour of the shell. In the late sixteenth and early seventeenth century their influence was widespread throughout Europe, especially in Italy, and many migrant Flemish workers applied their art in northern Italy and southern Germany, confusing the styles somewhat and clouding the exact origin of many pieces. This clouding became even more hazy in the eclectic nineteenth century. One of the most prominent of these migrant workers was Leonardo Van der Vinne of Antwerp who worked in Florence in the late seventeenth century and his simple marquetry foliage is often repeated in the ebonised marquetry pieces from Milan in the second half of the nineteenth century. Certain Spanish pieces can be found with a banding of ivory and ebony similar to the mirror on the next page which was probably brought to Antwerp by the Spanish, who acquired the technique from their Moorish conquerers, bringing certain aspects of the mudéjar *style to northern Europe. These pieces reflect the late seventeenth century style but are nineteenth century copies.*

1315 A small, seventeenth century style, side cabinet of ebony, ivory and tortoiseshell. The drawers are oak lined but a little crudely made. A highly decorative chest of drawers more likely to be used in a hall or living room than a bedroom.

c.1850

1316 This typical cabinet on stand was a very popular style in Spain as well as Antwerp, the home for fine cabinets the stands of which were often made in other countries. The whole of Europe demanded Antwerp cabinets which were sent out without a base, the base could then easily be made by local, less skilled craftsmen. The plain oak base of this cabinet is an early twentieth century replacement.

The cabinet c.1850

1317 The combination of two very Dutch features — the ivory and ebony barber's pole bandings and early seventeenth century style floral marquetry for which the Dutch are renowned. The effect is a very decorative but eclectic mirror that is extremely well made.

1880-1900

1318 A 'seventeenth century' occasional table incorporating all the best Antwerp features as a useful, conveniently sized little table. Once again — immaculately made.

1880-1900

1319 A fine marquetry centre table in the style of the mid-seventeenth century. Most period examples of these tables do not have drawers so that if one is seen with a drawer it is either a nineteenth century copy, of which there are many, or a seventeenth century table with a drawer added in the nineteenth century. The quality of this table is every bit as good as a period example, making it very difficult to tell, with any certainty, the true age.

c.1860 ✳

1320 A seventeenth century style Antwerp cabinet on stand with finely painted Italian views. Even the Italians had camels in the seventeenth century around the southern part of Italy and the Italianate views were almost certainly painted on this Flemish cabinet after it was exported to Italy. The base also is probably Italian which may account for the anomaly of square sections at the end of the barley twist legs and stretchers. Although this cabinet has been put in the northern European section, the value is in the decorative painted Italian panels.

1850-1870

1321 A very poor ebonised, i.e. stained wood, small side cabinet with painted pottery panels. Useful perhaps and quite capacious but hardly an elegant reflection of the eighteenth century.

c.1880

1322 (left) A Belgian carved cabinet in a vague imitation of the Louis XV provincial style, possibly from Liège. No space has been left free from the carver's chisel, which has worked religious passages and rustic peasant scenes into the four main panels. Having run out of further inspiration, the side panels are carved with extremely badly drawn leaves. A highly unsuccessful attempt at recreating French provincial furniture which is probably one of the most popular forms of French furniture.

1880-1900

1323 (above) A machine carved oak *semanier*. A large amount of this furniture was produced in Belgium as well as England and has little sense of style. There is a certain demand for this type of furniture in northern Europe but popularity is limited.

c.1880

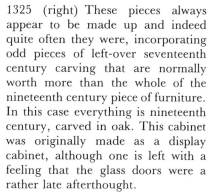

1324 (left) An extraordinary Gothic style cabinet painted with allegorical figures. There is no clear origin for the style of this cabinet, which is possibly best described as late nineteenth century Hispano Flemish with a little Venetian Gothic thrown in to complete the 'perfection'. Quite well made and unlikely to be repeated.

1860-1880

1325 (right) These pieces always appear to be made up and indeed quite often they were, incorporating odd pieces of left-over seventeenth century carving that are normally worth more than the whole of the nineteenth century piece of furniture. In this case everything is nineteenth century, carved in oak. This cabinet was originally made as a display cabinet, although one is left with a feeling that the glass doors were a rather late afterthought.

1880s

1326 A very plain and simple tortoiseshell and ebony-veneered side cabinet in a dark and gloomy seventeenth century style. It is interesting how the claw and ball feet have been carved. The claws are simply resting lightly on the balls instead of gripping them tightly as in eighteenth century similar examples — especially the English ones. Quite possibly the feet are later additions replacing the more normal flat bun foot.

1860s

1327 This carved Gothic oak extravaganza develops from the ordinary chest or coffer that later had a back attached so that the lid could be used as a rather uncomfortable seat. The lower part is carved in a fairly accurate Gothic style but the upper part is let down by the crests with the heavy crocketed arches above them. There must have been some very interesting little carved figures below each of the spires dividing the panels on the top and bottom, the gaps where they once stood can plainly be seen. It would be fascinating to know whether or not they were rare Gothic carved figures incorporated into a nineteenth century settle and removed in recent years by a knowledgeable punter.

1860-1880

1328 An ash and burr-walnut writing cabinet in a seventeenth Liègeois style with much in common with Antwerp and Augsburg. This most unlikely combination of woods proves to be most effective but the overall concept looks rather shaky on its multiple legs.

c.1900

1329 The form of this strange writing cabinet is of the typical French *secretaire à abattant* transformed into the Flemish late seventeenth century style with an overhanging cornice and frieze drawer rather commonly called a cushion drawer. The seaweed marquetry also became popular in England under the reign of William and Mary. This strange piece has had Queen Anne legs added to it, probably in the 1920s, and originally must have been on bun feet emulating the seventeenth century. It looks most unsatisfactory in its altered form.

c.1880

1330 (left) An extremely unusual walnut tall backed armchair, finely carved and designed in a very individual manner in the late nineteenth century art nouveau style. The exact origin of this chair is not certain. There is almost a Danish or Scandinavian feel about the reserved but stylish top-rail and carving. However, general opinion has it that this chair is a watered-down example of the highly developed Belgian art nouveau. Not likely to be found in a set.

c.1900

1331 (right) A very simple oak chair in an attenuated form of the style c.1690. The proportions are too thin and mean to be mistaken for a period chair. The stuffed drop-in seat is an eighteenth century innovation and therefore could never have been used in a late seventeenth century chair.

Early twentieth century

FLANDERS — Chairs

1332 (left) The epitome of a Flemish chair of the late seventeenth century. These chairs were made mainly in oak but sometimes in beechwood and occasionally in walnut. They became a very popular 'international' style and are found in Scandinavia and England. Note that the twist turned supports and the legs have a circular joint butting up to a square support. This typically European method of construction differentiates, in all periods, between Flemish and English chair construction. See detail below.

1850-1900

1333 A very much poorer quality oak chair with the most dreadful flat seat with a token amount of padding. The vine and grape carved čentre splat does not endear itself to comfort. Very much the poor brother of this type of popular chair. Probably a later example than above.

1880-1900

1335 (right) The low back chair was more common in the first half of the seventeenth century and was not as popular as the tall back reproductions of the second half of the nineteenth century. However, it is a much more satisfactory chair and far more sturdy than the vulnerable tall back. This chair is of oak and has carved *patera* on the square blocks on each of the front legs. The well worn leather upholstery gives a nice antique look and will probably suit most decors.

c.1900

1334 (above) Another uninspired later example of the 'seventeenth century' chair, also in oak. The double barley twist front stretchers are better finished than the very poor edging to the seat and the rather weak carving of the cresting. Compare no.968.

1880-1900

455

1336 A fine and very unusual dining table. The individual style is a good example of the power of patronage in the art of furniture making. This extending kingwood dining table was made for the fifth Earl Rosebery's yacht the *Czarina*. The highly individual style is an up-to-the-minute design in the art nouveau idiom using traditional methods of French veneering, with a strong architectural style of flying buttress supports and pierced copper mounts. The latter feature is a more English Arts and Crafts feature but the overall concept is most likely to be Belgian. It goes without saying that this elegant table is extremely well made. It has two extra leaves.

c.1900 (possibly as early as 1890)

1337 A very dumpy circular occasional table, ebony veneered and unusually heavy in both style and in weight! The segmentally veneered *scagliola* top and lapis panels on the capitals of the legs suggest that at one time the table was in Italy. Quite possibly it was exported to Italy for finishing, although this seems a little unlikely for such an uninspiring piece. The legs were popular in both Antwerp and Augsburg during the seventeenth century and possibly there is a heavy German influence.

c.1850

1338 An exceptional 'northern French' centre table in a very pure and restrained Louis XIV style. The carving really is a triumph of the woodcarver's art. The stamp underneath the frieze is that of a Mr. Rosel simply saying 'Rosel, Belgium'. There is little of the flamboyance normally ascribed to Flemish carvers. The Huguenots favoured a highly developed auricular style in the late seventeenth century which is not apparent here. A very sophisticated table with an excellent *brèche violette* marble top.

1850s? ✳

1339 The French Régence style most probably made in Belgium like the last table. This pier table has a massive marble top above very fine gilt and carved wood, every bit as well executed as it would have been in the 1720s. The gilding has that delicious slightly 'dusty' quality that is also found on the very best mercurial gilt metalwork.

1850s ✳

456

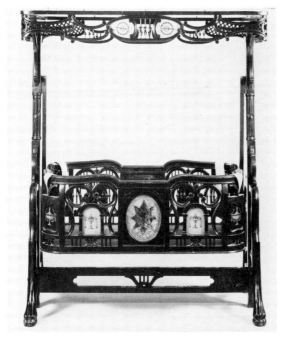

1340 A mahogany cradle incorporating painted glass and hardstone panels. It is difficult to establish the nationality with any certainty. The turned spindles appear on French and American furniture from the 1860s. The pierced 'C' scrolls incorporate rococo features into a heavy frame in a mechanical and surprisingly insensitive way which is surprising as a piece of furniture of this type is unlikely to have been made in large numbers and was quite probably a private commission.

1890s

1341 A carved oak 'court' cupboard in an imitation of what the late nineteenth century carvers thought was seventeenth century style. In this case, as quite often happens, the back panel supporting the cornice is a sixteenth century carved walnut panel of considerable quality. The panel is worth far more than the rest of the cupboard. Flemish carving of the late nineteenth century revival period is far freer than its English equivalent, without the attention to detail of either the carving or the interior.

Second half nineteenth century

1342 Another example of Flemish carved oak with considerable French influence. Settles of this type were made in large quantities throughout the second half of the nineteenth century and were made with little variation up until the 1930s. This one, in a moment of religious zeal, is carved with a Christian staving off the attack of a lion. The pierced cartwheels either side of the carved panel have a distinct northern feeling and are similar to the Breton turned roundels.

c.1900

457

1343 A very stately bed taking on the proportions of a Welsh tridarn, or three stage dresser. The style is a mixed early and mid-seventeenth century English and Flemish type, although the form could not have existed in any century but the nineteenth with its love for over-exaggeration and improving older styles. The two double-pierced obelisks are highly decorative on the footboard. The coving of the headboard is reminiscent of the medieval revival style of the English architect, Philip Webb, in the third quarter of the nineteenth century. Although a Flemish production, the English trade catalogues illustrated similar styles, especially the large firm Hampton's of Pall Mall.

Second half of the nineteenth century

A detail of the very worst of Flemish carving in the seventeenth century style that became so popular, indeed prolific in the second half of the nineteenth century. The oak graining can be seen quite clearly and was by far the most commonly used wood in recreating this style. Although the carving is quite well done by modern standards it is very poor by the standards that were easily possible in the nineteenth century and appalling by the standards of the highly skilled and individual Huguenot carvers.

1880-1920

This large bronze statue stands in the Square du Petit Salon in Brussels. It was cast to a design of Xavier Melly in 1882-1883 by the founder, J. Courriot. It is a somewhat pigeon-stained tribute to the vast output of the Flemish and Belgian chairmakers of the seventeenth century. The heavily studded seat of the chair owes much to the Spanish influence in the Low Countries in the seventeenth century. Note the circular stretcher joining the square leg — a feature illustrated in detail on page 455.

1344 A well made mixture of marquetry and well figured walnut. Most cabinet makers would be content with either the marquetry or the simple figuring of the wood. The style of this cabinet has developed along the lines of the French *encoignure*.

c.1870

1345 This corner cupboard is a copy of the archetypal Dutch neo-classical furniture popular c.1800. The inlay on this cupboard alone is enough to mark it as a late nineteenth century copy. The inlay is too weak, the tassels and drapes are far too stiff and no Dutch late eighteenth century cabinet maker would have allowed the fussy foliate designs on the pilasters. The wood, most unusually, is thuyawood from the Atlas Mountains.

c.1890 *

1346 Again the influence is very definitely French and the mounts are undoubtedly French exports. The delicate attenuated form of the marquetry is very unusual. Although this piece could in fact conceivably be French, it is possibly from Belgium or nearby Holland.

1860s

1347 A lacquered chest of drawers with a concave and a convex system of graduated drawers that was so popular in Holland in the middle of the eighteenth century. The carcass is well made in oak with fine drawer lines and, if it was not for the rather weak *chinoiserie* decoration, it would be a convincing example of eighteenth century furniture.

1880-1910 *

459

HOLLAND — Cabinets

1348 A large display cabinet with applied burr-walnut panels. The style is very similar to that popular in England and has a lot in common with English cabinets from the second half of the eighteenth century. There is also a lot in common with the American Grand Rapids style of the 1870s. These large cabinets are always sought after, almost regardless of nationality and decoration. This example is quite restrained with mainly small areas of leaf carving to complement the imposing architectural shape.

1870-1890

1349 The French influence of the *tambour* is often seen in Dutch furniture, especially in late eighteenth century examples, of which this is a copy. Note the English style handle that became popular in Holland in the late eighteenth century. The 'herring bone' and chequered banding are a reflection of the Dutch revival of interest in marquetry that had waned during the middle of the eighteenth century. This is a straightforward and not particularly good quality mahogany copy of a style c.1790.

c.1900 *

1350 An eclectic muddle in a mixture of English George III and French Louis XIV style but the overall design is typical of Dutch furniture in the third quarter of the nineteenth century.

1870s

1351 A simple highly 'Victorian' side cabinet in beautifully figured walnut with a token amount of rococo decoration that goes almost far enough to spoil the cabinet completely. The small oval panel does not give much of a display and makes one immediately suspicious of the fact that possibly there was a solid wooden panel in the cabinet originally. Although it is a shame for any piece of furniture to be altered from its original state, the cabinet will now be worth more and certainly be more useful. An unusual interpretation of the common French boulle small cabinet.

c.1860

1352 The well-figured burr walnut veneers of this cabinet in mid-eighteenth century style have probably saved it from the onslaught of the craze for marquetry that developed in a nostalgic revival in the 1880s. A plain and simple cabinet in a straightforward reproduction style. The apron, however, is a little eclectic and the applied wooden moulding at the bottom of the apron closely resembles that on the previous illustration.

1850s

1353 (right) Once again the style is of the mid-eighteenth century, underlining the comparatively small amount of new furniture made in a new style in the late nineteenth century. The barber's pole banding and complex drawer shape are typical of Dutch cabinet makers. This style of cabinet is often surprisingly small and in this instance about 1.90m high.

c.1880

1354 This beautifully made cabinet in well figured walnut is a rare example of true Dutch nineteenth century furniture, albeit in a beautifully executed French eclectic Régence and Louis XV style. The carving of the flowers is unusually delicate but the applied 'C' mouldings are similar to the first two illustrations on this page. The hinge, however, has a Spanish or Portuguese flavour and the overall effect is one of Iberian influence.

1860s

The finicky poor quality pressed brass metalwork on all four of these cabinets is very typical of Dutch metalwork and is repeated constantly on similar forms of furniture. It is unnecessarily fussy and 'bitty' and serves very little useful purpose. It appears to have been put on in a meccano type process like an erratic jigsaw puzzle. Each piece is lightly pinned and can easily work loose.

1355 The vase of flowers has a Franco-Dutch flavour and the whole cabinet is obviously based on the French nineteenth century examples imitating the rococo. The walnut is quite well figured but the veneers are very thin and poorly applied. The best feature is the longbow shaped section of the glass in the door which would be expensive to replace.

1860s

1356 Another similar example in almost every detail. The vase of flowers is obviously from a particular pattern. There is a feeling of a slightly inferior quality compared with the previous cabinet, mainly in that the metalwork is extremely spindly and the graining of the wood almost non-existent.

1860s

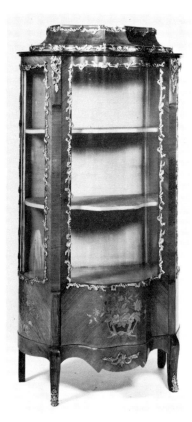

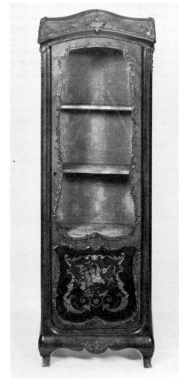

1357 (right) It is most probable that whichever country this *vitrine* was attributed to would deny it. It could have been made in France, Holland, Belgium, Spain or Portugal but the theory of the metalwork continues in a Dutch theme. One owner has decided that the woodwork was so poor that he has had the veneer painted with a thin eggshell finish. It is interesting how similar the leaves of the metalwork are to the leaves and foliage on Dieppe ivory furniture.

c.1900

1358 (left) A well made little cabinet imitating the style of a French mid-eighteenth century sedan chair. The roof is of a very familiar Dutch *bombé* form and it is surprising that the maker has not attempted to make the base of the door *bombé*. Arriving at the base of the cabinet he has had to invent a stand which looks a little incongruous.

1890s

HOLLAND — Chairs/Work Tables

1359 An unusual armchair from a drawing room suite in a style typical of Northern Europe imitating the English 'salon suites' in turn influenced by France and the Louis Revival. Few people ever seem to actually sit on a chair before they purchase it. They will always pick it up, look knowingly underneath, walk round it and admire it but rarely sit in it to see if it is comfortable. A chair that is immediately comfortable may look ugly to the admirer but it is worth its weight in gold.

1850s

1360 A rather plain little chair similar to French and English styles of the 1840s. They are seen in this rather watered-down style in most minor European countries and appear in Dutch and German catalogues up until the late 1880s.

Third quarter nineteenth century

1361 (right) A walnut workbox without the useful addition of a chess set inlaid on the top and with no provision for a capacious workbag. The column has a very Italian feel. Note the flat sided tripod legs.

c.1860

1362 (left) A good choice of mahogany veneer has been selected for this little work table that closely reflects popular English examples. The flat sides of the trestle supports and pierced stretcher are a normal indication of a northern European, i.e. north German or Dutch, origin. The embroidery on the workbag is taken directly from patterns exported in vast quantities from Berlin throughout the world.

1850s

HOLLAND — Tables

1363 A well made walnut centre table with a well-figured marquetry top in a fluid mixture of Dutch floral marquetry and French rococo. The shape and form owe much to English early nineteenth century furniture. A highly decorative table that is rarely seen on the market and would be very sought after.

c.1860

1364 On this turned beechwood occasional table the rings have been turned to simulate bamboo and then gilt. Tables of this type were made in large quantities, although few survive. They are to be found mainly in Dutch furniture catalogues although their exact origin is uncertain. The tripod form that, without the top, could be reversible, joined by a central ball, is inspired by the eighteenth century 'cat' or wool holder. The top would have had a material covering with a long fringe.

1860-1900

1365 A fine quality Dutch breakfast table that has developed naturally from the exquisite marquetry made in Holland in the late seventeenth century. The form is based on the English breakfast table but the segmented veneers and delicate baskets of flowers are Dutch in the extreme. The advantage of such a fine inlaid top is that it becomes a highly decorative piece of furniture when not in use and stored in the corner of a room. An English early nineteenth century example would have to rely entirely on the quality of the veneers for decoration.

1860s

1366 The top only is illustrated of this Dutch marquetry breakfast table, again veneered segmentally in walnut. Although there is more contrast in the stained woods the decoration has nothing like the freedom of the previous table and somehow feels more repetitive.

1860s

HOLLAND — Writing Desks

1367 A good honest copy of Dutch mid-eighteenth century furniture that has again survived the ravages of the fiendish marquetry inlayer of the late nineteenth century, indicating that perhaps this bureau was made after the rage had died down. Note the graduated concave and convex drawers that are in a very similar fashion to the chest of drawers no. 1347. In fact the shape is almost identical, with the boldly outset canted corners and flat sides contrasting with the complex front. As is a common feature with Continental furniture, as opposed to English, the pull-out supports for the flap (unfortunately nearly always called lopers) also usefully incorporate a small drawer, traditionally for candles and quill pens. Note the applied moulding on the apron which is repeated in various forms throughout this chapter.

c.1900 ✳

The next three secretaires are obviously influenced by the French secrétaire à abattant. *They appear in Holland and northern Germany and are extremely difficult to differentiate. The French examples are usually much plainer. In example 1370 we once again see the applied 'C' scroll moulding.*

1368 (below) This is very unusual, with the addition of a small display cabinet which makes it very useful indeed. The beautifully figured mahogany veneers are an indication of the return to a plainer style in the late Biedermeier period which tended to use the natural decoration of the wood as the main feature.

Late 1840s

1369 A faded mahogany secretaire. The very thin barley twist columns at the corners are a watered-down Dutch early seventeenth century feature but unfortunately this is no guarantee of the Dutch origins. The writing flap is beginning to crack badly on a horizontal plane which could be very expensive to repair.

c.1850

1370 A very plain example that would never be as popular as the previous two because of the lack of drawers at the base. Drawers are always more sought after than cupboards. The unusual poor quality rosewood veneers are nothing like as exciting as the previous mahogany veneers. Rosewood was in common use during this period but not often on such a large scale.

c.1850

DUTCH MARQUETRY — Bedrooms

The next six pieces of furniture are early nineteenth century examples in an Empire and Biedermeier style. In almost every case it is to be presumed that they were originally made in their figured mahogany or walnut veneers and seized by the inlayer towards the end of the century. It is unlikely that they would have been inlaid during their construction as they were made at a time of almost excessive simplicity where the natural figuring of the wood was ample decoration and there was no craze for marquetry. The Empire styles themselves had become popular by the 1880s and the early nineteenth century revival, alongside others, had started, especially in England, which had a major influence on Dutch furniture by the end of the nineteenth century as it had in the eighteenth.

1371 A toilet mirror or gentleman's shaving stand that has been inlaid at a later date. The shape is a fairly typical Dutch style of the first half of the nineteenth century before the great French influence began and eclecticism held sway.

Second quarter nineteenth century

1372 A similar story. The mirror may have been added at a later date, possibly at the time the marquetry was carried out. It is difficult to imagine quite how severe the table would have been without the marquetry. The chequered inlay on the mirror supports is a late eighteenth century feature and they could have been 'borrowed' from another piece.

Second quarter nineteenth century

1373 A free-standing looking-glass of odd proportions with appalling later inlay. The condition of this piece is very poor.

1840s

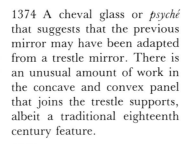

1374 A cheval glass or *psyché* that suggests that the previous mirror may have been adapted from a trestle mirror. There is an unusual amount of work in the concave and convex panel that joins the trestle supports, albeit a traditional eighteenth century feature.

1840s

1375 A traditional Empire style *lit bateau* drawing its form directly from France. Once again the marquetry has probably enhanced the overall effect.

Second quarter of the nineteenth century

1376 The foot, or the headboard, of a *lit bateau*. Both ends are always the same height so it is not possible to differentiate. It is tempting to think that the chequered inlay was original to the bed, being a late eighteenth century hangover, and not added with the bulk of the marquetry at the end of the nineteenth century. Not quite as gutsy as the previous bed with its boldly curved supports.

Second quarter of the nineteenth century

Most of the remaining Dutch marquetry pieces are late nineteenth century copies of earlier forms of Dutch furniture, except where indicated in the text, with the marquetry added when the item was made.

1377 A very anglicised form in the manner of the 1780s through to the 1820s. The fact that it is rosewood suggests that it is most probably a nineteenth century piece. The inlay is of good quality — at least on the drawers. The idea of the contrasting tulipwood veneers for the surrounding strapwork has not been soundly executed. Could it possibly be made up from old pieces when the inlay was carried out? Look at the 'stand like' appearance of the base and the *mid*-eighteenth century style of the overhanging top.

Second quarter of the nineteenth century

1378 A small bedside cupboard that leaves one very much unmoved. The whole appearance and design are dead, leaving very little to inspire one. The legs have been added to enable the floor area to be cleaned underneath. In the second half of the nineteenth century there was a great vogue for cleanliness throughout northern Europe and items of furniture which had for years rested on plinths, an early nineteenth century practice in itself, were raised up. At this time furniture of most countries was designed with a stand of some description to raise it off the floor for the purpose of hygiene.

Second quarter of the nineteenth century

DUTCH MARQUETRY — Cabinets

1379 This fine inlaid small side cabinet combines all the best features of Dutch furniture. The vase, flowers and leaves are exquisitely cut with delicately trailing tendrils in a pure late seventeenth century style. Great attention has been paid to the cresting and apron which are banded in ebony and ivory. An unusually fine quality cabinet.

Mid-nineteenth century

1380 A small *encoignure* in the style of the 1790s. At first glance it looks as though it is a period cupboard with the rococo foliage added a hundred years later. Certainly a late eighteenth century example would have had the familiar satinwood and ebony crossbanding and the chequered and barber's pole stringing and also the inlaid 'fluting' in the legs. In fact, the whole cupboard was made as a copy.

1890s

1382 A very unusual little box suitable for magazines, music or even logs and coal. Even the two flaps are based on Dutch mid-eighteenth century designs and are the shape of the typical chest of drawers.

1880-1900

1381 A rather gangly cabinet on stand in the late seventeenth century style. This clearly shows how the Dutch and Huguenot influence dominated English design in the reign of William and Mary during the 1690s. A poorly made piece — a 'genuine reproduction'.

1900-1920

1384 This is a simple Dutch 'chest of drawers' with a display cabinet added on the top, producing a very effective piece of furniture. In this case the marquetry is overdone and does not look right even to the untrained eye.

c.1880

1383 A rather conveniently sized straight fronted cabinet that originally must have had panelled doors in the lower part. Although in a very classical style from the third quarter of the eighteenth century, the whole piece is a copy. The marquetry around the lower doors is very untypical of Holland.

1880-1900

1385 (left) These small display cabinets above a chest of drawers were made in large numbers especially in this smaller size. Compare it to no. 1353 which, although plainer, is a prettier looking cabinet. However, flower power reigned supreme.

1880-1900

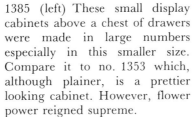

1386 This cabinet was made in the 1970s — yes, it is absolutely modern and made in Italy. The Italians, with all due respect, are the best 'copiers' of furniture and many of these pieces are on the market, probably having been sold quite genuinely 'without a date' and are now considered to be nineteenth century copies. Even the best dealers have been taken in. However, there is still a good market for such useful and decorative pieces.

1970s

DUTCH MARQUETRY — Chairs

Many thousands of these archetypal chairs in Dutch mid-eighteenth century style must have been made in the nineteenth and twentieth centuries, rarely appearing in long sets.

1387 This armchair is a mixture of floral marquetry, mainly on the legs, apron, arms and side supports and an etched decoration on the splat which includes the trumpet-playing *putti* and Prince of Wales feathers. The marquetry is in various woods with an occasional mother-of-pearl and/or ivory small flower head.

1880-1900

1388 A fine chair in a similar style but all the decoration is painted on to a Dutch East Indies satinwood ground. The use of satinwood instead of the more common walnut makes these unusual and very pretty chairs but they do not have the obligatory appeal of the more common chair.

c.1900

1389 A marquetry chair in all its glory. Why the legs have been incised with a rather novel and unpleasant decoration instead of inlaid, we will never know. The marquetry is not really very good quality but this appears to make little difference. Note that where the splat is coming away at the base it is held by two small dowels. An eighteenth century chair would have the splat held by a shoe and it would not be dowelled.

c.1900

1390 A very similar chair, at least with the legs decorated, but the whole effect is rather weedy; the marquetry totally unsympathetic.

1900-1920

DUTCH MARQUETRY — Chairs and Settees

1391 A much nicer quality chair with a lower back and without the rather unnecessary cresting. The chair is also heavier and stronger looking than the previous example. The slightly smaller back will make this much more popular.

1880-1900

1392 A hall seat in walnut that has been completely covered in marquetry but very effectively. As is common with Dutch marquetry panels, the flowers in two similar panels are almost invariably different and individually cut. They are not simply a repeat pattern of the opposing panel as with boulle or more mechanical marquetry. Not a very comfortable seat but unusual and a rare piece for anyone collecting marquetry furniture.

1880s

1393 A well made chair but not as old as it looks. There are no clues as to why this chair is modern that one can successfully glean from the photograph. The surface is very clean and shiny. There is no damage or inlay missing. No wear on the feet or greasy hand marks on the top-rail or seat-rail. The mask on the cresting has the rather benign look that faces cut, or indeed carved, by the modern hand seem to adopt.

1960s

1394 Both England and Holland, as well as the Iberian Peninsula, adopted the chair back settee in the eighteenth century. This fine triple chair back is literally three chair backs joined together. Although very similar in design, the individual panels and marquetry are all slightly different in interpretation. Like the hall seat above, this type of seat has little use today.

c.1900

1395 A useful and good sized bureau but with very heavy legs. The flap hardly seems to fit the serpentine shape of the top and the whole appearance is of a poorly made piece. The interior work of this type of Dutch reproduction furniture is often surprisingly crude, with heavy oak linings and poorly made dovetails or drawer pins.

c.1900

1396 This is the Dutch *bombé* form taken to an extreme. The top is reminiscent of early eighteenth century German cabinets. There is something very ungainly about this type of 'S' scroll leg which, made in square sections, always looks rather heavy. The writing flap supports are of course shaped to the same degree as the flap. The profuse marquetry is far too overdone and the musical trophy on the flap is too big — the spirit was willing but the flesh was weak.

c.1900

1397 Just flatten the top of the bureau and you have a standard chest of drawers. The writing part is simply the top half of any one of the *bureaux de dame* illustrated here. Although a considerable number of these bureaux were made in the eighteenth century and inlaid in the late nineteenth century, this one once again is a modern Italian example. The piece missing from the back left hand corner is simply over enthusiastic 'editing' in the dark room.

1970s

1398 A slightly better proportioned bureau but nevertheless not very well made. The marquetry of these desks is normally, like other Dutch furniture, inlaid on to a walnut ground but in this case very plain and cheap rosewood veneer has been used.

1880s

1399 This is an extension of the traditional Dutch late eighteenth century secretaire often found in satinwood with lacquer panels. Note the alternate light and dark ebony and satinwood banding on the cornice. The corbelled pilasters and the concave frieze drawer are later Empire and Biedermeier forms. This desk was made in the second quarter of the nineteenth century and all the inlay has been added in the late nineteenth century. It is not difficult to imagine it in its plain mahogany form. The veneers on the flap are very well-figured flame mahogany which would not have been chosen if the piece was to be inlaid when it was originally made.

Altered c. 1900   *£2,200 — £2,800*
                    in original form £1,200 — £1,800

1400 A very unusual design based on the principles of the French *bureau plat*. The traditional English style claw and ball foot was a very common Dutch feature in the middle of the eighteenth century. The irregular serpentine top is very similar to the shape of the lids on the little box no. 1382.

1900-1920   *£800 — £1,100*

1401 A small card table, again copying the ever popular mid-eighteenth century style. By now the shape is very familiar and unmistakably Dutch. This is quite a well made piece but the inlay, especially on the sides and legs, is very half hearted.

c. 1900   *£500 — £700*

1402 One of the most amusing inventions of Dutch furniture, the *opflaptafel*. Sometimes they were simply a commode with a lifting top, the top applied with small hinged shelves which fall open when it is lifted for the display of china, etc. The more sophisticated examples contained a cistern or tea urn with a bowl and drainage. The major disadvantage of these today is that one needs a large area in which to put them and if the top is going to be lifted then there must be nothing standing on it.

1880s   *£800 — £1,200*

Marble

(Country of origin in brackets)

Statuary Marble (Carrara, Italy)

Grey veined Carrara (Italy)

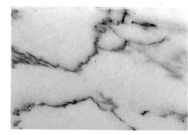

Branco verado (Portugal) (post-war only)

St. Anne (Pyrenees, France)

Bardiglio (Carrara, Italy)

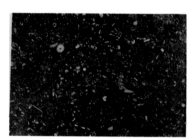

Granit Belge (Belgium). Also called Petit Granit

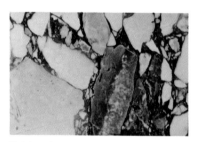

Brêche violette (Italy)

English style inlay of pietre dure

Florentine style inlay of pietre dure

The edge of a Florentine section

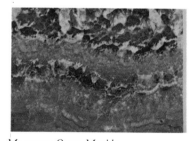

Moroccan Onyx Marble

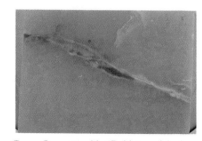

Green Onyx Marble (Pakistan, Mexico, Turkey)

Tinos (Greece)

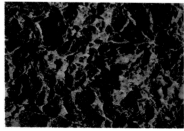

474

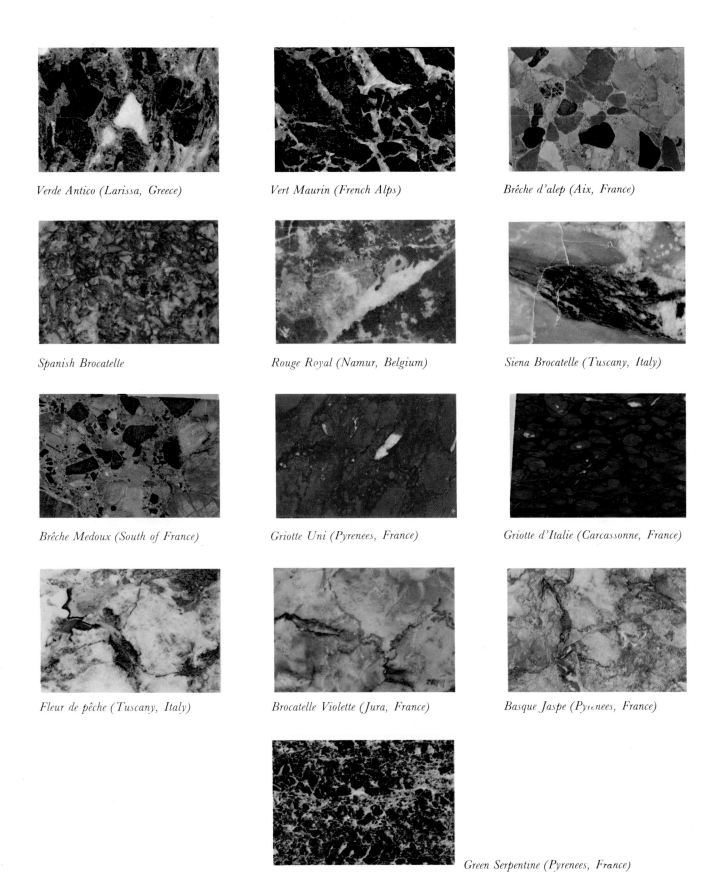

Verde Antico (Larissa, Greece)

Vert Maurin (French Alps)

Brêche d'alep (Aix, France)

Spanish Brocatelle

Rouge Royal (Namur, Belgium)

Siena Brocatelle (Tuscany, Italy)

Brêche Medoux (South of France)

Griotte Uni (Pyrenees, France)

Griotte d'Italie (Carcassonne, France)

Fleur de pêche (Tuscany, Italy)

Brocatelle Violette (Jura, France)

Basque Jaspe (Pyrenees, France)

Green Serpentine (Pyrenees, France)

1403 An unusual extending dining table from the second quarter of the nineteenth century with added marquetry. The semi-circular top sections open to accept extra leaves making, in this instance, a ten seater dining table which is a rare enough find in any style of furniture. The square tapering legs have been added and the top split to accept extra leaves, presumably towards the end of the nineteenth century when the marquetry was added. An ungainly table but useful, unfortunately in poor condition.

Altered c. 1900   *£1,550 — £2,100*

1404 A rather attractive small centre or breakfast table with a tip top. The larger table illustrated previously would originally have been of a similar form but nothing like as elegant. The table originally dated from the 1830s but has fallen into the hands of the *marqueteur*.

Inlaid c. 1900   *£450 — £650*

1405 A spindly card table of the type made in the third quarter of the eighteenth century but reproduced over one hundred years later. They are never very well made and the inlay is derisory.

1880s   *£220 — £320*

1406 This is a popular style of card table with a triangular flap that opens out to form a square playing surface, the gate-legged support can just be seen where it is warping at the left hand foot. These small tables fold completely and can be moved around the room or put away very easily. The fluted gilt legs became a new feature in the late 1770s.

c. 1900
£250 — £350

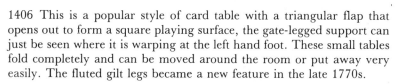

Details — 1760s or 1900s?

These four photographs are all taken of a Dutch drawer that was made in the late nineteenth century. The piece of furniture (a chest of drawers) was made with intent to deceive. The veneer is walnut on an oak ground. Oak has been traditionally used in the Low Countries as a carcass wood — softwoods were rarely, if ever, used. The drawer has lots of convincing wear, the odd ink stain and evidence of replaced hardware. The problem is that, as in most European countries, traditional furniture making techniques were continued alongside the machine made, mass-produced furniture and the old skills were never completely lost. Some pieces may have been quite genuinely made in a traditional, survival style in an old fashioned workshop. An apprentice, learning his skills as a boy of fifteen in 1825, might spend the next fifty years in his trade passing on his skills to the faker of 1885. These skills would have been passed to our apprentice by a craftsman who in turn learnt his trade in the eighteenth century.

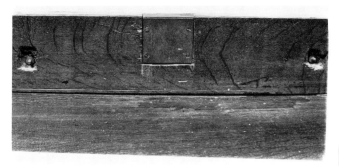

Two photographs showing the inside of the front of the drawer. Both the lock and the handles have been replaced — almost too obviously. The clever faker will not let himself be caught out by incorporating immaculate original ironwork. The medullary rays that are a salient and essential feature of certain cuts of oak can clearly be seen in these photographs. Why does the incised line at the bottom of the photographs stop dead between the lock and the right hand handle? The join between the drawer front in the first photograph and the side is far too clean to have survived like that since the mid-eighteenth century. Why should the top part of the drawer on that side be damaged?

Neither end of the drawer has any dovetailing, which is unusual in the eighteenth century. The front is lightly pinned but the other end has nothing in evidence — it is pinned from the back — not an original feature. The base of the drawer has the grain running from side to side instead of the more normal longitudinal grain. This may be more clearly seen in the first two photographs. Of course such a rule is only a general one, but useful nevertheless. The drawer runners have been replaced, which is an acceptable feature on an 'eighteenth century' drawer.

The conclusion must be that this drawer has been cut down from an eighteenth century piece of furniture to make a smaller and more convenient chest of drawers which will then sell for more. Old wood has been used to make the whole effect more convincing.

The lock tongue is only thrown once in common with all countries except for France. The whole lock has been let into the drawer and is completely encased. Most locks will be attached to the inside of the drawer, regardless of nationality. This has been let in simply because the drawer is bow-fronted and it would be difficult to effectively and neatly attach the lock to the inside of the drawer to a concave surface.

c.1900

OTTOMAN EMPIRE

Damascus to Cairo

1407 A card table of a very common form with a complicated triple top revealing firstly a chessboard and secondly a well inlaid for backgammon. The legs look most uncomfortable and have rather unsure origins.

First quarter twentieth century

This type of intricate and profuse geometric inlay was nearly always employed on the small amount of domestic furniture made on the Mediterranean coast south of Turkey down to Cairo. Occasionally pieces have been found with stamps saying 'Made in Syria'. The quality varies tremendously but the shapes are nearly always well-tried forms and vary little. A myriad of different woods, bone, ivory and mother-of-pearl are used in the marquetry, which is normally on an olivewood ground.

1408 An unusual centre table with fine quality inlay in a similar style. The angular legs and angular platform support are highly individual and a most original feature on what is otherwise a standard European shape. An exception to this is the half formed *merhabs* or prayer niches around the apron which are similar in shape to Turkish prayer rugs.

c.1900

1409 Another well made example of Arabian marquetry, this time in the form of a European style club chair. The apron yet again has a highly stylised *merhab*. The overall effect is very decorative and was greatly prized amongst those who wished to create Arab smoking rooms in the craze for Occidental living at the end of the nineteenth century. The damask cushion is surely a northern European addition!

c.1900

1410 Desks in this profuse marquetry are very rarely seen. The legs of this one are of almost exactly the same form as the legs of the card table except that these are of a diamond rather than a square section. The balustrade is very Italianate but there is no mistaking the seven panels of *mishrabeya* — the highly complex turned beadings that were originally designed to allow air to be passed through screens, thus creating a draught. The top is removable, allowing the table to be used for more than one purpose.

c.1900

1411 The small upper door of this cabinet is inlaid *Syndicat des Tramways du Caire* which gives us the nationality without any confusion. The Moorish influence is total but the form of this writing cabinet is very similar to Italian 'Moorish' furniture. The carcass is of olivewood with ebony, bone and mother-of-pearl geometric inlay. Strict adherence to the Moslem faith of the Ottoman Empire has resulted in a purely geometric inlay with no representations of animal life, human life or plant forms. This is the same on all the Ottoman art forms and is perhaps most noticeable on their prayer rugs.

c.1900

1412 A very Italian influence, in this case inlaid with a profuse decoration of flowers in mother-of-pearl instead of the normal bone or ivory. This chest was probably made in the south and is characteristically poorly made.

c.1880

1413 (left) A fine quality olive-wood writing desk veneered overall with an exotic decoration of mother-of-pearl parquetry, the drawers and cresting pierced with fine mother-of-pearl repeating patterns of heraldic lions and flowers. The general shape, bead and reel moulding at the sides, and stylised vases of flowers flanking the cresting, suggest an Indian influence. The desk could well have had Indian origins yet it is labelled 'Jousseph Sabet of Bethlehem' Was he a retailer or a maker?

1860-1890

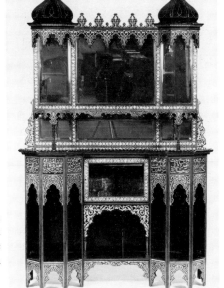

1414 (right) A piece of Moorish furniture inlaid in mother-of-pearl on an olivewood ground. It could have been made anywhere on the north African coast. The overall effect is highly decorative. Note the repeated multiple *merhabs*. The octagonal onion finials have a strong Byzantine influence which must originally come from the Turkish conquerors.

Late nineteenth century

RUSSIA

Russian furniture during the eighteenth century, although inspired by the same sources as much of Europe and supervised under the wide umbrella of Catherine the Great, herself a German princess, was constructed mainly in provincial centres. The great patron would have a team of craftsmen working at his country house and a peculiarly individual style of furniture began to develop, an individuality which extended well into the nineteenth century.

Russia's geographical location unquestionably lent a Scandinavian air to the shapes and styles of furniture which was often overdecorated with exaggerated curves and proportions. This exaggeration appears in furniture in increasing amounts as one leaves Paris, through Germany north east to Poland, Scandinavia and finally Russia. However, Russia especially retains an overdecorated simplicity difficult to compare with other, even north European, styles. Biedermeier, that totally European style of the early nineteenth century, was interpreted accurately from its Central European counterparts. Karelian Birch, a light, slightly oily wood, heavily grained with highly decorative well spaced knotting, was plentiful from the vast natural Karelian forests — an ideal material for the new style.

The ecstasies of the German rococo influence of the eighteenth century were repeated in the interpreted designs of Stakenschneider by Vasily Bosse in the White Palace. Mirrors and door panelling in gold on a white background almost grow into the comfortable Louis XV revival seat furniture.

Ernst and Peter Gambs were exponents of the revival furniture which had become popular by the 1830s. Formal restrained colours using the decorative qualities of mahogany, birch, walnut or poplar were matched to neo-Gothic, rococo and classical styles. Peter Gambs exhibited a fine porcelain and ormolu mounted tulipwood cabinet at the Great Exhibition in 'baroque' style.

Even the provincial atmosphere of Russian furniture was not exempt from mass-production and the subsequently easy interpretation of earlier styles.

Leo von Klenze, formerly Court Architect to King Jerome of Kassel and latterly Ludwig I of Bavaria, designed the New Hermitage c.1850 which was furnished and decorated with a surprising restraint, merging an Empire and classical style which looked back to the Directoire period in Rome rather than forward to the Regency revival styles in England of the 1880s. One room in the Hermitage incorporates the use of the highly decorative features of malachite, found in quantity in parts of Russia, on furniture and *ameublement*. The stone was thinly veneered and glued to furniture, vases and even walls, the effect being a delightful colour contrast to the finely burnished Russian *bronze doré* (see colour illustration no.2 on page 412).

Although the Tula iron works traditionally closed down on the death of Catherine the Great in 1796, a few fine examples of Russian steel furniture still survive dating from the beginning of the nineteenth century. Applied with burnished brass and copper, these rare items of furniture have a sophistication of their own. A good example is the dressing table set at the Pavlovskij Palace Museum in Leningrad.

Eclecticism continued throughout the century until a struggle to revert to traditional methods of arts and crafts was led by Prince Mamontov at Abramtsevo and Princess Tenisheva. A revival of interest in Russian crafts resulted in a purely national style based mainly on seventeenth century church decoration producing light pierced designs of an obviously Russian nature.

Many woods have been available although strangely little furniture appears to have been inlaid, unlike the beautiful geometric parquetry floors which were present in all of the most complete decorative Russian and Baltic floor schemes. This too was a traditional feature but one that had continued on formal seventeenth century lines and not part of a great European trend for revivals of an order which came before the age of machine production.

The workshops of Carl Fabergé produced a limited amount of furniture at the end of the nineteenth century and the very beginning of the twentieth. Very little of this exquisite furniture survives and the few pieces that occasionally come on the market are very sought after. This master designer's pieces are more than just furniture and must be considered as jewels to display jewels, as most of his furniture is purely made for the display of objects.

One of the best known Russian firms is that of Frederich Melzer whose designer Robert designed a Gothic library for the Winter Palace in 1894 and at the same time a heavy Renaissance style desk with a set of chairs reflecting a mixture of Hepplewhite and Morris designs. The private dining room was furnished in Louis XV style with a heavy, almost baroque, dining table. A few years later the firm was producing large numbers of art nouveau chairs of a deceptively simple form in stained birch or poplar. Many designs were of an eclectic style in a Sheraton/Hepplewhite manner almost indistinguishable from English versions. Others with tall backs are often seen in the Polish/Russian borders incorporating country scenes of troikas and snowscapes reflecting Russian everyday life.

The paucity of furniture made in Russia compared with the enormous output from other European countries made it a necessity to import large amounts of furniture, mainly from France and Germany. These imports were very heavily taxed however and few but the very rich could afford to pay the enormous import duties. In the 1880s, for example, the import duty applicable to furniture was the vast sum of eight hundred French francs per one hundred kilos of furniture — approximately forty times that of the import duties of furniture into France.

In Poland a progressive style had emerged known as the Zakopane Movement, with its roots in the Arts and Crafts Movement of England. However, traditional furniture continued to be made from various fruitwoods on large estates, as in Russia, for many years to come.

In 1898 the interest of Russia in the rapidly developing and changing feeling of design that was beginning to take the tired and weary old designs by the throat became channelled through a magazine that followed the lead of the *Studio* in England and various other European periodicals. The magazine was called *Mir Isskustva* and readily illustrated and discussed the progressive painters and designers of the time.

Russia's emergence into the twentieth century was limited by the ravages of the revolution but an establishment of local crafts groups had preserved traditional methods of manufacture.

Russian Designers, Architects and Makers

BAUMANN (fl.c.1810). Supervised workshops producing furniture to the designs of Carlo Rossi (q.v.).

BOBKOV, Vasily (fl.1830-1850). Furniture maker.

BOSSE, Vasily (fl. second quarter of the nineteenth century). Furniture decorator at the Hermitage, re-used the designs of Stackenschneider.

BRIULLOV (fl.c.1840). Built the Malachite Room at the White Palace.

FABERGÉ, Carl. The maker of fine objects who made a few items of miniature furniture in the Directoire style.

GAMBS, Heinrich (1765-1831). Influenced by David Roentgen. Court cabinet maker at St. Petersburg. His designs were widely popular and highly influential in Russia.

GAMBS, Peter (fl.1828-1850s). He took over from his father, Heinrich, c.1828, designing in an architectural Renaissance style. Probably exhibited at the Great Exhibition in 1851. Also worked with his brother Ernst.

KLENZE, Leo von (fl. mid-nineteenth century). A German furniture designer whose work and influence was brought from the German state courts to the Winter Palace in a formal mixture of Empire and Biedermeier styles.

LEBERDEFF (fl. early twentieth century). Exhibited at the 1905 Liège Exhibition. From St. Petersburg.

MELZER, Frederich and Robert (fl. mid-nineteenth century). Produced factory made furniture (also designs?).

MONTFERRAND (fl.c.1840). A designer at the Winter Palace.

MUSEUM OF SMALL INDUSTRIES (fl.c.1900). From Zemstvo. Exhibiting at the 1905 Liège Exhibition.

POLENOV (fl.1880s onwards). Supervised work for the patron of the crafts revival, Prince Sarva Ivanovich Mamontov at Abramtsevo.

ROSSI, Carlo (fl. after 1812). Italian architect brought in to re-design buildings and furniture after the defeat of Napoleon.

SMIRNOFF, Theodor-Michel (fl. early twentieth century). Place Lubianskaya, Moscow. Exhibited at Liège 1905.

STARCHIKOV, Nikolai. Patented a method of imitating mosaics with gesso.

TARASOV (fl.c.1840). Worked as a furniture maker for von Klenze (q.v.).

THOMON, Thomas de (fl. early nineteenth century). A Swiss architect whose influence was felt under the reign of Alexander I.

TIURIN (fl.1820s). A furniture designer at Arkhangelskoe.

TOUR, Andreas (fl.c.1840). Worked as a furniture maker for von Klenze (q.v.).

TULA IRONWORKS. The State Arsenal which produced fine quality steel furniture under Catherine The Great. Production is believed to have ceased at the end of the eighteenth century, at the death of the Empress, although certain pieces of steel furniture dating to the nineteenth century have been recorded, but are not proved to be from Tula.

VASSILIEFF & LUTZEDARSKY (fl. early twentieth century). A St. Petersburg maker exhibiting at the 1905 Liège Exhibition.

VORONIKHIN (fl.1820s). A Russian architect.

ZACHAROV (fl.1820s). A Russian architect.

Russia did not produce the vast quantities of furniture that the leading European manufacturing countries were able to mass-produce. There was no shortage of good workmanship available and the very few pieces of Russian furniture seen on the western market today are invariably well made. This is especially the case for pieces made in the second half of the nineteenth century which were often made for the International Exhibitions, hence their availability today.

1415 A very rare armchair of a highly individual nature in a heavy classical style held together by four entwined serpents, which are surprisingly crudely carved. The woods used are a highly burred and figured burr satin birch with inlaid ebony bandings. The snakes are of a light fruitwood which is easily carved. The slightly jokey appearance of this chair is reduced by the very handsome overall effect.

1860-1880

1416 Another bizarre chair. Russian furniture makers or, more precisely, chair makers seem to have expressed an unusual sense of freedom and individuality in their designs. This design, executed in elm and fruitwood, has its origins firmly embedded in agricultural tradition. The main support is a cart horse's harness or *douga,* the arms two very realistic axes — each with an ebonised axehead and lighter fruitwood shaft for added realism. The seat is 'held' by ropes and the back support is a *balalaika,* representing those rare moments for leisure allowed in harsh rural farming communities. The legend around the 'harness', carved in cyrillic reads approximately 'Go gently and you will go further'.

A similar chair is illustrated on page 190 in a book on Russian Furniture in the Collection of the Hermitage, published in 1973.

c.1900

1417 This type of stained and painted furniture is fairly frequently seen in Europe. Similar pieces, especially tables, are seen throughout the east of Europe, in Russia, Poland and Czechoslovakia. They are never well made and use very poor quality woods and paints.

Second half of the nineteenth century

1418 An elegant centre or tripod table with a malachite veneered top and malachite faceted bosses on the tripod supports. The pierced strapwork base is similar to Spanish ironwork of the seventeenth century and produces a highly decorative effect of the type perfected at the Tula Ironworks in the eighteenth century. A very rare table, although the construction is not quite of the quality that one would expect from a Parisian *fondeur*.

Mid-nineteenth century

Malachite veneered furniture is a speciality of the Russian makers and quite large quantities of this precious material have been exported to Europe. The strong green of the malachite contrasts beautifully with the metalwork of the supports and framework, which can either be of polished steel or good quality gilt bronze. A lot of plain pieces of furniture in the Russian style are now being dressed up with malachite veneers by western workshops and appear on the market as genuine nineteenth century malachite veneered items of furniture. However, the malachite now comes from the Congo and does not have the tight swirling grain of Russian malachite which can be easily identified (see page 412 illustration no.2).

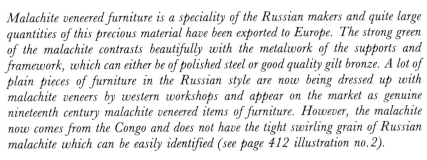

1419 (right) A large cupboard in a watered-down Empire style that closely follows the principles of Biedermeier. The wood is taken from the vast birch forests of Karelia. Almost the entire decoration is the knotting and figuring of the wood veneers producing a very pleasing effect and a light golden colour and the almost tacky feeling of chestnut. How much nicer this piece is without the addition of unnecessary *bronze doré* mounts.

c.1830

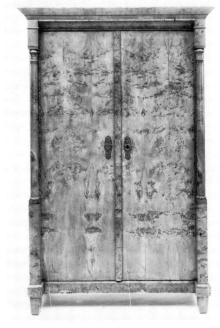

1420 (left) The style is late eighteenth century and the feeling is very Louis XVI. This little mahogany *bonheur-du-jour* is made in almost exactly the same way that it would have been originally c.1800. The white marble top, although itself a very French feature, was used in Russia to contrast against the dark well figured mahogany. Russian furniture often made a feature of contrasting woods and materials. Examples can be found in the Winter Palace and the Palace of Pavlovsk.

Mid-nineteenth century∗

1421 (right) An imposing giltwood and carved fire screen with an acid etched glass panel of Tsar Alexander looking just a little like a cut-out from a surrealist television programme.

Late nineteenth century

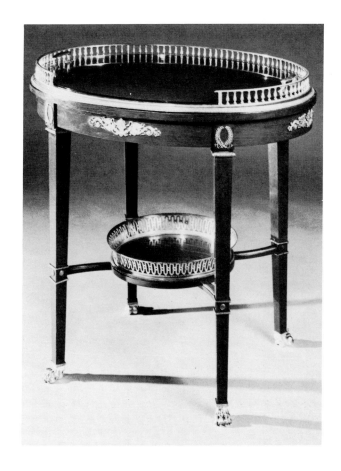

1422 A rare table by the maker of fine jewellery to the Imperial Russian Court, Carl Fabergé. It is in a traditional late Directoire/early Empire style that was popular in France a hundred years before this table was made. The delicate mounts are made of silver and no doubt the table was made to be used as a suitable item for displaying fine Fabergé objects. The workmaster responsible for the supervision and production of this little mahogany table made in Moscow was Julius Rappoport.

c.1900

1423 A macabre piece of furniture of fairly cheap stained woods carved realistically and cleverly into a grotesque memorial. It is dedicated ... 'Ivanovic Cheshcevi to Nickolay Ivanovic Kolemin' and dated 1838 and may well have been specially made by the one friend for the other in that year. It is certainly exceptionally rare, more suitable for a film company to use as a prop than for the average collector.

Second quarter nineteenth century

SCANDINAVIA

The nineteenth century taste in Scandinavia has three simplified phases comparable to, but more easily defined than, the rest of Europe. The light and airy interpretation of the Empire and Biedermeier styles of the early part of the century slowly became influenced by the great baroque revival which was popular from the 1860s, through the 'upholstered period' of the 1870s to the neo-Renaissance which lasted well into the 'nineties. An immediate reaction to these overbearing styles, which in execution and form were almost exactly the same as other Continental countries, is summed up by the painter Carl Larsson in the title of his book *Let Some Light In*. Larsson typified a revival of light airy rooms which, although still cluttered by today's standards, are not dissimilar to room plans of the early twentieth century.

The underlying light, airy feeling was heightened when the Cavaliers' Wing of Gripsholm Castle was opened up revealing remarkably fresh and delicate late eighteenth century rooms.

An eclectic style of furniture had prevailed since the eighteenth century. England had had a great influence as early as the seventeenth century; Dutch craftsmen had been employed by the large courts from the sixteenth century onwards. The carver and gilder, Burchardt Precht, produced numerous pieces in the late seventeenth century in Stockholm in French baroque style with a heavy influence from his native Germany — an influence which remained in evidence throughout the nineteenth century. Strong traces of this attenuated baroque style are found in Swedish furniture throughout the eighteenth and nineteenth centuries, notably in a love of over elaborate and disjointed pierced mirror crestings and drawer aprons which typify Swedish furniture. Influence from France was inspired by Swedish architects, notably Nicodemus Tessin and in Denmark by the French architect Nicholas Jardin.

Georg Haupt, probably the most notable Swedish cabinet maker of the late eighteenth century, brought an almost exact replica of the late Louis XVI neo-classical style to his native land after training in Paris.

Cabinet makers such as Gottlob Iwersson in Stockholm and Harsdorff of Copenhagen (himself a pupil of Jardin) brought the influences to Scandinavia which were to dominate the early years of the nineteenth century. The Napoleonic War had encouraged a need for developing nationalistic

A Scandinavian living room generously filled with cheap export furniture in varying styles. In front of the fireplace there is a Chinese export embroidered screen and numerous small tables with 'bamboo' and aesthetic ring turned legs. The stand in the corner of the room is an obvious export from Florence in the Italian Renaissance style. The two armchairs with their deep tassels would have been popular from the late 1870s onwards. The ebonised cabinet on the right in Louis XVI style is inlaid with brass stringing but very cheaply made, probably in France but not an export the French should be proud of. Note the pierced and carved picture frame above with a view of the Bay of Naples. Hundreds of these Italian carved and gilt-wood frames were made, normally these days called mirror frames. 1880s.

styles. Denmark developed its own Empire style firstly under Lorentz Wilhem Lundelius and in the middle of the century by C.B. Hansen and Professor Gustav Friedrich Hetsch, who was influenced by Percier and Fontaine, was responsible for the Christian VIII style. Artists at the Copenhagen Academy designed their own furniture in an over exaggerated neo-classical style mingled with the Christian VIII style.

The French influence dictated a need for a 'best room'. The ideal of each middle-class family was to have one room, perhaps little used, except on a formal occasion, where all the best furniture would be shown, to entertain only the most important. visitors.

For Denmark the 'best room' also served as a dining room which explains the curious secretaire/ sideboard known as the *chatol*. Until the middle of the century Scandinavian countries used beautifully figured veneers of mahogany, normally plain, but in Denmark and Norway marquetry designs or a simple inlay of exotic woods was employed.

Denmark had always been heavily influenced by the richness of decoration and generosity of form of German cabinet makers. The bold swollen baroque forms of German case work are readily identified in Danish commodes. The Kongelige Meubel Magasin set up in 1777 was a channel and centre for Danish cabinet work and joinery, helping to form a more nationalistic style. The map of Europe on page 8 shows the Schleswig-Holstein area still in Danish rather than German hands. Denmark had tested the might of the emerging German power in 1864 when trying to reassert its authority over Schleswig-Holstein and German and Austrian troops combined to oust Denmark for good. Norway followed the style set in Denmark with an overriding English, rather than German, influence. Both countries had a love for a particular almost 'cock-eyed' asymmetric decoration applied to chairs and other forms without any real feel for the origins of the rococo or auricular style. It is impossible to resist the temptation to think that this borrowed style has simply been 'plonked on'.

Ormolu or *bronze doré* was reserved for only the most expensive furniture. For years the Scandinavian craftsmen had imitated metal mounts, clocks and wall lights in carved and gilt wood, usually beech. The limited use of metal mounts was confined to thin brass *repoussé* handles of a thin and attenuated form similar to Dutch examples. A peculiar feature to Scandinavian furniture, especially in Sweden, is the use of thin brass fillets in the fluting so popular both horizontally and vertically on case furniture. These two points, coupled with the traditional use of a high fleshy knee on the 'cabriole leg' form of the sides of a baroque commode, distinguish Scandinavian furniture from its German and French origins.

Another 'native' feature especially in Sweden, with its origins firmly in the eighteenth century, is a peculiar type of square tapering leg that is slightly too thick at the top giving it a heavier and squatter look than the French or English equivalent.

Rooms were still painted white and the poorer families had painted furniture including chairs and mirrors in a style that had been popular in the late eighteenth century. Details would be picked out in green, blue and especially pink with gold or parcel gilding being used for highlights.

Oak drawer linings were used in the best case furniture and occasionally the whole carcass would be oak boned. However, normally pine would be used for the carcass with a mahogany veneer or occasionally a light indigenous wood would be used for veneers, such as maple or birch. The later neo-baroque love of dull stained oak turnings and veneer gave way to the cheaper use of birch which was readily available from vast local forests for mass-produced pieces. Parcel gilding was a highly favoured form of decoration especially in Denmark. The carved flowers on the apron of a commode, for example, would be gilt, leaving the natural grain of the wood as the main decoration.

The light *bois clairs,* especially polished birch of the Biedermeier style notably used in southern Sweden, gave way to a brief neo-Gothic form during the 1830s. A foretaste of this style can be seen in the elegant Gothic room built in 1828 at the Stockholm Palace. The style was elegant with attenuated forms and lancet arches but slightly heavy in form, incorporating serpentine outlines. Alongside Gothic was a neo-rococo decoration which consisted mainly of over-decorated Biedermeier forms applied with compressed sawdust 'carvings' similar to the manufacture of *bois durci* plaques in France. The exuberant vegetation of the rococo style took over as elsewhere in Europe, and grew into one of the most popular decorative influences. The over-decoration quite independently compares with the style as adapted in Spain. Similarly, painted Scandinavian furniture of this period compares with Spanish furniture white painted in a soft gentle tone and occasionally parcel-gilt with the rococo decoration still common in the 1860s.

Whereas in leading European manufacturing countries any lightness of form in a veneered rococo manner had degenerated into an eclectic form of

A Danish interior photograph with the familiar stove in the right hand corner of the room. On the far right there is a white painted longcase clock that is very much influenced by England and judging by the twist turned columns is no earlier than the 1840s, but with a movement and hood in the mid-eighteenth century English style. The pair of chairs in the foreground are English in George II style and look too heavy to be period examples.

The corner of a small library from a house in Copenhagen. The most interesting feature is the set of five small panels below the Chinese figure in the background which are decorated in a very English pre-Raphaelite style with Burne-Jones figures. The chair with the fox's pelt on the right hand side is very Danish in inspiration, similar to the designs of Herman Freund, and is neo-classical in style bearing a similarity to a Greek Klismos chair. The curtains behind it are in William Morris style. The table to the left of the neo-classical chair can just be made out and is extremely interesting, the tenons sticking right out with heavy graduated pegs holding them firm. The owner of this room obviously had a great feeling for the rustic and looks towards the Skønvirke style.

A wonderful glimpse into the interior of a house in Bergen during the 1880s. The room has already become Edwardian in style, cluttered with potted palms. There is very little room for anything else in the room. The young girl in the centre is employed in the traditional pastime for young ladies in the nineteenth century — embroidering. The bookcase in the far right hand corner is quite likely to be Dutch and is very similar in style to the large bookcase illustrated on page 460. The set of six balloon back chairs are of the type popular throughout Europe but the heavy moulded backs with vase splats in mid-eighteenth century style indicate that they are probably made in the Bergen area. The most fascinating feature is the heavy Gothic door frame with its attenuated spires and outset columns. This is matched by the pier mirror and console table in-between the two windows on the right. Scandinavian Gothic is rare and unusual. It would be interesting if either of these two features survive. The carpet looks like a cheap Indian carpet from Agra.

baroque by the late 1850s, Scandinavia still retained a lightness of furniture decoration and construction. Mahogany rococo forms suggest a comparison to similar pieces in America but otherwise there was a cleanness of line and elegance peculiar to Scandinavian products. A certain similarity to Russian furniture, some examples of which are now in the Hermitage, developed with the use of imported kingwood veneers on chairs and cabinets. These pieces have strange Louis XV proportions, applied with small porcelain plaques in Sèvres style, that look almost apologetic in their small size. The French ideas have been understood, but not imitated in design or execution. Decorative outlines were pretty and pert with a predominance of cane seats. Iron furniture for chairs and beds had been used in the 1840s but basketweave or rattan furniture was popularised from the 1850s onwards — almost anticipating the lightness of the latter part of the century which could have been hardly visible through the morass of baroque and Renaissance forms about to be introduced in the mass of engraved designs and imported furniture from England, France and Germany.

Louis XIV, XV and XVI generously mixed with Renaissance, baroque and Moorish styles, dominated Scandivanian taste from the 1860s to the 1890s. The upper and middle classes developed a preference for these imported styles, mainly as they were the only ones who could initially afford them. Boulle furniture was among the many imported styles but was only briefly popular and, a dangerous statement, apparently never copied by local craftsmen. When Norway became a separate country from Denmark in 1905 ties with England were heightened with the marriage of Princess Maud, daughter of Edward VII to Prince Carl of Denmark.

From the Oscar II *Klassical* style to the Gustavian heavy baroque style there was a native love of indigenous woods. The naturalistic style of cabinet making of the decade of the 1890s is typified in a magnificent buffet in Gothenberg Museum which is veneered in beautifully figured walnut.

Rooms were crammed with furniture; walls were often pine clad with tongued and grooved planks set with numerous hooks for the appendages of modern living. The court furniture makers, C.B. Hansen and J.G. Lund, furnished the Amalienborg Palace in Copenhagen with a mixture of Louis XV and XVI styles.

There was, however, some order to the use of these numerous styles. Rococo, a light and pretty form, for the bedroom and drawing room. The drawing room seat furniture, if gilding proved too costly, was often made of black-stained pear with gilt incising. The baroque and the Renaissance were for the formality of the dining room and men's smoking rooms. The love of simplistic forms made the Scandinavian countries one of the largest importers of Viennese furniture. From the 1880s onwards the Thonet and other bentwood factories exported huge amounts of furniture to Scandinavia which was, in many cases, assembled by the retailer.

By the time the Scandinavian manufacturers had

established a native style to combat total eclecticism a vogue for the Viking or Dragon style had taken hold. It became impossible to resist Russian knots and other Viking motifs akin to early Celtic designs. This *Fornordisk* Movement became mixed with a watered-down art nouveau style of a light and pretty nature without the rigour and strength of the work of leading Belgian and French exponents. Akseli Gallén-Kallela, a Finnish designer and illustrator, designed a weak form of art nouveau chair which, with its soft birchwood veneers, is more akin to the increasing popularity of the Biedermeier revival. The decoration of the upholstery of the chair refers

more to traditional Scandinavian decoration than the work of Paris or Brussels.

Changes at the turn of the century tended to be technical rather than stylistic but the independent spirit that had been retained by Scandinavian designers, mainly due to the comparatively short period of importation of machine made furniture, laid down the foundations of important twentieth century designs which, revived by the crafts movement, owe their beginnings to late eighteenth century and early nineteenth century craftsmanship and understanding of the use of materials.

A Swedish room with wallpaper after designs by Walter Crane. The cushion on the basket weave seat is embroidered in a very free naturalistic style. In front of the large cast-iron stove has been placed an ebonised over-mantel in a mixture of aesthetic and Renaissance revival styles. The writing desk on the left is a very simple late eighteenth century desk in a mixture of French and English styles.

Scandinavian Designers, Architects and Makers

ABILDGARD, N.A. (fl. early nineteenth century). A designer influenced by Biedermeier.

BERG, Johan Peter (fl. early nineteenth century). A Stockholm cabinet maker.

BIELSTEENS, Gustave. Trade label recorded on a commode c.1900.

BORCH, Martin (fl.1880s). An architect and furniture designer favouring the Renaissance revival.

BULL, Henrick (fl.c.1900). An architect and furniture designer in an eclectic but traditional style.

BURGESSEN, John (fl.c.1900). Exhibited at the 1905 Liège Exhibition. A maker from Christiana.

CARLBERG, Johan (fl.1830s). A Stockholm architect.

CHRISTENSEN, Carl Gustave (fl.c.1900). A Norwegian furniture maker and designer highly influenced by traditional runic motifs. A pine armchair, carved and painted, is at the Bethnal Green Museum.

COPENHAGEN ACADEMY (fl. first half of the nineteenth century). Many of the academy's artists designed their own furniture until the middle of the century.

EDEBERG, E.K. (fl.1860s). A Stockholm wood carver and furniture maker. Exhibited an eclectic carved oak cabinet and other furniture at the 1867 Paris Exhibition.

GALLEN-KALLELA, Akseli (1865-1931). A Finnish furniture designer who was primarily an illustrator. Worked in a distinctive style of a mixture of Biedermeier and art nouveau.

GOTEBORG (fl. second quarter nineteenth century). An upholstered 'gondola' chair.

GRONWALL, Johan Petter (fl.1816-1849). A Swedish chairmaker. Stamp IPG.

HANSEN, C.B. (fl.1850-1880). A Copenhagen manufacturer and court chairmaker. Made a splendid Gothic cabinet c.1880.

HOGLANDER, J.E. (fl. early nineteenth century). A chairmaker from Sweden.

JACOBSEN, M.E. (fl.1860s). A Stockholm architect and furniture designer. Worked in an eclectic vein for E.K. Edeberg (q.v.).

LARSSON, Carl (fl. late nineteenth century). An influential Swedish designer who reacted heavily against the cluttered rooms of the 1880s.

LINDEGREN, Axel (fl.c.1900 onwards). An architect designer in art nouveau style.

LUND, J.G. (fl.1850-1880). A cabinet maker to the Danish Court.

LUNDELIUS, Lorentz Wilhem (fl. first half of the nineteenth century). A Stockholm cabinet maker to the Royal Court. Working in an Empire and Biedermeier vein.

MUNTHE, Gerhard (1849-1929). A Norwegian designer working in an advanced art nouveau style from about 1895. Also complete polychrome rooms in Runic style.

PENGEL, J.J. (fl. early nineteenth century). Working in the early nineteenth century, copying from designs in *The Cabinet Maker's London Book of Prices*, 1793.

ROHDE, Johan (fl.c.1900). A painter turned furniture designer producing refined mahogany and satinwood pieces.

ROTHI, O-C. (fl.c.1900). Exhibiting at the 1905 Liège Exhibition.

SEVERIN & JENSEN (fl.1880s). Copenhagen manufacturers working a Renaissance revival theme.

1424 A Danish settee developed from the early nineteenth century. This style of settee always has a lidded well or compartment in the arms at either end and only appears in Denmark and Norway, usually in the second quarter of the nineteenth century. The mahogany veneers are not particularly expensive but the craftsmen have done the best they can with inferior materials. The inlay of the figures reflects the classical era and the work by Haupt and Furlough of the eighteenth century.

c.1840

1425 Another settee, this time without the lidded wells. It converts into a bed but can only be approached from the viewer's side as there is a spar of circular section behind the three bolster cushions. The veneers are in unusually variegated walnut.

c.1850

1426 (left) The theme of the figure on this beautifully figured mahogany door is similar to the settee in the first illustration. The waisted effect of the figuring on the door is most unusual and effective. The inlay is well executed but the design a little too attenuated and thin to be really effective. The architectural outline and the love of an arched door or *lunette* is a typical Danish feature associated with Danish Empire furniture. The marquetry is also typical of Denmark and is not found in quite the same way in Sweden or Norway.

c.1830

1427 This carved oak and walnut sideboard reputedly comes from the Royal Palace at Stockholm but it is uncertain whether it was actually made in Sweden. Certainly there is little evidence to suggest that it was made outside Scandinavia. The influence is obviously French with the well carved large figures in full relief, and hanging game. The vase and garlands of flowers are also French influenced. King Christian IX of Denmark had a love of this type of carved Renaissance and baroque furniture. This piece is illustrated in colour on page 312.

1880-1900

1428 The use of gilding in moderation contrasts with the wood, in this case painted satinwood. This technique was most commonly used in Denmark. In this instance there is a modest carved gilt-wood cresting similar to that of Spanish furniture during the same period. The Danish and Swedish furniture makers often reverted to the use of carved and gilt wood to ornament furniture where the French or German cabinet maker would use more expensive gilt-bronze castings. This is an unusual example of the English influence of Sheraton revival in the latter half of the nineteenth century.

1880-1900

1429 Once again the Danish cabinet maker has resorted to the cheaper use of carved and gilt wood as a decorative form — even the little corner mounts are gilt-wood. This commode follows traditional Danish forms of the second quarter of the eighteenth century with their American style block front and with the drawers supported on a stand in a very old fashioned style that had been dropped elsewhere in Europe some years earlier. The handles are a mixture of the English swan neck form, with French rococo ornament and of pressed brass that so typifies Dutch furniture.

c.1900

1430 This unusual item is in fact a *jardinière* with a zinc-lined container surrounded by a shelf for potted plants or cut flowers. The Greek key decoration is a reminder that neo-classicism had a powerful and early start in Denmark through a pupil of Nicholas Jardin, C.F. Harsdorff. The white painted surface with gilt decoration is a well-tried Scandinavian, especially Danish, form of decoration.

1880s

1431 A just recognisable watered-down French Empire style that had so much influence on the Continent. The plainness is a reflection of the severity of the Biedermeier style. The large bulbous column is an extraordinary size. The underside is stamped 'Kolping'.

c.1830

1432 (left) A very unusual but stylish side table in the Louis XV style painted with strapwork and chequered banding, the remaining surface marbled. The form is very French but the decoration is not typical of France but more reminiscent of Scandinavia. However, an interesting point is that the legs, if one looks closely on the inside of the back legs, are veneered kingwood. Perhaps this piece was painted some time after its original manufacture. The strongest argument against its being French is the unusual flat domed top.

Second half nineteenth century
£450 — £550

1433 (right) A Norwegian stove that has become, of necessity, a decorative piece of furniture. They were made in quantity in Norway, Sweden, Belgium and Germany. Cast in iron, they are brittle but most effective for their purpose. The decoration on these attenuated stoves became more and more elaborate as the century progressed and casting techniques improved. Sometimes the stoves, which were frequently tiled, reached right up to the ceiling.

c.1880   *£1,400 — £1,800*

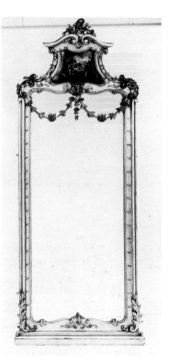

1435 A gilt and white painted mirror with a small *jardinière* below incorporating the unusual feature of *Vernis Martin* panels. The rococo motifs are quite strong and could possibly be a Dutch interpretation of the French eighteenth century style rather than Danish.

c.1900   £550 — £800

1434 A heavy but highly articulated rococo side table in carved pine, which has a very strong French influence. The top has the irregular knobbly shape of Holland and northern Europe. This French rococo style became very popular in Sweden in the late 1740s. Although an amusing piece of furniture, the finish is rather rough and ready. Similar furniture was made in Canada in the mid-eighteenth century.

1850s   *£250 — £400*

Woods

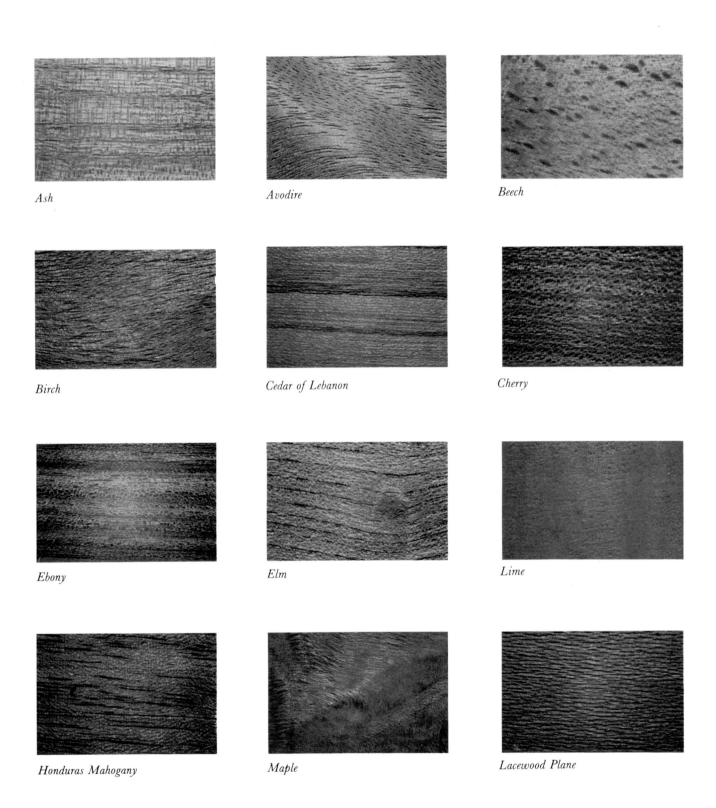

Ash

Avodire

Beech

Birch

Cedar of Lebanon

Cherry

Ebony

Elm

Lime

Honduras Mahogany

Maple

Lacewood Plane

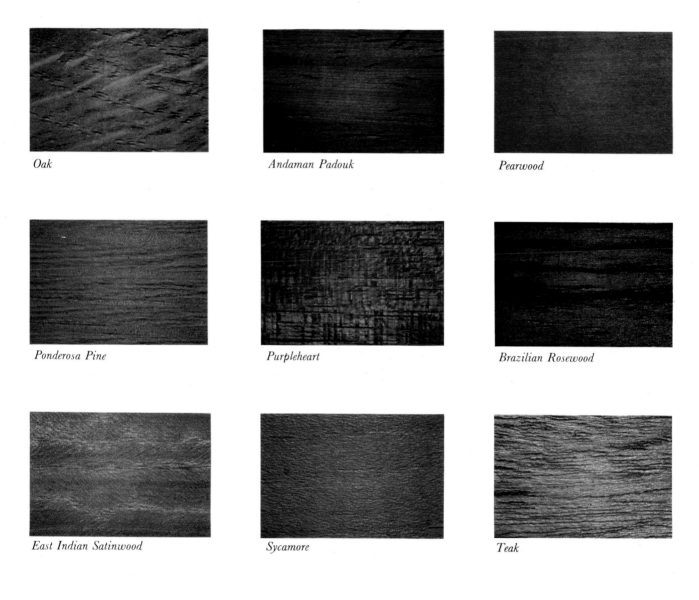

Oak

Andaman Padouk

Pearwood

Ponderosa Pine

Purpleheart

Brazilian Rosewood

East Indian Satinwood

Sycamore

Teak

Circassian Walnut

Zebrawood

1436 The high knees of this rather chunky small commode differentiate this style from the French rococo of the 1730s. This style with high *bombé* features became popular in Sweden from the 1760s. The parquetry decoration and weak handles are another well tried Swedish guideline. Another very Swedish feature is the three drawers.

Third quarter nineteenth century £550 — £750

1437 This is a copy of a commode made in 1771 by Gustaf Foltiern from Stockholm. Again the familiar Swedish parquetry and weak handles and the high chested form typify the Swedish commode. There is an additional feature of the serpentine thumb mouldings with brass fillets which is included on most pieces of mid-eighteenth century Swedish furniture that followed rococo outlines.

1900-1920 £350 — £500

1438 A Swedish fruitwood dining chair with ebonised mouldings. At first glance the chair looks French or English but closer inspection of the heavy apron and baroque style carving of the splat reveals the Scandinavian origins.

1860s £600 — £900 *for a set of six*

1439 A not very inspiring small commode painted white with gilt decoration and fluting, all in carved wood. The painted panels closely follow mid-nineteenth century porcelain panels from the Paris factories but the maker, or his patron, has not been able to afford the real thing. Probably Danish.

1870s £350 — £500

1440 A mystery painted cast-iron and wrought-iron garden chair. The 'C' scroll finials have a charming air. The whole design is highly individual. The cipher pierced into the splat has a distinctly Danish or Swedish feel about it. There was an ironworks at Malmö during the late nineteenth century and this could possibly be from that factory.

Late nineteenth century

1441 A Norwegian dining chair in mahogany. The style closely follows that of English and French examples popular in the middle of the nineteenth century. The Norwegian chairmaker has never been able to resist carved improvements to a plain and simple design. The result is much heavier than its contemporary counterparts.

1850-1880

1442 North German, Danish or even Dutch rococo revival of the 1850s and 1860s. The black, ebonised wood is rather foreboding on this type of Louis XV style parlour furniture, highly formal, even for the formal, stuffy third quarter of the nineteenth century. The three inset panels are porcelain painted with flowers — on a black ground.

1860s

1443 A light and attractive side chair with the familiar white painted and gilt decoration of Denmark. The rococo decoration is very weak, especially the flowers on the top-rail. The overall form is very suggestive and gutsy but a little out of control.

1860s

Marble

Marble has been used to decorate furniture mainly since the seventeenth century. The uses are either as small veneers applied to the carcass of furniture, especially in the Renaissance, to give an exotic jewelled effect or the more familiar inlaid table tops from Italy. The most common use is as the top of a commode, a pier or console table. The last practice was an everyday occurrence and was applied to furniture in France, Germany, Spain, England, Italy and Holland. Almost invariably French furniture from the eighteenth and nineteenth centuries will be topped by a marble slab of varying quality. This is often a useful differentiation between English and French furniture, where the differences become less obvious in the third quarter of the nineteenth century. The French will always use a marble top where the English prefer veneering.

True marble is formed by the movement of the earth in its mountain-building stage. The process is a combination of violent movement combined with intense heat.

True marble is metamorphic rock i.e., limestone formed in limey mud under water which has been recrystallised by heat and pressure during 'mountain building'. New minerals are formed and all previous fossil remains are destroyed, the new minerals form the decorative features that cause man to make such good use of this slowly evolved natural art form. Limestones in common use include Petit Granit, St. Anne, Rouge Royal, and Spanish Brocatelle.

White or statuary marble from Carrara is formed from pure limestone without fracturing. These marbles are almost exclusively from Italy, although similar types are found in the United States of America. However, American marble is not likely to be found on nineteenth century European furniture. White marbles from Carrara range in colour from pure white through to grey with a complete range of grey and white markings in between. Although the pure whites are used for indoor sculpture, grey veined Carrara is used for furniture slab tops as well as for outside sculpture, as the grey veined variety is far more weather resistant. Sometimes the Greek white marble is used as a cheap substitute for the pure white Carrara marble but it soon develops a yellowish hue.

The *breccia* marbles are marble that has been shattered by a natural process and then re-cemented. They can be identified by angular fragments on a dull ground.

Another type known as the conglomerates are not true marble but are fairly smooth, rounded marble fragments set in a later formed natural cement. They are re-cemented pebble beds with no heat or pressure being used as for the true marbles.

Scagliola is a plaster made of ground plaster of Paris or selenite which is coloured to give the effect of colourful marble or *pietre dure*. It can easily be identified as it is softer than nature's materials and far less durable. On older *scagliola* slabs the coloured decoration often wears through over a period of time showing the greyish cement-like qualities of the powder.

Pietre dure was made in numerous Italian towns in the seventeenth century including Florence, Rome and Venice. The technique was taken to Paris by the late seventeenth century and was practised in England in the eighteenth and nineteenth centuries. On the face of it Florentine and Derbyshire *pietre dure* look identical. The techniques are in fact fundamentally different. In Florence a thin veneer of black marble is taken and the shapes of the inlay are cut out, piercing the thin marble completely. The veneer is stuck on to a thicker, often white Carrara, marble slab and the marquetry of flowers or whatever decoration is inserted. Therefore, if it is possible to look at a section of *pietre dure* from the side, it will be seen as a veneer. Derbyshire marbleworkers chose the far more laborious process of taking a thick marble slab and cutting out the shapes of the flowers from the solid. Thus when it is inspected from the side it appears as a solid slab. Unfortunately it is rarely possible or practical to inspect *pietre dure* panels in this way as they are normally inset into a piece of furniture.

A widely used green 'marble' is serpentine, i.e. rocks made up of the mineral serpentine such as Tinos or *verde antico*. Another commonly used exception is the onyx marbles which are a specific limestone deposit formed by hot springs.

The furniture trade gives various names to different marbles that are not always the same names that the quarrymen use. This of course can, and does, give cause for confusion.

The term marble is widely used in the art and building trades for all stone that can be cut and polished for decorative purposes, regardless of their being true marbles, limestones, onyx or serpentines.

The colour guide on pages 474 and 475 gives a general indication as to the range of exotic colours and veining encompassing most of the stones used on furniture throughout the nineteenth century.

Bronze Doré (Ormolu)

A popular misconception is that anything eighteenth century is always better quality than anything nineteenth century. This ill-informed comment is very often applied to gilt metalwork and if it is will often land the person who uses this as a guideline in trouble. Nineteenth century gilt-bronze can be every bit as good in quality as eighteenth century work — as techniques developed the later work often surpassed the eighteenth century. It is true however that more eighteenth century *bronze doré* is seen finished to a better standard, the nineteenth century makers did not always keep to the consistent standards of their forebears.

The term ormolu is taken from the French *or molu* meaning ground or powdered gold. It is constantly used in England but is not a term that a Frenchman would understand today. The equivalent in France is *bronze doré* or gilt-bronze. Another French term for ormolu is *chrysocale* or Pinchbeck, an alloy of copper and zinc with a gold-like appearance that was in common usage in the nineteenth century, having been widely used in England by Christopher Pinchbeck in the early eighteenth century. In Paris a merchant named Leblanc made a similar type of metal alloy with a deceptive gold appearance, sometimes coated with a very thin water gilt gold wash to give the gold a more realistic appearance.

The true term for ormolu — a term inadvertently termed by Josiah Wedgwood in the 1770s — is *dorure d'or molu, i.e.* gilding with powdered gold. In England an alloy was developed that was very similar to French mercurial gilt-bronze, this metal was essentially very similar to brass, itself an alloy of copper and zinc. The advantage of the English process was that the alloy itself did not need further gilding as it did in France. So the world ormolu should be used only when referring to English metalwork and not to French mercury gilding. As the English had their own high quality alloy, fire-gilding with mercury was not often used. Matthew Boulton's firm of Boulton and Fothergill used the English alloys consistently, to the very highest standards — considered to be at least as good as the French fire-gilding.

The paste of mercury and powdered gold was applied as an amalgam, sometimes with enough liquid mercury to enable it to be applied with a brush for ease of use and application. The heating of the metal with its applied paste vaporises the mercury leaving the gold fused to the metalwork. Since the second half of the nineteenth century fire-gilding has not been used very much but in controlled conditions it can be used for restoring or matching up. Modern methods of electro-deposits are much safer and far less toxic but none can equal the lovely dusty colour of fire-gilding.

Colour detail photographs showing various qualities of metalwork are illustrated on pages 413 and 432.

Woods

A short list of woods most commonly found in the manufacture or decoration of furniture in Europe in the nineteenth century. Turn to pages 494 and 495 for colour details of various woods.

ALDER — *alnus glutinosa*. Northern Europe. Normally fairly plain but found with burrs similar to burr maple. Used for marquetry and veneers, especially in Sweden.

ALMOND — *prunus arnygdalus*. Used for marquetry in France. Similar to plum. French: *bois d'amandier*.

AMARANTH — *peltogyre paniculata*. Purple colouration or hue. Used for veneers and marquetry in France. French: *bois d'amaranth*.

AMARILLO. Many varied species. Found in Brazil. A yellow red colour in an unpolished state. Other names include kingwood, raspberry jam wood, *amarillo vinhatico*. French: *bois de jaune*.

AMBOYNA — *pterocarpus indicus*. East Indies. The only common usage in Europe for this popular wood is when the veneers are highly burred. The colour when polished varies from a reddish brown to a golden hue. Usually lighter in tone with closer excrescences than thuya. Used consistently on French and English furniture in the third quarter of the nineteenth century, especially on Louis XVI style furniture instead of thuya (q.v.).

AMYRIS — *amyris balsamifera*. Tropical America. Used as small sections of veneer and is very similar to sandalwood (q.v.). French: *bois de Rhodes*.

APPLE — *malus genus*. Europe. Used for treen and in the solid in provincial furniture. Also used as a veneer in the mid-nineteenth century. A light pinky/tan colour. Often confused with cherry. French: *bois de pommier*.

ASH — *fraxinus excelsior*. Europe. Good for steam bending although not commonly used in the later mass-production of bentwood furniture by Thonet or J. & J. Kohn. Often found with burrs exploited on veneer for a decorative effect. Hungarian ash was very popular in the second quarter of the nineteenth century, especially in Austria. (Also used a great deal by the English firm of Holland & Son.) The effect of a water mark on the grain gives Hungarian ash a distinctive difference from its less heavily marked western European variety. French: *loupe de frêne*.

AUSTRIAN PINE — *pinus negra*. Often termed black pine.

AVODIRE — *turraenthus africana*. West Africa. Known as West African satinwood. Became used more widely at the end of the nineteenth and beginning of the twentieth centuries. Similar to sycamore. Little or no growth ring evident. Often used as a veneer on a diagonal plane to heighten the decorative effect. (Used considerably in England.)

BAMBOO — *genus Bambusa*. Not commonly used. The genus consists of a wide variety. Became more popular as the love of the Orient became stronger in the middle of the nineteenth century. Mostly bamboo was imitated with turned pine or beech, as bamboo is difficult to work and join.

BEECH — *fagus sylvatica*. Europe. Medullary rays appear as dark flecks. Liable to worm. A widespread use especially for chair frames. Often used as a base for simulating more expensive imported woods. Used for bentwood furniture. French: *bois de hêtre*.

BIRCH — *betula alba*. Europe. An even fine grain. Used for turning and cabinet work, as well as plywood in Northern Europe. French: *bois bouleau*.

BITTER ORANGE — *citrus aürsantium*. Used in small amounts in France for marquetry. Larger veneers seen on German and Scandinavian furniture. French: *bois d'oranger*.

BITTERWOOD — *simarbuba amara*. A wide genus, little used. French: *bois blanc*.

BOXWOOD — *buxus sempervirens*. Europe. A very hard grain used for tools and instruments. Commonly seen as stringing and sometimes for marquetry. French: *bois de buis*.

BRAZILIAN MAHOGANY — *swietenia macrophylla*. A commonly used mahogany, imported into Europe in the latter part of the nineteenth century.

BRAZILIAN ROSEWOOD — *dalbergia nigra*. Widely used. Very strong markings. Often called Palisander (q.v.).

BRAZILWOOD — *caesalpinia*. Tropical Americas. A hardwood that looks rather like walnut (q.v.). Difficult to work, sometimes used for treen. Found in Portugal and Spain. French: *bois de brésil*.

BROOM — *cystisus scoparius*. A sparse wood found in Europe. Very occasionally used for small sections of contrasting veneers.

BROWN EBONY — *brya ebenus*. Partridgewood (q.v.).

BURR. An abnormal growth found on trees that reproduce by stooling. The veneers are not very strong but are highly prized and very decorative and taken from a wide variety of trees.

CALAMANDER — *diospyros quaesita*. East Indies. Also known as Coramandel (q.v.). From the ebony family. A heavily striped variegated brown/yellow.

CAMPHORWOOD — *cinnamomum camphora*. India. Fragrant, olive coloured wood with black striations. Used for carcass work. Not common in Europe, mainly Britain.

CEDAR — *thuja plicata* (Western Red Cedar). A wide genus. Used for drawer linings on the best furniture. Fragrant. Most commonly used in England. Occasionally seen in France.

CHERRY — *prunus avium*. Used for decorative work. A fine oily grain. Often has an elegant but sparse dark knotting. Used widely on the Continent and Scandinavia, especially for large areas of veneers. Austrian Cherry: *prunus mahaleb*. A genus found in Austria and southern Germany. A lighter more marked veneer popular on Biedermeier furniture. Known as Perfumed Cherry. French: *cerisier*.

CHESTNUT — *castanea vulgaris*. Europe. Similar to oak without medullary rays. Known as Spanish Chestnut. Mainly used for large veneers in Southern Europe but popular in France. French: *le châtaignier*.

CITRON — *citrus medica*. Mediterranean. A soft yellow grain. Popular for small areas of softly coloured veneer especially in France. French: *citronnier*.

COCONUT — *cocus nucifera*. From the Indian palm called Porcupine Wood. A highly distinctive close grained wood that is very durable. Used rarely. Occasionally seen in France between the 1920 to 1940 period.

CORAMANDEL. Indian ebony. India and the East Indies. Also Calamander (q.v.). Also spelt Coromandel.

CYPRESS — *cupressus sempervirens*. Southern Europe. Sometimes used for furniture especially in rustic Mediterranean furniture in Italy. Has a red/tan colour. Also used sparingly in Austria, France and Southern Germany.

DAMSON — *prunus institia*. Compares to plum (q.v.). In rare occasions used as a substitute for tulipwood (q.v.). French: *le prune* or *le prune de damas*.

EBONY — genus of *diospyros*. A highly varied hardwood. Used sparingly for veneers. Other types in common use are Calamander (q.v.), Coramandel (q.v.), Marblewood, Macassar Ebony, Partridgewood (q.v.). French: *ébène* or, with green hues, *ébène verte*.

ELDER — *sambucus nigra*. Occasionally used for inlay, especially in France. French: *bois de sureau*.

ELM — *ulmus procera*. Europe. A strong workable wood with distinctive grain markings and well marked growth rings. Used in the solid or occasionally as a carcass wood. Burr elm common. French: *bois d'orme*.

GRANADILLO. A name given to Partridgewood (q.v.).

HAREWOOD. 1. A well figured sycamore or maple dyed to a green hue with ferrous sulphate. 2. A name given to satinwood which seasons to a silvery green.

HAZEL — *corylus arvellana*. Used for country furniture or veneers in Austria and Germany. Straight grain with a pink hue unpolished. French: *bois de coudrier* or *bois de noisetier*.

HOLLY — *ilex aquifolium*. Europe. Used extensively for marquetry and stringing. A white colour. French: *bois de houx*.

HORNBEAM — *carpinus betulus*. Europe. Used for carcass work, especially in France when the carcass is to be ebonised (*bois noirci*). Used for inlay in Northern and Central Europe.

JACARANDA. Brazil. Similar to rosewood (q.v.).

JUNIPER — *juniperus communis*. High areas of Northern Europe. Used for veneers and turnings, especially in Sweden.

KARELIAN BIRCH — A well-figured wood. Vast quantities of this tree were found in the Finnish forests of Karelia. Popular for Russian furniture in the second quarter of the nineteenth century. Called Mesur Birch — markings attributed to insect damage.

KINGWOOD — *dalbergia spp*. Tropical Americas. A genus of the rosewood family (q.v.). Also called violet wood because of hues. Variegated colours from brown to black. Used for veneers in a huge amount of Paris furniture, the veneers made up of small sections, usually diagonally. The term Kingwood was introduced into England in the nineteenth century — previously, in the seventeenth century, it was known as Princes' Wood. A substitute is sometimes made from Spanish Elm. French: *bois violette*.

LABURNUM — *laburnum vulgare*. Europe. Straight grained but highly decorative. Compares to the grain on pearwood (q.v.). Used as oyster veneer but not common in the nineteenth century. French: *bois d'aubour* and *faux-ébénier*.

LACQUER TREE — *rhus vernicifera*. Japan. The sap is used for lacquer in decorative panels.

LARCH — *larix decidua*. European variety. Used for rustic furniture. A knot-free oak-like grain. Used in Hungary and Siberia. French: *bois de mélèze*.

LAUREL — *laurus nobilis*. Mediterranean regions. Used for inlay. French: *bois de laurier*.

LIGNUM VITAE — *guaiacum officinale*. Central Americas. Very hard and heavy. Not common. Sometimes found in Paris marquetry work. French: *bois de gaiac*.

LIME — *tilia europaea*. Austria, France, Germany, Holland and Russia. A light wood with little grain. Used for carving (and some drawer linings?). French: *tilleul*.

MAHOGANY — *swietenia mairophylla*. Many different types. Originally from Cuba, which is the hardest and easiest to carve. Honduras was less expensive and used at the beginning of the nineteenth century. At the beginning of the twentieth century substitutes were imported from Africa, although some African mahogany began to appear on the market in the second quarter of the nineteenth century. Used extensively for veneers with a wide variation of grain and colouring. French: *acajou*. Also Plum Pudding Mahogany (*acajou moucheté*). A common light and dark straight grained variety is often seen and is more likely to be African mahogany (*acajou satiné*).

MAPLE — *acer saccharum*. Northern Europe. Used for veneers. Has a straight fine grain. Often used to veneer the inside of better pieces. Bird's Eye Maple from Germany, Poland and Russia, sometimes called Peacock's Tail. French: *bois d'érable*. Burr Maple: *broussin d'érable*. Bird's Eye Maple: *érable moucheté* or *érable oeil d'oiseau*.

MEDULLARY RAYS. A tissue formed against the growth rings in a tree, especially in oak and beech. Useful signs for identifying woods.

MULBERRY — *morus nigra*. Europe. Highly distinctive growth rings with soft silky burrs. Used in small amounts for veneers.

OAK — *quercus pendunculata; q. robur; q. sessiliflora; q. petraea*. Europe. A highly durable wood that is easy to work and carve in comparison to its strength. Identified by the highly marked Medullary rays (q.v.) that resist deep staining and are often seen as a light, very hard fleck on the wood surface, depending upon the angle of the cut of the plank. Corrodes iron, hence the practice of using dowells (Fr: *Goujon*). Used on a wide scale for carcass work, drawer linings and in the solid. Most common in France (apart from Britain). FUMED OAK — oak darkened by ammonia fuming. LIMED OAK — oak applied with a paste of lime chloride. POLLARD OAK — a cultivated 'burr' from the poll or top of a trunk. French: *bois de chêne*. Pollard oak: *bois de chêne étêté*.

OLIVE — *olea europa*. Southern Europe. Used for turning and sometimes veneers, especially in Italy. A hard wood of a yellow/brown hue with dark streaks. Oily touch. French: *bois d'olivier*.

PADOUK — *pterocarpus dalbergiodes*. Burma and Africa. Often used in the solid. A very hard and heavy wood with a deep red colour, often mistaken for mahogany. Not common in the nineteenth century. Sometimes spelt 'Padauk'.

PALISANDER. Brazilian Rosewood or Jacaranda (q.v.). Used for veneers, usually fairly small sections. French: *bois de palissandre*.

PARTRIDGEWOOD — *caesalpina granadillo*. Central Americas. A heavy hardwood with dark flecks alternating with light markings on a chocolate brown base. Looks like partridge feathers. Also called Pheasant wood or Cabbage wood. Used in small sections for decorative veneers. French: *épi de blé*.

PEAR — *pyrus communis*. Europe. Similar to lime (q.v.) with a fine even texture. Used for carving and for some carcass work. A favourite wood for carving by Fourdinois (q.v.). Principally found in the Tyrol, Switzerland and adjoining areas.

PERSIMMON — *diospyros virginiana*. Central Americas. Used for golf clubs in the nineteenth century.

PINE — *pinus spp*. A wide group of softwoods found extensively in Europe, especially in hilly or mountainous regions. In the nineteenth century a huge amount was imported into Europe from Canada. Used mainly as cheap carcass furniture. Some harder varieties from Canada used for exterior cabinet work to benefit from the hard reddish streaky grain. Used in France for simulated bamboo furniture. French: *pitch-pin*.

PLUM — *prunus domestica*. Italy, Southern France and Spain, also Sweden. A highly decorative wood used for wide crossbandings or veneers to make use of the even light and dark wide bands of striped colouration. French: *bois de prunier*.

PLYWOOD. Layers of veneer glued together. Used by English cabinet makers in the mid-eighteenth century. The use of three or more thin sections of wood glued together with the grain of each section running in a different way makes the wood incredibly strong. In common use in the early twentieth century. In the nineteenth century mainly used by the better makers for strengthening galleries on furniture and fretwork. A laminated form of plywoods was used by Michael Thonet in Vienna in his early bentwood forms, often incorporating iron for extra strength.

POLLARDING. A method of producing highly decorative veneers similar to birds by the constant cutting off of young growth from the poll of a tree.

POPLAR — *populus canescens*. Europe. Compared to willow with a white and grey lustre. An Italian variety is known as black poplar. Used in solid in Europe and in Biedermeier furniture. Burr poplar looks like a softer form of amboyna (q.v.).

PORCUPINE WOOD — *cocus nucifera*. From the coconut palm tree. A very hard and decorative wood that looks like a cross section of porcupine quills. Occasionally seen for small tables in the 1920-1940 period.

PURPLE HEART — *peltogyne porphyrocardia*. Tropical America. A close grained wood used for inlay and veneers. Also called Amaranth Palisander or Violet Wood. French: *bois d'amarante*.

ROSEWOOD — *dalbergia spp*. Central Americas. The most commonly seen of the *dalbergia* genus. A hard, dense wood used considerably for veneers especially in the second quarter of the nineteenth century.

SABICU — *lysiloma sabicu*. West Indies. Often called horseflesh. Looks very like mahogany with pronounced, even growth rings. Not common. Not to be confused with Fiddle Wood or Savana Wood known as *bois côtelet* in France.

SANDALWOOD — *santalum album*. India. A light, oily, aromatic wood of a yellow-brown hue that is easy to work. Also called Amyris Wood. French: *bois de santal*.

SATINWOOD (i) *Fagara flava*. The West Indian variety with a straight or irregular grain, slightly aromatic, used in the middle of the nineteenth century. (ii) *Chloroxylon swietenia*. The East Indies variety, most commonly seen in the latter part of the nineteenth century and early twentieth century. Has a very straight grain giving a striped effect of light and dark hues. Imported by Dutch ships and used considerably in Northern Europe and Scandinavia. See Avodire (q.v.).

SERVICE TREE — *pyrus torminalis. p. sorbus*. Found in Europe and North America and called the Wild or True Service Tree. Used for inlay and occasionally in the solid. French: *bois de sorbier* or *bois de cormier*. Sometimes confused or substituted with the Rowan Tree, *sorbus acuparia*, which compares to Mountain Ash. French: *bois des oiseleurs*.

SILVER BIRCH. European birch (q.v.).

SNAKEWOOD — *brosium aubletti* or *piratinera guianensis*. West Indies. Rarely used as a decorative part of marquetry or sometimes for wider veneers. Identified by black spots and maroon colouring until polished. Many other names including Tortoiseshell Wood, Leopard Wood, Letter Wood. French: *bois de lettres; de lettres de Chine; lézard; d'amourette moucheté*.

SPINDLE TREE — *euonymus europeae*. Europe. Fine white grain similar to Boxwood (q.v.). Used in marquetry and for stringing. French: *bois de fusain*.

SPRUCE — *picea spp*. Europe and North America. Used as a substitute for pine in carcass work.

STRAWBERRY TREE — *arbutus unedo*. Southern Europe. Occasionally used for treen.

SWEETWOOD — *pradosia lactescens.* Tropical Americas. Very streaked. Used occasionally for bentwood furniture.

SYCAMORE — *acer pseudoplatanus.* European variety. A lustrous yellow coloured wood with a fiddle-back grain pattern. Used as veneers especially in France and also Germany. Also used in marquetry. See Harewood (q.v.). French: *bois de sycomore.*

TEAK — *tectona grandis.* India and Burma. A very hard and heavy wood seen in the solid in colonial furniture. Burma teak used a great deal in recent years for veneers. Not common in European furniture.

THUYA — *tetraclinis articulata, callitris quadrivalis.* North Africa. Found in the Atlas Mountains. A brittle wood cut for its highly burred decorative veneers. The eyes of the veneers are very dark with an overall silky finish in a light chestnut brown colour. Used a great deal in France in the second half of the nineteenth century. Often mistaken for Amboyna (q.v.) and vice versa. An expensive wood formed by cultivation and repeated cropping. The gum is fragrant and used for making varnish, called sandarac.

TULIPWOOD — *harpullia pendula.* From Australia, not used until the twentieth century.

TULIP WOOD — genus of *dalbergia.* Brazil. See Rosewood (q.v.). Scented, fleshy pink to mid-tan hue. Highly striped and variegated and fades to a soft patination. Widely used in Paris as a decorative veneer of banding, especially as a contrast to Kingwood (q.v.). French: *bois de rose.*

VIOLET WOOD. Known in England as Kingwood (q.v.). Light and dark elliptical striations. French: *bois violette* or *bois de violet.*

WALNUT — *juglans regia.* Indigenous to Southern Europe. Now found in a wider area of Europe. A very wide variation of brown tones with black markings along the growth rings common. Can vary from a pale golden colour with little grain to contrasting gold/black with marked grain. Italian Walnut usually has a black pigment. Easy to work, used on a large scale for carving and veneers. Highly decorative burrs are sought after. In Italian Renaissance revival furniture of the third quarter of the nineteenth century often used in the solid. French: *noyer.*

WILLOW — *salix alba.* Europe. A wide species. Whitish colour often used for wickerwork.

YEW — *taxus baccata.* Europe. A rich orange colour with a good waved well marked grain. Often burred and used for decorative veneers. Very occasionally used in the solid. In rare occasions yew is stained black and called German Ebony.

ZEBRA WOOD — *astronium fraxissiofolium.* South America. Only found in small sizes and used for contrasting veneers. Very hard and durable with a straight but light and dark grain in bands. Also called Kingwood (q.v.), Locustwood, Tigerwood and *goncala alves.* French: *bois serpent.*

Major Nineteenth Century Exhibitions

The industrial power enjoyed by the major manufacturing countries of the nineteenth century was ostentatiously put on display at a series of International Exhibitions. The range of products was immense, from agricultural machinery to fine furniture, from exquisite jewellery to immense statuary. All manufacturing nations were invited to take part in these proud displays, each country exhibiting the pride and joy of its produce. The wares of France, Germany, America and Great Britain extended over vast halls, those of smaller countries taking only a more modest stand. The displays were only of items of the very finest quality, often sent as gifts to Royal personages, or enjoying Royal patronage. Even Kings and Emperors, however, were not immune from bartering and records of the Paris *expositions* clearly indicate that Napoleon III rarely paid the craftsman's asking price!

It is difficult to imagine the splendours of these magnificent displays. It would hardly be economically viable to mount such a show today, the joyful exhibits of the 1951 Festival of Britain being no match for the quality of items chosen for the nineteenth century displays. In Paris, the first of many industrial products exhibitions was staged in the Louvre courtyard during 1797. It was not, however, until the Crystal Palace Exhibition in London during the year 1851 that other countries were invited to exhibit on an 'international' scale. The specially constructed iron and glass 'railway station' was a flamboyant expression of smug wealth and supremacy, the theme of which was taken up and repeated by other countries on an ever increasing scale throughout the second half of the century. France traditionally held her major exhibitions every eleven years during the second half of the nineteenth century.

The exhibitions set their own style and the immense quantity of furniture designs had a major influence on everyday, mass-produced, pieces. The furniture itself was truly international. French designers worked for English firms exhibiting in Paris, combining some of the best workmanship with the most fashionable of contemporary designs.

As the century progressed the exhibitions became more specialised and towards the end exhibitions of varying size were being held to promote the new styles and designs that began to emerge above the over-exuberant muddle of revival styles.

List of Major International Exhibitions

1797	Exposition des Produits de l'Industrie at the Louvre. These exhibitions continued almost every year until the middle of the century.
1818	Kunst und Zeichnungsanstalt – first of many annual exhibitions in Munich
1843	Rome
1844	Esposizione Dei Produtti Dell'Industria Francese, Pirigi
1845	Vienna
1851	Crystal Palace Exhibition, London
1852	London
1853	New York
1855	Exposition Universelle, Paris
1859	Exposition Universelle, Paris
1861	Industrial Arts Exhibition, Paris
1861	Metz
1862	London
1865	International Exhibition, Oporto
1865	Retrospective Exhibition at the Musée Rétrospectif, Paris
1866	Amsterdam
1867	Exposition Universelle, Paris
1871	South Kensington Exhibition
1872	International Exhibition, London
1873	International Exhibition, Vienna
1876	Philadelphia Centennial Exhibition
1878	Exposition Universelle, Paris
1882	Exposition Rétrospective, Palais de l'Industrie, Paris
1884	Exposition Universelle, Paris
1888	Italian Exhibition, London
1888	Arts and Crafts Exhibition Society, first of five exhibitions, London
1889	Exposition Universelle, Paris. (The Eiffel Tower was opened as part of this exhibition)
1891	Le Salon du Champs de Mars, Paris
1892	Munich Exhibition
1893	Chicago Columbian Exhibition
1894	La Libre Esthétique. First of a series of Exhibitions by the Brussels group, 'Les Vingt'
1895	'Salon de l'Art Nouveau', Paris. A shop opened on 26th November by Samuel Bing.
1895	Exposition Historique et Militaire de la Révolution et de l'Empire
1895	'L'art dans tout'. First of a series of exhibitions by a group of art nouveau designers called 'Les Cinq' (later to become 'Les Six')
1896	Congress of Vienna Exhibition by Osterreichisches Museum für Kunst und Industrie Biedermeier.
1897 the	'La Maison Moderne', Paris. A shop opened by Belgian designer Henry van de Velde
1898	Munich Exhibition in the Glaspalast (Biedermeier decoration included)
1898	Vienna – Biedermeier
1899-1900	Deutsche Werkstätten Exhibition of Industrial Art, Dresden
1900	Exposition Universelle, Paris
1902	Turin Exhibition
1905	Liège Exhibition
1905-1906	Deutsche Werkstätten Exhibition of Industrial Art, Dresden
1910	Exhibition of Typen möbel (or unit furniture) by the Deutsche Werkstätten, London

Bibliography

Hverdagens Stole by Eric Larssen, 1957.
Mobilier Louis Philippe, Napoleon III by Colette Lehmann, 1978.
Chefs-d'oeuvre des grands ébénistes published by the Musée des Arts Décoratifs, 1951.
Storia dell'Arredamento by Alberto Clementi, 1952.
Egerer Reliefintarsien by Heribert Sturm, 1961.
Le Mobilier Liègeois by Joseph Phillippe, 1962.
Zweites Rokoko 1830-1860 by Marianne Sweig, Anton Schroll & Co., 1924.
The Art of Furniture by Ole Wanscher, 1968.
Le Meuble de Style by C. E. Rava, 1956.
Mobili Italiani dell'Ottocento by Valentino Brosio, 1962.
Das Deutsche Zimmer der Gothik by Georg Hirth, 1880.
Paris Exhibition Catalogue 1990.
Wegner Möbler by Johannes Hansen, 1970.
Late Nineteenth Century Art by Hans Jürgen Hansen, 1972.
Hungarian Furniture by Magda Barany-Obershall, 1939.
Bauernmöbel in den Alpen by Frans Colleselli, 1974.
The Practical Book of Italian, Spanish & Portuguese Furniture by Harold Donaldson Eberein, 1927.
Svenska Möbler I Bild 1830-1930 by Ernst Fischer, 1950.
Meubles de estilo español by Juan de Lozoya, 1972.
Le Magazin de Meubles Catalogue 1865-1875.
Le Mobilier Napoleon III by Jacqueline Viaux – *Revue de l'Ameublement*, May 1965.
Les Ebénistes Parisiens 1795-1870 by Denise Ledoux-Lebard, De Noeble 1965.
The Amazing Bugattis published by the Design Council, 1979 (*Carlo Bugatti 1856-1940* by Philippe Garner).
Chats on Old Furniture by Arthur Hayden, Fisher Unwin, 1907.
Encyclopedia Britannica.
Historical Tables 58 B.C.- A.D. 1978 by S. H. Steinberg, Macmillan Press, 1964.
Pioneers of Modern Design by Nikolaus Pevsner, Pelican Books, 1960.
Biedermeier Furniture by Georg Himmelheber, Faber, 1974.
Art at Auction 1973-1974, Sotheby Parke Bernet (*French Furniture in the Saleroom and Outside* by Sir Francis Watson, K.C.V.O., F.B.A.)
Dictionary of Antiques by George Savage, Barrie & Jenkins, 1970.
Italian Renaissance Furniture by Wilhelm von Bode, pub. William Helburn Inc., 1921.
The Price Guide to Antique Furniture by John Andrews, Antique Collectors' Club, 1978.
Bauernmöbel by Anton von Kugler, Battenberg Verlag München, 1979.
Le Prix des Meubles d'époque 1860-1956 by Jannine Capronnier, Libraire Armand Colin, 1966.
World Furniture edited by Helena Hayward, Hamlyn, 1965.
Die Kunst des Deutschen Möbels by Heinrich Kreisel and Georg Himmelheber, *Volume III*, pub. C.H. Beck, 1973.